EVERY DAY
REMEMBRANCE DAY

ALSO BY SIMON WIESENTHAL

Max and Helen
The Sunflower
The Murderers Among Us

EVERY DAY REMEMBRANCE DAY

A Chronicle of Jewish Martyrdom

SIMON WIESENTHAL

Henry Holt and Company
New York

First published in the United States in 1987 by
Henry Holt and Company, Inc., 521 Fifth Avenue,
New York, New York 10175
Distributed in Canada by Fitzhenry & Whiteside Limited,
195 Allstate Parkway, Markham, Ontario L3R 4T8.
Originally published in France under the title *Le Livre
de la Mémoire Juive*

Library of Congress Cataloging in Publication Data
Wiesenthal, Simon.
Every day remembrance day.
Bibliography: p.
Includes index.
1. Jews—Persecutions—Anniversaries, etc.
2. Holocaust, Jewish (1939–1945)—Anniversaries, etc.
I. Title.
DS123.W47   1987   940.53'15'03924   86-12085
ISBN 0-8050-0098-4

First American Edition

Designed by Susan Hood
Printed in the United States of America
10 9 8 7 6 5 4 3 2 1

ISBN 0-8050-0098-4

For my grandchildren
Rachel, Dan, and Yoram

There will always be Jews as long as they remember. There is no greater sin than to forget.

In 1942 when the Jewish poet Layser Aychenrand escaped from the deportation train to Auschwitz and reached Anne-masse on the Swiss border without documents, the customs officer questioning him asked his age. He answered: "I am two thousand years old. . . ."

This book is not a calendar in the ordinary sense of a calendar you use every day. It is a book commemorating horror, arranged by date; it is the story of Jewish martyrdom, of suffering; it is a document that shows what man is capable of doing to man. This calendar relates the atrocities committed against the Jewish people over two thousand years.

CONTENTS

Map showing the concentration camps in occupied Europe appears on page 34.

ACKNOWLEDGMENTS

I should like to thank the following friends for their kind help in the preparation of this calendar: Professor Dr. Friedrich Heer, Vienna, for his advice and for reading through the material; Gerald Bender, Chicago, for the dates regarding blood libel; Walter Bick, Toronto, for the dates of the Petlyura pogroms in the Ukraine; Dr. Florence Guggenheim, Zürich, for the dates of Jewish history in Switzerland; Jules Huf, Vienna, for dates in Holland at the time of the Nazi occupation; Erich Kulka, Jerusalem, for dates in the Nazi era in Czechoslovakia; Dr. Herbert Rosenkranz, Jerusalem, for the dates of the Nazi era in Austria.

I also wish to thank my secretaries Mrs. Mona Braune, Mrs. Rosa-Maria Austraat, and Mrs. Dorothea Huf for their dedicated work, and the Jewish Documentation Center in New York for its financial support.

EVERY DAY
REMEMBRANCE DAY

INTRODUCTION

The history of the Jews can be traced back over a period of about four thousand years. The great migration of peoples in the twentieth century before the common era forms the backdrop to the oldest times of biblical history. The Semitic nomads, notably the Amorites, who left the desert and settled down to civilization formed one part of the great coming and going of peoples. Israel's patriarchs, Abraham, Isaac, and Jacob, were probably tribal leaders of such nomadic groups. The Bible narrates the events of many centuries before their time. It was when the various immigrant groups had come together as a nation, the nation of Israel, that the individual patriarchal figures were combined into a single line of ancestry.

The first historical mention of Israel tells of its destruction: An inscription of the victorious Pharaoh Merneptah describes his conquest in 1223 B.C.E.

In the darkness of the earliest history of the Jews (before chronicled time), on which we shall never throw any light, there shines one outstanding figure: Moses.

Moses the liberator! Moses who in the Bible's vision leads the Hebrews out of Egypt to the threshold of the "Promised Land" of Canaan. Was Moses actually an Egyptian? Several Jews, including Sigmund Freud, and many enemies of the Jews maintain he was. His Egyptian name certainly suggests this.

Whatever Moses' nationality, as long as Jews are alive they will have to come to terms with this extraordinary figure as the Bible portrays him.

The Jews were shepherds, always ready to move on. They believed in a God who went ahead to lead them, a God of the Way. Even after they had formed settlements, the Israeli tribes continued to think of themselves as a wandering people, led by God.

As for Moses, the site of his grave is unknown. The Bible says God himself buried him. The Jews who were annihilated in the Holocaust have no graves either—they lie deep in our memory.

Moses had a pact with God, who had appeared to him on the sacred mountain, Mount Sinai, and handed him the tablets bearing the Commandments. We do not know where Sinai, Moses' Sinai, was, the holy mountain that was a place of pilgrimage for the nomads.

But we know that mankind, if it lays claim to being human—humanely human—lives according to the Ten Commandments.

The people of the pact were members of twelve tribes: Reuben, Simeon, Judah, Dan, Naphtali, Gad, Asher, Issachar, Zebulun, Benjamin, Manasseh, Ephraim. The tribes were named after, and considered descended from, the sons of the patriarchs Jacob and Joseph. In the land they had conquered with great effort, vanquishing their enemies both within Canaan and beyond its borders (for a long time their most dangerous foes were the Philistines), it was not until the period of the Judges that a certain stabilization set in. The Judges, leaders in the fight against neighboring peoples, owed their authority to a manifestation of Godly grace. The Bible portrays them as men who represented the direct rule of God, full theocracy. God himself, not the priests, not temple lords, shall rule over the people—God alone.

God reveals himself through the Judges, who are directly filled with his spirit (*ruách*). This direct rule of God could not last. According to the biblical account, the last and most important Judge, Saul, anointed himself king at the urgings of the Elders. This first king of Israel died a violent death. But the works of this troubled man lasted long after his death and were carried on by his successor, David. The Star of David, chosen by the murderers of the Jews as a symbol to brand the victims of their persecution and destruction, is today the symbol on the flag of Israel, the Jewish State.

Solomon, the "Prince of Peace" (971–932 B.C.E.), a vivid figure of extremes, was of great historical importance. He is portrayed critically by the authors of the Bible. Jewish self-criticism and Jewish soul-searching come to the surface in the stories about this king who created in his time a kind of humanism and enlightenment that spread and gathered strength in the turbulent centuries after him. Following his death, during the reign of his son Rehoboam, the Empire was divided; it had already started to disintegrate when Rehoboam was proclaimed king in Shechem. The ten northern tribes formed a state retaining the name of *Israel*—a state that lasted until the fall of Samaria in 721 B.C.E. The dynasty of David continued to reign over the southern kingdom, now called Judah, until the Babylonian imprisonment, starting in 586 B.C.E.

When the tribes of Israel, under Sargon II, were forced into exile in Mesopotamia by the Babylonians in 720 B.C.E., they were able to continue their spiritual and cultural development. Four hundred years later, the Jews living in exile in Babylonia numbered nearly one million. From there they partially dispersed throughout several countries in Asia. Jews lived in "the land of the two rivers," the cradle of the Babylonian exile, for nearly two and a half thousand years until they were forced to leave Iraq after the founding of the State of Israel.

The Empire of Judah fell with the conquest of the Neo-Babylonian Empire in 605 B.C.E. The great prophet Jeremiah, highly regarded in the nineteenth and twentieth centuries by Jews, Christians, and nonbelievers of all hues, proclaimed that the rule of Babylon would last seventy years. His prophecy largely came true.

The Jews took on the specific character that follows them throughout history during the time of the Babylonian Captivity from 596/586 to 538 B.C.E. The nation of Jews destined as God's people was originally the product of a catastrophe: the destruction of the Temple in Jerusalem by Nebuchadnezzar in 568 B.C.E., when the Kingdom of Judah was rent apart and its people forced into exile in Babylon.

From the time of the destruction of the Judaic state by the Romans in 70 C.E., until the founding of the State of Israel in 1948, the Jews lived in a permanent state of exile, in the galut.*

It was during the Babylonian captivity, when about 20 percent of the population was forcibly dragged into exile, that for the first time in the history of the Jewish people a Zionist longing for the land of their fathers became noticeable. Psalm 137, verse 5, says: "If I forget thee, O Jerusalem, let my right hand forget her cunning."

After the return from exile, the Temple was rebuilt under the rule of the Persian King Cyrus. The Persians retained their hold of the empire until it was conquered by Alexander the Great in 331 B.C.E.

The Greek empire under the Seleucids, the descendants of Alexander the Great, granted the Temple priests of the city-state of Jerusalem special rights (that they would also be allowed to keep under the Romans). But eventually Antiochus IV tried to suppress Judaism. The Jews rose up against the Seleucid profanation of the Temple and the abolition of their religious privileges in the Maccabean War. Judas Maccabaeus conquered Jerusalem in the autumn of 164 B.C.E. His victory is still celebrated today on Hanukkah, the Jewish festival of the consecration of the Temple.

The state of forced banishment as opposed to the Diaspora, the wandering.

The Roman Pompey deposed the last Seleucid king in 65 B.C.E. Thereafter Rome became the destiny of the Jews; they tried to maintain their own identity, first in pacts with the Romans, then in a relationship of dependency in varying degrees. Herod the Great, who, although hated by Orthodox Jews, was a politician of great standing, ordered magnificent new buildings that changed the face of Jerusalem and the Empire of Judea, of which he was proclaimed king in 40 B.C.E. After his death the tension between Jerusalem and Rome increased. The Jews went to war with the Romans, the mightiest military power of the Ancient World. Titus, son of Emperor Vespasian, laid siege to Jerusalem from April to August in the year 70 C.E. Titus's victory culminated in his taking the seven-branched golden candelabrum and the loaves of shewbread out of the Temple and bearing them in triumph to Rome. The Titus Arch, still standing in Rome today, graphically portrays these events.

In 73 C.E. the fortress of Masada was conquered by the Romans. The whole garrison committed suicide. This suicide set the example for the collective suicides committed by the Jews during the time of the Crusades and later in German towns. Masada: a place of commemoration never to be forgotten.

There will always be Jews as long as they remember.

There is no greater sin than to forget.

Even as Jewish rule in Jerusalem ended tragically, the Jews were successful in spreading and multiplying throughout the Ancient World to the length and breadth of the Roman Empire.

But before the end of the Jewish state, a unique personality appeared on the political and religious scene: Jesus of Nazareth, a religious reformer, a revolutionary who suffered the usual fate of all revolutionaries. He was condemned to death by the Romans, who were rulers of the Jewish state at the time, and crucified according to the law. This event was to play a greater part in the history of the Jews than Jesus' contemporaries ever dreamed of.

His disciples later saw in him—quite against his intentions—the founder of a religion, and in their memories of him (in the Gospels) they created the basis for a new religion, namely Christianity, which blamed the Jews for the death of Jesus.

When the early Christians fled from persecution by the Romans, they sought refuge in the synagogues. Such details deserve to be recorded, for, when the tables were turned, Jews sometimes found safety in Christian churches too. But this cannot hide the fact that the persecution of the Jews was often the work of the Church.

Belief in witches and sorcerers goes back of course to antiquity, but it was not until the Middle Ages—in the fourteenth century—that this belief began to spread in a most sinister way. In many countries it exists even today. The situation became fatal for the Jews when monks adopted this superstition and turned it into dogma, which they set down in fat books. This drove the people into the hands of the magicians, who then incited them to take the law into their own hands. As was only to be expected this led to massacres, of course, of Jews—witches and devils also celebrate their sabbath, just like the Jews.

Such was the situation when at the beginning of the fourteenth century the Dominicans marched into the arena to "fight against false doctrines." In their campaign they leaned heavily on the efficient apparatus of the Inquisition. The institution of the Inquisition lent the Christian persecution of the Jews a bureaucratic character. The denunciator thus became the prototype of a "good Christian"—just as under the Nazis or Communists.

Spanish Catholicism is a unique politico-religious phenomenon. It set itself the goal of "purging" the Spanish nation of Jews, Arabs, Lutherans, and other Christian noncon-formists by means of the royal and ecclesiastical Inquisition. When the Inquisition was set up in Spain—and it was the Dominican order that ran this instrument of the Church—the institution took on characteristics that are very similar to those of the SS in the Nazi state much later on. The French historian Poliakov put this very succinctly—it became a state within a state.

The Inquisition and the Castilian monarchy became business partners with regard to the property of the victims of the Inquisition. The rich—particularly rich baptized Jews—were always considered suspicious characters and were therefore in danger. The popes were unable, despite great efforts, to put a stop to the practices of the Spanish Inquisition. The mass forced baptisms in Spain in 1391 meant that the newly baptized, the *Conversos*, were accepted into the Church, although in their innermost beings they remained Jews. The year 1391 is a year full of massacres of Jews who refused to be baptized. Many Church leaders did not condone these massacres and openly condemned them, but their voices remained unheard. Marranos—baptized Jews who really remained Jews—and their descendants can be traced into the twentieth century in Spain.

In 1412 Pope Martin V declared in a papal bull that forced baptism was not Christian baptism, but this bull had no effect. A long line of fanatical priests appeared in Spain, among them a man named Vinzenz Ferrar, who gave the Jews a choice: death or baptism. Not until 1834 was the Inquisition officially abolished in Spain. The number of its victims is officially estimated at several hundred thousand, the majority of whom were of Jewish descent. But this estimate only takes into account those who died at the stake. The secretary of the Inquisition, Juan Antonio Lorente, who was in charge of the Inquisition archives, published in 1817 a history of the institution and gave the figure of those burned to death as 341,021.

The French-Jewish historian Poliakov calls the Inquisition a "soul police" and sees in the way it was run the first signs of political brainwashing as it is practiced nowadays by dictatorships in various countries. This brainwashing uses both "bitter" and "sweet" terror. It works on the principle of the carrot and the stick, with promises and torture.

The popes—with few exceptions—spoke out against the massacres of the Jews, but at the same time they warned Christians not to fraternize with Jews and in this way supported the manifold forms of discrimination. Ecclesiastic councils decreed that it was better for a Christian to die than to be treated by a Jewish doctor and recover from his illness—no Christian should owe his life to a Jew. However, in the Middle Ages the popes often had Jews as their personal physicians because they combined the wisdom of ancient Greek, Jewish, and Arab medicine.

The Jews were never driven out of Rome, but they were forced to live in ghettos under many personal restrictions. The Papal States, which in the nineteenth century horrified even the "Christian powers" in Europe with their barbaric practices (imprisonment, persecution, terror), kept their Jewish ghetto longest. Even in the bulls of safety that were issued by the popes, it was only the physical life of the Jews that was protected. They were still condemned to eternal damnation and Christians were only forbidden to actually kill them. In the papal bulls we find also the notion of "eternal slavery" which the Jews brought on themselves by their "own guilt." The mere safety of their lives is afforded them, but as an act of special—and undeserved—"Christian mercy."

Over the centuries the Inquisition developed a life of its own, removed from kings and popes (except in the Papal States). It became a cancer cell in the body of the Church. Many grand inquisitors were excommunicated, but continued to carry out their work as if nothing had happened. A certain parallel evolved toward the end of World War II when Heinrich Himmler tried to create a basis for bargaining with the Allies by stopping the gassing. Many of his own men simply ignored his orders.

Anti-Judaism presented the Jews as evil beings—nothing could change this status, neither "goodwill" nor "mercy." Their "bad blood" was the root of all evil. If somebody was disliked, one did a bit of investigation to see if he wasn't of Jewish descent. Further "proof" of his "guilt" was then superfluous.

Special mention must be made of the founder of the "Aryan Christ," the "non-Jewish Christ," who can be seen as the ideological forerunner of the "German Christ" who was the figurehead of a movement within the Evangelical Church in the Nazi era. In 1547

Archbishop Juan Martinez Siliceo of Toledo, who, like many anti-Semitic priests in France and Austria in the nineteenth and twentieth centuries came from a farming community, wrote a tract which was to have dire consequences. The tract took as its subject the "purity of Spanish blood," the *limpieza de sangre*. His main purpose was to expose many Spanish high priests, bishops, and aristocrats as being of Jewish descent. In the *limpieza de sangre* an early form of the Aryan certificate was created, without which one very soon could not live in Spain.

The obsession with "purity of blood" took on the form of an underground civil war. Everywhere people were on the move collecting proof of their own "purity" of blood and of the "impurity" of their enemies' blood. This internal poisoning of Spain had consequences right into the twentieth century.

Racial discrimination became part of the law—the *limpieza de sangre* had to be produced on all occasions and in all spheres of life, social, economic, and political. In the sixteenth and seventeenth centuries, when other European countries experienced a general economic growth, Spain was concerned with "race research" and suffered an economic decline.

Christian universalism died in Spain as soon as the "race question" appeared. The blood of Jews and Moslems was declared to be not equal to that of Christians. So the Jews who had converted to Christianity suffered further discrimination from several laws which declared them not "complete" Christians. The inquisitors gave as "evidence" of the guilt of many of their victims that they were the children of baptized Jews, and therefore not "full-blooded Christians." The Spanish blood laws served as a model for the Nazis' "Aryan certificate" centuries later; the Spanish "blood purity certificate" affected seven generations and the first draft of the Nazi law pertaining to the Aryan certificate also demanded proof of seven generations. But that proved impractical in Germany where, unlike in Spain, families were not so settled; they rarely lived in one place for seven generations, so the "proof" could not be found. For this reason the Nazis gave in and restricted the "blood hunting" to three generations.

The idea of a common ancestry of all mankind was the true foundation of the Christian belief, but the practices of the Inquisition and militant Catholicism took the idea to absurd extremes.

As late as 1772 a Spanish teacher could not get permission to teach without an Aryan certificate.

Not until the present day has it been possible to openly combat the traditional anti-Judaism in Spain. Franco intervened on behalf of Sephardic Jews in the Balkans whom he regarded as the descendants of Jews driven out of Spain in 1492. The Nazis had to give in under protest, enabling Franco to save a large number of Jews from their hands.

The anti-Semitism of the nineteenth and twentieth centuries is the terrible offspring of the anti-Judaism of antiquity, which was expounded principally by Greek intellectuals, early on in Alexandria and later in Rome. The attitude of these intellectuals of ancient times sprang from a strange inferiority complex of the same sort found in the anti-Judaism of French intellectuals since the sixteenth and seventeenth centuries. The word "anti-Semitism" was coined in 1879 by the German Wilhelm Marr, whose Hammer publishing house printed anti-Semitic books. Friedrich Nietzsche left Hammer for this reason; he saw in anti-Semitism the cancerous evil of a decaying society. It is interesting that this modern kind of anti-Semitism—which goes back two thousand years to the "Christian" anti-Jews—appears very early on both on the right and the left of the political spectrum, with drastic consequences right to the present day, both in the East European states and in Western Europe.

The German radical left-wing intelligentsia in 1863 was as anti-Semitic as their great-grandchildren in 1968. In 1863, Bruno Bauer's book *The Jews in Exile* appeared. For him the Jew is the expression of evil in the world. In his writings on the "Jewish question" and "the capacity of Jews and Christians today to become free," Bruno Bauer, a friend of Karl Marx, denied the Jews the right of assimilation and equality with Christians.

Was Karl Marx, the baptized Jew, the anti-Jew, an anti-Semite? Was he possessed by that legendary "self-hatred" which the philosopher Theodor Lessing (who was murdered by the Nazis) found the tragic fate of our time?

In the nineteenth and twentieth centuries, Marxist, socialist and communist Jews fled the confinement of the ghetto, out of the world of their fathers into the vision of the "World of Freedom," into a secularization of the ancient Jewish belief in the Messiah. But not infrequently they awoke from their dream to become the strongest critics of a perverted "Marxism."

Stalin, who shortly before his death ordered a small-scale "Final Solution" (in the prosecution of Jewish doctors) that was never carried out, regarded the Jews as his harshest critics.

What we call "anti-Semitism" has been happening to the Jews for two thousand years and more, ever since they were driven or deported from the land that belonged to them. In contrast to modern times—particularly under the Nazis or Stalin—after the conquest of foreign territories and the deportation of the original inhabitants, the ancient rulers left their subjects to live in peace and allowed them to build up their communities again in the new settlement areas.

As this calendar shows, the story of the persecution of the Jews has always been directed by Christians: first of all by the Roman Catholic Church, then by the Orthodox Church. These Churches plunder the Bible, the most precious element of Jewish life, the unique treasure of Jewish identity, and use it for their own ends. Friedrich Nietzsche was the first to openly comment on and criticize this theft. The official theology of the Catholic Church considers Rome "the true Jerusalem" and the Church "the true Israel." In the eyes of the Church the Jews forfeited their history and their means of salvation by killing Jesus. Real and effective political and religious reconciliation of the Christian Church with the Jews will only become possible when—as indeed both Protestant and Catholic theologians are nowadays demanding—the backbone of "Christian" anti-Judaism, anti-Semitism, and anti-Zionism is broken.

The history of the persecution of the Jews is—as will become clear from this calendar—at the same time a history of Christianity. The acts of persecution against the Jews were from the very beginning acts of revenge against that part of the Jewish community which refused to recognize Jesus (even though the first Christians were actually Jews).

The murder of six million Jews brought a change of heart to the Catholic Church, because after the mass murders they could not ignore the fact that the murderers of the Jews were at least partly people with a Christian education and also that Nazi propaganda had employed all the reproaches of the Church against the Jews.

The fact that Jews and Christians both had to suffer under the Nazi regime played a not inessential role. There were also thousands of Catholic priests who were with the Jews in the camps and many among them who did not survive. In the relations between the Church and Judaism, "Auschwitz" became a turning point.

One of the first to recognize this was Pope John XXIII, who initiated a reconciliation of the Church with the Jews. In 1965, his successor, Pope Paul VI, published the Second Vatican Council's Declaration "Nostra Aetate" ("In Our Time"), which states that the relations between the Catholic Church and Judaism should be completely changed.

With this Declaration the Roman Curia officially broke with the age-old Catholic doctrine that the Jews were collectively guilty of the murder of Jesus Christ and remained so, and that salvation from the suffering of mankind is never possible without confession of faith in Christ (Extra ecclesiam nulla salus—no salvation outside the Church).

This Declaration "Nostra Aetate" was supposed to annul the ancient Church theories about Judaism without reserve, and a friendly dialogue, even a cooperative basis between Catholic and Jewish theologians, should have been recommended and introduced. Jewish theologians certainly looked forward to a reduction of the tension between the two religions, but had no great expectations and wanted to wait quietly for reactions to the Declaration.

On the Catholic side, a Vatican Secretariat on Religious Relations with the Jewish People was established under the direction of Augustin Cardinal Bea, a German cardinal kindly disposed toward Jews; after his death control went to the Dutch cardinal Johannes Cardinal Willebrands. The activities of the commission spanned twenty years, with representatives of American, European, Israeli, and Latin American Jewish organizations participating in this dialogue.

A counterreaction also came about in conservative Catholic circles, especially after the death of Pope John XXIII, and they tried to slow down and restrict the dialogue. Moreover, attempts were made to play down the Holocaust and return to the thesis that Judaism and Christianity should have "no parallel paths for the salvation of man."

The uncertainty caused by internal developments in the Church manifested itself in the new Vatican document, "Notes on the correct way to teach about Jews and Judaism in the Catechism." But Cardinal Willebrands took the edge off these "notes" by referring to the unspeakable suffering of the Holocaust and to the parallels of the theologic doctrines of salvation. Only in reference to recognition of the State of Israel did the Vatican stand by its earlier critical viewpoint. It is worth hoping that this dialogue will develop even further. After all, the state of war that prevailed between the Catholic and Jewish theologies for almost two thousand years has abated and relaxed, and that alone signifies enormous progress.

It is thanks to Pope John XXIII that paragraphs of the liturgy that concerned the Jews and that were offensive and inciting were removed. But the new formula adopted reflects a compromise dictated by political considerations and by resistance on the part of the clergy. Succeeding popes—up to the present Pope John Paul II—have continued the process of reconciliation and understanding.

Pope John XXIII's position is suggested by the text of a penitential prayer he is thought to have composed shortly before his death:

"We now acknowledge that for many, many centuries we were blind to the beauty of Thy Chosen People and in his face did not recognize the features of our elder brother. We acknowledge that the mark of Cain is upon our brows. For centuries Abel has lain in blood and tears because we forgot Thy love. Forgive us the curse which we unjustly pronounced upon the name of the Jews. Forgive us that we crucified Thee for the second time in cursing them. For we knew not what we did. . . ."

The compiling of a calendar such as this one necessitated first and foremost a definition of what can be seen as the underlying pattern of this particular history. Six factors recur like leitmotifs throughout these events. They can be regarded as the preconditions or main causes of the persecution. They are:

Hatred
Dictatorship
Bureaucracy
Technology
Crisis or War
Minority as Scapegoat

Hatred

We live in an era of worldwide hatred in extreme forms on a religious, political, and social level. In the twentieth century, the "century of barbarism," this hatred is of a particularly aggressive, murderous kind that uses all the means that a technological and industrial society has at its disposal. Hate propaganda is in the press, on the radio, on TV and in films (Goebbels was the first to use film propaganda against the Jews), everywhere in the mass media.

The story of mankind is a story of migration and emigration. In the last centuries—and in modern times, particularly in Africa and Asia—people have been driven out of their settlements, and those driving them out often did not hesitate to murder as well. Over the centuries people came and went, moving from one place to the next, from country to country, voluntarily or under force; and everywhere they went they met others, mingled with them, and drew them into their community or were themselves absorbed—or annihilated. Some of these tribes and peoples have left no trace of themselves or their activities and we know nothing about them except their name.

And there were the Jews, who are in every way a notable exception in the history of emigration. The immigrant Jews, those who had been deported and those who came to join them, never mingled with the natives of their new land. They felt the differences between them very deeply, differences of belief and laws as well as religious customs, and this feeling of being different was passed on from one generation to the next and became one of the primary reasons why the Jews were disliked or hated.

Their monotheistic religion was one factor that separated them from others. Jews as a nation did not mix with other nations or tribes mainly because the laws of the Torah forbid them to marry people of other beliefs.

As far back as ancient times there existed a conflict with the rest of the population of the Roman Empire who were strongly influenced by Greek and Roman conceptions of culture and religion, and this too contributed to excesses fueled by hatred, a fact stressed by the Jewish historian Josephus Flavius roughly two thousand years ago. The way the Jews held on determinedly to their faith even outside the traditional center of their religion demonstrates clearly the fundamental character of this monotheism.

The Jews were the only monotheists in the Roman Empire, whose other subjects adhered to a multiplicity of religious creeds, cults, and sacrificial customs, even human sacrifice! The Jews believed in an invisible God, a God so holy that his name may not be spoken out loud. All the "names" that the Jewish faith gives to its God are substitutes, including "Jehovah," or "Yahweh," so defamed in anti-Semitic propaganda of the nineteenth and twentieth centuries which maintained that it was the name of the devil, or rather that it was the very devil himself, "the father of the devil Jews." Being different from others in matters of religion bred animosity.

In the vast Roman Empire, the Jewish religion was a "religio licita," permitted and recognized by law. The Jews were allowed to build synagogues and to celebrate their holy days. This did not change even when the Romans destroyed the Temple in Jerusalem in 70 C.E. and by so doing did away with the apparatus of the Jewish state.

With the coming of Christianity, which began as a Jewish sect, the situation changed drastically, for now there were two monotheistic religions within the Roman Empire. The early Christian communities were made up largely of Jews who had been converted to Christianity. As it took three centuries for Christianity to spread over the whole of the Roman Empire, it was inevitable that the first Christians were called "Jewish Christians." For the most part they lived strictly according to Jewish laws and settled particularly in Syria, Greece, and Spain.

"Jewish Christians," whose tragic fate was to be crushed between the non-Jewish New Christians and the synagogue, remained in the Near East right up to the tenth century, as recent research in Israel has proved.

Christianity was "invented" by the apostle Saul-Paul, who throughout his life bore the name Saul as a Jew and the name Paul as a Roman citizen. He openly confessed that he was not interested in the Jew Jesus, his contemporary. He combined a religiosity based on the mysterium with his own experiences (including the "apparition of Jesus" on the road to Damascus) to form a religion which fought long and hard to eventually become the official Christianity of the World Church. Paul himself long remained a suspicious figure to many Christian communities who did not really find him credible.

At first the Roman authorities were unable to distinguish between the two creeds. But Christianity did not want only to convert the Jews, it wanted to take its teachings to the heathens. *Heathen* is an ominous word which still plays a fatal part in the Church's missionary work in Africa and Asia in the twentieth century; it implies a denunciation of all other forms of belief and religions. In his magnificent translation of the Bible into German—that unique monument to German-Jewish symbiosis—Martin Buber uses in stead the biblically correct phrase "tribes of the world" (*Welstämme*—in the Latin translation of the Bible it is *"gentes"*).

Jesus was declared a god by Paul. That was the beginning of the break. Harsh words against the Jews followed. As time went by, instead of theological debate such as Paul had used, the rift grew wider as animosity deepened and the Jews were reviled and cast out.

The Jews were accused of being "murderers of God." Theological anti-Semitism grew from this attitude, becoming integrated into the Easter liturgy.

John Chrysostom (345?–407) created the notion of collective guilt which makes the whole Jewish nation responsible for Jesus' death. Christianity was in the middle of an identity crisis, and the theory about the murder of God was designed to help it out of its predicament. In early Christian times hostility toward the Jews became an important element of the faith—a welcome distraction from the internecine quarrels among the various Christian groups.

In that era, the fatal theological concept of the "Jewish nation as murderers of God" was utilized particularly by Roman Catholicism.

But in our day the Roman Catholic Church has changed its view—especially since the pontificate of Pope John XXIII—and little by little, the Jews are being exculpated of the death of Jesus.

The so-called Constantine turning point, when Emperor Constantine the Great— himself a murderer many times over and no Christian—declared Christianity the state religion, paved the way that would lead tragically to the Inquisition and to legal discrimination against Jews everywhere. But the attacks against the Jews which began in the fourth century can be viewed in the light of the bloody, merciless battles within Christianity itself, patriarch against patriarch, bishop against bishop, and theologian against theologian. They found distraction by turning to attack the Jews together.

The first outrages committed against Jews by Christians in this era took place after church sermons branded Jews as the "murderers of the Lord" and "assassins of God." The outrages against Jews in Asia Minor, where numerous Jews lived, were later described by the Jewish historian Poliakov as part of the anti-Semitic tradition of Byzantium and, one thousand years later, as "typical of the Muscovite Empire."

The fanatical anti-Jewish sermons preached by the Church fathers in the fourth century in Asia Minor served as an example to anti-Semitic National Socialist propaganda and played a dominant role in more recent Church policy—until the second Vatican Council.

Christians hated the Jews and thought that by so doing they were honoring Christ. They revered the Bible and heaped curses upon its authors.

Hatred of the Jews grew as they came to be regarded as the cause of every catastrophe— if there was too much rain or too little, if the harvest was poor, earthquakes, floods, fire, famine, lightning, the plague, everything was laid at the door of the Jews; even though as many Jews were among the victims of such catastrophes as the rest of the population, the Jews were responsible for all calamities.

The accusations against the Jews reached a peak when they were said to be holding secret meetings to plan the destruction of the Christian community. This horror story of a worldwide Jewish plot was prevalent for many centuries, again and again resulting in massacres; in modern times it found its ultimate expression in the fabrication of *The Protocols of the Elders of Zion* by the Petersburg Ochrana, the czar's secret police. Even when the Protocols were proved to be a forgery, this did not prevent the Nazis republishing them in the 1930s for propaganda purposes. Even today many Christians still believe that *The Protocols of the Elders of Zion* are genuine and they are constantly being published in new editions particularly in Arab countries and in South America, where they play a sinister role in the anti-Semitism that continues to be fueled by immigrants from Europe.

Absurd accusations were invented against the Jews that were diametrically opposed to all the principles of the Jewish religion, such as the tale of "ritual murders," according to which the Jews slaughter Christian children and drink their blood or use it in the preparation of matzohs at Passover. Many popes spoke out against the propaganda of "blood libel," but to no avail; this fairy tale was believed from the Middle Ages right down to the recent past, which is why the disappearance of a child frequently led to acts against the Jews inspired by hatred.

The belief in "ritual murders" continued under the surface in Christian nations until the modern era. An article published on September 9, 1960, in the Soviet newspaper *The Communist*, the organ of the regional committee of the Communist party in Dagestan, maintained that the Jews use not only Christian but also Muslim blood in the preparation of matzohs.

In a letter written on December 9, 1954, Dr. Paul Rusch, the bishop of Innsbruck, declared to Catholics in Vienna: "Now, from a purely historical point of view, no consensus of opinion has been reached by historians about the ritual murders . . . From a more general point of view we must however bear in mind that it was after all the Jews who crucified our Lord Jesus Christ. . . ." This disastrous belief in the Jews being "murderers of Christ" has been exposed as a lie by theologians of all the main Christian churches. On the other hand, however, many books have been written by theologians in which they encourage the hatred of the Jews by bringing forth unverifiable accusations against which the Jewish minority was powerless. All these unfounded accusations against the Jews were later taken up again and amplified by the Nazis who transformed them into particularly effective propaganda—ignoring the logic of historical evolution whereby a society that wanted to be "free of Jews" would ultimately have to become equally "free of Christians."

The segregation of the Jews, their ghettoization, stigmatization, and indescribable humiliation (as it was practiced by the National Socialists from the very beginning) can be traced back to the Christians, primarily to militant Catholics. The popes—the representatives of Christ on earth—have admittedly never called for the destruction of the Jews, but they welcomed their degradation, because in the humiliated Jews the world could see the proof of the punishment that is visited upon all those who reject Jesus. This attitude prevailed for roughly fifteen hundred years. It is only very recently, after the Nazi catastrophe engulfed not only Jews but the whole world, that the Church has begun to rethink its point of view. This process was and is very painful for many Christians; discussions in the Protestant Church in the Federal Republic of Germany over the last decade have shown how strongly respected theologians cling even today to the old, terrible clichés.

In the eighteenth century the methods of persecution of the Jews became more subtle and sophisticated. In the early nineteenth century German Jews like Heinrich Heine and Ludwig Börne felt this acutely and documented it for the first time in journalistic and poetic works. Many Jews reacted by shutting themselves off in the ghetto, by striving for a renewal of Jewish orthodoxy, in which the Sabbath and family are hallowed, and by generally leading an exemplary moral life. Others, such as Moses Mendelssohn, a prominent Jewish philosopher, chose another way and fought for emancipation and "Germanization." Mendelssohn's great dream of a German-Jewish symbiosis, which was born in the sociopolitical atmosphere of the eighteenth century, was brought to an abrupt end in the twentieth at the height of its upswing.

In the eighteenth and nineteenth centuries Germany was flooded with anti-Jewish literature. Inflammatory pamphlets and leaflets that skillfully combined pornography with anti-Semitism denounced the Jews as the personification of evil. Such pamphlets became the most effective means of hate propaganda in the twentieth century, appealing to the basest instincts of both the frustrated petty bourgeoisie and, unfortunately, children and young people. When National Socialism began to turn itself into a state religion, its propaganda leaders were able to build on a centuries-old tradition. Defamatory pamphlets of this kind were also very popular with enemies of the Jews outside Germany; they were exported and translated into many languages.

On the other hand, French anti-Jewish writings were imported early on to Germany and Austria and became ammunition in the arsenal of the "Christian Socialists" who were openly anti-Semitic.

Poliakov writes of the "streams of ink" that preceded the "streams of blood," or accompanied them. The slogans of anti-Jewish propaganda acted as a stimulus to attack and to kill.

Earlier on, another theologian, Martin Luther, had played a fatal role in the attitude adopted toward the Jews by proposing in his pamphlet *Of the Jews and Their Lies* to burn down the synagogues, to confiscate Jewish books, and to forbid the Jews to pray to God. Furthermore, the provincial princes should expel the Jews from their territories.

Martin Luther had changed his views, much like the founder of Islam, Mohammed. As a young man, friendly toward the Jews, he hoped that they would convert to the Christianity he was revitalizing, but through disappointments he became, like Mohammed, more and more fanatically hostile to the Jews. Luther's anti-Jewish writings were rediscovered for the first time by anti-Semitic Protestant Germans in the nineteenth century.

The notorious anti-Semite Julius Streicher—originally a teacher—who in his newspaper *Der Stürmer* ("The Attacker") fanned the flames of hatred with pornographic anti-Jewish illustrations and inflammatory articles, cited his "teacher" Martin Luther during the Nuremberg trials that followed the collapse of the Third Reich.

At the beginning of the eighteenth century accusations against the Jews that had existed for centuries, such as desecration of the host and ritual murders, surfaced again. This had a paralyzing effect on the ability of the Jews to live together with their neighbors. The popes tried to combat such accusations by refusing to make martyrs out of the children who had supposedly been murdered by the Jews.

On April 17, 1937, Eugenio Cardinal Pacelli (later Pope Pius XII) preached a sermon in Rome against the "antico popolo deicido," the God-murdering nation of the Jews. In 1944, during the deportations of Jews from Slovakia to Auschwitz, Rabbi Michael Dov Weissmandel had an audience with the apostolic administrator in Bratislava, Giuseppe

Burzio, and, asking him to intervene with the Slovakian president Josef Tiso (who was a Catholic priest himself), mentioned the innocent blood of Jewish children. Burzio answered: "There is no innocent blood of Jewish children in the world. All Jewish blood is guilty. This is the punishment that has been awaiting you, because of that sin."

The much-discussed silence of Pope Pius XII over the mass murder of the Jews in World War II must be understood in this context.

The common origins of the religions were suppressed and only recently "rediscovered" by Protestant and Catholic theologians. On the initiative of Pope John XXIII, the curse of the Church was removed from the Jews at the Second Vatican Council.

To sum up: The National Socialists did not invent anything new in the measures they took against the Jews; they simply took over existing models, such as the proof of Aryan ancestry, the stigmatization of the Jews, and the burning of their books, borrowing them from the Church. The fatal "J" for "Jew" on German passports was invented for Himmler by the Swiss chief of the Aliens Police, Dr. Rothmund. He wanted to reduce the number of Jewish refugees entering Switzerland and his idea was accepted with enthusiasm by the Germans. Legal action was never taken against Dr. Rothmund for this innovation, which cost the lives of many Jews.

Dictatorship

In the two thousand years of persecution of the Jews, dictatorship has taken many different forms. In ancient times the absolute ruler turned his unlimited power against the Jews, as we know from the Book of Esther describing the Iranian-Persian empire. Later it was the turn of emperors, kings, bishops, and generals to rule until the dictators of modern times took over: party leaders and bureaucrats who became the lords over life and death. Within the boundaries of their rule they could exercise and abuse their power to the utmost against a minority like the Jews, to degrade, humiliate, persecute or destroy them; to use this minority as a punching bag on which to get rid of all pent-up vexations, no matter how petty. They locked them up in ghettos to keep them under control. Jews were forced to pay a head tax and to submit to all sorts of other tax burdens. They became the vassals of bishops, princes, and kings. If for their part these rulers were in debt to the Jews, they never even dreamed of repaying their debts. It was so simple to get rid of such creditors by expelling them from their territory. Expulsion was often used as a method of quickly doing away with both debts and creditors. The difficult situation in which many Jews found themselves as moneylenders to princes was portrayed—and perverted—very effectively during the Nazi era in the film *Süss the Jew*.

In the Middle Ages, Jews in Germany were declared the property of the emperor, kings, and bishops, which meant that everything they owned also became the property of the rulers. In this way they could seize whatever they wanted that belonged to a Jew, because it belonged to them "legally"—that is, in accordance with the law that they had specially created for this purpose.

The French kings, for example, ensured one source of income for themselves by decreeing—entirely against the will of the Church—that baptized Jews would lose their property. In the second half of the fourteenth century, Jews who were expelled from Germany found refuge in Poland under the reign of King Casimir the Great. Casimir issued several tolerance edicts which guaranteed the safety of the Jews. The Jews in turn provided Poland, which at that time was solely an agricultural sociey, with material goods and with badly needed craftsmen.

Over the centuries it was always the Catholic Church that put pressure on Poland's kings to restrict the rights of the Jews. Anti-Semitism on the part of the Church has had tragic consequences in Poland right up to the present day.

Bureaucracy

Nowadays when the word bureaucracy is mentioned we think of the swarm of desk clerks who make life difficult for us in our day-to-day dealings with them. But here our concept of bureaucracy comprises not only these functionaries but all those who carry out the orders of state, political, corporate, and ecclesiastical institutions.

The two elements we have looked at so far, hatred and dictatorship, could never be effective without these executive organs as accomplices. Again and again bureaucrats have been the ideal conductors of hatred, ready to carry out any and every order. Those who stirred up the people against the Jews and who prepared the funeral pyres were bureaucrats.

It was the monks who started the murders of Jews in Spain and in the Rhineland during the Crusades. In England and in France in the twelfth and thirteenth centuries monks were present when outrages took place. Of course, they also spearheaded the anti-

Jewish measures adopted during the Inquisition in Spain from the fourteenth to the sixteenth century; and later in the sixteenth century they supported the anti-Jewish movement in Germany which was led by the baptized Jew Johannes Pfefferkorn.

The Cossacks who slaughtered the Jews and the men who ran the machinery of destruction in the Nazi era—the warders in the ghettos and concentration camps, the members of execution squads—in short, all those who carried out orders to suppress, degrade, and finally kill the Jews, belonged to the bureaucracy.

Over the centuries, of course, their outward appearance changes: in this calendar we find them in various costumes, as monks, as ringleaders of the mob, as Cossacks, SS men, and KGB catchpoles.

"Modern" mass society has resulted in the enormous growth of bureaucracies. These often develop a dangerous mind of their own, in which the terror they exert exceeds in inhumanity the orders of their superiors. Thus arises the attitude of the SS nobodies in the camps and the low-level clerks in consulates who refused visas to fleeing Jews even though the quota laid down by their governments was not full.

Technology

Modern technology provides the practical instruments for mass murder—"progress" makes possible the partially successful "final solution to the Jewish question," then a "final solution to the question of mankind." Individuals can easily, that is, with relatively primitive means, be transported from life to death. But the millionfold murder committed in the Nazi era was only possible because of modern technical inventions. Five hundred years ago rulers and exponents of the destruction of the Jews, such as the Inquisition, looked for new ways to kill as many people as possible at once. A throttling machine was ordered, which was supposed to kill seven people at a time, but the technical limits of the age proved insuperable. So a new attitude gained ground: if the Jews could not be destroyed physically, then they should at least be extinguished spiritually and mentally. They should be reduced to the choice between two alternatives: death or baptism.

Because mass destruction was technically impossible, mass expulsion followed. Often the Jews beat their executioners to it—many Jewish communities committed collective suicide; there will be several examples in this calendar. The dying Jews spoke with their last breath the same prayer (widui) spoken by Jesus before he died. Protestant and Catholic theologians have been greatly affected by this fact over the past two decades, once they crossed the threshold of fear and began to think about the "Jewish Jesus."

The Nazis had all the highly developed technology of our times at their disposal. First they tried it out on small groups and then they used it to kill millions of Jews and other people who were "unfit to live."

The technocrats, scientists, researchers, and technicians who invented poison gas and tested its possibilities for practical use in the First World War, enabled Hitler and his followers to come very close to realizing their vision of a human race "free of Jews." We know today that for Hitler the destruction of the Jews became more and more urgent and even took priority over military victory in the war, which became objectively impossible after Stalingrad and El Alamein.

Crisis or War

Again and again, we notice, those institutions and personalities who sought to persecute and destroy the Jews bided their time and waited for an opportune moment for acts of this kind. In late antiquity and in the early Middle Ages the widespread campaign against "heresy" played right into their hands. Jews were seen as the "forefathers" of such "heresy." After the heretics and their families had been murdered, it was the Jews' turn to die, for setting a "bad example."

The Crusades were an invention of Roman Christianity, to be precise of Pope Urban II, in the late eleventh century, although the roots of the idea go back as far as the tenth century. These wars were originally intended to provide an outlet for the French aristocracy and to turn the tide of their suicidal disintegration by giving them a common goal outside France. The Eastern Church has never known Crusades and their theologians look down on the "Franks" (as Christians are known to this day in Islamic and Asian countries), interpreting their acts as plundering campaigns which were intended to conquer rich Constantinople and later the "Holy Land."

By the thirteenth century the Crusades had come directly under the orders of the popes, who used them to attack political opponents or "heathens" in Eastern Europe and heretics in southern France.

The crusaders destroyed whole Jewish communities in their path or drove them out of places in which they had lived for centuries. Occasionally there were apostates who had turned their back on Judaism and became cheerleaders in the service of anti-Jewish propaganda. One such example was the Dominican Father Donin who in the thirteenth century propagated the legend of ritual murders. The history of Jewish suffering is filled with apostates who tried to improve their own position by becoming opponents of Jews. Such renegades played a particularly fatal role in Germany, in the Austrian Empire, and in South America.

Those who had received material gains when the Jews were driven out often became their murderers when they tried to return, not least because they were a reminder of their evil deeds. This mechanism was prevalent particularly in the Middle Ages but also much later, notably after the collapse of the Third Reich; for example, in Poland, where Jews returning home and wanting their property back were murdered outright. Again and again Jews bore the brunt of crises and wars, and again and again the Jews were accused of collaboration with the enemy. In Spain, for instance, they were accused of being in league with the Arabs or of having incited them to invade the Spanish peninsula.

Between 1357 and 1360 a third of the population of Europe died from the plague—the Black Death. Jews, of course, were just as badly hit by this terrible epidemic as everybody else, but they became the scapegoats, particularly as the catastrophe was regarded as the work of the devil and the Jews as his followers. Neither papal bulls nor attempts by princes to protect the Jews could stop such accusations.

In the Thirty Years War the Jews were the scapegoats for both sides. When the Swedes marched into Poland and left the Jews unmolested that was merely another "proof" that the Jews were in league with the Swedes, acting as their spies.

In Poland the Jews were lucky enough to have a kind of self-rule and there were no limitations on where they could settle. The Jews played an important role in the country's turbulent history and endured the strokes of fate side by side with the non-Jewish population. However, Jews were often the first targets of anti-Polish attacks. This applies particularly to when the Ukrainians under their commander Bogdan Chmielnicki rebelled against Poland in 1648 and 1649, when the Ukraine was a Polish dependency. The uprisings spread from the Ukraine toward central Poland; both Poles and Jews were brutally murdered en masse by Chmielnicki's bands, so that as time went by the Ukraine became almost "free of Jews." The number of Jews murdered by Chmielnicki and his troops is estimated at several hundred thousand; an exact figure cannot be given owing to the lack of reliable statistics about the population. The murders by Chmielnicki's hordes traumatized the East European Jews, leaving them paralyzed, their spirit of resistance destroyed. When the Brownshirts of the Nazis appeared on the scene they seemed like the descendants of Chmielnicki.

In Russia in the nineteenth century four geographical areas were laid down for Jews to settle: the Ukraine, Belorussia, Latvia, and Lithuania. They were forbidden to live in the large towns like St. Petersburg or Moscow.

When the czarist regime lost the war against Japan in 1905 and discontent spread throughout the land, the bad humor of the Russians was channeled into anti-Jewish pogroms under the motto: "Beat the Jews, save Russia!"

It is often the case that the same man is regarded by one nation as a "freedom fighter" and by another as a "murderer." Many of the struggles for independence fought by the Ukrainians to free themselves from the Russian or Polish yoke began with murders of Jews. Particularly in areas claimed by two nations as their territory, innocent Jews were victims in the struggle for power. The National Socialists continued this tradition without interruption.

The historical fanatical anti-Judaism of Poland, the Ukraine, Slovakia, and Hungary—where at certain times there were as many as half a dozen anti-Semitic political parties—played right into the hands of the National Socialists and their murderous bands.

When Hitler invaded the Soviet Union and declared war against the United States, he made his war into a world war, which is what finally enabled the Nazis to put their plans for the destruction of the Jews into practice. The extermination of eleven million Jews had already been planned at the conference in Wannsee where the Final Solution was determined. In this context we must remember that Heinrich Himmler himself in 1944 gave several speeches to high-ranking SS leaders and generals stating the number of millions of Jews who had already been killed.

The war, which because of state security measures and the necessity for military secrecy effectively cut off whole regions from the eyes of the world, allowed the Nazis to keep the secret of the mass murders—even to a large extent from their own people—with the hope that final victory would "justify" the crimes. Under the code name K44 an international anti-Jewish congress was planned for autumn 1944. Professors from satellite states and from the occupied territories were to take part and the murders of the Jews justified. The conference was to have been held at Cracow, but the Soviet offensive put an end to the plan.

Minority as Scapegoat

After the Jews were driven out of Palestine, the Promised Land, they dispersed to all the provinces of the Roman Empire: from Spain to the Orient, from the British Isles to the border of the Sahara. Very early on they reached Central Asia and China. Everywhere they went they were a minority and had to try to survive as Jews. But only after the fall of the Roman Empire did the Jews really become aware of their precarious status as a minority group. The tolerant attitude of the Roman world was succeeded, in the Christian epoch, by the fanaticism of a new creed which had become the state religion in many parts of Europe. From the fourth century on, the Jews' existence became very difficult because they were forced to live under the pressure of the Christian State Church. After the conversion of Constantine, Christianity became the official religion of the empire—a process seen by religious nonconformists in the Middle Ages and by Protestant and Catholic theologians today as a fatal turning point that perverted the Gospel by changing the whole nature of the glad tidings into a message of threats and drudgery. Constantine's conversion was also to be a turning point in the fortunes of the Jews.

The storming of the synagogues began in the fourth century in Italy (in Rome) and in Africa. Ambrose, Augustine's teacher, one of the strongest personalities of the Roman Church, warned the Christians: to speak to a Jew is a sin.

The legal code of Emperor Theodosius II treats Jews with suspicion. This language was new for Roman law. The legislation of Justinian I, inordinately effective in Europe long after the Middle Ages, completed this evolution by depriving the Jews of their civil rights. In the ninth century the Roman Church's liturgy for Good Friday was changed: the genuflection in prayer "for" the Jews ("oremus et pro perfidis judaeis") was suspended, the word "perfidis" taken literally and employed in its worst meaning. Not until Pope John XXIII was this fateful curse-prayer removed.

One of the worst measures against the Jews was adopted at the Fourth Lateran Council in 1215. The council created the Papal Inquisition and prescribed that Jews had to wear distinguishing marks. Thomas Aquinas carried on the teachings of Pope Innocent III. The Jews were condemned by God to eternal slavery as a punishment for the death of Christ. The Church, kings, and princes therefore have the right to dispose of the property of Jews as they see fit.

Thereafter in Italy, France, Germany, and the Balkan countries Jews were forced into the role of scapegoats for every imaginable calamity.

The circular badge, forerunner of the Yellow Star, became obligatory as well as a certain kind of dress the Jews had to wear so that they were easily distinguished as members of a minority—their "sign" was an eye-catching stigma. In addition, restrictions were imposed with regard to the professions they could practice; certain professions were forbidden to them and others were forced upon them. An absurd Church dogma forbade Christians to earn money by usury, declaring usury a deadly sin, and made the despised

Jews do all money dealing. The "Jewish usurer"—an anti-Semitic catchword to the present day—is a product of the Roman Church. The application of "usurer's interest" stemmed from the insecurity of Jewish existence: the Jews could never be sure that they would get their money back from their Christian rulers.

In the Islamic world, too, excesses of a more minor kind took place against the Jews; attacks against the Koran were always given as the reason. In many Islamic countries, both Jews and Christians had to wear a distinguishing mark—the Jews yellow, the Christians blue.

In retrospect, generally speaking—exceptions prove the rule—a kind of symbiosis between the two civilizations resulted from the cohabitation of Jews and Muslims.

In Spain, in the "world of the three rings" which inspired Gotthold Lessing to write his parable *Nathan the Wise*, a symbiosis of four civilizations developed: Arab, Islamic, Jewish, and Christian. There was a closeness between Christians and Jews which was never to be achieved again and which provided, on the basis of the philosophy and science of late antiquity, the foundations for the first Christian universities in the twelfth century.

The Islamic-Jewish symbiosis has repeatedly been disturbed by Islamic fanatics and, in our century, with the rise of Arab nationalism, has been completely destroyed. One only has to think of the Arabic translations of *The Protocols of the Elders of Zion* and Hitler's *Mein Kampf* in this context.

When Granada capitulated in 1492 the Islamic rulers reached an agreement with the Castilian kings ensuring the safety and protection of the rights not only of Muslims but also of Jews—an agreement that the Castilian kings violated in spite of their oath.

The Jews were the scapegoats whenever anything unpleasant happened to medieval man, and this custom continued on into the Renaissance. They were the target of collective hate right up to modern times when people gradually began to reconsider their prejudices against the Jews. Only partially and at certain times have they ever overcome them.

The great French Revolution did not bring with it—as has often been claimed—the full liberation of the Jews. Leading fathers of the French Revolution and the Enlightenment were anti-Jewish. The French Revolution demanded from the Jews that they give up their specific Jewish identity; only in this way could they become good citizens, real citizens, of the Republic.

National Socialism represents a horrendous regression into the darkest Middle Ages, but it was equipped with twentieth-century technology that made it possible for the Nazis to actually carry out what the enemies of the Jews in the Middle Ages had only dreamed of, only accomplished partially and in isolated towns and villages.

It should be noted, though, that in the midst of the Nazi propaganda against the Jews after Hitler's assumption of power, Pope Pius XI expressed his opposition against National Socialism in the 1937 encyclical "With Burning Concern." The Nazi party saw this encyclical as a challenge by the Catholic clergy. Later, especially after the war began and the Nazis were committing their atrocities against humanity, certain priests in Germany, Austria, and the occupied territories preached from their pulpits against National Socialism, and many of them were either imprisoned or had to pay with their lives for defending the innocents being persecuted.

These were the foundations on which the anti-Semitism of the National Socialists built. "Once a Jew, always a Jew" was the Nazi motto. The figure of the Jewish Christ, however, was problematic, which is why they undertook to make Jesus "Aryan" at this time. Perhaps he had even been a member of a Germanic tribe that had emigrated to Palestine.

This doctrine of the "Aryan Christ" originated in Spain and was adopted by German Protestant theologians and pastors who found much support among the "German Christians." Even today there are "pious" Catholics who ingenuously declare that Jesus was only a half-Jew, the son, after all, of God the Father in heaven.

Today it is fairly certain that Christianity as a whole would have been the next target of the Nazis if history had left them enough time. This next phase—eventual persecution of the Christians—was completely ignored by Christian Nazis as a possible prospect for the future. Unfortunately the leaders of the world churches drew no conclusions from what they certainly knew better than their flocks—which makes all the more contemptible their attitude during the catastrophic events.

If the six components set out above can be substantially regarded as the prerequisites for the intentions and actions of the opponents of Judaism, we must then ask the question: How did the Jews react to all this?

Their reactions ranged from armed rebellion when the Jews still lived in Palestine and armed acts against the Nazi hordes to a specific willingness to suffer which is particularly characteristic of the time when Jews lived in ghettos under the spiritual influence and leadership of the rabbis; in those circumstances given the choice between baptism and death they chose death.

This "traditional" Jewish passivity which was continually encouraged by the rabbis and declared by them to be the only way a Jew could "live" in this evil world—in which God himself had allowed a Hitler to exist—had a catastrophic effect, paralyzing all action. The only counterbalance was the resistance of many young Jews who escaped from the house of their fathers in the shtetl, the Jewish settlement. For a long time, Sabras, young Israelis, reproached their parents for not having fought back, which they regarded as the real reason for their feelings of guilt.

The Jews fled in the face of "the Jewish question." They sought a refuge where there was no such thing, but as soon as they had settled down, the persecution started again.

The way the Jews avoided the "Jewish question" in the nineteenth and twentieth centuries is one of the saddest chapters of Jewish history. Well respected, rich, and—so they thought—influential Jews in Germany, Austria, France, Hungary, and so forth, did not want to face reality and did not understand the danger Hitler posed to them. Austrian and German Jews believed him to be merely a successor of the Viennese mayor Dr. Karl Lueger, whom Hitler indeed revered. Lueger had on occasion expressed his support for anti-Semitism, but this was mainly election propaganda, and after coming to power in Vienna he strictly forbade the persecution of "his Jews." The equation Hitler = Lueger did not work.

There were two fundamental ways of "solving the Jewish question": physical annihilation or assimilation, that is, baptism. While the former—in the sense that it was a "final solution"—requires no further comment, the latter makes very clear how strong the discrimination against the Jews really was.

For a long time only a very few Jews tried to save their lives by being baptized. The great temptation to gain a ticket to success in the Christian world by baptism did not become a burning question until the nineteenth and twentieth centuries. Before this time it was mainly Spanish Jews who tried to attain security in this way; but the persecution did not stop, for even after "Christianization" they were still regarded with suspicion. So there remained nothing for them to do except to try and shake off their newly imposed faith and become Jews again. This is demonstrated particularly clearly in the fate of the Marranos in Spain. Until the present day they are strongly conscious of being Jewish: grandchildren and great-grandchildren remember those who were forced to change their faith and turn their back on the religion of their forefathers. The history of the Marranos at the height of the Inquisition illustrates the fate of the Jews who were "converted to Christianity." Many Marranos tried to escape the clutches of the Inquisition by emigrating to far-off places. Their flight led them as far afield as South America or the Portuguese colonies of India, such as Goa. The influx of Jews, converted or not—beginning with Columbus's men—must be seen from this perspective, which the Spanish historian and philosopher Salvador de Madariaga y Roso aptly described.

In the course of two thousand years no people has been persecuted or had to face death as often as the Jews. Their willingness to suffer, as already mentioned, did not subside until the doors of the ghettos were burst open during the emancipation movements of the nineteenth and twentieth centuries when new ideas were conquering the world and a restructuring of society was already inevitable. Nevertheless, one must remember that it was often only "islands" of enlightenment, often only individuals or small parts of the population that were influenced by the new ideas. The masses—the working class and the middle classes—remained for the most part enslaved to the old anti-Judaism, which started to take on increasingly political overtones and to find expression in the political parties.

In the Nazi era Jews were not allowed to vote; no alternatives were left open for them. The Jew realized that not even baptism would "wash him clean" of his Jewishness. This knowledge drove many assimilated Jews to suicide.

In the Middle Ages during the persecutions that accompanied the Crusades, many laments were written which express no protest, but only humiliation, subjugation, and submission to fate. Every Jew tortured or killed by anti-Semites, a victim of passive resistance, was regarded as a martyr—which is an example of how a virtue can be made of necessity.

The bewitching beauty of the medieval laments, which have become part of the Jewish liturgy and form an integral part of the High Holy Days service, and the poetic songs from Spain and the countries of the Holy Roman Empire cannot hide the harsh fact that the fatalism which is their very soul and which finds its expression in deepest piety and total devotion to God's will has catastrophic consequences.

For centuries it rendered the Jews vulnerable, for the very thought of armed revolt was rejected as an act of disbelief.

The Jews believed that they should not combat the destructive will of their foes. So they tried to be superior in other ways, for example in the many fields of knowledge or in material things, for they knew money had often been the means of saving them from expulsion or indeed death. The Jews' love of gold and jewels and all other movable goods is an attribute of flight. Knowledge and money were supposed to help them survive, in spite of their enemies.

Since the eighteenth century, there has been a kind of burning ambition in Jews which is characterized by outstanding achievements in science—for a long time mainly in medicine—and the arts. (Goethe called the young Mendelssohn, sitting on his lap, his "consoling David".) In this way a Jew could gain equality and respectability; occasionally he was even made a nobleman.

Over half the world's population today was born after World War II, and the number of people who personally experienced National Socialism is decreasing day by day, while the number of those who know nothing about it grows. In the whirlpool of everyday life and its problems, much is forgotten; but this "forgetting" is often really a "suppressing." One doesn't want to have anything to do with the old stories. Furthermore, many people nowadays know nothing or only very little of the facts. And least of all are they capable of seeing specific events of the recent past in the framework of a continuous development lasting for thousands of years. This horrifying lack of knowledge is revealed again and again when one talks both to Christian theologians and atheists as well as to so-called "ordinary people."

For many people the persecution of the Jews began with Hitler, when actually he represented merely the culmination point. But even this modest "knowledge" often becomes nothing but a cliché of existential noncommitment. Today, in the era of nonstop news reports and information inflation (the mass media and most of the newspapers only report the news in summary form), we know precious little about what really happened. In such an atmosphere Hitler's campaign of destruction against the Jews has also become an "episode"—an episode that does not really affect us anymore and that certainly has no power to mobilize us to action, to take steps here and now against genocide, torture, and expulsion.

For our children and grandchildren the millions of victims are nothing but a statistic that leaves them cold; they cannot begin to comprehend it because the number exceeds the bounds of all imagination.

For many people who participated personally in the Nazi crimes, the inconceivability of the atrocities committed seems in itself to have been part of a calculated plan. An episode during the Nuremberg trials in 1947, which I attended, throws some light on this. An SS troop leader, a witness for the prosecution, told me about a conversation which had taken place in the SS Officers' Club in Budapest in autumn 1944, shortly before the withdrawal of the Nazi troops from Hungary. Adolf Eichmann was talking to several SS officers of equal rank as himself. One of them asked how many Jews had been killed. Eichmann answered: "About five million." Then another SS leader, who had no illusions anymore about the coming end of the war and its outcome, asked: "What will happen when the world asks about these millions of dead?" Eichmann apparently snapped back: "One hundred dead are a catastrophe, one million dead are nothing but a statistic." I'm afraid I can only confirm this point of view.

This calendar is thus intended to help prevent the millions of victims disappearing into the abstraction of statistics and at least partially to give them back their true status. If one young reader pauses to think about the fates of these people hidden behind the statistics, then the purpose of this book will have been at least partly fulfilled.

At the time of the decline of the Roman Empire, the percentage of Jews in its total population was about 7 percent to 8 percent. It is estimated that they numbered about 4 million, including those living in Mesopotamia. In Palestine there were about half a million Jews at the time of Jesus.

In roughly 2,000 years, because of persecution, forced mass baptism, assimilation, and mass annihilation in the Nazi era, the number of Jews increased from 4 to only 14 million (at the time of this writing). Compare, for example, these figures with the population of the British Isles, which over the same period has grown from about 1 million people to 55 million, even though they too suffered plagues and wars. If the Jews had been able to grow in numbers as the Britons did, there would today be over 200 million Jews in the world.

What would such a world be like? What cultural potential would 200 million Jews represent? To visualize this we need only look at the blossoming of Jewish intellectual life in Germany in the eighteenth and particularly in the nineteenth and twentieth centuries, which produced a great number of creative personalities: scientists of all disciplines, physicians, chemists, physicists, sociologists, political scientists, and psychologists, and also poets, writers, prominent literary critics, state reformers, economists, and jurists. The oft-quoted names of Marx, Einstein, and Freud are merely the tip, not of an iceberg, but of a creative potential the size of a continent which broke free from the ghetto and left behind the miserable existence of deprivation and confinement.

The centuries-old history of the Jews is that of a people left over after catastrophes. The Jews always remained: after Egypt, after Babylon, after the Roman victory over ancient Israel, after Spain and the persecution of the Middle Ages, after Hitler. But the Bible and the Prophets have decreed: They will survive.

Just as I was finishing this manuscript, I received news which gave me great encouragement: Pope John Paul II visited the synagogue in Rome. After almost two millennia the pope took this step, and in the history of Jewish-Christian relations it is like the light at the end of the tunnel. I, together with many others who wish for communication and understanding, hope that that light will continue to grow.

As can be seen from many examples in this calendar the persecutors of the Jews often deliberately chose Jewish feast days for their coercive measures, and this was intended to attack the Jews not only physically but in their spirit and in their faith. Favorite dates were the Yom Kippur feast and the Jewish New Year. We also know that it was often after Sunday sermons that incited mobs attacked the Jews within or outside of the ghetto walls and brutally mistreated them.

The dates of the calendar are according to the Julian Calendar up to 1582, and thereafter the Gregorian Calendar is used. The reader will perhaps find it interesting that the Christians used the Jewish Calendar for the first three centuries.

It is obvious that not all the dates can appear in detail in this calendar; for many events we know only the year or the season. When we sift through archive material we continually come across new dates, find new information.

So it is possible—and indeed probable—that this book will have to be revised as our knowledge grows.

The book has no end—it is designed to grow, for research continues to fill in the dates and the facts of the tragedy that has accompanied the Jews for two thousand years.

—*Simon Wiesenthal*
Vienna

First page of the Book of Exodus, from an illuminated manuscript.

We remember

CONCENTRATION CAMPS
IN OCCUPIED EUROPE
1939–1945

...... Borders in 1933
✷ Extermination camp
★ Concentration camp
▽ Ghetto
▼ Transit camp
☆ Labor camp

Scale of miles
0   350

Map designed by Jeffrey L. Ward

JANUARY

January 1

1940 The Jews of Lodz, Poland, are concentrated in the old city and in the Baluty quarter.

1941 Four hundred Jews from the hospital and the home for the aged of Kalisz, Poland, are murdered in specially constructed gas vans.

1942 The Nazis begin a massacre of the Jews of Eupatoria on the Crimean Peninsula, Ukrainian S.S.R. But the Jews have friends among the Gentile population who offer them shelter. Because of their help it takes the SS two weeks to kill 1,300 Jews.

In Turka, Lvov province, Poland (today Ukrainian S.S.R.), the first large Aktion against the Jewish community takes place—500 Jews are shot on the spot.

A transport with about 1,000 Jews from the ghetto of Lodz, Poland, reaches the Chelmno extermination camp. The deportees are gassed immediately after their arrival.

Jewish organizations in the ghetto of Vilna, Poland (today Lithuanian S.S.R.), found a Jewish resistance movement under the leadership of Yizchak Wittenberg, Joseph Glazman, and Abba Kovner. First it is active only in the ghetto itself, but later outside as well.

A ghetto is set up in Kamionka, a suburb of Bedzin, in Silesia, Poland. The Jews are interned to await deportation to the extermination camps. Until summer 1943, numerous small deportations to Auschwitz take place.

1943 The Germans deport 3,000 Jews of Iwje, district of Novogrodek, Belorussian S.S.R., to Borisov, where they all perish.

1944 The last 200 Jews of Kozlov, Kielce province, Poland, are deported to the Auschwitz extermination camp.

1945 In an Aktion which lasts for two days SS men drive more than 200 Jews out of their apartments in Budapest, Hungary, and shoot them.

January 2

1235 The corpse of a Christian is found on the road between the towns of Lauda and Bischofsheim, Germany. Suspicion falls on the Jews of Bischofsheim, and before a judicial inquiry can be carried out the townspeople and the clergy slaughter men, women, and children of the Jewish community. On the same day eight Jewish notables from Lauda and Bischofsheim are put on trial for the same offense. They are tortured, found guilty, and executed.

1920 For the second time within three months Bobrovitsy, district of Tschernigov, Ukrainian S.S.R., is raided by units linked to Simon Petlyura's Ukrainian National Army. In the pogrom that follows 38 Jews are slain, 16 are wounded and mutilated so that eight of them die later. Many Jewish women are raped—often several times.

1940 In Chrzanov, Cracow province, Poland, a ghetto is set up. Jews have been living there since the sixteenth century. In 1940 the town numbered 8,000 Jews.

1942 Returning to the ghetto of Lvov, Poland (today Ukrainian S.S.R.), a working brigade of 60 Jews is led to a prison where they are shot the next day.

January 3

1941 From the environs of Grojec, Poland, 1,000 Jews are brought to the Grojec ghetto.

1942 Jews of Sabac, Nis, and Kragujevac, Central Serbia, Yugoslavia, are deported to the Sajmiste camp, near the Yugoslavian capital Belgrade.

1943 The Nazis execute 120 Jews from Opoczno, province Kielce, Poland. They are the last of the 3,000 Jews living in Opoczno before the German invasion.

In the ghetto of Czestochova, Poland, an armed group of Jewish resistance fighters under the leadership of Mendel Fiszlewicz takes on the Nazis who want to enter the ghetto. In the fighting, 20 Nazis are killed and 25 resistance fighters die. As a retaliatory measure, the SS shoots 250 Jews.

January 4

1349 The plague ravages the town of Ravensburg, Germany. Knowing they will be blamed, the Jews flee to the castle. A mob sets fire to it, killing the Jews inside.

1941 Brought to the ghetto of Gora Kalvarya, Poland, are 300 Jews. Jews have been living in the area since the seventeenth century. Gora Kalvarya was called New Jerusalem because so many Jewish scholars originated from it.

From Rudki, Poland, 300 Jews are deported to the ghetto of Warsaw.

1942 In Brody in the province of Lvov, Poland (today Ukrainian S.S.R.), a ghetto for 6,500 Jews is set up. Now they are all subjected to arbitrary restrictions by the Nazis.

January 5

1895 In a humiliating ceremony, Alfred Dreyfus, a French officer of Jewish origin, is publicly demoted after being found guilty of high treason on vague and contradictory evidence. His trial before the court-martial in Paris has provoked anti-Semitic riots all over France. Dreyfus is exiled to Devil's Island for life imprisonment. Three years later, the famous author Émile Zola publishes an article in which he accuses the denouncers of Dreyfus of malicious libel, but only in 1906 is the plot against Dreyfus by anti-Semitic officers uncovered. The Court of Appeal rejects the evidence against him as completely unsubstantiated. Dreyfus is reinstated in the French army.

1919 Colonel Palienko's troops, the Ukrainian National Army's "Battalions of Death," pass through the town of Berdichev, Volhynia (today Ukrainian S.S.R.). The Jewish community is subjected to methodical looting, the Jewish militia disarmed, and its members shot. Jews attending a funeral are shot by the rampaging soldiers.

1920 Units under the command of Romaschko, an ally of the Ukrainian National Army, carry out a pogrom in the town of Novaya Bassan in the district of Tschernigov, Ukraine, in which 43 Jews are slaughtered.

1943 In a surprise Aktion, the ghetto of Radomsko in the Polish province of Lodz is liquidated by the Nazis. Hundreds of Jews die in the fighting. The rest, about 4,000, are deported to the Treblinka extermination camp where they are murdered. A small group manages to escape, some of them to the ghetto of Warsaw, where they later will take part in the uprising in April 1943.

In the course of an Aktion against the ghetto of Miedzyrzec Podlaski, district of Lublin, Poland, the Jews are deported to the Treblinka and Majdanek extermination camps.

More than 15,000 Jews become victims of a two-day Aktion in the ghetto of Lvov, Poland (today Ukrainian S.S.R.). They are driven to the sandpits at Piaski, northwest of Lvov, where they are shot. Among the victims are the last president of the Jewish Council, Dr. Eberson, and other council members.

1945 The last deportation train leaves Berlin, Germany, destined for the Auschwitz extermination camp.

A convoy with about 40 Italian Jews who had been imprisoned at Risiera di San Sabba, in the only Nazi concentration camp on Italian territory, leaves for the German camp Ravensbrück.

January 6

1497 The Jews are expelled from Graz, capital of the Austrian province of Styria, following an edict by Emperor Maximilian I. Jews began settling in Graz as early as 1160, only thirty years after the foundation of the town itself.

1943 From Zarki, Kielce province, Poland, 3,500 Jews are deported to the Auschwitz extermination camp.

Of the 2,300 Jews of Lubaczov, Ukrainian S.S.R., only a few have survived the previous Aktionen of the Nazis. On this day, SS men drive the last few hundred Jews out of their houses and murder them.

From the ghetto of Ujazd, Poland, 2,000 Jews are deported to the Treblinka extermination camp.

Konskie, Polish province of Kielce, is declared "free of Jews." The remaining 300 Jews are deported to Szydlowiec. There they are murdered along with the local Jews.

The SS and the Ukrainian police slaughter 1,200 Jews of Narajov, Ternopol district, Ukrainian S.S.R., outside the town.

After the liquidation of the ghetto of Gorlice in Poland, originally housing several thousand Jews, only workers living in the factory buildings have remained. On this day they are sent to the forced labor camps of Muszyna and Rzeszo.

1945 In the course of an Aktion in Budapest, Hungarian Fascists, members of the Arrow Cross, drive 160 Jews to the bank of the Danube where they shoot them.

Agitators arrive from Tripoli, the capital of Libya, in Zanzur, 50 km away, aiming to incite the Muslim population against the Jews. In the resulting anti-Jewish riots about half of the 150 Jews of Zanzur are murdered.

The last execution of an inmate of Auschwitz takes place.

The Nazis deport 400 Jewish women, inmates of the Sered camp in Slovakia, Czechoslovakia, to the Ravensbrück concentration camp in Germany.

1942 In Chmielnik, Poland, the local police perpetrate a massacre of Jewish inhabitants. Afterward the Jewish Council is dissolved by the head of the police.

1943 A deportation train with 101 Jews leaves Vienna, the capital of Austria, its destination the Theresienstadt concentration camp in Czechoslovakia.

1945 A group of Hungarian Fascists breaks into the Janos Sanatorium in Budapest, where they brutally pull Jewish patients out of their beds, killing several.

January 7

1942 The new governor of Odessa, G. Alexianu, decides to rid Odessa, the capital of Transnistria, Ukrainian S.S.R., of Jews.

Several hundred Jews are murdered by the SS near Svieciany, Vilna district, Lithuanian S.S.R.

1943 The SS takes 500 Jews from the ghetto of Grojec, Poland, into a forest near Gora Kalvarya, where they are shot.

On this and the following two days, 4,000 Jews from the ghetto of Augustov, Poland, are deported to the Auschwitz extermination camp.

January 9

1942 The deportation starts from the Theresienstadt ghetto in Czechoslovakia toward the east. 1,000 Jewish men, women, and children are deported to Riga, Latvia, and about 400 Jews to the neighboring concentration camp of Salaspils where they are murdered.

In Klodava, Poland 1,100 Jews are murdered by the SS; 1,800 are sent to the Chelmno extermination camp.

1945 The Jewish patients of the Charite polyclinic in Budapest, Hungary, are pulled out of their beds by members of the Hungarian Fascist Arrow Cross brigade. They are driven to the banks of the Danube where they are shot.

January 8

1919 In the town of Zhitomir, Volhynia province, Ukraine, Ukrainian troops begin a pogrom that lasts six days. The troops belong to the Ukrainian National Army under supreme commander Simon Petlyura. They slay 53 Jews and wound 19.

January 10

1943 The Nazis deport 6,000 Jews imprisoned in the forced labor camp in Sandomierz, Poland, and 2,500 Jews from the ghetto of Sandomierz to the Treblinka extermination camp where they are gassed.

The Kopernik labor camp near Minsk Mazoviecki, Poland, is liquidated by the SS. The Jews show active resistance and in the course of the battle some SS men are killed.

The ghetto of Bochnia, Poland, is liquidated and 3,500 Jews are murdered by the Nazis.

1944 From Vienna, 6 Jews are deported to the Theresienstadt concentration camp in Czechoslovakia.

January 11

1941 The ghetto in Domaczow, Belorussian S.S.R., is liquidated, and 2,000 Jews are murdered by the SS.

1942 From Vienna, 1,000 Jews are deported to the ghetto of Riga, Latvia.

1943 A deportation train leaves the Westerbork transit camp in the Dutch province of Drenthe carrying 750 Jews to Auschwitz.

The ghetto of Augustov, Poland, is liquidated; 5,500 Jews are driven into the forest of Szczabre where they are shot.

From Vienna, 100 Jews are deported to the Theresienstadt concentration camp in Czechoslovakia.

1944 A transport with 1,037 Jewish inmates leaves the Westerbork transit camp in the Dutch province of Drenthe for the Bergen-Belsen concentration camp.

1945 Hungarian Fascists of the Arrow Cross carry out a pogrom in Budapest, Hungary, murdering 43 Jewish inhabitants of the ghetto. They also storm the Jewish hospital of Budapest, pull the patients—men, women, and children—out of their beds, and murder them, along with the doctors and nurses. Only one nurse survives.

January 12

1349 The Black Death reaches Friedrichshafen, Germany. The Jews are accused of having poisoned the wells in order to kill the Christians and are murdered by the mob.

1412 Proclamation of the Castilian Edict containing 24 articles "contra Judaeos"—"against the Jews." Among those articles is one ordering the creation of ghettos in all Spanish towns.

1493 This is the last and irrevocable date for all Jews to leave Sicily, then part of the Spanish Kingdom. Every remaining Jew is liable to the death penalty. Up to this day, Jews have been living in Sicily for about 1,500 years.

1942 From Bugaj, Poland, 600 Jews are deported to the Chelmno extermination camp where they are murdered.

In Brdov, north of Warsaw, Poland, 600 Jews are massacred in an Aktion by the SS and security police.

The deportation of the Jews of Odessa, Ukrainian S.S.R., begins. They are brought to the forced labor camps of Berezovka and Golta. The deportations last five weeks. Nearly 20,000 Jews are murdered.

1943 A deportation transport of 1,000 Jews leaves Berlin, the capital of the Reich.

The Nazis begin to deport the 20,000 Jews from the forced labor camp of Zambrov in the Polish province of Bialystok. In groups of 2,000 they are sent to Auschwitz in night trains.

The liquidation of the Wolkovysk camp in the province of Grodno, Soviet Union, takes place, and 1,000 Jews are deported to Auschwitz.

1944   Arrival of 23 Jewish deportees from Trieste, Italy, at the Auschwitz extermination camp, Poland, where they are murdered immediately.

A deportation transport arrives from Lodz, Poland, at Auschwitz. The 95 deportees are murdered immediately after their arrival.

A transport with 1,000 Jews from the Stutthof concentration camp, Poland, are transported to the Auschwitz extermination camp. They are murdered shortly after their arrival.

January 13

1298   During the war between Adolf of Nassau and Albrecht of Habsburg, both pretenders to the German crown, the people of Rufach in Alsace (today France), accuse the Jews of their town of siding with Adolf, whereas they themselves are partisans of Duke Albrecht. They massacre the Jews, slaying them or burning them on piles of wood.

Jews being burned at the stake. German woodcut of 1493.

1675 An auto-da-fé is held in Lisbon, Portugal, in which the effigies of 6 fugitive Portuguese Judaizers (secret practitioners of Judaism) are burned, together with a refugee from Madrid.

1943 From the ghetto of Przytyk, Poland, 1,000 Jews are deported to the Treblinka extermination camp.

From the ghetto of Szydloviec, Poland, 5,000 Jews are deported to the Treblinka extermination camp.

From the labor camp in Radom, Poland, 1,500 Jews are sent to the Treblinka extermination camp.

1945 Several Jews are arrested in Budapest, Hungary, by the Hungarian Fascist Arrow Cross. After their arrest the Jews are murdered.

1948 The de facto leader of Soviet Jewry, Solomon Mikhoels, chairman of the Jewish anti-Fascist committee, Moscow, Soviet Union, is assassinated, probably on the orders of Stalin. As director of the Yiddish theater in Moscow, his productions had brought him world fame.

1953 The arrest of 9 well-known doctors, 6 of them Jews, in Moscow, Soviet Union, is announced. The doctors have allegedly confessed to the assassinations of two Soviet leaders and the planned murder of several leading officers of the Soviet army, as well as planning espionage and terror against the Soviet Union in the service of the United States and Zionism.

The death of Stalin on March 3, 1953, puts an end to the "Doctor's Plot." Later it will be announced that all accused had been found "not guilty" and set free.

January 14

1942 In Szczakova, Poland, a Jew is hanged by the Gestapo—the German Secret Police—as a retaliatory measure.

From Izbica Kujavska, Poland, 1,000 Jews are deported to the Chelmno extermination camp, where they are murdered.

1943 In an Aktion lasting several days, some of the 8,000 Jews from the ghetto of Lomza, Poland, are deported to the Auschwitz extermination camp. The rest are murdered outside the town in the forest of Galczyn.

1945 At the Orthodox Jewish Hospital in Varosmajor, Hungary, 150 patients and medical personnel are massacred by gangs of the ultrarightist group, Nyilas.

January 15

1755 The last person to be burned for Judaizing, secretly practicing Judaism, in Lisbon, Portugal, is Jeronimo José Ramos, a merchant from Braganza. Having escaped the auto-da-fé of September 24, 1752, he was recaptured and finally sentenced to death as a nonrepentant.

1919 Units under Kozyr-Zyrko, linked to Simon Petlyura's Ukrainian National Army, carry out a pogrom against the Jews of Ovrutch, Ukraine; 32 Jews are massacred.

1920 In the town of Gogolevo, in the district of Tschernigov, Ukraine, the Ukrainian National Army under Romaschko stages a pogrom against the Jewish population in which 42 Jews are murdered, 6 gravely wounded.

1921 The village of Dumanovka in the district of Kiev, Ukraine, is the site of a pogrom carried out under Strukovtsy, leader of a unit linked to the Ukrainian National Army. The unit kills 4 Jews.

1942 From the Theresienstadt concentration camp in Czechoslovakia 1,000 Jews are deported to the ghetto of Riga, Latvia. Upon their arrival 924 of them are brought to a nearby forest where they are shot.

1943 The SS catches and shoots 27 Jews who have been living in Bilgoraj, province of Lublin, Poland. In the forest surrounding the town, young Jews have formed a resistance group. They fight the German occupiers unceasingly and manage to survive until the end of the war.

2,500 Jews from the ghetto of Jaryczov Novy, Galicia, Poland, are shot by the SS and the Ukrainian police.

Two transports with 1,632 Jews—including 287 children—leave the Mechelen transit camp in Belgium for the Auschwitz extermination camp in Poland. Only 11 of these people will survive until the liberation of the camp in 1945.

1944 The twenty-third transport with 625 Jews—among them 62 children—leaves the Mechelen transit camp for Auschwitz. In the same transport are 351 Gypsies, of whom only 12 will survive until the liberation of the camp in 1945.

January 16

1349 In the course of the Black Death Persecutions, the entire Jewish community of Freiburg, Germany, men, women, and children, is burned at the stake. The accusation here, too, is poisoning of wells by the Jews in order to kill all Christendom. Their property falls to the municipality of Freiburg.

Similarly, the Jews of Basel, Switzerland, are burned alive in a wooden hut, constructed for this purpose on a small island in the Rhine River. Only the children are spared, having been taken away from their parents to be baptized and raised as good Christians.

1605 A large auto-da-fé is held in Lisbon, Portugal, of 155 New Christians, descendants of the Jews forcibly baptized in 1497, when mass baptism of the Jews of Spain was at its cruelest. This time the Inquisition does not demand their blood, but the king of Spain, Philip III, being in great need of money, confiscates all their wealth, condemning them only to public repentance.

1942 From Lodz, Poland, 3,000 Jews are deported to the Chelmno extermination camp, where they are murdered.

1943 1,000 Jews are deported from the Ostroviec ghetto in the Polish province of Kielce to the forced labor camp of Sandomierz.

From the ghetto of Grodno, Poland (today Belorussian S.S.R.), 2,000 Jews are deported to the Auschwitz extermination camp.

1944 Before the arrival of the Soviet army, the 400 Jewish inmates of the Sandomierz camp, in the province of Kielce, Poland, are murdered by the SS.

January 17

1942 The Nazis murder 22 Jews in Eupatoria on the Crimean Peninsula.

The Jews of Zaandam, Netherlands, are ordered to report for resettlement in the Jewish quarter of Amsterdam. Bringing only the allowed hand luggage, 270 Jews report. The Nazis intern 98 stateless Jews living in Zaandam in the Westerbork camp.

1944 A deportation transport of 417 Jews from Mechelen, Belgium, arrives at the Auschwitz extermination camp in Poland. They are murdered immediately after their arrival.

1945 The SS leadership orders the evacuation of Auschwitz to prevent the prisoners from falling into the hands of the Soviet army.

The Swedish diplomat Raoul Wallenberg is arrested in Budapest, Hungary, by the Soviet police and taken to the Soviet Union. At great personal risk he saved tens of thousands of Hungarian Jews from the hands of the Nazis by providing them with Swedish passports. His fate is unknown.

The labor camps of Skarzysko-Kamienna, Mielec, and Plaszow (all in Poland), are liquidated. Of the total of 15,000 Jewish internees, 10,000 of them are shot, 5,000 transported by train to the Buchenwald and Ravensbrück concentration camps in Germany.

Prisoners riot in the Chelmno extermination camp in Poland, and 46 Jewish inmates are shot.

Interior of the old synagogue at Metz. (Frauberger)

January 18

1670 A 3-year-old Christian child from Metz, France, has disappeared. Raphael Levy, a Jew, is accused of having killed the child in a ritual murder. He is tortured but maintains his innocence. When the dead child is found and proved to be the victim of a wild animal, Levy thinks that he will soon be free. Instead, he is condemned and burned alive at the stake. Following this the Christian inhabitants of Metz write to the king of France, demanding the expulsion of the Jews from their city. Their wish is granted.

1943 From the ghetto of Warsaw, Poland, 6,000 Jews are deported to the Treblinka extermination camp, where 1,000 are shot on the spot.

In the Dutch province of Drenthe, 748 Jews leave the Westerbork transit camp in a transport to the Auschwitz extermination camp in Poland.

The 200 Jews remaining in the ghetto of Sokolka in the Polish province of Bialystok are murdered and the town is thus declared "free of Jews." A few young Jews manage to escape to Warsaw, where they will participate in the ghetto uprising in April 1943.

1944 On this day, 870 Jews are deported from the Westerbork transit camp to the Theresienstadt concentration camp in Czechoslovakia.

In Buczacz, Poland (today Ukrainian S.S.R.), 300 Jews who have been hiding in the forest are murdered by the Nazis.

1945 The evacuation of the labor camps surrounding Auschwitz to the Gross-Rosen concentration camp begins. Many of the prisoners are shot on the march.

On a death march, 3,000 Jews leave Auschwitz for Geppersdorf in Germany. On arrival at their destination in March 1945, only 280 Jews are still alive.

January 19

1942 In an Aktion carried out by Hungarian Fascists, hundreds of Jews from the seaside resort town of Strand, Yugoslavia, are sent on a death march and murdered.

A deportation transport with 1,000 Jews from Vienna arrives in Riga, Latvia. About 70 or 80 young Jews are selected to work in a forced labor camp; the rest of the deportees are shot in Bikerneku, the "Birch Grove."

1945 From the camp of Gwizdzilny, Poland, 24 Jewish women are shot by the SS in a forest near Skarlin.

In Mokre Slaskie, Poland, the SS murders 15 prisoners who are too weak to continue their evacuation march from the Auschwitz extermination camp. In nearby Brzezce, the same happens to 17 prisoners. Most of the victims are Jews.

January 20

1942 The historical Wannsee Conference for the Final Solution takes place near Berlin, Germany. Under the chairmanship of Reinhard Heydrich, head of the Reichssicherheitshauptamt (Reich Central Security Office), and in the presence of many important government representatives, as well as Adolf Eichmann, the executor of the entire project, the annihilation of 11 million European Jews is decided and planned.

1943 A transport with 2,000 Jews is sent from the Theresienstadt ghetto in Czechoslovakia to the Auschwitz extermination camp in Poland. Immediately after their arrival, 1,760 men, women, and children are driven into the gas chambers; 160 men and 80 women are interned in the Auschwitz II-Birkenau camp.

1944   The first deportation convoy of the year leaves the camp at Drancy, France, with 1,155 Jews for Auschwitz. Immediately after their arrival, 864 deportees are gassed. Of the rest, only 47 men and 17 women survive and are liberated by the Soviet army in 1945.

The Nazis take 70 old Jews from the Jewish home for the aged in Trieste, Italy. Their destination is unknown, but not one of the Jews will return.

1945   The Nazis shoot 4,000 Jews in the Auschwitz II-Birkenau camp.

January 21

1268   In St.-Antoine, near Paris, a forcibly baptized Jew is arrested by the municipal power for having relapsed to Judaism. As he bravely remains faithful to his Jewish belief, he is burned at the stake.

1349   The Black Death Persecutions with their false accusations against the Jews reach the Jewish community in Feldkirch, in the Austrian province of Vorarlberg, bringing great sufferings upon its members. Accused of poisoning the wells in order to extinguish Christendom, the Jews are burned at the stake.

The same fate befalls the Jews of Messkirch in the German province of Baden. Well poisoning is a common accusation during this period.

1919   The Jewish community of Bobrynetz, in the Ukraine, suffers a pogrom carried out by units of Simon Petlyura's Ukrainian National Army, in which 10 Jews are murdered, many more wounded or mutilated.

1938   The Rumanian government abolishes the minority rights of Jews. Consequently many Jews are deprived of their Rumanian citizenship.

1941   The Iron Guard, the Rumanian Fascist military organization, revolts against the Rumanian head of state, Antonescu. In the course of this revolt a pogrom is carried out against the Jews of Bucharest in which 120 members of the Jewish community are murdered.

1942   Hungarian Fascists start a riot in Novi Sad, in the Voivodina province of Yugoslavia. This serves as a pretext for a three-day Aktion against the town's Jewish population, in which 1,400 Jews are driven out of their homes. Some of them are shot in the streets, the others are driven to the banks of the frozen Danube River. There they are shot, men, women, and children, and pushed through the holes chopped in the ice. Jews have been settling in Novi Sad since the sixteenth century.

1943   During the night the Jewish psychiatric hospital Het Apeldoornse Bos near Apeldoorn in the Dutch province of Gelderland is evacuated by the SS. The SS deports 869 patients and 52 members of the medical personnel to the Auschwitz extermination camp in Poland.

A further deportation takes place from the Grodek Jagiellonski ghetto in the province of Lvov, Poland (today Ukrainian S.S.R.). 1,000 Jews are sent to the Belzec extermination camp.

January 22

1349   The Jewish community of Speyer on the Rhine in Germany is destroyed in the persecutions engendered by the plague. On January 22, the mob gathers and storms the Jewish quarter. Some Jews lock themselves in their houses and set fire to them; others are murdered by the mob. A few allow themselves to be baptized in order to save their lives. A small number are able to flee to neighboring communities like Heidelberg and Sinzheim. Out of fear of contamination the mob puts the corpses into empty wine barrels and throws them into the Rhine. All Jewish property is seized or destroyed, including the Jewish cemetery.

1941 Within three days, 3,000 Jews of Piaseczno, Poland, are deported to the ghetto of Warsaw.

1942 In a forest near Golinka, Poland, 6 Jews are shot while looking for food.

1943 From the Westerbork transit camp in the Dutch province of Drenthe, 921 Jews are deported to the Auschwitz extermination camp in Poland.

17 Jewish workmen who have been employed by the German headquarters in Dzisna, Belorussian S.S.R., are murdered.

A raid code-named "Aktion Tiger" is carried out by the Nazis in Marseilles, France, destroying the old quarter of the city. The inhabitants, mainly Jews, are deported to the camps of Compiègne and Drancy to await their further deportations to Auschwitz.

1945 During an evacuation march from Auschwitz, 3 Jews, among many others, are shot by the accompanying SS guards.

January 23

1639 The Spanish Inquisition was established in South America too, where many Conversos,

children of forcibly baptized Jews, emigrated in the hope of being able to practice Judaism more freely there. In 1519 Inquisitors for the Latin American colonies were appointed by the Supreme Tribunal in Spain.

On January 23, 1639, a great auto-da-fé is held in Lima, the capital of Peru. Of the 72 accused of Judaizing, 63 are condemned to be burned at the stake, the others sentenced to penalties of varying severity.

The most prominent of the condemned is Francisco Maldonado da Silva who called himself Eli Nazareno and had been languishing in the Inquisition prison for thirteen years.

1943 Of the 2,000 Jews from the Theresienstadt ghetto in Czechoslovakia deported to the Auschwitz extermination camp in Poland, 1,800 of them are gassed immediately upon arrival; 200 young men are selected to work in the I. G. Farben factory in Buna-Monowice, known as Auschwitz III.

Emblem of the Lima Inquisition.

A deportation convoy with 516 Jews leaves the Westerbork transit camp in the Dutch province of Drenthe for Auschwitz.

A Jew doing forced labor for the Germans in the Bizerte camp in Tunisia is shot by a Nazi guard.

January 24

1942 Several hundred members of the Jewish intelligentsia of Kolomyja, Ukrainian S.S.R., are assembled and murdered.

A large-scale Aktion against the Jews of the Bogdanovka camp, Transnistria, Ukrainian S.S.R., begins, lasting two weeks.

1943 Twenty-five cattle cars with patients from the Jewish psychiatric hospital Het Apeldoornse Bos near Apeldoorn in the Dutch province of Gelderland arrive in the Auschwitz extermination camp in Poland. They are murdered and their corpses burned in special fire pits.

A working brigade of 110 Jews are shot by the SS in a sandpit near the Janovska camp in Lvov, East Galicia, Poland.

January 25

1338 The Armleder persecutions, so-called after the piece of leather worn by the peasantry instead of the metal armor of the knights, are carried out by bands of peasants and adventurers who threaten the Jewish communities in Franconia and Alsace between 1336 and 1339. Armed with saws, shovels, and clubs, with a cross and a flag carried before them, the Armleder massacre the Jews of Rufach, Alsace. The meadow where the slaughter took place is still called Judenmatt—Jew's meadow.

1941 From Jeziorna, Poland, 250 Jews are deported to the Warsaw ghetto.

1943 From the ghetto of Jasionovka, Poland, 2,120 Jews are deported to the Auschwitz extermination camp.

1944 From the Westerbork transit camp in the Dutch province of Drenthe, 949 Jewish inmates are deported to Auschwitz.

1945 The Stutthof concentration camp in the district of Gdansk, Poland, is liberated with only a small number of survivors.

January 26

1531 An earthquake in Santarém, Portugal, terrifies the inhabitants. In the aftermath, monks incite the people to riot against the town's Jews. Thus in the middle of a bitterly cold winter the Jews are driven into the mountains. Many perish because of the cold and the lack of food. The survivors later return.

1942 A deportation transport with 1,196 Jews leaves Vienna, Austria, for Riga, Latvia.

The synagogue in Rufach, Alsace, built in the fourteenth century.

In a mass execution in Obecse, Delvidek, in Yugoslavia, Jews and Serbs are murdered together. In two days 200 people—100 of them Jews—are murdered by Hungarian soldiers under the high command of Fcketehalmy-Czeydner.

1943   From the Theresienstadt ghetto in Czechoslovakia, 1,000 Jews are deported to the Auschwitz extermination camp in Poland. Immediately, 770 are sent to the gas chambers; 130 young women are sent to work in the camp Auschwitz II-Birkenau, 100 men to the subcamp Goleszov. Of this transport, 39 persons will survive until 1945.

The SS raids the ghetto of Stanislavov, Poland (today Ukrainian S.S.R.), and rounds up 1,000 people who are old, ill, or without a work permit. All are murdered at the Jewish cemetery.

1945   A death march of 1,000 Jewish women begins from Neusalz, a forced labor camp in Silesia, Poland, to the Flossenbürg concentration camp in Germany. The march lasts six weeks. Only 200 women arrive on March 11.

January 27

1942   Hungarian Fascists carry out a raid in Stari Becej, a village near Novi Sad in Voivodina in Yugoslavia. They murder more than 100 Jews.

After the British conquest of Benghazi, Libya, the port is soon recaptured by the Italo-German army. This results in immediate attacks on the Jewish community, systematic looting of Jewish shops and the proclamation of a deportation order. Subsequently almost all Jews of Benghazi are deported to Giadi, a camp in the desert 240 km south of Tripoli, where they have to perform forced labor under inhuman conditions, including a typhoid epidemic—562 of them perish.

1943   In the ghetto of Grodek Jagiellonski, Lvov province, Poland, 1,300 Jews are shot by the SS.

In the ghetto of Pruzana, Poland (today Belorussian S.S.R.), a Jewish underground resistance movement has been set up. The Nazis learn of it and decide to liquidate the ghetto. On January 27 the deportation of the Jews begins with 2,500 Jews being sent to the Auschwitz extermination camp. Some of the Jews offer fierce resistance.

January 28

1943   After an Aktion lasting two days, the SS sends several hundred Jews from the ghetto of Wolkovysk, in the province of Grodno, Poland, to the Auschwitz extermination camp.

Nine Jews from Vienna, Austria, are deported to the Theresienstadt ghetto in Czechoslovakia.

1945   In Malki, in the Polish district of Brodnica, 75 Jewish women are shot by SS men.

January 29

1942   In the Domanevka concentration camp, Ukrainian S.S.R., 2,000 Jews are murdered by the SS.

1943   From Berlin, 1,000 Jews are sent to the Auschwitz extermination camp in Poland.

Over 1,000 Jews from the Theresienstadt ghetto, Czechoslovakia, are deported to Auschwitz. Immediately, 820 men, women, and children are sent to the gas chambers; 80 women are selected for hard labor in the Auschwitz II-Birkenau camp, 120 young men for work on road construction.

From the Westerbork transit camp in the Dutch province of Drenthe, 659 Jews are deported to Auschwitz.

January 30

1349 The Jewish community of Ulm, Germany, suffers the consequences of the Black Death. At first the municipal council protects the Jews against the infuriated mob, but finally gives in. The Jewish community of Ulm is annihilated.

The Jewish community of Freiburg in Breisgau, Germany, is accused of well poisoning in order to spread the plague and thus kill Christians. All Jews are burned at the stake except the pregnant women and children. According to the custom of the time, the children were baptized in order to save their souls from hell.

1544 A decree issued by King Ferdinand I expels the Jews from the towns in Austria holding the privilege "De Non Tolerandis Judaeis," the right to exclude Jews.

1942 From the ghetto of Otvock, near Warsaw, Poland, 150 youngsters are deported to the recently opened Treblinka extermination camp.

1944 A transport from Milan, Italy, arrives at the Auschwitz extermination camp in Poland. The 563 Jewish deportees are gassed a few hours after their arrival.

January 31

1941 From Pruszkov, Poland, 1,000 Jews are deported to the Warsaw ghetto.

1942 In Krzemieniec, Poland (today Ukrainian S.S.R.), a ghetto is established. The Jews have to leave their homes in order to resettle in the ghetto area, where they are completely isolated from the rest of the population.

Several hundred Jews from Kharkov, Ukrainian S.S.R., are massacred in the vicinity of Drobitzky Yar.

1943 The ghetto of Pruzana in the district of Brest, Poland (today Belorussian S.S.R.), is liquidated. Pruzana is thus "free of Jews." Four days before, the Germans had begun to clear the ghetto at full speed. Every day 2,500 Jews were deported to the Auschwitz extermination camp. A small group of young men manages to flee into the woods from where they fight the Germans.

FEBRUARY

February 1

1194 In Neuss, Germany, a mentally disturbed Jew kills a young Christian woman in a fit of madness, in front of many witnesses, Jews as well as Christians. The Christians present kill the madman at once, as well as 6 uninvolved bystanders, Jews of high esteem in the community.

1919 Petlyurian units carry out a pogrom against the Jewish inhabitants of Malina, in the Russian district of Kiev. Three Jews are massacred and twenty severely injured.

1941 By order of Alois Brunner, one of Adolf Eichmann's deputies, the Jews in Vienna, where all Jews from Austria have been assembled, are to be deported to the camps in Poland beginning February 1, 1941. Each transport will carry 1,000 people.

The 4,000 Jews of Sochaczev, Poland, are deported to the Warsaw ghetto and share the fate of the other Jews in the ghetto. Jews have been living in Sochaczev since the beginning of the fifteenth century.

1942 In the town of Kursk, Soviet Union, 100 Jews are murdered by German soldiers.

In Cherven, Soviet Union, 1,800 Jews are murdered by SS men.

The Nazis decree that all unemployed Jews in the Netherlands must report to the authorities. The 175 Jews who follow the order are interned in the SS labor camp of Ellecom in the Dutch province of Gelderland. They are cruelly mistreated and some of them are murdered. The remaining Jews are later deported to the Westerbork transit camp.

1943 1,000 Jewish inmates of the Theresienstadt concentration camp in Czechoslovakia are deported to the Auschwitz extermination camp in Poland. Immediately, 782 Jewish men and women are gassed; 155 men and 64 women are selected for labor in the camp Auschwitz II-Birkenau. Another 50 men are transferred to the subcamp Swientlochowice to work on road construction at the beginning of June 1943. Only 29 of them survive until the end of the war.

1,500 Jews are taken from the Minsk ghetto in Belorussian S.S.R. They are shot at the mines of Maly Trostyanets.

Having survived the previous deportations, the last 200 Jews of the ghetto of Jedrzejov in the Polish province of Kielce are shot.

An Aktion lasting two days takes place in Buczacz, in the province Ternopol, formerly Poland, today Ukrainian S.S.R. 2,000 Jews are brought to the hill of Fedor where they are murdered. The ghetto is liquidated and only a small number of Jews remain in a labor camp.

1944 Five Argentinian Jews are deported from Vienna, Austria, to the Bergen-Belsen concentration camp in Germany.

Deported to Bergen-Belsen are 908 Jews from the Westerbork transit camp in the Dutch province of Drenthe.

1945 Four Jews are deported from Vienna, Austria, to the Theresienstadt concentration camp in Czechoslovakia.

February 2

1189 As the result of a quarrel between a Jew and a recent convert, riots break out against the Jewish community of Lynn, England. Jews are butchered or burned in their houses. Part of the town is completely destroyed by fire.

1942 In the Rakov ghetto, in the district of Novogrodek, Belorussian S.S.R., 2,000 Jews are burned in their houses.

Nazis massacre 500 Jews in the village of Shamovo, Ukrainian S.S.R.

1943 SS men massacre 1,000 Jews in the Rakov ghetto.

The Nazis deport 890 Jewish internees from the Westerbork transit camp in the Dutch province of Drenthe to the Auschwitz extermination camp in Poland.

In Zychlin in the province of Lodz, Poland, 181 Jews are shot by the German Schutzpolizei.

February 3

1939 A bomb planted by a Hungarian Fascist explodes in a synagogue in Budapest, Hungary, during services. One man is killed and several others injured.

1943 1,000 Jews are deported from the Grodek Jagiellonski ghetto in the Polish province of Lvov (today Ukrainian S.S.R.), to the Belzec extermination camp, where they are all murdered.

From Berlin, the capital of the Reich, 950 Jews are deported to the Auschwitz extermination camp in Poland.

Nearly 1,000 Jews are murdered in the course of an Aktion against the Jewish community of Boryslav, Poland (today Ukrainian S.S.R.).

1944 The second transport in the year 1944 leaves the Drancy transit camp in France and 1,214 Jewish men and women are deported to Auschwitz. Immediately after their arrival, 985 of them are sent to the gas chambers. Only 38 survive until the liberation of the camp.

February 4

1919 Units of the Ukrainian National Army under Simon Petlyura carry out a pogrom in Jelissavetgrad, in the Russian district of Kherson. In the course of two days 22 Jews are massacred, 50 more severely injured.

1942 400 Jews are murdered in the town of Liepaja, Latvian S.S.R.

1943 In Novogrodek, Belorussian S.S.R., SS men murder 450 Jews.

February 5

1840 In one more recent case of alleged ritual murder, known as the Damascus Affair, seven Jews are arrested in Damascus, Syria. After one of their friars and his servant disappear, the Capuchins accuse the Jews of having killed them in order to use their blood for the Passover rituals.

In the subsequent investigation two of the falsely accused Jews die under torture. After the intervention of several well-known European Jews, including Moses Montefiore and Adolphe Crémieux, the surviving Jews are liberated, but they will never be acquitted of the alleged crimes.

1942 From Suchovola, Poland, 2,000 Jews are deported to the Grodno ghetto.

1943 In Bialystok, Poland, a ghetto was set up by the German army on August 1, 1941. On February 5, 1943 the first Aktion begins. In one week, through the twelfth of February, about 10,000 Jews are deported to the Treblinka and Auschwitz extermination camps and about 1,000 Jews are murdered on the spot. Jewish resistance fighters—led by Eliahu Boraks—manage to kill a number of SS men. Zvi Wider, a member of the Jewish Council of Bialystok, commits suicide when he learns that the other members of the council provided the Gestapo with a list of persons to be deported.

The Nazis murder 200 Jews in the Chodorov ghetto in East Galicia, Ukrainian S.S.R.

February 6

1189 The riots of Lynn in Norfolk spread to the English town of Norwich. The populace starts rioting against the Jewish community. Many Jews escape to the bishop's castle. Those who remain in their homes are murdered, their property looted.

1194 In Neuss, Germany, five days after the murder of a mentally disturbed Jew who had killed a Christian woman in a fit of madness, his family is arrested by the judges. They are tortured but, with the exception of the madman's young sister, they do not allow themselves to be baptized. The mother is buried alive and the uncles are broken on the wheel.

1481 The first auto-da-fé in the Castilian town of Seville, Spain, is held. Six men and women, all honorable and respected citizens of Seville, are burned alive for Judaizing, secretly practicing the Jewish faith.

1484 The first auto-da-fé is held in Ciudad Real, Spain, by the Inquisition Tribunal, established there for the province of Toledo. Four Conversos—children of Jews forcibly baptized in the persecutions of 1391—are accused of Judaizing, and burned at the stake as nonrepentants.

1919 Units of the Ukrainian National Army under Simon Petlyura carry out a pogrom in the town of Balta, Ukraine; 27 Jews are massacred, many wounded and Jewish women are raped.

1942 A train transport with 997 Jews leaves Vienna, capital of Austria, for Riga, the capital of Latvia.

The small ghetto of Sierpc, in the province of Warsaw, Poland, is liquidated. Its 3,500 Jews are

Ancestor of the Yellow Star: red-and-white circular badge worn by French Jews in the thirteenth and fourteenth centuries. Sometimes the disk was yellow. (From a fourteenth-century French miniature)

transported to the Mlava ghetto from where they are deported, all together, to the Auschwitz extermination camp. Only 20 of the villagers survive the war.

1943   The Nazis liquidate the camp of Peresieka in the Polish province of Grodno (today Belorussian S.S.R.). They shoot all the artisans. A group of 50 Jews escapes into the forest, where they form a partisan group.

In Salonika, Greece, the wearing of the Yellow Star becomes obligatory on the orders of two assistants to Adolf Eichmann, the head of the Jewish department of the Gestapo in Berlin, Dieter Wisliceny and Alois Brunner.

1944   There is a transfer of 1,000 Jewish inmates of the Dora-Nordhausen concentration camp in Germany to the Majdanek concentration camp in Poland.

February 7

1919   For two days troops of Simon Petlyura's Ukrainian National Army pass through Volkovintsy in the district of Podolia, Russia, where they carry out a pogrom against the Jewish community of the town. They flog all the Jews they can get hold of.

For two days the 4th railway battalion carries out a pogrom against the Jews of Vassilkovo in the district of Kiev, Ukraine. The troops slaughter 50 Jews and wound a great number. The battalion is allied with Petlyura's Ukrainian National Army.

1940   The German police invade the Zychlin ghetto in the Polish province of Lodz and murder several hundred Jews in the streets. Most members of the Jewish Council and their families are among the victims. The Jewish ghetto police, too, are liquidated by the Germans.

1942   Several hundred Jews of the Stolpce ghetto in the Polish province of Minsk (today Belorussian S.S.R.), are taken to the Jewish cemetery and murdered there.

February 8

1940 The German police order all Jews of Lodz, Poland, to move into the Balnty ghetto.

1944 From the Westerbork transit camp in the Dutch province of Drenthe, 1,015 Jewish internees are deported to the Auschwitz extermination camp in Poland.

1945 During the night, 180 deportees from the Buchenwald concentration camp in Germany, among them many Jews, are shot on the way from the Mauthausen train station to the Mauthausen concentration camp in Upper Austria because they cannot walk any farther in the deep snow.

ported to the Auschwitz extermination camp in Poland. Immediately after their arrival, 816 of them are gassed. Only 28, seven of them women, survive until the liberation of Auschwitz by the Russian army in 1945.

The local committee of the Union générale des israélites de France (U.G.I.F.) is liquidated by Klaus Barbie, head of the Gestapo in Lyons. He has 86 Jews arrested and immediately deported to Auschwitz. Among them is the father of the minister of justice under President François Mitterand, Robert Badinter. The last survivor of this raid died in 1985 after having given evidence for the Klaus Barbie trial.

1,184 Jewish internees are deported from the Westerbork transit camp to Auschwitz.

February 9

1919 The town Belaya-Tserkov in the Ukraine is struck by a pogrom carried out by units of Simon Petlyura's Ukrainian National Army. Many Jews are massacred, others wounded, and many Jewish women and girls raped.

1941 In Amsterdam, Dutch Nazis, supported by German soldiers, attack Jews who refuse to comply with anti-Jewish regulations. Several young Jews offered resistance; 19 are arrested and deported, most to the Mauthausen camp in Austria and to the Auschwitz extermination camp in Poland, where they perish.

1942 From Utrecht, Netherlands, 150 Jews who do not hold Dutch citizenship and 30 Jewish children of German nationality are transported to the Westerbork transit camp.

1943 From the Drancy transit camp in the German occupied zone of France, 1,000 Jews are de-

February 10

1942 In Leczna, Poland, 4 Jews are hanged and 1 is shot by the Gestapo. They had left their camp in order to look for food.

1943 In the ghetto of Stryj, Lvov, Poland (today Ukrainian S.S.R.), 2,000 Jews are shot.

1944 1,500 Jewish men and women interned in the Drancy transit camp near Paris are deported to the Auschwitz extermination camp in Poland. Immediately after their arrival, 1,229 of them are gassed. Only 42 men and 24 women will survive until the liberation of the camp in 1945.

February 11

1943 998 Jewish men and women are deported from the Drancy transit camp in France to Auschwitz extermination camp in Poland. Upon arrival 802 of them are gassed; only 11—among them 1 woman—will see the liberation of the camp by the Soviet army in 1945.

The second convoy deporting the foreign Jews still remaining in Drancy leaves for Auschwitz. Altogether 1,600 Jews of foreign nationalities are deported in the two convoys leaving Drancy on February 9 and 11. Left in Drancy are 2,200 French Jews.

February 12

1486 The seat of the Inquisition Tribunal is moved from Ciudad Real to Toledo, Spain. A plot against the Inquisition by some Conversos is betrayed and in the first auto-da-fé held by the recently moved tribunal, 750 persons of both sexes are led in a procession through the streets of Toledo. Most of them are punished financially and stripped of all civil rights. About 50 are condemned to death and burned at the stake.

1940 The first deportation of Jews from Germany takes place.

In the Waski Las woods near Severynovo, Poland, about 500 people are shot by the Gestapo, the SS, and German civilians. Many Jews are among the dead.

1941 In Amsterdam, the Nazis erect a ghetto in the Jewish quarter.

In Amsterdam, a Jewish Council is established by order of the Germans. The Jewish Council is allowed to publish a newspaper, in which all regulations and warnings issued by the Nazis have to be printed.

1942 In Brailov, a little town in the Ukrainian S.S.R., 3,000 Jews are murdered by the Nazis.

1943 The Nazis kill 40 Jews in Tluste, Galicia, Poland (today Ukrainian S.S.R.).

February 13

1941 From Grodzisk Mazoviecki, Poland, 3,600 Jews are deported to the Warsaw ghetto.

1943 Herded into cattle cars, 1,000 Jewish men and women are deported from the Drancy transit camp in the German-occupied zone in France to the Auschwitz extermination camp in Poland. On arrival 689 of the convoy are immediately sent to the gas chambers. Only 13 of them—among them one woman—survive until the liberation of the camp by the Soviet army in 1945.

The Nazis decide to deport from Drancy the Jews of French citizenship as well, even though the question of the French Jews has not yet been settled between the French and German authorities. The former have not consented to the deportations; nevertheless 1,000 French Jews are deported to Auschwitz.

February 14

1349 Accused of poisoning the wells, the entire Jewish community of Strasbourg, Alsace, is condemned to death. A huge fire is lit and the 2,000 Jews of the town, adults as well as youngsters, are burned alive.

1436 The rights of settlement and dwelling for all Jews in Zurich, Switzerland, are annulled "for the greater glory of God and the Virgin Mary."

1919 Soldiers of Petlyura's Ukrainian National Army enter Stepantzy, Ukraine. The soldiers rape 50 Jewish women, while their husbands and fa-

Facade of the Church of Santa María la Blanca in Toledo, Spain; formerly a synagogue. (From Amador de los Rios, *Monumentos*)

thers are imprisoned; 9 of the women are so gravely wounded that they die the same day.

1943 In Kosow, Poland, 1,800 Jews are murdered by the SS.

The last inmates of the ghetto of Kolomyja, Ukrainian S.S.R., totaling 1,500, are brought to the forests near the village of Szeparowce and murdered. Kolomyja is declared "free of Jews." Only about two dozen of its 15,000 Jews survive the Nazi era.

February 15

1919 Units of the Ukrainian National Army under the command of Semosenko march into Proskurov, Ukraine. They slaughter 1,500 Jews.

A priest who asks them to stop the massacre is slain in front of the church.

1940 Jews fom Stralsund, North Germany, are deported to the east, to the so-called protectorate of Lublinland, where most of them perish.

About 1,000 Jews from the North German town of Stettin (today Poland), are deported to the protectorate of Lublinland, where most of them perish.

1941 A deportation transport with 996 Jews leaves Vienna, for Opole and Pulavy in the so-called General Government region of Poland.

1943 The second Aktion is carried out in the Brazlav concentration camp in Transnistria,

Ukrainian S.S.R. (the first having taken place in September 1942). The German and Russian guards shoot 30 Jews.

1944 From the Westerbork transit camp in the Dutch province of Drenthe, 773 Jewish internees are deported to the Bergen-Belsen concentration camp in Germany.

1945 From Vienna, 7 Jews are deported to the ghetto and concentration camp of Theresienstadt, Czechoslovakia.

February 16

1349 During the night of February 16, all Jews are expelled from Burgdorf, on the Emme, in the Swiss canton of Berne. As they are charged of having spread the plague, the nobleman Eberhard von Kyburg drives them off his lands, confiscating all their property.

1919 Units of Petlyura's Ukrainian National Army carry out a pogrom in Felshtin, Ukraine, that lasts for two days. 485 Jews are massacred. Another 142 are wounded, most of whom die soon thereafter. All Jewish property is looted.

Insurgents under the hetman* Sokolovski, ally of Simon Petlyura and the Ukrainian National Army, carry out a pogrom in Radomysl in the Russian district of Kiev. Many Jews are massaced and many others seriously wounded and mutilated.

1920 Units of the Ukrainian National Army under Colonel Romaschko reach Bobrik in the district of Tschernigov. The soldiers kill 7 Jews and wound many others.

Cossack chief.

1943 Majdanek, Poland, is officially designated a "concentration camp."

From Westerbork transit camp, 1,108 Jewish internees are deported to the Auschwitz extermination camp in Poland.

600 Jewish women, children, and old people are taken from the ghetto in Boryslav, Poland (today Ukrainian S.S.R.) to the municipal slaughterhouse, where they are massacred.

February 17

1349 The Black Death Persecutions reach the small town of Mengen in the German province of Würtemberg. The townspeople murder all the Jews and then completely destroy the Jewish quarter.

1941 The Jews of Zyrardov, in the province of Warsaw, and 1,000 other Jews from the surrounding area are forced to leave the town. They are brought to Warsaw where they share the fate of the Jews of the ghetto. Zyrardov is declared to be "free of Jews."

1942 From Belz, a small town in the district of Lvov, Ukrainian S.S.R., 1,000 Jews are sent by the Nazis to the Belzec extermination camp. Jews have been living in Belz since the sixteenth century. Among Jews, Belz is well known as the birthplace of a famous rabbinical dynasty, the Roke'ah family.

1943 The final Aktion against the Jews in the Chrzanov ghetto, in the Polish province of Cracow, begins.

February 18

1943 The 1,000 Jews remaining in the Chrzanov ghetto in the Polish province of Cracow, are deported to the Auschwitz exterminaton camp. Only 12 Jews survive the atrocities of the camp until the liberation by the Soviet army in 1945.

In an Aktion carried out by the Nazis, the victims are 693 old or sick Jews and the staffs of forty-three homes for the aged and hospitals in The Hague, Netherlands. The Jews are arrested and sent to the Westerbork transit camp in the Dutch province of Drenthe.

1945 More than 500 Jews throughout Germany who have been protected up to now by their marriage to a Christian are arrested and deported to the Theresienstadt concentration camp in Czechoslovakia.

February 19

1349 During the persecutions accompanying the Black Death massacres of Jews reach even the remotest spots in Germany. The entire Jewish community of the village of Saulgau is slaughtered.

1919 Units of the Ukrainian National Army reach the town of Novomigrod, Ukraine. In the pogrom they carry out against the Jewish community 100 Jews are massacred.

1941 From Vienna, 1,010 Jews are deported to Kielce, Poland.

1942 On a day since known as Bloody Thursday, 40 Jews of the Radom ghetto in the Polish province of Kielce are shot in the streets by the Nazis.

Professor August Hirt proposes to Himmler the selection of 80 Jews from the Auschwitz extermination camp in Poland for the skeleton collection of the University of Strasbourg. They have to be killed by injection and their corpses boiled in order not to damage the skeletons. Himmler agrees. This collection of skeletons is part of a planned "Jewish Museum."

1943 From Berlin 1,000 Jews are deported to Auschwitz.

February 20

1349 Duke Albrecht of Austria energetically protects his Jewish subjects against the persecution resulting from the Black Death epidemic and the superstitions of the time. But confronted with ultimata from all sides, and the threat of seeing his Jewish subjects slaughtered, he decides to preserve his sovereignty by assuming the role of executioner himself. So the Jews are burned at the stake in Schaffhausen and in Thurgau, Switzerland.

1941 This is the first day of the liquidation of the Plock ghetto in the Polish province of Warsaw. About half of the Jewish population is assembled and deported to the Dzialdowo labor camp.

From Blonie, Poland, 2,000 Jews are brought to the Warsaw ghetto.

1942 Jewish men from the Anhaltelager (prisoners' camp) in Nis, Serbia, Yugoslavia, are shot on the nearby hill of Bubanj.

From Zbaraz, Poland (today Ukrainian S.S.R.), 600 old and sick Jews are sent on a march toward Ternopol. They are shot on the way.

February 21

1941 From Warka, Poland, 3,000 Jews are deported to the Warsaw ghetto.

1943 In the Protestant and Catholic churches of the Netherlands a pastoral letter is read, condemning the persecution of the Jews. On February 17 this letter was sent to the deputy of the Reich.

1945 In Plömnitz, Germany, a camp for women is set up adjoining the Buchenwald concentration camp.

In the Bavarian town of Ganacker, a concentration camp for men is set up. It belongs to the Flossenbürg camp and will be evacuated on April 24.

February 22

1349 The persecutions accompanying the Black Death reach Schaffhausen, Switzerland. All members of the Jewish community, with their rabbi Aaron ben Moshe, are burned at the stake.

After the Jewish community of Schaffhausen, that of Zurich becomes the target of the Black Death Persecutions. Although the town council tries to protect the Jews, in the end they give in to the pressure of the mob. The Jews of Zurich are burned at the stake.

1501 An auto-da-fé takes place in Toledo, Spain. A Converso (a Jew forcibly converted to Catholicism) who calls herself a prophetess is arrested by the Inquisition. Her followers are also arrested and condemned to death; on February 22, 38 are burned at the stake.

1941 In response to persistent agitation and resistance activity, the Nazis seal off the Jewish quarter in Amsterdam. They arrest 400 Jewish men and deport them to the concentration camps at Buchenwald and Mauthausen where—with the exception of 2 or 3 survivors—all of them will perish.

1943 In retaliation for an accident in which a Jew injured a Ukrainian, the Jewish community of Stanislavov, Ukrainian S.S.R., is annihilated by the SS and the Ukrainian police. 10,000 people are massacred in the Jewish cemetery. The Jewish resistance movement, led by Oskar Friedlander and Auda Luft, battles the Nazis.

3,500 Jews of Jendrzejov, in the province of Kielce, Poland, are deported to the Treblinka extermination camp.

1944 A transport with 86 Jews from Narva, Estonia, arrives at the Auschwitz extermination camp in Poland. The deportees are killed immediately after their arrival.

A transport with 462 Jews from Fossoli, Italy, arrives at Auschwitz. The deportees are murdered within a few hours of their arrival.

February 23

1349 The persecutions of Jews during the plague epidemic reach Switzerland. Many Jewish communities are exterminated. On the charge of well poisoning, the people of St. Gall burn all Jews at the stake.

1484 The second auto-da-fé takes place in Ciudad Real, Spain, lasting two days. On the first day about 15 Jewish men and women are burned at the stake for Judaizing, secretly practicing Judaism. The bones and effigies of 20 more Jews, already deceased, are also burned.

1501 A Converso woman from the town of Herrera, Spain, has been arrested because she pretended to be a prophetess. All her followers, men and women, are arrested and condemned to death. On February 23, 67 of her female followers are burned at the stake in an auto-da-fé in Toledo.

1941 Deported to the Warsaw ghetto are 2,700 Jews from the Grojec ghetto in central Poland.

1942 The deportation of the Jews from Odessa, Ukrainian S.S.R., is accomplished. Forty-three trains carry a total of 19,582 Jews to the concentration camps. In each transport about 50 Jews die on the way, as a result of the inhuman conditions. Odessa is proclaimed "free of Jews."

Two Jews are hanged by the Gestapo in Leczna, Poland.

1943 In the Dutch province of Drenthe, 1,101 Jewish internees of the Westerbork transit camp are deported to the Auschwitz extermination camp in Poland.

February 24

1147 At the beginning of the Second Crusade most of the Jewish communities in Germany, remembering the massacres of the First Crusade, ask the German King Conrad III and the bishops for protection and seek shelter in their bishop's or their town's fortress. The Jews of Würzburg, Germany, have totally trusted in the protection of the bishop. When troops of Crusaders arrive on February 24, excesses against the Würzburg Jewry break out, during which 20 Jews are murdered and many injured.

1349 The Black Death Persecutions reach the German town of Dresden on the Elbe River. All the Jews of the town are driven together and burned at the stake.

1484 On this second day of the auto-da-fé in Ciudad Real, Spain, another 15 Jewish men and women are burned alive on the charge of having lived according to the Jewish faith, while the bones and effigies of twenty more Judaizers are burned on specially erected pyres.

1590 Francisca Núñez de Carvajal is burned alive at the stake in Mexico City, Mexico. She is a member of the famous Carvajal family that has included governors of New Spain (Mexico), who refused to abjure their Jewish faith. Francisca Núñez de Carvajal has been imprisoned for three years before her execution in the course of which she was tortured several times.

Torture of Francisca Núñez de Carvajal in Mexico, 1590. (From Palacio, *El Libro Rojo*)

1942 The Jewish refugee boat *Struma* is sent to the bottom of the Black Sea with 709 passengers aboard. The boat came from Constanza, Rumania, arrived in Istanbul, but was sent back by the Turks. It is still not clear whether the Germans or the Soviets torpedoed the boat.

1942 Jewish intellectuals and notables in Tunis are arrested by German soldiers of the occupation army in Tunisia. Among the arrested is Victor Cohen-Hadrian, chief of finances of the Jewish community of Tunis; Dr. B. Levy; the journalist S. Moatti; O. Silvera, an official of the ministry of finances; and 20 prominent French Jews. They will be deported by airplane to concentration camps in Europe. Victor Cohen-Hadrian will be murdered in the Auschwitz extermination camp in Poland.

1944 A transport with 41 Jews leaves Vienna for the Auschwitz extermination camp in Poland.

February 25

1941 All Jews from Gora Kalvarya, a town southeast of Warsaw, Poland, are sent to the Warsaw ghetto.

The first and largest demonstration by non-Jews in a German occupied country against the persecution of the Jews, takes place in the Netherlands, in the form of a three-day general strike. Nine people are killed, about 50 severely wounded, and 200 are arrested and tortured. The towns of Amsterdam, Hilversum, and Zaandam are fined 18 million guilders. The mayors and the members of the city councils are replaced by Dutch Nazis.

1942 In Vjazjma, Soviet Union, 25 Jews, among them one physician, are shot by the Nazis.

The German army entered Tomaszov Lubelski in the Polish province of Lublin on September 13,

1939—but after two weeks withdrew and left the town to the Soviets. However, in accordance with the newly drawn borders the Soviets gave the town back to the Germans several days later and 4,500 Jews fled to the Soviet Union. Most of the 1,500 Jews who remained in the town on February 25, 1942, are deported to the Cieszanov labor camp, where all of those will perish.

The Jews of Lvov, Poland (today Ukrainian S.S.R.), are classified in three groups: A, B, and C. Group A includes all artisans, who are provided with permits. They have to wear armbands with the Star of David and the letter A in the middle. The permit means temporary safety. The Jews of the two other groups are shot.

1943 A deportation transport leaves Vienna for the Theresienstadt concentration camp and ghetto in Czechoslovakia.

1944 From the Westerbork transit camp in the Dutch province of Drenthe, 811 Jewish internees are deported to the Theresienstadt concentration camp.

A transport of 41 Jews from Vienna arrives at the Auschwitz extermination camp in Poland. Four of them are singled out and tattooed with numbers; the other 37 are gassed.

February 26

1941 A deportation convoy with 1,049 Jews from Vienna leaves for Opole in the so-called General Government region of Poland.

1943 From Berlin, 900 Jews are deported to the Auschwitz extermination camp in Poland.

1944 A transport with 54 Jews from Sosnoviec, Poland, arrives at Auschwitz. The deportees are murdered immediately after their arrival.

A transport with 26 Jews from Berlin arrives at Auschwitz and the deportees are murdered immediately after their arrival.

1945 The last transport of 6,000 inmates of the Gross-Rosen concentration camp in Silesia (today Poland) leaves for the west. Their first stop is the Buchenwald concentration camp in Germany; their final destination is Mauthausen, a concentration camp in Austria. Only 1,200 of the 6,000 will survive the journey.

February 27

1919 In the town of Ananiev in the district of Kherson, Russia, units of Petlyura's Ukrainian National Army start a pogrom against the Jewish population and 14 Jews are massacred.

1942 In the ghetto of Wlodzimierz (today Ukrainian S.S.R.), 250 Jews are arrested. Under the pretext of forced labor they are deported to Kiev. No trace of them will ever be found.

1943 Jews previously working in the war industry in Berlin are deported to the Auschwitz extermination camp in Poland.

February 28

1670 The Jews of Vienna are expelled from the town by an edict of Emperor Leopold I.

1942 The liquidation of the Jewish women and children of the Sajmiste camp, near Belgrade, Yugoslavia, begins. In groups of 100 the victims are brought into large, covered vans where they are suffocated by exhaust gases.

In the village of Lepel in Belorussian S.S.R., 1,000 Jews are murdered by the Nazis.

Members of the SS murder 36 Jews in the town of Feodosiya, Ukrainian S.S.R.

MARCH

March 1

1349 The Jewish community of Worms on the Rhine, which is one of the oldest in Germany, is reached by the Black Death Persecutions. The alderman of Worms sentences the Jews to death at the stake, but they set fire to their own houses and more than 580 die in the flames.

1919 Units of Petlyura's Ukrainian National Army carry out a pogrom in Skvira in the district of Kiev, Ukraine. They slaughter 13 Jews and gravely wound 8.

1940 This day is known as Bloody Thursday in the history of Lodz in central Poland. The German army organizes a pogrom against the Jewish population of Lodz for not moving into the ghetto quickly enough. Several Jews are slain and the others are driven into the ghetto without being able to bring any belongings.

1941 On this day Plock, a town in the Polish province of Warsaw, is declared "free of Jews." Starting from February 20 until March 1 about 7,000 Jews are marched to the Dzialdowo camp.

The old synagogue at Worms. (C. Gross Mayer)

Jews from several small neighboring communities are forcibly driven to other camps. All will perish.

From the ghetto of Skiernievice, Poland, 4,300 Jews are deported to the Warsaw ghetto.

1942 In Belowschtschina, in the Soviet district of Starodub, 800 Jewish women and children are shot by the Nazis.

The ghetto of Krzemieniec in the Polish province of Volhynia (today Ukrainian S.S.R.) is hermetically closed and strictly guarded. The Jews in the ghetto are cut off from any supply of food and water and they begin to starve.

1943 In the center of the ghetto of Minsk—the capital of Belorussian S.S.R.—5,000 Jews are driven into a large pit and killed. Among the victims are the children of the ghetto orphanage. The members of the Jewish Council were forced to dig the pit.

1945 The last transport from the Risiera di San Sabba camp near Trieste, Italy, arrives at the Dachau concentration camp in Germany. The transport consists of Jews and Italian partisans.

March 2

1704 An auto-da-fé is performed in the Portuguese town of Coimbra. The descendants of Jews baptized centuries earlier are accused of practicing Judaism secretly. Some are sentenced to death at the stake.

1941 In Imielnica, the Gestapo shoots 25 Jews from Plock, Poland.

1942 In the ghetto of Minsk, an Aktion begins and 5,000 Jews are murdered. A Jewish resistance group battles the SS and the Russian collaborators.

From the ghetto of Krosniewiece, Poland, 900 Jews are deported to the Chelmno extermination camp.

1943 Jewish internees, 1,105 of them, are sent from the Westerbork transit camp in the Dutch province of Drenthe to the Sobibor extermination camp in Poland.

A train convoy with 1,000 Jewish men and women crammed into cattle cars leaves France. They are of various nationalities and had been assembled in the Drancy camp in France for further deportation. Their destination is the Auschwitz extermination camp in Poland. Immediately after their arrival, 881 of them are gassed. Only 8 of them will survive.

March 3

1349 The Black Death Persecutions reach the Jewish community of Constance on the Bodensee, Germany. The Jews are accused of well poisoning; the wells of the Jews are walled up, and 330 Jews are burned in a special wooden house. Only a very few members of the community will survive these days.

1941 In Amsterdam, Netherlands, the first Jew falls victim to the persecutions of the Nazis: Ernst Cohn, a refugee from Germany, is shot.

1942 In the ghetto of Zychlin in the Polish province of Lodz on the eve of Purim, the Nazis drive together the remaining Jews. The aged and the sick, who are not able to climb up into the trucks, are shot on the spot. The entire Jewish population of Zychlin (over 3,000) is deported to the Chelmno extermination camp where they are murdered. Zychlin is "free of Jews."

The German army carries out the first large-scale Aktion against the Jews of Dolhinov, Belorussian S.S.R. The army arrests 1,500 Jews and takes them outside the town where they are shot. Their corpses are burned.

1943 A transport with 75 Jews leaves Vienna for the Auschwitz extermination camp in Poland.

During the night of March 3 the German army raids a number of towns in Macedonia, Greece (today Bulgaria): Cavalla, Drama, Comotini, Alexandroúpolis, and Xanthi. 5,000 Jewish men, women and children are forcibly assembled in Drama and then deported to the Treblinka extermination camp in Poland. Also 3,000 Jews of the Baron Hirsch ghetto in Salonika, Greece, are deported to Auschwitz, and all Jews from East Thracia, including those from the island of Samothrace, are arrested by the Nazis.

1944 Jewish internees—732 of them—are sent from the Westerbork transit camp in the Dutch province of Drenthe to Auschwitz.

1945 During the disinfection procedure, 182 Jews die in the Ebensee concentration camp in Austria. They had been evacuated from the Gross-Rosen concentration camp in Silesia.

March 4

1649 After the election of a new king of Poland in Warsaw, in which the Cossack leader Bogdan Chmielnicki played a decisive role, his Cossack hordes return to the Ukraine and continue their slaughter of the Jews. In the town of Ostrog they massacre at least 600 Jews.

1942 The last 400 Jews of Donetsk, Ukrainian S.S.R., are murdered by the SS.

The Nazis kill 3,000 Jews from the Belorussian S.S.R. town of Baranowicze and the surrounding area.

1943 A deportation convoy with 1,003 Jewish men and women leaves the Drancy transit camp in the German occupied zone of France. They are sent to the Majdanek extermination camp in Poland. Immediately after their arrival, 950 of the deportees are gassed; only 3 men survive until

the liberation of the camp in 1945 by the Soviet army.

March 5

1328 The county of Navarre, Spain, tries to become independent of France. As a result of the political tensions massacres of Jews occur all over Navarre. On March 5, a Sabbath, a massacre begins in the town of Estella with one of the largest Jewish communities of Navarre. Several thousand Jews are slaughtered.

1332 When in the small town of Überlingen, Germany, the corpse of a Christian boy is found who has been missing for some days, the Jews are immediately accused of killing him. The townspeople also suspect the Christian cemetery caretaker of having sold the boy to the Jews. The Jews are tortured and they "confess." The caretaker commits suicide. The Jews of Überlingen flee into their synagogue, which is set on fire, and 300 to 400 Jews perish in the burning building.

1941 A convoy with 381 Jews leaves Vienna for Modliborzyce in Poland.

1942 Three Jews are hanged in public in the Olkusz ghetto in the Polish province of Cracow, on the charge of having left the ghetto to look for food. The German police force other Jews to set up the gallows and carry out the execution.

1943 Among the 132 men and 86 women who arrive at the Auschwitz extermination camp in Poland there are Jews from Vienna.

In Chmielnik, Poland, 1,300 Jews are murdered by the SS.

March 6

1648 The rebellion of Bogdan Chmielnicki and his Cossack hordes against the Polish aristocracy begins. In the course of about two years more than 200,000 Jews are massacred in the Ukraine and in Poland.

1919 Units of Petlyura's Ukrainian National Army under the command of Diatchenko, carry out a pogrom in Hachtchevaty, in the district of Podolia, Ukraine. In two days 21 Jews are slaughtered and several gravely wounded. It is the fourth pogrom in this town in a series of five within half a year.

1943 The second deportation train to the Majdanek extermination and concentration camp in Poland leaves Drancy in France. The cattle cars are crammed with 998 Jewish men and women who are sent east. Immediately after their arrival, 950 of them are gassed and only 4 survive until the liberation in 1945.

March 7

1190 Crusaders setting out for the Holy Land attack the Jewish community of Stanford, England, considering it a good deed to kill the "murderers of our Lord." The wealth of the Jews is probably not a minor motive, too. The Jewish houses are plundered, some Jews are murdered, and many mistreated. The crusaders flee before the royal officials can get hold of them.

1691 An auto-da-fé is held in Palma de Mallorca on the Balearic Islands, Spain. There are 24 New Christians accused of practicing Judaism secretly; they had already fallen victim to the Inquisition five years earlier. At that time they managed to escape; now they are called to do penance and are incarcerated.

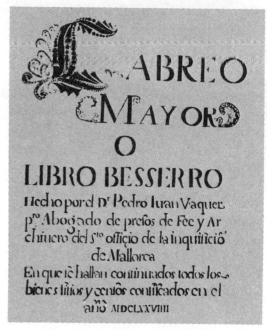

Title page of the first volume listing property confiscated from the Jews by the Mallorca Inquisition in 1679 and 1691.

1941 All over Germany, Jews are seized for forced labor.

1942 From the Mielec ghetto in the Polish province of Rzeszov, 2,000 Jews are deported. The old ones are shot on the spot, the young Jews sent to the Pustkow labor camp.

1943 The ghetto of Radoszkowice, Poland (today Belorussian S.S.R.), is liquidated. The Nazis murder 300 Jews, but 50 young Jews succeed in fleeing to the nearby forest, where they join a group of partisans named Revenge. Very few of them survive until the end of the war.

1944 On this one day, 9,971 Jews are gassed in the Auschwitz extermination camp in Poland. Intact Jewish families have been deported from the Theresienstadt concentration camp in Czechoslovakia to Auschwitz to prove to the visiting Red Cross teams that "Jews are not mistreated in Auschwitz." When the Red Cross teams have gone the Jews are sent to the gas chambers.

Crammed into cattle cars, 1,501 Jewish men and women are deported from the transit camp of Drancy in the German occupied zone of France to Auschwitz. Immediately after their arrival, 1,311 of them are gassed; only 25 survive until the liberation of the camp in 1945.

The Jewish historian Emanuel Ringelblum, originally from Buczacz, is tracked down by the Gestapo in Warsaw, Poland. He and his family are tortured and subsequently killed. He had written the tragic history of the Warsaw ghetto on thousands of pieces of paper which he managed to hide. These papers were found after the war and make an invaluable historical record.

March 8

1942 In the course of a three-day Aktion, 7,000 Jews from the ghetto of Kutno in the Polish province of Lodz are deported to the Chelmno extermination camp where they all perish.

Several hundred Jews from Kopyczynce and Koropiec are brought to the ghetto of Monasterzyska, Ukrainian S.S.R., and murdered there.

1943 Four trains crammed with 4,000 Jews leave Thracia in Greece. After several days they arrive at the Treblinka extermination camp in Poland.

The SS murders 1,200 Jews of Radoszkowice, Poland (today Belorussian S.S.R.).

All Jews of East Thracia, Greece, are deported by train to Treblinka.

March 9

1422 A certain John of Seelau, an agitator, is beheaded on the order of the magistrate of Prague, Bohemia, Czechoslovakia; after that the townspeople start rioting, assaulting the town hall and looting the houses of the town councilors. Then they turn their attention to the Jewish quarter, plundering the Jewish houses and killing many of the inhabitants.

1496 Emperor Maximilian I issues an edict saying the Jews have to leave Central Austria by September 14 of the same year. This particularly affects the Jews living in the province of Carinthia.

1919 Units of Petlyura's Ukrainian National Army carry out a pogrom in the town of Kalinovka in the district of Podolia, slaying 10 Jews.

1936 A pogrom breaks out in the Polish town of Przytyk. An anti-Semitic campaign has incited the populace until on March 9 they gather to march toward the Jewish quarter with the police on their side. Every Jewish house is destroyed and set afire; 3 Jews are murdered, 20 to 30 gravely injured.

1942 An Aktion is carried out by the German police in the camp of Cihrin in the district of Berezovca in the Ukrainian S.S.R. 722 Jews are rounded up and shot on the spot.

1944 During the night, 3,792 Jewish men, women, and children of the so-called family camp of Auschwitz II-Birkenau, Poland, are gassed and cremated. They were the rest of two deportation transports with 5,007 prisoners from the Theresienstadt camp in Czechoslovakia that arrived on September 6 and 8, 1943. More than 1,200 had died from mistreatment by the SS guards and the kapos (prisoners who supervised other prisoners).

March 10

1925   Hugo Bettauer, a Jewish writer from Vienna, dies sixteen days after an attempt on his life by an Austrian National Socialist. He was famous for his book, *The Town without Jews*. The assassin will be acquitted in the subsequent trial on the grounds of not being accountable for his actions. Bettauer is the first Jewish victim of the Nazis in Austria.

1943   From the Westerbork transit camp in the Dutch province of Drenthe, 1,105 Jewish internees are deported to the Sobibor extermination camp in Poland.

1944   A deportation transport with 84 Jews leaves Vienna for the Theresienstadt concentration camp in Czechoslovakia.

March 11

1919   The 151st Nalivaiko regiment of the Ukrainian National Army carries out a pogrom in the town of Uchomir in the region of Podolia; another follows within three weeks. During them, 3 Jews are choked to death and another 10 are severely injured.

Insurgents under the command of their hetman Sokolovski carry out a second pogrom in Radomysl in the district of Kiev, Ukrainian S.S.R., where they had already massacred Jews the previous month. The pogrom lasts three days; 33 Jews are murdered and many are wounded or mutilated by saber cuts.

1941   The Nazis transport 2,000 Jews from Plock, Poland, to the ghetto of Tomaszov Rawski in the Polish province of Lodz. The number of Jews in this ghetto is now 15,000. Every day dozens of Jews die from the mistreatment by the Nazis.

1942   From the Theresienstadt concentration camp in Czechoslovakia, 1,001 Jewish men, women, and children are deported to Lublin, Poland. They stay several weeks in this transit camp and are then deported to the extermination camps of Chelmno, Belzec, and Sobibor in Poland, where they perish. Of this transport, only 7 will survive until the liberation in 1945.

The Germans shoot 850 Jews from Radoszkowice, Poland (today Belorussian S.S.R.). The remaining 350 Jews are set up in a ghetto.

1943   The Germans arrest all Jews of Skoplje, the capital of Yugoslavian Macedonia. Together with the other Jews of the province they are locked in an empty factory. About 215 people are left there without food and sanitary facilities.

1944   300 Jewish women and children from north Dalmatia, who have been interned in Gospic, Yugoslavia, are deported to the Croatian concentration camp of Jasenovac. None of them will survive.

March 12

1421   Under Albert V, Archduke of Austria, Emperor of Germany, and King of Bohemia (1411–1430), the persecutions of the Jews in his realm begin. They are accused of desecrating the host, and those who don't submit to baptism are condemned to death. The persecution culminates in the burning at the stake of 120 Jewish men and 92 Jewish women in Vienna. The Jewish community of 1,400 members ceases to exist. This event is later known in Jewish tradition as the Wiener Gesera (Vienna persecution).

1940   About 160 Jews from Schneidemühl, Germany (today Poland), are deported to the east, to the so-called Lublinland, where most of them perish.

1941 A deportation transport with 995 Jewish men, women, and children leaves Vienna for Lagov and Opatov in Poland.

1944 The program to exterminate 760,000 Hungarian Jews in the Reichs-Sicherheitshauptamt (Reich Security Headquarters) in Berlin is halted. A week later the Nazis invade Hungary.

March 13

1605 An auto-da-fé is held in Lima, Peru, and 19 persons are accused of Judaizing (secretly practicing Judaism); 6 are burned in effigy, 3 are burned at the stake, and 16 are "reconciled," that is, they promise to repent. They have to do public penance and are deprived of all their civil rights.

1919 A pogrom is carried out in Samgorodok, in the district of Kiev, by units of Petlyura's Ukrainian National Army. They murder 4 Jews.

1938 Hitler marches into Vienna—the annexation of Austria by the Reich is accomplished and the tragedy of the 200,000 Austrian Jews begins. On the same day prominent Jews from Vienna and the Austrian provinces are arrested, including the president of the community Desider Friedmann, the vice president Robert Stricker, and the director Josef Loewenherz.

1942 The SS rounds up and shoots 650 Jews of the Hulievca camp in the Ukrainian S.S.R.

In the Polish town of Belchatov in the province of Lodz the police hang 10 Jews on Narutowicza Square.

1943 In a two-day Aktion, the Cracow ghetto in Poland is liquidated: 2,000 Jews are deported to the Auschwitz extermination camp; 700 are shot on the spot.

Another crematorium is set in operation in Auschwitz.

A transport with 113 Jews leaves Munich for Auschwitz.

To guarantee that the Jews obey German orders, 100 prominent Jews of Salonika, Greece, are taken hostage.

March 14

1191 The Jewish community of Bray, France, falls victim to a defamation spread by the townspeople. The Jews are accused of having executed a murderer by crucifixion, mocking Jesus Christ. King Philip Augustus hurries with his troops to Bray; the Jews must choose between baptism and death. About 100, almost the entire Jewish community, are burned at the stake.

1473 During a procession of the Catholic Church anti-Jewish riots break out in Cordova, Spain. The Jewish quarter is sacked and all Conversos murdered. A decree issued after the riot henceforth prohibits Conversos from settling in Cordova.

1723 The Portuguese Inquisition holds an auto-da-fé in Coimbra. Among the victims accused of Judaizing (secretly practicing Judaism) is the pharmacist Francisco Diaz of Braganca, a town near the Spanish border where hitherto many clandestine Jews have found shelter. Diaz remains steadfast until the end and is consequently burned alive as a nonrepentant. The other victims of the auto-da-fé are repentant and are therefore sentenced to imprisonment only, after all their goods are confiscated.

1919 The Nalivaiko regiment, a unit of Petlyura's Ukrainian National Army, carries out a pogrom in Berchad, massacring 9 Jews. The number of wounded is unknown.

1942 From Szadek in the province of Lodz, Poland, 800 Jews are deported to the Chelmno extermination camp.

1943 The Nazis gather the Jews of Salonika, Greece, and tell them that they will be sent to Poland to start a new life there. They are allowed to take 20 kg of personal luggage with them. The Nazis cram them into trains and deport them directly to the Auschwitz extermination camp in Poland. They all perish.

The remaining Jews of Sambor in the Polish province of Lvov (today Ukrainian S.S.R.) are assembled at the Jewish cemetery. Mothers are forced to leave their children on an open square and to watch them being shot. In all, 900 Jews are murdered; only a small number manage to escape.

March 15

1391 After the sermon of a monk who is notorious for his hatred of Jews, the people of Seville, Spain, start attacking the Jews. In spite of the intervention of the city aldermen, the chief of police, and two judges many Jews are murdered. King Henry II intervenes to stop the killing for the moment but it recurs even more violently three months later.

1919 Units of Petlyura's Ukrainian National Army carry out a pogrom in Strichevka in the Russian district of Podolia. They murder 8 Jews, severely wound 1, and rape many Jewish women and girls.

In the town of Dubno in the province of Volhynia, Ukraine, units of the Ukrainian National Army under Setcheviki carry out a pogrom. They murder 15 Jews.

1939 The Germans occupy the town of Olomouc in the province of Moravia, Czechoslovakia, and burn down the synagogue. At the outbreak of World War II about 3,500 Jews are living there. The first Jewish settlements in Olomouc date back as far as to the beginning of the eleventh century.

1942 In an Aktion which lasts several days, 15,000 Jews from Lvov, Poland (today Ukrainian S.S.R.), are deported to the Belzec extermination camp, where they perish. The selections for this deportation are carried out in the Sobieski School on the edge of the ghetto district.

Seven hundred Jews—classified as not able-bodied by the Germans—are deported from the Zolkiev ghetto, Polish province of Galicia (today Ukrainian S.S.R.), to Belzec.

1943 The first train convoy with Jewish deportees leaves the Greek town of Salonika. Crammed into forty cattle cars are 2,800 Jews; they are taken to the Auschwitz extermination camp in Poland. Altogether more than 40,000 Jews from Salonika are sent to certain death in Auschwitz. Two thousand years ago Jews were already settling in Salonika.

600 Jewish men are sent from the Zolkiev ghetto to the Janovska labor camp in Lvov.

215 Jews assembled in an empty plant near Skoplje, Yugoslavia, are deported to the Treblinka extermination camp in Poland. None of them will survive.

In revenge for the murder of an SS man in Lvov, Poland (today Ukrainian S.S.R.), 1,000 Jewish internees are taken from the ghetto and shot by the Nazis.

1944 From the Westerbork transit camp in the Dutch province of Drenthe, 210 Jewish internees are deported to the Bergen-Belsen concentration camp in Germany.

March 16

1474 Persecutions against the Conversos (children of those Jews who were forcibly baptized during the persecutions of 1391) break out in Spain. They are accused of Judaizing, secretly practicing Judaism. On March 16, armed bands march through the streets of Segovia, Spain. They break into the houses of Conversos, plunder and murder every Converso they can get hold of. The castellan of Segovia finally intervenes; otherwise the whole community would be annihilated.

1919 Units of Petlyura's Ukrainian National Army stay for three days in the village of Belochitz in the province of Volhynia, Ukraine, carrying out a pogrom. They massacre 16 Jews and wound another 2.

1920 Bands of insurgents under Tiutiunnik, an ally of Simon Petlyura, reach the town of Dachev in the province of Kiev; in the subsequent pogrom 22 Jews are massacred and 31 wounded.

The little town of Golta in the district of Podolia, Ukraine, is reached by units of insurgents under their hetman Tiutiunnik. In the pogrom that follows, 10 Jews are murdered.

1945 The last Jew of Prague, Czechoslovakia, is deported to the Theresienstadt concentration camp, raising the number of Jews that were deported there to 46,067.

March 17

1190 Rioting against the Jews of York, England, breaks out. The populace is stirred up by crusaders and aristocrats. The Jews flee into the town's castle. The armed crowd besieges the castle for six days. On the eve of March 16 the more courageous Jews commit suicide. The 500 survivors, who open the gates on March 17 in order to accept baptism, are all massacred by the rioters. Thus the Jewish community of York is annihilated.

1905 At the instigation of the clergy, Jewish passersby are beaten up in the streets in Saratov on the Wolga, Russia.

1942 Another transport with 1,000 Jewish men and women from the Theresienstadt concentration camp in Czechoslovakia arrives at the Izbica transit camp in Poland. Of the group, 300 young men are singled out and sent to the Janowice labor camp. The remaining 700 Jews are either shot or deported to the Belzec extermination camp. Only 3 people of this transport will survive until the liberation in 1945.

The ghetto of Ilya, north of Minsk, Belorussian S.S.R., is liquidated by the SS, and 900 Jews are massacred. Joseph Rodblatt, the chairman of the Jewish Council, heads the armed resistance movement. Together with a group of young Jews he manages to escape into the forests.

The Belzec extermination camp in the Polish district of Lvov is opened and two transports—one from Lublin and one from Lielec—with over 6,000 Jewish deportees arrive there. The camp will be closed in June 1943. In autumn 1942 the burning of the corpses of the mass graves begins and in spring 1943 the barracks are pulled down and the whole territory leveled.

The Gestapo hangs 17 Jews in Leczyca, Poland.

The deportations of the Jews of Lublin, Poland, to Belzec start. About 15,000 Jews are affected. Every day 1,500 Jews are deported.

1943   In a sandpit, the Nazis murder 1,500 Jews from the ghetto of Lvov, Poland.

Another transport with 2,800 Jews from Salonika, Greece, is made ready to be sent to the Auschwitz extermination camp in Poland. Finally they are deported to Birkenau instead, where they are murdered.

From the Westerbork transit camp in the Dutch province of Drenthe, 964 Jewish internees are deported to the Sobibor extermination camp in Poland.

March 18

1190   One day after the terrible massacre of the Jews in York, crusaders slaughter 57 Jews in St. Edmund, England. They consider it an act of piety. However, a motive not to be ignored is the wealth of some members of the Jewish communities, which will provide the crusaders with the financial means for their undertaking.

1349   During the Black Death period, the Jews of Baden in the Swiss canton of Aargua are falsely accused of well poisoning. Consequently part of the Jewish community is slain, the rest burned at the stake. The first Jews settled in Baden in the thirteenth century.

The Black Death epidemic causes massacres of Jews almost everywhere in Europe. When the Christian population of Rheinfelden in the Aargua canton begins to threaten the Jews, Duke Albrecht of Austria, to whose territory the Aargua belongs, tries to protect them by sending them to his castle in Baden, where the Jews of Baden are, he believes, already safe. On March 18 they are sacrificed

to the infuriated mob who overrun the castle and slaughter them together with the Jews of Baden.

1496   Emperor Maximilian I decrees that the Jews must leave the Austrian province of Styria, and the towns of Wiener Neustadt and Neunkirchen, by January 6 of the following year.

1919   Again the Jews of Ovrutch in Volhynia, Ukraine, fall victim to a pogrom. This time troops of Petlyura's Ukrainian National Army stay in the town for three days. They massacre 20 Jews and rape many Jewish women.

1942   The Nazis start murdering the patients of the Jewish hospital of Belgrade, Yugoslavia. They take them out of the hospital in groups of 85 and close them in gas vans in which they are suffocated. This Aktion lasts several days; 800 Jews are murdered.

1945   The Nazis send 1,075 Hungarian Jews to the Theresienstadt concentration camp in Czechoslovakia.

March 19

1941   In the course of one week 4,500 Jews of Lowicz in the Polish district of Lodz are brought to the Warsaw ghetto.

1942   The Nazis round up 400 Jews of Novomoskovsk, Soviet Union. They are shot in sandpits near the town, on the other side of the Samara River.

In the course of two days 2,500 Jews of Kazimierz, Poland, are deported to the Belzec extermination camp.

This is the last day of the Aktion against the Jews of Mielec in the Polish province of Cracow. In the course of four days 7,800 Jews are either shot or sent to extermination camps.

1943 1,000 Jews of Wilejka, Poland (today Lithuania), are taken to the Vilna ghetto.

The Nazis begin to liquidate the Braslav camp in Belorussian S.S.R. A resistance group tries to defend themselves, barricading their houses. They fight as long as they can but all resistance fighters and several others are killed in the fighting. Only 40 Jews from Braslav will survive until the end of the war. They had already fled and joined the Russian partisans when the anti-Jewish measures of the Nazis began.

1944 German troops occupy Budapest, the capital of Hungary. In this period 184,000 Jews live in Budapest, about 10 percent of the whole population. The first anti-Jewish measures are decreed by the German occupiers. The tragedy of the Jewish community begins.

1945 The Flossenbürg concentration camp in Germany is evacuated by train transports to the Bergen-Belsen concentration camp. Many deportees perish on the way.

1946 In Lublin, Poland, Chaim Hirschmann, 1 of the only 2 survivors of the Belzec extermination camp, is murdered.

March 20

1942 From the Zolkiev ghetto (today Ukrainian S.S.R.), 700 Jews are deported to the Belzec extermination camp.

The Nazis deport 2,000 Jews of Rzeszov, Poland, to Belzec.

From the Rohatyn ghetto, Polish district of Stanislavov (today Ukrainian S.S.R.), 2,000 Jews are taken to the border of town and killed, then hurriedly buried in a mass grave.

1,500 Jews from the Rava Ruska ghetto in the Ukrainian S.S.R are deported to Belzec, where they perish.

1943 The SS executes 127 Jewish intellectuals of Czestochova, Poland.

1944 The Majdanek extermination and concentration camp in Poland is evacuated. All sick Jews are immediately deported to the Auschwitz extermination camp, where they are gassed.

A transport with 45 Jews leaves the Theresienstadt concentration camp in Czechoslovakia for the Bergen-Belsen concentration camp in Germany.

March 21

1349 At the time of the Black Death, the Jews are commonly held responsible for the spread of the plague by well poisoning. Thus many Jewish communities are annihilated. Count Frederick of Thuringia advises the townspeople of Mühlhausen, Thuringia, Germany, to kill all Jews in the town, ". . . as they had set out to destroy all Christendom . . ." Consequently all Jews are slain, among them Rabbi Eliezer.

In connection with the Black Death Persecutions the Jews of Erfurt, Germany, are massacred. Led by the guildmasters, a crowd carrying a flag and a cross march on the Jewish quarter. The Jews try bravely to defend themselves, but when a hundred of them are slain, they set fire to their houses and perish in the flames.

1881 Riots break out against the Jews of the village of Walegozulowo near Balta, Russia.

1941 In Cracow, Poland, the Nazis set up a ghetto planned to hold 20,000 Jews, 6,000 of them from small neighboring villages.

1942 An Aktion takes place in the ghetto of Lublin, Poland. The Jewish inmates are ordered to report to the authorities. Those who stay in their hiding places are hunted by the SS. Some are killed on the spot, others taken directly to the deportation trains awaiting them.

1943 Deported to the Belzec extermination camp are 1,200 Jews of Buczacz, Ternopol district, Poland (today Ukrainian S.S.R.).

March 22

1349 At the time of the Black Death Persecutions, the Jews of Fulda, Germany, hide in three houses, but the townspeople find and massacre them. Earlier the Jews had sought aid from the abbot but the abbot's servants joined the murderers. Only a few Jews survive.

1919 For the second time within two months a pogrom is carried out in Zhytomir in the district of Volhynia, Ukraine, by units of Petlyura's Ukrainian National Army. They murder 317 Jews; many others are wounded and mutilated.

1941 Marshal Henri Pétain, head of the French State in Vichy, orders that prisoners build the Transsaharan Railway. Among them are a great number of Jews who—doing extremely heavy work—die of exhaustion.

1942 The Nazis seize the doctors and workers of the Jewish hospital of Belgrade, Yugoslavia, and kill them.

1943 A first transport with 2,400 Jews leaves Skoplje, Yugoslavia, its destination the Treblinka extermination camp in Poland.

1944 Under the leadership of Shlomo Kuszniz, the Jews of the Koldyczevo camp in Belorussian S.S.R. rise up against their oppressors. They kill 10 SS men and several hundred prisoners manage to escape.

The SS massacre an unknown number of Jewish children in Liepaja, Latvia.

1945 When the Red Army approaches Köszeg, Hungary, the town is evacuated and all the Jews in the military labor camp are murdered. Thirty-five ill and emaciated Jews are locked in the barracks and gassed by German commandos specially equipped for this purpose. Afterward the corpses of the Jewish victims are buried in mass graves.

March 23

1939 The German army occupies Memel, Lithuania. The tragedy of the Jews living there begins.

1942 The local police, supported by the Hlinka Guards, a Slovak copy of the Nazi SS, start rounding up the Jews of Bratislava, capital of Slovakia, Czechoslovakia. Hundreds of Jews are arrested and deported to the Sered labor camp. The Hlinka Guards were founded in honor of the Catholic priest Andrej Hlinka, who died in 1938.

1943 At six o'clock in the morning the deportation of the Jews of French nationality detained in the Drancy camp in France begins. 780 Jews from Marseilles, and 580 non-Jews who have been accused of violating the anti-Jewish laws, are packed into the trains for Auschwitz extermination camp in Poland.

On the same day 4,000 Jews from Marseilles, and 994 other Jewish men and women, are deported from Drancy to the Sobibor extermination camp in Poland. Of the 994, 950 are gassed immediately after their arrival; none of the remaining 44 will survive until the liberation of the camp by the Russian army in 1945.

Jewish internees—numbering 1,250—are deported from the Westerbork transit camp in the Dutch province of Drenthe to Sobibor.

1944 1687 Jews from Joanina, Greece, are deported to Auschwitz.

500 Jewish internees in Westerbork are deported to Auschwitz.

The Russian army marches into Buczacz, Ukrainian S.S.R. About 800 Jews leave their hiding places in the forests and elsewhere. However, the Russians stay only one week and cannot take the Jews with them on their withdrawal. The invading Germans murder nearly all the Jews of Buczacz. Only 100 Jews survive until the end of the war. Another 300 who were deported by the Russians survive in the Soviet Union.

March 24

1606 An auto-da-fé is held in the town of Évora in Portugal. It is initiated by the Portuguese Inquisition. Several people accused of Judaizing, secretly practicing Judaism, are burned at the stake.

1942 Deportation transports with Jews from the towns of Würzburg, Jülich, and Fürth leave Germany for Piaski, a transit camp in Poland. From there 586 Jews are deported to the Belzec extermination camp, where all of them perish.

The Nazis arrest 83 Jews in Bad Kissingen, Germany, and the surrounding area, to be deported

to the transit camps of Izbica and Piaski. From there they are sent to Belzec.

From the Izbica Lubelska camp, 2,000 Jews are deported to Belzec and murdered there. Among them are many deportees from Austria and Czechoslovakia.

In Kolomyja, Ukrainian S.S.R., three different ghettos are set up by the Germans. Each is surrounded by barbed wire and strictly guarded. Jews from smaller communities in the surrounding areas are deported and interned in these ghettos.

1943 In "Piaskownia," a sandpit in Lvov, Poland (today Ukrainian S.S.R.), the Nazis shoot 350 children and old people from the ghetto. Some of the injured children are buried alive.

1944 In the caves of Ardeatina in Rome, Italy, the Nazis murder 335 Italians. Among the victims are 57 Jews.

The German army carries out a large-scale raid on the 550 Jews living in the region of Chalkis, Thessalia, Greece. They are arrested and crammed into trains, their destination the Auschwitz extermination camp in Poland. None of them will survive.

The Nazis announce extra food supplies for the Jews of Athens, Greece, will be distributed at the synagogue. The 800 Jews who come for it are arrested. They are interned in the camp of Haidon.

March 25

1350 In the town of Eger, Bohemia, Czechoslovakia, the crowd is stirred up by the sermon of a Franciscan. They start looting and the whole Jewish community is slain—only Meir, the architect of the local synagogue, his mother and his wife survive.

1919 Units of Petlyura's Ukrainian National Army carry out a pogrom in the town of Romanov in Volhynia, Ukraine. They massacre 8 Jews and wound a great number.

Troops of the Ukrainian National Army reach the town of Tetiev, Ukraine, and 2,000 Jews take refuge in the synagogue. The soldiers set fire to it and the building burns to the ground. Many other Jews are murdered by soldiers with sabers. Altogether 4,000 of the 6,000 Jews of Tetiev are massacred.

1942 In September 1941 the first ghetto of the Polish province of Galicia was erected in Ternopol (today Ukrainian S.S.R.) and 12,500 Jews were interned there. On March 25, 1942, the first Aktion takes place when 1,000 Jews are taken to a forest near Ternopol, where they are shot by a German commando.

Members of the SS arrest 105 Jews in the Glebokie ghetto, Poland (today Belorussian S.S.R.), and shoot them. After this murder the young Jews of the ghetto seek contact with the Soviet partisans operating in the forests.

A transport with several hundred Jews from Bratislava, Czechoslovakia, leaves the Sered labor camp. Their destination is the Auschwitz extermination camp in Poland.

1943 The second transport with 2,500 from Skoplje, Yugoslavia, is sent to the Treblinka extermination camp in Poland.

The ghetto of Zolkiev, in the Polish province of Galicia (today Ukrainian S.S.R.) is liquidated; 2,000 Jews are murdered. 100 young Jewish men and 70 Jewish women are deported to the labor camp in Janovska in Lvov.

A convoy with 1,008 Jewish men and women leaves the Drancy transit camp in the German occupied zone of France. Their destination is the Sobibor extermination camp in Poland. Immediately after their arrival, 970 of them are gassed; only 5 men survive until the liberation by the Russian army in 1945.

1944 In a large-scale Aktion, many Jews of Athens, Greece, are arrested and deported by the SS to Auschwitz.

March 26

1481 After the establishment of the Spanish Inquisition in the Convent of San Paulo in Seville on January 2, 1481, the first auto-da-fé takes place there—17 Conversos, children and even grandchildren of the Jews forcibly baptized in 1391, are burned at the stake. They are accused of Judaizing, secretly practicing Judaism.

1601 Mariana, the youngest daughter of the famous Converso family of Carvajal, the "dynasty" of governors of Mexico, is burned at the stake in Mexico City. She was the last of her family, most of whom died at the stake in 1596.

1919 A unit under the leadership of Setcheviki, an ally of Petlyura's Ukrainian National Army, joined by peasants of the region, carries out a pogrom against the Jewish inhabitants of Isnuchpol in the province of Volhynia, Ukraine. The killing and looting of Jewish property lasts until April 4 and 23 Jews are tortured and murdered. Many are injured and mutilated; 20 Jewish women are brutally raped.

1938 In a public declaration in Vienna, General Field Marshal Hermann Goering announces the first anti-Jewish measures for Austria, long planned for by the Nazi leadership.

Execution of Mariana de Carvajal in 1601.

killed the child in a ritual murder. Three Jews of Valréas are immediately seized, tortured, and burned at the stake. However, other Jews of the district are also rounded up, tortured, and finally burned at the stake.

1605 An auto-da-fé takes place in the Portuguese town of Évora. A secret Jew—a so-called Judaizer—is turned over to the secular justice by the Portuguese Inquisition to be burned alive at the stake.

1942 The Jewish intellectuals and notables arrested by the Nazis in a house-to-house raid in Paris on December 12, 1941, are deported to the extermination camps in the east.

A train convoy with 1,112 Jewish deportees from the Compiègne transit camp in France leaves for the Auschwitz extermination camp in Poland. At this time French-Jewish citizens are still protected, so the convoy consists mainly of Jews of foreign nationalities. Only 19 of the 1,112 Jews survive until the liberation of Auschwitz in 1945.

1942 The first deportation with 2,000 Jews leaves Bratislava, Slovakia, Czechoslovakia, for the Auschwitz extermination camp in Poland.

The first transport from Poprad, Slovakia, leaves for Auschwitz with 999 Jews. Many others will follow.

1943 Victor Lellouche, a Tunisian Jew from Ferryville, interned in the Bizerte camp of Tunisia, is driven out of the camp by three German guards, who return with his mutilated corpse in the evening.

March 27

1247 A little Christian girl is found dead in Valréas, France. The rumor spreads that the Jews

1944 A deportation convoy with 1,000 Jewish men and women leaves Drancy, France, for Auschwitz. On their arrival 480 of them are immediately sent to the gas chambers. Only 185 of the rest of this deported group—among them 60 women—will survive until the liberation of the camp in 1945 by the Russians.

The Jewish policemen of the Riga ghetto in Latvia, under the command of Levine, actively support the Jewish underground movement of the ghetto. The Gestapo discovers their activities and orders all 140 policemen to the Kommandantur.* There they are tortured and 40 of them, those in responsible positions, are shot. The others are sent back to the ghetto.

Headquarters of the German occupation.

In an Aktion lasting two days, 2,000 Jews are murdered in Kaunas, Lithuania. Most of the victims are children and old people.

1979 A terrorist bomb explodes in a Jewish restaurant in Paris, wounding 26 people.

March 28

1871 A pogrom breaks out in Odessa, Russia, lasting for four days.

1900 In Konitz, Germany (today Poland), the body of a young man is found and a number of Jews are charged with the crime of ritual murder. Anti-Jewish riots break out and the synagogue is attacked. Finally, one of the accused, Moritz Levy, is sentenced to four years' imprisonment. Later he will be pardoned by Kaiser William II. The Jewish population of Konitz declines because many of them are economically ruined by the anti-Semitic agitation.

1919 In a pogrom carried out by soldiers of Zaporosjski in Tschernigov, Volhynia, Ukraine, 1 Jew is slain.

1942 From Drohobycz, Poland (today Ukrainian S.S.R.), 1,500 Jews are deported to the Belzec extermination camp, where they all perish.

1944 From Risiera di San Sabba concentration camp near Trieste (the only German camp in Italy), a deportation transport leaves for the Auschwitz extermination camp in Poland. Included are 25 old and sick Jews from a nursing home in Trieste.

From Boryslav, Poland (today Ukrainian S.S.R.), 600 Jews are deported to the Plaszov camp near Cracow, from where they are transported to Auschwitz.

March 29

1283 A blood libel brings the Jewish community of Mulrichstadt, Franconia, Germany, the same fate as their brethren in Mainz. Members of the community are burned at the stake.

1881 A pogrom breaks out in Balta, Ukraine. The local population, along with the peasants of the surrounding villages, destroys the Jewish quarter and loots all their property. Many women are raped and many Jews are murdered.

1891 All Jews are expelled from Moscow, Russia.

1919 Barzna, a town in the district of Tchernogov, is raided by bands of insurgents linked to Simon Petlyura's Ukrainian National Army. Two Jews are slaughtered, 1 is injured.

1942 The Nazis take 365 Jewish patients of the psychiatric asylum in Kiev, Ukrainian S.S.R., to the forest of Kirillow, where they are murdered in gas vans. Another 120 Jewish patients are murdered later on.

The first deportation train leaves Paris for the Auschwitz extermination camp in Poland.

1943 Several hundred Jews, mainly women and children, are shot in the Belzyce labor camp in the Polish province of Lublin, and 600 men and women are transferred to the Budzyn concentration camp.

The third transport leaving Skoplje, Yugoslavia, takes 2,500 Jews to the Treblinka extermination camp in Poland.

1985 In a bombing at a Paris theater during a Jewish film festival, 18 people are killed.

March 30

1942 The SS murders 200 Jewish inmates of the Trawniki labor camp in the Polish district of Lublin.

1,000 Jews of the Kalusz ghetto, Poland (today Ukrainian S.S.R.), are taken out of the ghetto and deported to the Belzec extermination camp.

1943 A deportation transport with 101 Jews from Vienna leaves for the Theresienstadt concentration camp in Czechoslovakia.

From the Westerbork transit camp in the Dutch province of Drenthe, 1,255 Jewish internees are sent to the Sobibor extermination camp in Poland.

1945 In Germany, 9 Jewish women escape from the Ravensbrück concentration camp. They are rounded up by the Nazis and murdered the same day.

March 31

1283 In the German town of Bad Kreuznach, the Jew Ephraim ben Eliezer ha-Levi is broken on the wheel.

1310 In Paris, a Jew who probably was baptized by force is burned at the stake. He relapsed into Judaism and consequently is punished by death.

1349 In the small town of Mellrichstadt in Lower Franconia, Germany, 4 Jews are burned at the stake. Their names have been passed on to us: Nehemia ben Yachiel, Eliezer ben Yoez, Samuel ben Yechiel and Isaac ben Gerschom.

1492 According to the royal decree issued by the Spanish monarchs Ferdinand and Isabella, all Jews must leave the Spanish territories within four months. If they are found in Spain after this period (later prolonged to August 3), they are to be killed.

1941 A ghetto is set up in Kielce, Poland, for 28,000 Jews, 3,000 of them from Lodz. As a result of the insufficient sanitary conditions and the lack of space, 4,000 Jews die the same year of a typhus epidemic. At the same time, Jews continue to be brought into the ghetto from the province—in spite of the lack of space.

1942 The first deportation transport with Jews from Opole Lubelskie, a little town in the Polish province of Lublin, leaves for the Belzec extermination camp. At the outbreak of World War II, in addition to the 4,000 Jewish residents of the town, 2,000 Jewish refugees from Austria and 2,500 Jews from Pulavy live in Opole Lubelskie.

In four transports, 6,000 Jews are deported from the ghetto of Stanislavov, Poland (today Ukrainian S.S.R.), to the Belzec extermination camp.

The Gestapo attacks the Minsk ghetto in Belorussian S.S.R., in order to crush the resistance in the ghetto. The head of the resistance, Hersh Smolar, manages to escape.

1943 A deportation transport with 85 Jews leaves Vienna for the Treblinka extermination camp in Poland.

APRIL

April 1

1629 An auto-da-fé is held in the Portuguese town of Évora. The Portuguese Inquisition accuses several persons, descendants of forcibly baptized Jews, of Judaizing, secretly practicing the Jewish religion.

1899 When the corpse of a Christian girl is found in a wood near Polna, Bohemia, Czechoslovakia, violent anti-Jewish agitation starts. The Jews are falsely accused of blood libel and the 22-year-old Jew Leopold Hilsner is arrested, tried, and sentenced to death. Only through the intervention of T. G. Masaryk, later the first president of Czechoslovakia, the sentence is commuted to life imprisonment. An imperial amnesty sets Hilsner free in 1916.

1938 The first deportation transport leaves Vienna with 151 prominent citizens, among them 60 Jews, including the leaders of the Jewish community. Their destination is the Dachau concentration camp in Germany.

1940 The Germans decree that 35,000 Jews have to leave Cracow, Poland, within three months.

Many of them must leave without any of their property. Only 15,000 Jews are allowed to stay.

1941 The ghetto in Chmielnik, Poland, is set up by the Nazis. The 10,000 Jews who make up 80 percent of the town's population are crowded into a small space, where many die of hunger and epidemics. The old synagogue is destroyed immediately after the invasion of the Nazis. Jews have been settling in Chmielnik since the sixteenth century.

1942 Another 1,000 Jewish men, women, and children are deported from the Theresienstadt concentration camp in Czechoslovakia to the Piaski ghetto near Trawniki. Groups of men have to do construction work under SS guard. Further transports coming from Germany raise the number of internees to about 7,000. As a result of the miserable living conditions epidemics break out and cause a high death rate.

1943 A deportation transport with Viennese Jews arrives in the Treblinka extermination camp in Poland. Among the deportees there is a sister of Sigmund Freud.

Seder plate from eighteenth-century Germany. (Israel Museum)

Departure of a transport with 72 Jews from Vienna to Theresienstadt.

1944 A deportation transport with hundreds of Greek Jews arrives at the Auschwitz II-Birkenau extermination camp. Immediately after their arrival, 1,500 men, women, and children are sent to the gas chambers.

April 2

1265 In Koblenz on the Rhine, Germany, a pogrom takes place in which 20 Jews—among them children—are murdered.

1279 The Jews of Rothampton, England, are accused of having crucified a Christian child.

Consequently, many Jews are cruelly put to death in London. Their corpses are hanged in public.

1642 An auto-da-fé is held in Lisbon, Portugal, in which 86 persons are accused of being Judaizers, descendants of Jews that were baptized by force some centuries ago, who still secretly practice the Jewish religion. Two of them are burned alive, 4 are garroted before being burned and another 80 are made galley slaves.

1940 In an Aktion that lasts from April 2 to April 4, several hundred persons are murdered by the Gestapo in a forest near Rossoszyca in the Polish district of Sieradz. There are 179 Jews among the victims.

1942 SS members murder 64 Jews in the town of Feodosiya on the Crimean Peninsula.

From the ghetto of Kolomyja, Ukrainian S.S.R., 1,000 Jews are deported to the Belzec extermination camp in Poland.

1943 The Zloczow ghetto, East Galicia, Poland (today Ukrainian S.S.R.), is liquidated. All inmates of the ghetto are shot in Jelechowice or sent to the Belzec extermination camp.

1944 From Athens, Greece, 1,500 Jews are deported from the Haidon camp to the Auschwitz extermination camp in Poland. In this convoy are also Italian, Spanish, and Portuguese Jews; their cars are uncoupled along the way and sent to Bergen-Belsen concentration camp in Germany. The survivors of this horrible journey—altogether 155 persons—are ultimately sent to Magdeburg, where they will be saved by the American army just when they are going to be shot by the SS.

April 3

1349 In Constance on the Bodensee, Germany, a baptized Jew called Nasson (Nathan) and his two sons set fire to their house, because they are not willing to abjure their faith.

1919 The 61st regiment of "Gaissin," a unit of Petlyura's Ukrainian National Army, carries out a pogrom in Uchomir in the province of Podolia. The unit murders 5 Jews and severely wounds another 10.

1941 In Benghazi, a port in Libya, Jews are attacked by young Arabs released by the Italians, who had recaptured the city.

1942 From Tlumacz, Ukrainian S.S.R., 1,200 Jews are deported to Stanislavov, where they are murdered.

The last 129 Jews of Augsburg, Germany, are sent to the east, their destination the Belzec extermination camp in Poland. Jews have been living in Augsburg since the thirteenth century.

In the course of two days 10,000 Jewish women and children from Austria, Hungary, Germany, and other countries are shot in the forest of Bikerneku, near Riga in Latvia.

1944 The Hungarian government decrees that all Jews have to wear the Yellow Star.

1945 The Nazis murder 497 Jewish forced laborers in Bratislava, Slovakia, (today Czechoslovakia), at the approach of the Soviet army.

The Jewish inmates of the Ohrdruf labor camp in Germany set out on foot for the Dachau concentration camp; 500 perish on the way.

Inmates of the Dora-Nordhausen concentration camp, Germany, among them many Jews, are deported to the Theresienstadt concentration camp, Czechoslovakia. During the transport, 300 of them perish.

April 4

1878   On the eve of Passover, 9 Jews are arrested in Sachkhere, Georgia, Russia, accused of having killed a little Christian girl for ritual purposes. The arrests are followed by severe agitations against the Jews. In March of the following year the accused Jews will be acquitted by the court of Kurtaisi.

1942   From the Horodenka ghetto, Ukrainian S.S.R., 1,500 Jews are assembled and murdered.

The first convoy with 1,000 Jews leaves the ghetto of Sniatyn, in the province of Stanislavov, Poland (today Ukrainian S.S.R.), for the Belzec extermination camp.

A ghetto is set up in Braslav, Belorussian S.S.R., into which all Jews from Braslav as well as from the surrounding communities like Dubinovo, Druja, Druysk, Miory, and Turmont are driven. The ghetto is divided into two parts, one for the able-bodied, the other for the unemployable ones. The Jews in the ghetto are subject to severe restrictions and attempts to flee always result in the death of the desperate victim.

In Sarny, Volhynia, Ukrainian S.S.R., a ghetto is set up. In addition the Jews have to pay a fine of 250,000 rubles on very short notice. Hostages are taken to force the Jews to pay.

1943   In Svieciany in the district of Vilna, Lithuanian S.S.R., 3,500 Jews are murdered by the SS.

1944   The twenty-fourth convoy of 625 Jews—among them 62 children—leaves the Mechelen transit camp in Belgium for the Auschwitz extermination camp in Poland. Only 147 people will survive until the liberation of the camp in 1945.

A convoy with Jewish deportees which left the Risiera di San Sabba camp near Trieste, Italy, on March 28 arrives at Auschwitz. Most of the Jews are gassed on arrival, the rest compelled to do forced labor. None of them will survive.

April 5

1919   The Poles execute 35 prominent Jews from Pinsk, Poland (today Belorussian S.S.R.).

1942   The 4,000 remaining Jews in the ghetto of Lublin, Poland, are deported to Majdan Tatarski.

1943   In the Zloczow ghetto in East Galicia, Poland (today Ukrainian S.S.R.), 5,000 Jews are massacred.

Making matzohs for Passover. (Amsterdam Haggadah of 1695)

The Nazis massacre about 300 Jews from the villages of Soly and Smorgonie on the railway embankment of Ponary Station near Vilna, Poland (today Lithuanian S.S.R.).

About 3,500 Jews from Monastir, Macedonia, Yugoslavia, are sent by the Bulgarian occupation administration to the Treblinka extermination camp in Poland.
Jews were already settling in Monastir at the time of the Roman Empire. They enjoyed a vibrant economic, social, cultural, and religious life.

Hostages are executed in Salonika, Greece, in the Jewish quarter the Nazis have made into a ghetto. The Nazis shoot 3 young Greek Jews 18 years old in front of all the Jews of the quarter. They had tried to escape into the forest.

1944   From Fossoli, Italy, 559 Jews are deported to the Auschwitz extermination camp in Poland.

From the Westerbork transit camp in the Dutch province of Drenthe, 101 Jewish inmates are deported to the Bergen-Belsen concentration camp in Germany.

A transport with 240 Jewish internees leaves from Westerbork for Auschwitz.

From Westerbork, 289 Jewish internees are deported to the Theresienstadt concentration camp in Czechoslovakia.

In Ponary, Poland (today Lithuanian S.S.R.), 450 Estonian Jews are shot by the SS.

April 6

1679   The first auto-da-fé is held in Palma de Mallorca on the Balearic Islands, Spain. The Inquisition accuses 50 persons of secretly practicing Judaism. They are so-called New Christians, descendants of forcibly baptized Jews. All of them are sentenced to life imprisonment.

1903   A pogrom breaks out in Kishinev, Moldavia, initiated and organized by the local authorities and the Russian government. In two days, 49 Jews are murdered and more than 500 are injured; 2,000 families are left homeless.

1941   German troops invade Yugoslavia and Greece. Another 145,000 Jews come under Nazi rule.

1942   From the Otwock ghetto in the Polish province of Warsaw 400 Jews are deported to the Karczev labor camp, where they all perish.

1943   From the Westerbork transit camp in the Dutch province of Drenthe, 2,020 Jewish internees are deported to the Sobibor extermination camp in Poland.

1944   In Izieu, France, Klaus Barbie—head of the Gestapo in Lyons—orders the arrest of 44 children who have been placed there by the recently dissolved Union générale des israélites de France (UGIF). These children are later sent to the Auschwitz extermination camp in Poland.

April 7

1720   An auto-da-fé is held in Madrid, Spain, shortly after a secret synagogue has been discovered in which twenty families have held Jewish services for some years. On this day, 5 Jews are burned at the stake.

1919   According to an article in *The New York Times*, in the Ukrainian town of Felshtin 800 Jews are murdered and 400 are wounded and mutilated by units of Petlyura's Ukrainian National Army. On the same day another pogrom occurs in the town of Proskurov and even more Jews are murdered there.

Insurgents under the leadership of Struk, an ally of Petlyura, carry out a pogrom in Meschigorie in the district of Kiev, Ukraine. They drown 94 Jews in the Dnieper River.

1941 The Jewish population of Radom, in the Polish province of Kielce, is confined to two ghettos. At the outbreak of World War II, 30,000 Jews live in Radom—one third of the population. Jews have been living in Radom since the seventeenth century.

1943 The Nazis murder 800 Jews in Trembovla, East Galicia, Poland (today Ukrainian S.S.R.).

750 Jews from the Skalat ghetto in the Polish province of Ternopol (today Ukrainian S.S.R.) are driven out of town. They are shot and hurriedly buried in mass graves.

Jews are taken out of the Zbaraz ghetto, Poland (today Ukrainian S.S.R.), and murdered outside of town.

The garrison headquarters of the Chelmno extermination camp, Poland, is liquidated and the crematoria in the forest are blown up. Only a few persons are retained to eliminate all traces. In spring 1944 new barracks and crematoria are set up in the forest again.

April 8

1484 In Arles, France, monks incite the townspeople against the Jews. The Jewish community

is attacked and about 50 Jews are forced to accept Christianity. The others are murdered.

1941 In the course of an Aktion that lasts one week, 25,000 Jews are rounded up in the streets of the Warsaw ghetto, Poland, and sent to various forced labor camps in the region. Most of them will perish.

1942 The SS murders 1,500 Jews in Korzeniec in the Polish district of Vilna.

In the course of two days, 2,800 Jews of Kariv, Poland, are deported to the Sobibor extermination camp.

1943 In the course of two days, 2,300 Jews of Rudki in the Polish province of Warsaw are murdered by the SS and the Ukrainian police.

1945 All Jewish inmates of the Buchenwald concentration camp, Germany, are sent on a march to the Flossenbürg concentration camp.

April 9

1941 A ghetto is set up in Czestochova, a town 205 km southeast of Warsaw, Poland. The Jews are crammed into the ghetto, where for lack of space and provisions they suffer from hunger and epidemics.

1942 A deportation train with 998 Jews leaves Vienna for Izbica in Poland.

A ghetto is set up in the town of Volyn, Ukrainian S.S.R. The Jewish inhabitants are divided into two groups: the able-bodied and the unemployable. Only 400 Jews are classified as "able-bodied"; the others will be murdered.

From Lubartov, Poland, 800 Jews are deported to the Belzec extermination camp, where they all perish.

1943 During the night, 800 Jews from Rotterdam, Netherlands, are seized by the Nazis and deported to the Westerbork transit camp in the Dutch province of Drenthe. From there they go to the Auschwitz and Sobibor extermination camps in Poland.

Several hundred Jews who have been deported from Komarno in the Polish province of Lvov (today Ukrainian S.S.R.), to Rudki, are murdered there, together with 1,500 Jews of Rudki.

In Kozova, Galicia, Poland (today Ukrainian S.S.R.), 420 Jews are murdered by the SS and the Ukrainian police.

April 10

1349 The Black Death Persecutions reach the town of Meiningen in the German province of Thuringia, where Jews have been living since the thirteenth century. Some of the Jews living there are killed by the populace, who accuse them of well poisoning. The survivors of this first massacre are murdered some months later.

1882 A pogrom breaks out in Balta in the Russian province of Podolia (today Ukrainian S.S.R.). All Jewish houses are looted, 40 Jews are massacred, 170 are wounded, and 20 Jewish women are raped. Altogether 1,250 Jewish dwellings and shops are razed, and 15,000 Jews—among them many children—are reduced to begging.

1919 Units of Petlyura's Ukrainian National Army carry out a pogrom in Emiltchine, in the province of Volhynia, Ukraine. They murder 6 Jews.

1941 The Germans occupy Zagreb, the capital of the Yugoslavian province of Croatia. At once they start to arrest Jews. Jews have been living in Zagreb since the thirteenth century and the Jewish community's cultural life has been quite active. Notable artists, doctors, scientists, and intellectuals have originated here. At the time of the German invasion the Jewish population numbers 12,000 people.

1942 From Radziev Kusawski in the Polish province of Warsaw, 800 Jews are deported to the Chelmno extermination camp.

The Catholic bishops of the Netherlands publish a pastoral letter protesting the increasing injustice the Jews have to suffer. In particular they condemn forced labor.

The Nazis send 1,750 Jews from Leczyca in the Polish province of Lodz to the Chelmno extermination camp. The Jewish community was established in Leczyca in the middle of the fifteenth century under the protection of the Polish kings. On September 7, 1939, the Nazis occupied the town.

The Nazis begin an Aktion against the Jews of Kuty, in the Polish district of Stanislavov (today Ukrainian S.S.R.). There are 950 Jewish victims. Jews have settled in Kuty since the eighteenth century. At the beginning of World War II the town numbers about 3,000 Jews.

From the village of Uchanie, Poland (today Ukrainian S.S.R.), 1,650 Jews are deported to the Sobibor extermination camp, where all of them will perish.

1943 Heinrich Himmler, the head of the SS, the German police, and the Gestapo, forbids the use of the code word "Sonderbehandlung," special treatment, in connection with the murder of the Jews. Instead, he recommends the term "Durchschleusung," a sort of transportation to the other world, in the language of the murderers.

The Nazis arrest 45 Jews in Utrecht, Netherlands. They are brought to Amsterdam from where they are deported to the Westerbork transit camp in the Dutch province of Drenthe.

April 11

1649 The climax of the Mexican Inquisition is marked by a great auto-da-fé in Mexico City, in which 109 persons are accused of being Judaizers, descendants of forcibly baptized Jews who still secretly practice the Jewish faith. Of that group, 75 are burned in effigy; 13 are burned at the stake, all but one garroted beforehand. The only person burned alive, because he doesn't repent, is Tomas Trevino of Sobremonte.

1940 All the Jewish and Polish intellectuals of Zychlin, in the Polish province of Lodz, are arrested by the Nazis and deported to different concentration camps from where none of them ever will return.

1941 Hungarian Fascists occupy Subotica, a town in the Yugoslavian district of Backa in the Voivodina. Some young Jews offer resistance; about 250 of them are subsequently shot by the Fascists. Jews have settled in Subotica since the middle of the eighteenth century. At the time of the occupation there are 6,000 Jews.

1942 250 Jews who were outside the ghetto are arrested in Zablotov, in the Polish district of Stanislavov (today Ukrainian S.S.R.). They are deported to an unknown destination.

On the evening before Passover, the Nazis call the Jewish inhabitants of Zamosc in the Polish province of Lublin to assemble in the marketplace.

Several hundred are murdered on the spot, and 3,000 Jews are deported to the Belzec extermination camp, where all of them will perish. Jews have been living in Zamosc since the sixteenth century, including famous Jewish scholars. In 1939 there are 12,000 Jews resident in the town; 5,000 of them succeed in escaping to the Soviet Union during the short period of the Soviet occupation of the town.

1945 In Randegg, a small town in Austria, 100 Jewish men, women, and children of Hungarian origin are murdered.

April 12

1463 A crusade is organized after the fall of Constantinople to the Turks in 1453. The crusaders, beggars, monks, peasants, and adventurers set out on April 12, 1463. They have gathered in Poland and march toward Cracow, where they attack the Jewish population—30 Jews are murdered, many wounded. Only those who take refuge in the house of the bishop, Jan Gruszynczki, and the magistrate, Jacob Dembinski, are safe.

1725 An auto-da-fé takes place in Cordova, Spain. Catharina de Reyna y Medina, the widow of Gabriel de Torres of Bordeaux, descendant of a famous Jewish family, and her son Antonio Gabriel de Torres are accused of Judaizing, secretly practicing the Jewish religion. They are burned at the stake.

1941 German troops invade Belgrade, the capital of Serbia, Yugoslavia. The first anti-Jewish measure is the confiscation of Jewish property. Jews have to leave their houses. The Yugoslavians of German origin move into the Jewish apartments and shops. The Ashkenazic synagogue is turned into a brothel, the other synagogue into a storeroom for confiscated Jewish property. Jews have been living in Belgrade since the thirteenth century. In 1941 Belgrade numbers 12,000 Jewish inhabitants.

1942 Beginning of the first deportation of Jews from Krasnik in the Polish province of Lublin, in which 2,000 Jews are deported to the Belzec extermination camp, where they will perish. Jews have been living in Krasnik since the sixteenth century. At the outbreak of World War II the town numbered 5,000 Jewish inhabitants.

1943 The Nazis shoot 2,000 Jews of Brzezany, Poland (today Ukrainian S.S.R.), who are still alive. At the time of the German invasion 1,500 Jews were living there.

1945 One day before the liberation of Vienna by the Soviets, 9 Jews are discovered and shot.

April 13

1891 A few days before Passover, the eight-year-old daughter of the Jewish tailor Sarda of Corfu, in Greece, disappeared and is found dead on April 13. In spite of the child being Jewish, a rumor spreads immediately that she was Christian and had been adopted by Sarda to be ritually killed for Passover. The rural population is inflamed and starts plundering and beating up the Jews. Finally the Jews are besieged in their ghetto as well as in the island's fortress.

1941 In an Aktion in the town of Osijek, Hungary, fascists of German descent and members of the Ustashi* loot Jewish property. They demand 20 million dinars. The Jews are driven out of the town, the synagogue burned down and the Jewish

*Ustashi: Croatian nationalist organization that collaborated with the Nazis.

cemetery devastated. Jews have been living in Osijek since the seventeenth century. At the time of the German occupation, 2,584 Jews were living in Osijek.

1942 250 Jews of Chrzanov in the Polish province of Cracow are deported to the transit camp of Turobin.

After the resettlement of the Jews from the small communities near Wlodzimierz, Poland (today Ukrainian S.S.R.), the number of Jews interned in the ghetto rises to 22,000. The first step toward the extermination of these Jews is made in dividing them into two groups: the "able-bodied" and the "unemployable." From this day on, "unemployables" are taken out of town daily and murdered.

1943 From the ghetto of Bobrka, Poland (today Ukrainian S.S.R.), 3,000 Jews are deported to the Belzec extermination camp.

Jewish internees—1,204 in number—are sent from the Westerbork transit camp in the Dutch province of Drenthe to the Sobibor extermination camp in Poland.

The Nazis murder 2,000 Jews in the Buczacz ghetto, Ternopol, Poland (today Ukrainian S.S.R.).

1944 From the Drancy transit camp in France, 1,500 Jewish men and women are deported to the Auschwitz extermination camp in Poland. Immediately after their arrival, 265 deportees are sent to the gas chambers; only 105 men and 70 women will survive until the liberation of the camp by the Russian army in 1945.

April 14

1859 Anti-Jewish riots break out in Galatz, Rumania. They are probably instigated by local Greeks.

Synagogues are looted, Jewish houses and shops are destroyed, and many Jews are murdered.

1942 In Riga, Latvia, 300 Jewish patients from the principal mental hospital are brought to the nearby Bikerneku forest and shot.

1943 From the Siedlce labor camp in Poland, 500 Jewish internees are deported to the Treblinka extermination camp. A small group manages to escape into the forest, where they offer armed resistance against the Nazis until the end of 1943.

In an Aktion carried out by the SS and the Ukrainian police in Sambor, Poland (today Ukrainian S.S.R.), 1,000 Jews are murdered.

1944 German task forces arrest 150 men of the Jewish community of Baja on the Danube, Hungary, and deport them. About 2,000 Jews are living in Baja at this time. The Jewish community has existed since the beginning of the eighteenth century.

A deportation transport leaves Athens, Greece, for the Auschwitz extermination camp in Poland.

April 15

1881 A pogrom breaks out in Jelissavetgrad, Russia.

1938 Riots against the Jews arise in Dabrova Gornicza, in the Polish province of Katovice. Many Jews are injured and a lot of Jewish property is destroyed.

1940 The German Ministry of the Interior decrees that Jewish hospitals situated in the Nazi-administered area have to be incorporated in the euthanasia program.

1941 The Nazis arrest the Municipal Council of Salonika, Greece, and institute anti-Jewish laws. Salonika has had a Jewish community for 2,000 years. At the time of the German invasion about 50,000 Jews are living in Salonika.

1942 From Paskuda, in the Polish province of Lublin, 100 Jews are deported to the Treblinka extermination camp.

1943 The Nazis massacre 600 Jews from Kopyczynce, in East Galicia, Poland (today Ukrainian S.S.R.).

1944 A group of Jewish prisoners in Ponary, Poland (today Lithuanian S.S.R.), whose task is the effacement of all traces of the mass murders, tries to escape—25 of them are killed, 15 of them succeed.

1945 The Bergen-Belsen concentration camp in Germany is liberated by the British troops. They find 40,000 survivors and 13,000 dead, most of them Jews.

Sent on a march to the west are 40,000 prisoners from the Oranienburg-Sachsenhausen concentration camp in Germany. Thousands perish on the way. At the same time 17,000 female inmates of the Ravensbrück concentration camp (also in Germany) are sent on a march to the west, without a definite destination.

A transport leaves the Neuengamme concentration camp near Hamburg, Germany; 1,000 Jews are brought to the Ebensee labor camp. The "journey" lasts two weeks and many of the deportees perish on the way.

Pogrom in Russia in 1881. (Collection Roger-Viollet)

April 16

1497 The king of Portugal orders all Jewish children under the age of 14 taken away from their parents. They are sent to distant parts of the country, where they are baptized and brought up as Christians.

1919 The regiment of Nalivaiko, a unit of Petlyura's Ukrainian National Army, reaches Gorchtchik, a town in Volhynia, Ukraine, and one Jew is murdered.

1941 The Nazis occupy Sarajevo, the capital of Bosnia-Herzegovina, Yugoslavia. They storm the Sephardic and other synagogues, plunder and devastate the sanctuaries. The prayer books are burned. Jews have been living in Sarajevo since the middle of the sixteenth century. Their cultural, economic, and religious life flourished. When the Nazis occupy Sarajevo the town numbers about 10,500 Jews.

The Nazis shoot 133 Jews at Mont-Valérien, near Paris, because of their participation in the Resistance.

1942 Von Alvensleben, the SS Polizeiführer (SS chief of police), reports to Berlin that the Crimean Peninsula is "free of Jews." Jews have been living in Crimea for more than two thousand years.

The ghetto of Gostynin, Poland, is liquidated. About 2,000 Jews are deported to the Chelmno extermination camp. Only a few Jews will survive the period of the Nazi occupation. Jews have been settling in Gostynin since the beginning of the eighteenth century.

April 17

1942 The ghetto of Pinsk, Poland (today Belorussian S.S.R.), is reduced in space, and 400 Jews are shot.

From Sanniki, Poland, 250 Jews are deported to the Chelmno extermination camp, where all of them will perish.

1943 From the town of Avignon, in the south of France, 20 Jews are brought to the Drancy transit camp, from where they will be deported to the Auschwitz extermination camp in Poland.

In Kozova, Galicia, Poland (today Ukrainian S.S.R.), 500 Jews are murdered by the SS and the Ukrainian police.

From Leshniov, Poland, 250 Jews are brought to the Brody transit camp.

1944 During the Jewish festival of Passover the SS encircles the Hungarian town of Nyiregyhaza and arrests all the Jews. They join the Jewish inhabitants of 36 communities in the surrounding area in one overcrowded ghetto of 18,000 people.

April 18

1266 In Mare-du-Parc, near Rouen, France, a Jew who converted to Catholicism is put to trial. It is not known whether this conversion was of his own free will, but he has returned to Judaism and remains loyal to his faith until he is burned alive on April 18.

1389 A massacre against the Jews of Prague, Bohemia (today Czechoslovakia), breaks out. Shouting "death or baptism," the mob storms the Jewish houses. When the Jews refuse to be baptized, several thousand are massacred, their corpses burned together with the cadavers of animals.

1905 A pogrom breaks out during the Passover season in Bialystok, Russia (today Poland), and lasts two days. Cossacks assault Jews in the streets and in the synagogues.

1939 Slovakia adopts Germany's anti-Jewish laws for itself.

1942 From Ceske Budejovice, Bohemia, (Czechoslovakia), 909 Jews are deported to the Belzec extermination camp in Poland, where they perish. Jews first settled in this town in the fourteenth century. At the outbreak of World War II about 1,500 Jews live in Ceske Budejovice.

A transport with 1,000 Jewish men, women, and children leaves the Theresienstadt concentration camp in Czechoslovakia. Some of them will be interned in the camp near the village of Sawin in the Polish province of Lublin. The majority of them dies of a typhus epidemic. The survivors are deported to the Sobibor extermination camp where they perish. Of this transport only 3 women will survive until the liberation of the camp by the Soviet army.

1943 An uprising breaks out in the ghetto of Javorov in Galicia, Poland. After that 3,489 Jews

Old synagogue at Bialystok.

are massacred by the Nazis. Only a few Jews, who have been hidden in bunkers, manage to survive.

1944 From Munkacs, Hungary (today Ukrainian S.S.R.), 13,000 Jews are ordered to leave their homes and assemble in town to await deportation. Many of them have to wait in the open air, exposed to the elements.

April 19

1283 A Christian child is found dead near Mainz on the Rhine, Germany, during Easter. A relative gathers a crowd, accusing the Jews of having killed the child in a ritual murder. They approach Mainz where they break into Jewish houses, looting them, and 10 Jews are murdered. The stolen goods are confiscated by Emperor Rudolf I.

1343 The Jewish community of Wachenheim, Germany, is struck by a ritual murder accusation. All Jews are burned at the stake.

1506 Anti-Jewish riots break out in Lisbon, capital of Portugal. A crowd of 10,000 Portuguese, enlarged by German, Dutch, and French sailors from the harbor, enters the Conversos' quarter (Conversos are Jews who converted to Christianity) and slaughters men, women, and children. Several pyres are set up in different places of the town, and dead as well as living are burned on them. The massacre lasts until April 23 and about 3,000 Conversos are murdered. The governor of Lisbon tries in vain to intervene in the name of King Manuel.

1919 In Vilna, Poland (today Lithuanian S.S.R.), Polish legionnaires carry out a pogrom which continues for four days. They loot Jewish houses, set the Jewish quarter on fire, and murder several hundred Jews. Hundreds of others are arrested and tortured. The famous Jewish writer Weiter is among the dead.

In a second pogrom carried out by Petlyura's Ukrainian National Army in Romanov, in the province of Volhynia, Ukraine, 11 Jews are murdered.

1942 1,500 Jews of Ciechocinek in the province of Warsaw, Poland, are deported to the Chelmno extermination camp.

1943 800 Jews from Borszczov, in East Galicia, Poland (today Ukrainian S.S.R.), are massacred by the Nazis.

The Nazis start to liquidate the ghetto of Warsaw, Poland, planning within two days to send all Jews to the Treblinka extermination camp. The Jewish underground resistance fights ferociously and the Nazis have to call for reinforcement. Regular troops under the command of General Jürgen Stroop are employed. Mordecai Anielewicz leads the Jewish resistance fighters in the ghetto.

The twentieth transport of 1,631 Jews—among them 262 children—leaves the Mechelen transit camp in Belgium for the Auschwitz extermination camp in Poland. Only 150 of all these people will survive until the liberation of the camp in 1945.

1944 The Jews of Nagykanizsa, Hungary, numbering about 2,700, are concentrated in a ghetto. Jews have lived in this town since the beginning of the eighteenth century. The Jewish community is known for its flourishing religious, cultural, and economic life.

1945 In Scheibbs, Austria, 15 Jews, deportees from Hungary, are shot and burned.

April 20

1017 A considerable number of people are killed by a heavy storm raging in Rome, Italy. Pope Benedict VIII is told that the Jews have insulted the image of Christ in the synagogue and thereupon he has a number of Jews beheaded. According to the Christian annals the storm dies away at once.

1298 In the little town of Roettingen in Franconia, Germany, the German knight Rindfleisch instigates the first massacre of Jews. He incites an armed crowd to take revenge for alleged desecration of the host and massacres all 21 Jews of the community, burning them alive.

1506 The massacre of the Jews of Lisbon, Portugal, begun the day before, continues with even greater cruelty, as people from the surrounding countryside arrive to participate in the plundering and slaughtering. In all, 1,000 Jews are killed.

1639 A Christian child has disappeared on the Wednesday before the Jewish Passover holiday. When the tramp Thomas falsely confesses that he sold the child to the Jews of Leczyca, Poland, two Jews from the town, called Meir and Lazar, are tortured and subsequently executed.

1941 The Jews of Belgrade, capital of Serbia, Yugoslavia, are ordered to register with the authorities, and wearing of the Yellow Star becomes obligatory—9,145 Jews are registered.

1942 In Germany the Jews are forbidden to use public transportation.

1943 Jewish internees—numbering 1,166—from the Westerbork transit camp in the Dutch province of Drenthe are deported to the Sobibor extermination camp in Poland.

In honor of Hitler's birthday, 30 Jews are shot at a gorge near the sandpits of Piaski. They are doctors, lawyers, and engineers who have been interned in various outposts of the Janovska camp in Lvov, Poland (today Ukrainian S.S.R.).

1944 A ghetto is set up in Maramarossziget in Hungary, in which the Jews are ordered to settle.

In Ponary near Vilna, Poland (today Lithuanian S.S.R.), Jews who have been forced to burn the dead in order to eliminate the traces of the Nazis' crimes revolt. Almost 100 Jews are killed, but 15 manage to escape.

April 21

1349 In the course of the Black Death Persecutions the Jewish community of Würzburg, Germany, is accused of well poisoning. The Jews set fire to their houses and perish in the flames. Rabbi Goldknopf and David and Moshe ha-Darshan, the directors of the local yeshiva (the Talmud school) are among those killed.

1920 Several Jews are driven out of their home by a detachment of soldiers in Vilna, Poland (today Lithuanian S.S.R.). One of them is shot immediately, another is tied to a horse and dragged to death in the streets.

1941 The Sajmiste concentration camp near Belgrade, Yugoslavia, is set up. Until the end of June 1942 about 15,000 Jews will be murdered in gassing vans that are camouflaged as Red Cross trucks.

1942 300 Jews of Oszmiany, Belorussian S.S.R., are deported to the Vilna ghetto.

1944 In an Aktion that will last three days the Jews of Ungvar, Ukrainian S.S.R. have to assemble in the courtyard of a plant, in which the Jews of the surrounding area have also been crowded. The number rises to 25,000, who have to await their further deportation under most inhuman conditions.

April 22

1919 Units of Petlyura's Ukrainian National Army pass through the town of Krasnostav in the province of Volhynia, Russia. They stay for two days carrying out a pogrom in which 3 Jews are slain and almost all Jewish men are publicly flogged.

1941 The Nazis enact measures against the 4,000 Jews of Skoplje, Yugoslavia. Jews have been living in Skoplje since Roman times.

1942 Deported to the Janovska labor camp are 1,000 young Jewish men from the ghetto of Javorov, Poland (today Ukrainian S.S.R.).

From Osencin, in the Polish province of Warsaw, 750 Jews are deported to the Chelmno extermination camp.

About 3,000 Jews from the ghetto of Wloclavek, Poland, are deported by the Nazis to the Chelmno extermination camp, where all of them will perish.

1945 Uprising of the 600 inmates of the Jasenovac concentration camp in Yugoslavia. Of these, 520 are murdered, only 80 manage to escape—including 20 Jews.

A *Passover seder*. (From a seventeenth-century Haggadah)

April 23

1283 Outbreak of a massacre against the Jews of Rochenhausen, in the German province of Pfalz—13 Jews are slaughtered, others are forcibly baptized.

1338 The Jews of Pulkau, Lower Austria, are accused of host desecration. The crowd attacks the Jews, massacres them and burns their corpses. The Jewish houses are looted. From Pulkau the riots will spread to other towns in Lower Austria.

1679 An auto-da-fé is held in Palma de Mallorca, Balearic Islands, Spain. Put to trial are 52 Judaizers, descendants of forcibly baptized Jews who are still secretly practicing the Jewish faith. They are condemned to prison and their property is confiscated by the Church and the Crown.

1905 A pogrom breaks out in Shitomir in the province of Volhynia, Ukraine, which will last until April 26. With the help of soldiers, Jewish houses are looted—22 Jews are massacred, 60 are gravely wounded. Among them are many members of the Jewish self-defense organization.

1936 This night the British authorities evacuate the Jewish inhabitants of Hebron, Palestine, as they are not able to guarantee their safety from the hostile Arab population. The Jewish community has existed there since the sixteenth century and was destroyed for the first time in 1929 by Arab rioters, then rebuilt in 1931.

1942 Eight hundred Jews of Mielec, Poland, and 1,000 Jews of Vienna are deported to Wlodava in the Polish province of Lublin where they have to live in the ghetto. Jews have been living in Wlodava since the sixteenth century. At the outbreak of World War II about 6,000 Jews were living there.

After being gathered in the synagogue, 600 old and sick Jews of Skalat in the province of Ternopol, Poland (today Ukrainian S.S.R.), are taken to the train station. They are sent to the Belzec extermination camp.

Another transport with 1,009 Jewish men, women, and children leaves the Theresienstadt concentration camp in Czechoslovakia for Lublin in Poland. There 350 Jews will be selected to be sent to the Majdanek extermination camp. The other 659 will be interned in the Piaski ghetto. In June 1942 they will be sent to the Sobibor extermination camp. Only 8 will survive until the liberation in 1945.

April 24

1288 The Jews from the town of Troyes, France, are accused of ritual murder. During the Jewish feast of Passover, a dead body has been placed in the house of a Jewish notable of Troyes, Isaac Chatelain. The inquiry is carried out by the Franciscan and Dominican orders and 13 Jews, most of them members of the Chatelain family, sacrifice themselves in order to save the community. They are burned at the stake on April 24.

1905 A group of 14 young Jews from Tschudnowo, Ukraine, leave for Shitomir to help defend their Jewish brethren against the hostile crowd.

Passing through Trojanowo, 10 of them are brutally murdered by the peasants.

1920 In a pogrom in Hodorkov, district of Kiev, Ukraine, units of Petlyura's Ukrainian National Army under the command of Generals Sokolski and Ogorodnikov slaughter about 700 Jews and injure 800 within twelve hours.

1941 A ghetto is set up in Lublin, Poland, and 34,000 Jews are crowded into it. Leaving the ghetto is prohibited. Another 10,000 Jews will be sent to smaller ghettos in the district of Lublin.

In Schluda, near Libau, in Latvia, 40 Jewish women are shot by the Nazis. These women had been working with the Schupo (security police).

1942 Since they do not hold working papers, 600 Jews from Kossov, Ukrainian S.S.R., are deported to the Kolomyja ghetto. Several hundred Jews from Kuty in the Polish district of Stanislavov, who are considered too old or too ill for work, are also deported to the Kolomyja ghetto. On the march many of the deportees will die. All but 20 Jews remaining in Zablotov, in the Polish district of Stanislavov are transferred there as well.

The Gestapo hangs 10 Jews in Warta in the Polish district of Sieradz.

A deportation transport with 650 Jews leaves Nuremberg, Germany, for the Belzec extermination camp in Poland.

1943 In the course of an Aktion, 4,000 Jews are murdered in Izbica, in the Polish province of Lublin.

An Aktion against the 3,500 Jews of Javorov, Poland (today Ukrainian S.S.R.), is carried out. Part of them are murdered, part of them deported to the Janovska camp in Lvov.

April 25

1302 A rumor spreads that the Jews of Magdeburg, Germany, have made a sculpture of Christ, which they crucified. The mob attacks the Jewish quarter, massacres 7 Jews and loots their houses. Magdeburg has had a large and important Jewish community since the thirteenth century.

1920 A pogrom against the Jewish community of Tsibulev in the Russian district of Kiev is carried out by units of Petlyura's Ukrainian National Army. They brutally massacre 3 Jews.

1942 A deportation transport with 105 Jews leaves Bamberg, Germany, for the Belzec extermination camp in Poland, where they arrive a few days later. They all will perish in the camp.

From the Theresienstadt concentration camp in Czechoslovakia, 1,000 Jews are deported to Warsaw, Poland, where they are lodged in a synagogue. A group of men is selected to be sent to the Rembertov camp to work in agriculture. The rest of the Jewish deportees are taken to the Treblinka extermination camp where they are killed. In 1944 those Jews working in the Rembertov camp will attempt to escape but most of them will be shot by the SS. Only 8 of them will survive.

1943 An unknown number of Jews—including many children and women—are shot in the forest of Bikerneku near Riga, Latvia.

1944 A convoy with 160 Jews leaves the only Nazi concentration camp in Italian territory, Risiera di San Sabba near Trieste, for the Auschwitz extermination camp in Poland.

1945 Italy is liberated. However, the Germans continue to hunt the Jews in this area until the last minute of war. So, on April 25, 6 Jews are shot by the Nazis near Cuneo.

In Delfzijl, Netherlands, 2 Jews who have been hiding until that time are found by the Nazis and murdered on the spot.

April 26

1343 A ritual murder accusation is raised against the Jews of Germersheim, Germany. Thereupon, the town's whole Jewish community is burned at the stake.

1881 Outbreak of pogroms in the entire Kiev area, lasting until May 4. The atrocities against the Jews are the result of anti-Semitic propaganda encouraged by the governor, General Drenteln. There are 762 Jewish victims.

1933 The Gestapo (Secret Police of the Reich) is founded.

1944 The Jews of Munkacs, Hungary are concentrated in a ghetto consisting of two brickworks with no sanitary facilities. Jews have been living in this town, which has produced a number of famous rabbis, since the second half of the seventeenth century.

A deportation train with 19 Jews leaves Vienna for the Auschwitz extermination camp in Poland.

1945 The Stutthof concentration camp near Danzig, Poland, is evacuated. The internees are transported by ship to Lubeck, Germany. The journey lasts one week and many of them perish on the way.

Victims of a Kiev pogrom.

April 27

1940 Heinrich Himmler, the head of the German police and the Gestapo, orders the foundation of the Auschwitz concentration and extermination camp in Poland. Auschwitz will play an infamous role in the history of Jewish martyrdom. The number of people murdered in this camp is between 2½ and 3½ million. These victims are mainly Jews, but Gypsies and people of other European nations figure among them.

1942 A deportation train with 998 Jews leaves Vienna for Wlodava, Poland.

About 2,000 Jews from the Wloclavek ghetto in Poland, the remainders of the 13,500 Jewish inhabitants of this town, are deported to the Chelmno extermination camp. They are murdered immediately after their arrival. The ghetto is completely destroyed: Wloclavek has thus become "free of Jews."

1,000 Jewish men, women, and children from the Theresienstadt concentration camp in Czechoslovakia are sent to the Izbica ghetto in Poland. About 400 Jewish men are transported to the Lublin labor camp. After the liquidation of the Izbica ghetto the rest of the Jews of this transport will go to the Majdanek extermination camp. All—except one woman—will perish in the camp.

In a raid on the ghetto of Tomaszov Rawski in the Polish district of Lodz, 100 Jews are arrested and shot, among them members of the Jewish underground movement.

1943 From the Westerbork transit camp in the Dutch province of Drenthe, 196 Jewish internees are deported to Theresienstadt.

Jewish internees—numbering 1,204—are sent from the Westerbork transit camp to the Sobibor extermination camp in Poland.

From Vienna, 2 Jews are deported to Theresienstadt.

1945 The SS massacres 1,000 Jews with machine guns at the Marienbad railway station in Czechoslovakia. They form part of 2,775 Jewish prisoners on march from Rehmsdorf, a camp adjoining Buchenwald, to the Theresienstadt concentration camp. Another 1,200 die on the way, so that only 575 arrive at their destination.

April 28

1919 In the town of Dubovo in the province of Kiev, Ukraine, units of the Ukrainian National Army carry out a pogrom, looting Jewish houses and killing 38 Jews.

1942 In an Aktion that lasts several days, 2,000 Jewish men, women, and children are deported from the Theresienstadt concentration camp in Czechoslovakia to Zamosc in Poland. Able-bodied men are selected for construction work. Old people, women, and children are interned in the Komarov ghetto before being sent to the Chelmno extermination camp, where they will be murdered. Only 24 of these 2,000 deportees will survive until 1945.

1943 The ghetto of Ozmiani, Lithuania (today Belorussian S.S.R.), is liquidated. Part of the 2,500 Jewish inmates are deported to the Vilna ghetto, part to labor camps in the surrounding area, while many of them are massacred in Ponary.

From Izbica, Poland, 300 Jews are deported to the Sobibor extermination camp.

1944 A deportation transport with 79 Jews leaves Vienna for Theresienstadt.

A deportation transport with 1,000 Jews from Budapest, capital of Hungary, arrives at the Auschwitz extermination camp in Poland.

The 11,830 Jews in Kosice, Czechoslovakia, are collected and resettled in the houses of a quarter consisting of eleven streets. Later, their quarter will be reduced to only three streets. In the end they will have to live in the space of a brickyard and the four fields that surround it.

A group of Jewish internees is deported from the Kistarcsa internment camp, 15 km northeast of Budapest, Hungary. In this camp are imprisoned Jews who have been caught by the Nazis in so-called individual operations (Einzelaktionen). On April 28 the first transport with 1,800 Jews leaves Kistarcsa for Auschwitz.

1945 The International Red Cross comes to terms with the SS to save 150 Jewish women from the Ravensbrück concentration camp in Germany; they are sent to Sweden.

April 29

1938 Severe excesses against Jews in Vilna, Poland (today Lithuanian S.S.R.). Several Jews are injured and their property destroyed.

1940 In Warsaw, Poland, the Nazis start to surround one quarter with a wall. This quarter is destined to become the future ghetto. Its surface is 840 acres. It is intended not only for the Jews of Warsaw but also for Jews from the provinces.

1942 In Amsterdam, Netherlands, the Nazis supply 500,000 Yellow Stars to the Jewish Council to be distributed to all Jews in Holland above the age of six. Wearing them is obligatory.

The SS hangs 7 Jews in the town of Chrzanov in the Polish district of Cracow, because they have baked bread illegally.

1943   The last 330 Jews interned in the camp in Leczna in the Polish province of Lublin are deported to the Sobibor extermination camp.

1944   A transport with 1,004 Jewish men and women leaves the Drancy transit camp in the German occupied zone of France. The destination of this convoy is the same as so many before: the Auschwitz extermination camp in Poland. Immediately after their arrival, 904 of them will be gassed; only 37 men and 25 women will survive until the liberation in 1945.

1945   The Dachau concentration camp in Germany is liberated by the American army. Over 40,000 people have perished in this camp, more than two thirds of them Jews.

April 30

1349   The Black Death Persecutions reach the small town of Radolfszell on the Bodensee, Germany. Accused of well poisoning, the Jewish community is exterminated, probably burned at the stake.

1679   The third auto-da-fé in a series of five within one year is held in Palma de Mallorca on the Balearic Islands, Spain. There, 62 persons are accused of being Judaizers, descendants of Jews forcibly baptized some centuries ago who still practice the Jewish faith secretly. They are sentenced to incarceration for life. Their property is confiscated by the Church and the Crown.

1940   The ghetto of Lodz, Poland, in which 164,000 Jews are crowded together in the space of only 4 square kilometers is encircled with barbed wire and wooden fences in order to separate this part from the rest of the town. The ghetto is also guarded by a special police, the so-called Schutzpolizei.

1941   Enactment of the first racial laws by the pro-Nazi government in Zagreb, Croatia, Yugoslavia. The Jews are prohibited to work in government offices and the wearing of the Yellow Star becomes obligatory.

1942   The deportation of the Jews of Wloclavek in the Polish district of Warsaw to the Chelmno extermination camp begins. In the course of one week nearly 20,000 Jews will be sent to that extermination camp where they all will perish.

In an Aktion, 300 Jews are killed by the SS in Grybov in the Polish district of Cracow.

A transport with 1,000 Jews leaves the Theresienstadt concentration camp in Czechoslovakia for the ghetto in Zamosc, Poland.

The Nazis deport 200 Jews from the village of Brzesc Kujavski, Poland, to Chelmno, where all will perish.

1943   The 400 Jews from the town of Florina, Macedonia, Greece, are deported by the German

Menorah found on a glass vase in the Jewish catacombs.

army to the town of Verria. Later they will be transported to Athens, the capital of Greece, in order to be sent to the Auschwitz extermination camp in Poland.

About 2,000 Jews are deported by the Nazis from their native town of Wlodava in the Polish province of Lublin to the Sobibor extermination camp.

MAY

May 1

1265 The Jewish community of Sinzig, Germany, is annihilated as predicted by the proselyte Abraham, who is burned at the stake in December 1264. The 61 Jewish men, women, and children are driven into the synagogue, which is set on fire.

1691 During an auto-da-fé, 25 New Christians—baptized Jews—are accused of secretly practicing the Jewish religion in Palma de Mallorca, Spain. They are garroted and burned at the stake.

1920 Units of the Ukrainian National Army massacre 32 Jews, wound 5, and rape several Jewish women in Vassilkovo in the Soviet district of Kiev.

1940 The ghetto of Lodz, Poland, is set up by the Nazis and the Jewish population of the town is commanded to leave their homes and resettle there.

1942 From Dortmund, Germany, 2,100 Jews are deported to the Belzec extermination camp in Poland.

The SS kills 22 Jews in Feodosiya on the Crimean Peninsula, Ukrainian S.S.R.

The SS and local collaborators shoot 4,000 Jews in Dünaburg, Latvian S.S.R.

From Lasoczyn, province of Kielce, Poland, 200 Jews are brought to the Lazarov camp.

The inhabitants of the ghetto in Dolhinov, Belorussian S.S.R., which is set up on May 1, will be murdered one month later. Only 500 Jewish craftsmen are temporarily exempt and some young Jews manage to flee to join partisan groups.

1943 The last 100 Jews in a forced labor camp in Wegrov, in the Polish province of Warsaw, are killed by the Nazis.

The remaining 2,500 Jews from the ghetto of Brody, Ukrainian S.S.R., are deported to the Majdanek extermination camp. A few dozen Jews manage to flee and join a group of partisans.

Over three days, 5,600 Jews of Wlodava in the Polish district of Lublin are deported to the Sobibor extermination camp.

Drawing by Simon Wiesenthal. Mauthausen, 1945.

Replica of the Jewish star printed and distributed by the Dutch Resistance in 1942. It reads, "Jews and non-Jews stand united in their struggle." (Jewish Historical Museum, Amsterdam)

May 2

1919   Petlyurian units of the Ukrainian National Army slay 5 Jews, rape Jewish women, and beat many others with sabers during their first pogrom in Orinin, in the province of Podolia.

1942   The Nazis murder 3,000 Jews from Dunayevtsy, a town near Kamenets-Podolski in the Ukrainian S.S.R.

From this day onward all Jews in the Netherlands are ordered to wear the Yellow Star which costs four Dutch cents and a quarter of a textile ration ticket.

1943   The ghetto of Miedzyrzec Podlaski in the Polish province of Lublin is liquidated and more than 3,000 Jews are deported to the Treblinka ex-termination camp with the exception of 200 skilled workers who stay behind.

The ghetto of Lukov in the Polish province of Lublin is liquidated and all Jewish inhabitants of the ghetto are killed.

1945   The Red Cross takes over the Theresienstadt concentration camp in Czechoslovakia.

Members of the SS shoot 223 Hungarian Jews in the local Jewish detention camp in the village of Hofamt Priel, Austria.

May 3

1096   Soldiers of the First Crusade surround the synagogue in Speyer, Germany, which has one of the oldest Jewish communities in Germany, in order to kill the Jews after the service. The Jews inside have been warned but 11 Jews who are found outside are massacred.

1679   During the fourth auto-da-fé held in Palma de Mallorca, Balearic Islands, Spain, 46 persons are accused of being Judaizers, descendants of forcibly baptized Jews who are still practicing the Jewish religion. They are condemned to perpetual incarceration and all their property is confiscated by the Church and the Crown.

1919   During a pogrom carried out in Gornostaipol, Ukraine, 13 Jews are forcibly drowned by the troops of Simon Petlyura's Ukrainian National Army and some loosely linked Cossack troops.

1920   Petlyura's troops massacre 14 Jews and rape many Jewish women during a pogrom in the town of Miastkovka, Podolia.

1939   In Hungary the so-called second Jewish Law is enacted, which prohibits all Hungarian Jews

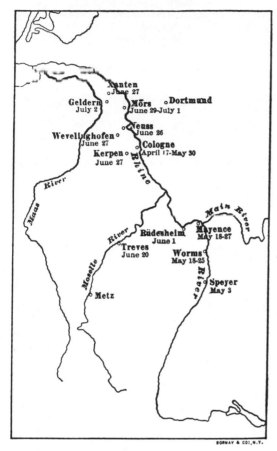

Xanten
June 27

Geldern °
July 2

Mörs °
June 29-July 1

° Dortmund

Neuss
June 26

Wevelbghofen °
June 27

Kerpen °
June 27

Cologne
April 17-May 30

Rhine

Maas

River

River

River

Moselle

Main River

Rüdesheim
June 1

Mayence
May 18-27

Treves
June 20

Worms
May 18-25

Rhine River

Metz

Speyer
May 3

BORWAY & CO:, N.Y.

Map of the Rhine region, showing dates and sites of anti-Jewish action during the First Crusade, 1096.

from working as or becoming judges, lawyers, teachers, and members of parliament.

1942 The members of the Jewish Council in Bilgoraj, district of Lublin, Poland, are shot because of their refusal to cooperate with the Gestapo.

1944 Added to the 12,000 Jews who have already been concentrated in a brickyard in Cluj (Kolozsvar), Hungary, are 10,000 more Jews. They will all be deported to the Auschwitz extermination camp in Poland.

In Nagyvarad (Grosswardein), Hungary, 35,000 Jews are deported from the overcrowded ghetto to Auschwitz.

1945 Sinking of the prisoner ships *Cap Arcona* and *Thielbech* near Neustadt, Germany. Many Jews are among the victims.

In the village of Persenbeug, Austria, 233 Hungarian Jews from Debrecen are shot. Their corpses are burned.

May 4

1941 The Hungarian authorities intern about 3,500 Jews in the ghetto of Subotica, in the Backa district, annexed from Yugoslavia.

1942 The deportation of the Jews from Bilgoraj, Poland, to the Belzec extermination camp begins.

The gassings in the Auschwitz extermination camp in Poland begin. The number of victims will be between 2 and 3.5 million people.

The Sobibor extermination camp in Poland is erected and ready for the gassings. In the first year and a half of its existence, 250,000 Jews are murdered.

1943 From the Westerbork transit camp in the Dutch province of Drenthe, 1,187 Jewish internees are deported to the Sobibor extermination camp in Poland.

May 5

1624 An auto-da-fé takes place in Lisbon, Portugal. Antonio Homem, a descendant of Jews forcibly baptized some centuries ago, who was caught officiating at a Jewish ceremony with a group of other New Christians, is accused of Judaizing—secretly practicing Judaism. He and several other members of this group are burned at the stake.

1942   630 Jews from Dabrova Gornicza in the Polish province of Katovice are deported to the Auschwitz extermination camp where they are murdered.

1943   The Nazis shoot 30 Jews in the Salaspils concentration camp near Riga, Latvia.

1945   The concentration camp in Mauthausen, Austria, is liberated by the American army, which finds 3,000 unburied dead bodies lying between the barracks.

May 6

1543   The first auto-da-fé is held in Tomar, Portugal, after the establishment of an Inquisition tribunal in 1540. The fortunes of the executed Judaizers, descendants of upper-class Jews forcibly baptized some centuries ago but according to the accusation still practicing Judaism, are confiscated by the Crown.

1691   A secret synagogue is discovered in Palma de Mallorca, Balearic Islands, Spain, and the Judaizers are punished. In the main auto-da-fé, 25 persons are killed; 22 are garroted before being burned. Raphael Valls, the spiritual leader of the group, and his principal disciples, Raphael Benito Terongi and his sister Catalina Terongi, are burned alive.

1892   During a two-day pogrom, 20 Jews are killed and many others are wounded in Lodz, Po-

land. Many houses are looted and set on fire by the mob.

1941   During an Aktion, 57 Jews from Vlasenica, a village in Bosnia-Herzegovina, Yugoslavia, are arrested and slain outside of the village.

1942   From Vienna, 994 Jews are deported to Minsk, Belorussian S.S.R.

Jews from the ghetto of Deblin, Poland—2,500 of them—are deported to the Sobibor extermination camp, where they all perish.

May 7

1919   During a pogrom 82 Jews are slaughtered and 12 are wounded in Brazlav, Podolia. The pogrom is led by hetman Tiutiunnik and his units, allies of Simon Petlyura and his Ukrainian National Army.

1942   The Nazis deport 800 Jews from the ghetto of Grodek, situated between Lvov and Przemysl, Poland (today Ukrainian S.S.R.), to the Janovska camp in Lvov.

From the ghetto of Josefov, Poland, 1,000 Jews are deported to the Sobibor extermination camp. Also sent are 2,500 Jews from the ghetto of Ryki, Poland, to be murdered in Sobibor.

1943   The last 370 Jews of Novogrodek, Grodno district, Poland (today Belorussian S.S.R.), are shot. Before this Aktion the Jews had dug a tunnel through which about 100 of them managed to flee. They fought against the Nazis and against Belorussian collaborators.

From Zagreb, Yugoslavia, 1,000 Jews are deported to the Auschwitz extermination camp in Poland.

May 8

1919 During a pogrom 39 Jews are massacred In Raigorod in the province of Podolia, by units linked to Simon Petlyura's Ukrainian National Army.

1942 3,500 Jews from the ghetto of Konskovola, Poland, are deported to the Sobibor extermination camp. Also sent are 1,500 Jews from the ghetto of Baranov and 1,500 Jews from Markuszov, Poland.

The German municipal police killed 100 Jews in Szczebrzeszyn in the Polish province of Lublin.

The Jews from Lipniszki, Traby, and Duoly, Poland, of whom there are only 1,250 left following an Aktion, are transferred to the Lida ghetto in the Polish province of Grodno (today Belorussian S.S.R.).

1943 The Jewish resistance in the ghetto of Warsaw, Poland, continues. The uprising of the Jews began on April 19, but the Nazis have conquered the center of the resistance and 100 resistance fighters, among them their leader Mordecai Anielewicz, die on May 8.

May 9

1919 During a pogram lasting one week, 400 Jews are slaughtered and many Jewish women are raped in Trostyanets, Ukraine, under the command of Drewinski of the Ukrainian National Army.

1942 In Poland, 800 Jews from the ghetto of Lubartov and 1,500 Jews from the ghetto of Markuszov are deported to the Sobibor extermination camp.

The SS murders 2,000 Jews in Szczuczyn, in the Novogrodek district of Belorussian S.S.R.

The SS deports 600 Jews from Rozanka to Szczuczyn, and murders them there.

Deported from Bedzin, Silesia province, Poland, to the Auschwitz extermination camp are 8,000 Jews. Many of them had originally come from the Auschwitz region and had fled to Bedzin.

In the course of two days the SS murders 1,100 Jews of Voronova, Novogrodek district, Poland (today Belorussian S.S.R.).

The SS murders 1,500 Jews of Orlovo, Novogrodek district, Poland (today Belorussian S.S.R.), in the forest of Borainik.

A transport with 1,000 Jews leaves the Theresienstadt concentration camp in Czechoslovakia for the Ossovo ghetto, Ukrainian S.S.R.

1943 The Nazis shoot 660 Jews in Skalat, in the Polish district of Ternopol (today Ukrainian S.S.R.).

1944 All Jews from Heves, Hungary, who number 10,000, are deported to Bagölyuk near Egercshei.

May 10

1427 The Jews of Bern, Switzerland, are expelled from the town "for the honor and greater glory of the Lord, his Mother and all the Saints."

1484 Lives are lost and great damage is done to the Jewish community of Aix-en-Provence in southern France when bands of marauders from the neighboring provinces attack.

1682 Miguel (Isaac) da Fonseca, Antonio de Aguiar (alias Aaron Cohen Faya) and Gaspar (Abraham) Lopez Pereira are accused of being Judaizers—descendand of forcibly baptized Jews who practice Judaism secretly—and are burned at the stake in an auto-da-fé in Lisbon, Portugal.

1883 During a pogrom 100 Jewish residences and businesses are completely destroyed in Rostov-on-Don, Russia.

1920 During an eight-day pogrom, 100 Jews are slaughtered and many wounded by bands of insurgents under Stepanski, an ally of Simon Petlyura's Ukrainian National Army, in Jashkov, Kiev province, Ukraine.

1933 Book burnings take place in Germany, involving mainly books by Jewish authors and by authors whom the Nazis dislike. The book burnings are supported by students who take books out of the libraries and by publishers who make the books available.

Sentence of the Portuguese Inquisition against Miguel Henriques da Fonseca, who was burned alive, having publicly professed the Law of Moses after being convicted of heresy and apostasy. Lisbon, 1682.

1940 From the Polish region of Zaolzie, 600 Jews are deported to a ghetto in the town of Zaviercie in the province of Katovice.

The Germans occupy the Netherlands. At this time 140,000 Jews live in the country, 10,000 of them Jewish refugees from the Nazis. The occupiers begin to issue anti-Jewish regulations.

The first Jewish community in the Netherlands came into existence in 1492. By the seventeenth century Amsterdam was one of the most important centers of Jewish life in Europe.

1942 From the ghetto of Brzezany, Poland, 5,000 Jews are deported to the Chelmno extermination camp.

In the course of two days, 2,000 Jews are murdered by the SS in Radun, Poland.

The SS murders 500 Jews in Sluzevo, Poland.

1,500 Jews are deported from Sosnoviec, in the Polish province of Katovice, to the Auschwitz extermination camp.

The last deportation of Jewish women and children leaves the Sajmiste camp near Belgrade, Yugoslavia. Because they are married to Gentiles, 6 Jewish women remain. The 8,000 Jews from Semlin are killed in specially constructed trucks, which suffocate them by exhaust from the motor.

1943 In the Salaspils concentration camp near Riga, Latvia, the remaining Jewish craftsmen are shot by the Nazis.

May 11

1942 The Gestapo hangs 2 Jews in Bedzin, Silesia, Poland.

Deported from Vienna, 1,000 Jews arrive in Minsk, Belorussian S.S.R., where they are led to freshly dug pits near the station and shot.

1943   Jewish detainees numbering 1,446 are deported from the Westerbork transit camp in the Dutch province of Drenthe to the Sobibor extermination camp in Poland.

1944   During a several-day Aktion, 15,000 Jews from Kassa in north Hungary and its surrounding area are deported to the Auschwitz extermination camp in Poland.

In an Aktion lasting several days, 15,000 Jews, who are assembled in the ghetto of Satoraljaujhely, Hungary, are deported to Auschwitz.

May 12

1020   On Good Friday, an earthquake followed by a hurricane ravages Rome, Italy, and Pope Benedict VIII has a number of Jews arrested for alleged host desecration. They all "confess" under torture and are burned at the stake.

1919   In Uman, Ukraine, 170 Jews are massacred, many are wounded, and several Jewish women are raped when allies of the Ukrainian National Army under the leadership of Klimenko carry out a pogrom lasting five days.

Units linked to the Ukrainian National Army massacre 314 Jews and rape 2 Jewish women during a large pogrom carried out in Gaissin, in the province of Podolia, Ukraine.

1942   In Poland, 2,750 Jews from Turobin and 1,000 Jews from the village of Zolkievka are deported to the Sobibor extermination camp.

From Sosnoviec, Poland, 1,500 Jews are deported to the Auschwitz extermination camp.

A transport with 1,001 Jews leaves from Vienna for Izbica, Poland.

The SS deports 2,500 Jews from Krasnostav, Soviet Union, to the Treblinka extermination camp in Poland.

2,500 Jews from the German provinces of Saxony and Thuringia arrive in the ghetto of Belzyce in the Polish province of Lublin, bringing the total number of Jews to 4,500.

The remaining 2,000 Jews in the ghetto of Gabin in the Polish province of Warsaw are deported to the Chelmno extermination camp.

1943   Szmul Zgyielbojm, member of the Polish National Council in exile in London, commits suicide as a protest against the indifference of the Allies to the fate of the Jews in Poland, who fight against the Nazis in the ghetto of Warsaw.

1944   About 1,200 Jews from the town of Bonyhad, Hungary, where they had settled in the middle of the eighteenth century, are forced into a ghetto.

May 13

1728   When a baptized Jew, Jan Philipowicz, wants to return to the Jewish faith, the Church orders the arrest of all Jews of Lvov, Poland. Most Jews manage to flee, but the brothers Chaim and Joshua Reizes and a rabbi are imprisoned. The rabbi manages to escape and Joshua Reizes commits suicide. Chaim Reizes is publicly tortured and then burned at the stake with his brother's corpse.

1919   Units of insurgents under the leaders Chepel, Sarantcha, and Volynets, allies of Simon Petlyura's Ukrainian National Army, carry out a pogrom in Litin in the region of Podolia, Ukraine. The pogrom lasts until May 15 and 8 Jews are slain.

Troops of the Ukrainian National Army carry out a pogrom in the town of Ivantchik in the province of Podolia, Ukraine, killing 2 Jews and wounding 1.

1942 In the village of Sineljnikov in the area of Dnjepropetrowsk, Soviet Union, 200 Jews are arrested by the Nazis and shot.

1943 In the course of ten days 3,500 Jews are murdered by the SS and the Ukrainian police in Przemyslany, Lvov district.

1944 The deportation of 25,000 Jews from Ungvar, and its vicinity in the Ukrainian S.S.R., to the Auschwitz extermination camp in Poland begins and lasts several days.

May 14

1919 During a pogrom, 20 Jews are massacred and many are mutilated by sabers and whips in Olgopol in the province of Podolia, Ukraine. The commanders are Tchaly and Zabolotny, linked to Simon Petlyura's Ukrainian National Army.

In the train station at Kirilovka, Russia, 18 Jews are slaughtered by units under Commander Chepel, linked to the Ukrainian National Army.

During a pogrom lasting five days, 33 Jews are brutally killed by units of insurgents under their hetman Zeleny, ally of Simon Petlyura, in Berchad, Podolia, Ukrainian S.S.R.

1941 The French police arrest 3,747 Jews of Polish, Czechoslovakian, and Austrian nationality

on the order of Eichmann's deputy Dannecker. They are sent to the two camps of Pithiviers and Beaune-la-Rolande. During the two years of the camps' existence, thousands of Jews are deported from there to the transit camp Drancy and farther on to the Auschwitz extermination camp in Poland.

1942 From Gorzkow, Poland, 1,200 Jews are deported to the Sobibor extermination camp.

1,700 Jews are deported from Brzezany, Poland, to the Chelmno extermination camp.

May 15

1919 During a three-day pogrom, 4 Jews are massacred and many are wounded by units linked to Simon Petlyura's Ukrainian National Army, under the command of Volynets, in Hachtchevaty in the province of Podolia, Ukraine.

During a pogrom, 10 Jews are massacred and many seriously wounded in Monastiristch in the region of Podolia, Ukraine, by units under the command of Klimenko, linked to the Ukrainian National Army.

During a pogrom lasting five days, 23 Jews are massacred and many injured by units linked to the Ukrainian National Army, in Khmelnik in the province of Podolia, Ukraine.

1940 After the Germans invade The Hague in the Netherlands, 30 Jews commit suicide.

1941 The Nazis murder 12 Jewish prisoners of war in Biala Podlaska, Poland.

1942 Jewish resistance fighters escape the ghetto of Stolpce in the province of Minsk, Belorussian S.S.R., and join partisans in the forest.

A deportation train with 1,006 Jews starts from Vienna for Izbica, Poland.

1943 In one week, 14,000 Jews are deported from Piotrkov, Poland, to the Auschwitz extermination camp.

1944 The first deportation of Jews begins from the brickyard of Kosice, Slovakia (today Czechoslovakia), to Auschwitz.

In the German occupied zone of France, 878 Jewish men and women are deported from the Drancy transit camp to the Kaunas concentration camp. Only 16 men will survive until the liberation.

The deportation of 26,000 Jews forcibly detained in Munkacs, Hungary (today Ukrainian S.S.R.) begins, and 14,000 of them are deported to Auschwitz.

The first deportation transport with 3,400 Jews leaves Nagyszöllos, Hungary, for Auschwitz.

May 16

1942 After an Aktion in the ghetto of Pabianice, Poland, carried out by the SS, in which 150 Jews are killed, 8,000 Jews are deported to the Chelmno extermination camp.

1943 From the ghetto of Warsaw, Poland, Jürgen Stroop, the SS general who put down the Jewish rebellion, announces that "The Jewish district doesn't exist anymore" and in celebration the Great Synagogue in Tlomacka Street is blown up.

1944 From the Theresienstadt concentration camp in Czechoslovakia, 2,500 Jewish men, women, and children are deported to the so-called family camp Auschwitz II-Birkenau in Poland. Like

the other inmates, they are accorded certain privileges until they are gassed on the night of July 11/12.

The first deportation transports of Hungarian Jews arrive at the Auschwitz extermination camp.

518 Jews are deported from Fossoli, Italy, to Auschwitz.

May 17

1942 Jewish men, women, and children numbering 2,000 are deported from the Theresienstadt concentration camp in Czechoslovakia to Lublin, Poland, and to the Sobibor extermination camp.

From the ghetto of Zaviercie, Katovice province, Poland, 2,000 Jews are deported to the Auschwitz extermination camp.

1943 From Berlin, 395 Jews are deported to Auschwitz.

1944 A Jew is deported from Vienna to the Theresienstadt concentration camp in Czechoslovakia.

May 18

1096 Troops of the First Crusade arrive in Worms on the Rhine, Germany. The wealthy Jews receive protection—after payment—from the bishop of Worms in his own castle. The other 500 Jews, who stay in their houses, are slaughtered. The town is looted and the Torah scrolls are burned. Among the victims are Rabbi Solomon and his family.

1721 An auto-da-fé is held in Madrid, Spain, where descendants of forcibly baptized Jews are

Breastplate for the Torah scrolls in a synagogue at Schön-hausen, Germany.

accused of being "Judaizers," secretly practicing the Jewish religion. Among the victims is an old woman of 96, Maria Barbara Carillo, who is burned alive.

1919 During a three-day pogrom, 14 Jews are massacred, 9 wounded, and 15 Jewish women and girls are raped in Ivankov in the district of Kiev, Ukraine, by units under the command of Struk, ally of Simon Petlyura and the Ukrainian National Army.

1942 During a large-scale Aktion, 180 Jews are shot and 350 are deported to labor camps from the ghetto of Tlumacz, Ukrainian S.S.R.

The Germans arrest 2,000 Jews from the Wolkovysk ghetto in the Polish province of Grodno (today Belorussian S.S.R.), and kill them outside of town. This gives rise to a Jewish underground, which works with the partisans in the forest.

Deported to the Sobibor extermination camp are 1,000 Jews from the Siedliszcze ghetto in Poland.

1943 Jewish internees numbering 2,511 are sent from the Westerbork transit camp in the Dutch province of Drenthe to Sobibor.

1944 From Vienna, 4 Jews are deported to the Theresienstadt concentration camp in Czechoslovakia.

Having deported 160 Jews from the Drancy transit camp in France, the Nazis shoot them in the Proyanovska labor camp in Kaunas, Lithuanian S.S.R.

May 19

1942 600 Jews from the Grodek Jagiellonski ghetto in the Polish province of Lvov (today Ukrainian S.S.R.) are deported to the Janovska concentration camp.

1943 The liquidation of the Busk ghetto in the Polish province of Galicia (today Soviet Union), takes place. About 1,500 Jews are killed.

Berlin, the capital of the Reich, is declared "free of Jews."

1944 A transport with 238 Jews leaves the Westerbork transit camp in the Dutch province of Drenthe for the Bergen-Belsen concentration camp in Germany.

From the Westerbork transit camp, 453 Jewish detainees are deported to the Auschwitz extermination camp in Poland.

The twenty-fifth transport, with 507 Jews (among them 58 children), leaves the Mechelen transit camp in Belgium for Auschwitz. From this convoy, 132 people will survive until the liberation of the camp in 1945.

May 20

1940 The Auschwitz-Birkenau extermination and concentration camp is set up in the Cracow district of Poland.

1942 From Vienna, 986 Jews are deported to Minsk, Belorussian S.S.R.

1,540 Jews of Belz, Poland (today Ukrainian S.S.R.), are deported to the Belzec extermination camp.

In the course of an Aktion that lasts for two days, 3,400 Jews are deported from Brzezany, Poland, to the Chelmno extermination camp.

1943 The Ukrainian police murder 200 Jews in two days in Moravica, Volhynia, Ukrainian S.S.R.

1944 The seventy-fourth deportation convoy of cattle cars leaves French territory bringing 1,200 Jewish men and women, assembled and detained in Drancy, to the Auschwitz extermination camp in Poland. Immediately after their arrival, 904 are gassed.

May 21

1919 The Haidamacks (Cossacks and peasants) of Simon Petlyura, high commander of the Ukrainian National Army, carry out a pogrom in Orinin, Podolia province, Ukraine, in which 16 Jews are slain, many beaten with sabers, and several Jewish women raped.

Units of the Ukrainian National Army, under the command of Alexander Udovichenko, carry out a four-day pogrom in Urmini, Ukraine.

1921 In Jaffa and Tel Aviv, Palestine, 34 Jews are massacred by the Arabs, among them the famous Hebrew author Joseph Brenner.

1942 From the Olkusz ghetto in the Polish province of Cracow, 1,000 Jews are deported to the Auschwitz extermination camp. Smaller groups

have already been deported to various concentration camps.

From Ozorkov, Poland, 2,000 Jews are deported to the Chelmno extermination camp.

2,200 Jews from the town of Korzec, Poland (today Ukrainian S.S.R.), are taken outside of town and shot. Moshe Krasnostavski, chairman of the Jewish Council, commits suicide as a sign of protest against the Nazis and the Jewish Council organizes a resistance group. About 50 Jews manage to flee into the woods.

Young Jews from the ghetto of Lida, Poland (today Lithuanian S.S.R.), flee to the Naliboki forest and there join other resistance groups under the leadership of Tuvia Bielski.

In an Aktion lasting three days, 4,300 Jews from Chelm, Poland, are sent to the Sobibor extermination camp. Among them are also 2,000 Jews from Slovakia who had been deported to Chelm earlier.

1943 The last message is received from the fighters in the Warsaw ghetto uprising.

The Gestapo shoots 1 Jew in Mochy, Poland, as he leaves the camp to look for something to eat.

1944 The Gestapo interns 260 Jews from the Greek island of Crete in Iraklion. They are later loaded on a ship which is purposely sunk by the Germans.

May 22

1919 During a pogrom, 20 Jews are massacred by the Ukrainian National Army in Rovno in the Volhynia district.

1942 From the Ozorkov ghetto, Poland, 300 Jewish children are deported to the Chelmno extermination camp. The secretary of the Jewish Council, Mrs. Mania Rzepkovitch, refuses an exemption for her son, who goes with the others.

In the course of the last Aktion in the Dolhinov ghetto, Belorussian S.S.R., the SS kills 4,500 Jews but spares the lives of 500 skilled workers.

The Nazis deport 1,000 Jews from the Polish town of Tyszovce to the Belzec extermination camp.

1943 The Nazis take 1,000 Jews from the ghetto of Stryj, Poland (today Ukrainian S.S.R.), and shoot them in the Jewish cemetery.

1944 From the ghetto of Munkacs, Hungary, 12,000 Jews are deported to the Auschwitz extermination camp in Poland.

The Jews from the area of Harangod and Nyirjes, Hungary, are assembled at the train station in Nyiregyhaza, Hungary.

May 23

1536 The second bull issued by Pope Paul III establishes the Inquisition tribunals in Portugal, paving the way for the most brutal killing.

1919 In the region of Podolia, Ukraine, 6 Jews are massacred when units linked to the Ukrainian National Army, under their leader Chepel, carry out a pogrom in Novo-Konstantinov.

1938 A transport with 120 people, among them 50 Jews, leaves Vienna for the German concentration camp Dachau. The Jews are particularly mistreated by the guards during the transport.

1942 A Jew is hanged by the Gestapo in Warta in the Polish district of Sieradz.

The first group of 2,000 Jews are deported from the Wlodava ghetto, Lublin province, Poland, to the Sobibor extermination camp.

1943 The ghetto of Przemyslany, Lvov province, Poland (today Ukrainian S.S.R.) is liquidated and the town is declared "free of Jews."

In Jezierzany, Poland (today Ukrainian S.S.R.), 700 Jews are murdered by the SS and the Ukrainian police.

May 24

1241 In Frankfurt on the Main, Germany, a quarrel breaks out between Jews and Christians over the conversion to Catholicism of a Jewish boy whose parents object. The fight escalates and 180 Jews are killed.

1420 The Jews in Austria are arrested en masse: 800 are expelled; 1,000 are imprisoned for host desecration in Enns, Upper Austria. The Jews are threatened with death if they don't become baptized.

1944 The camp in Biala Podlaska, Lublin province, Poland, where 300 Jewish artisans still remain, is liquidated and the Jews are deported to the Majdanek concentration camp.

When the deportation trains crammed with Hungarian Jews stop at the Slovakian railroad station of Kysak, en route to the Polish concentration camps, the escorting German guards rob and massacre several Jews.

The 2,700 Jews of Papa, Hungary, are rounded up in a concentration camp set up on the grounds of a factory. Jews have lived in Papa since the eighteenth century.

May 25

1096 Soldiers of the First Crusade besiege the castle of the bishop of Worms on the Rhine, Germany, in which about 300 Jews have found shelter. Those who don't accept forced baptism are slaughtered or commit suicide. Among the victims are the rabbi of Worms, Simcha ben-Isaac ha-Cohen, and the scholars Alexandri ben-Moshe and Isaac ben-Eljakim.

1556 A trial for host desecration takes place in Sochaczev, Poland. A Polish maidservant has accused her master, the Jew Benjascha, and four other Jews, his alleged accomplices. Three of them are tortured and on May 25 Benjascha is burned at the stake despite orders for his release from the Polish King Sigismund August.

1737 After an auto-da-fé in Lisbon, Portugal, 12 persons are burned at the stake for being Judaizers, descendants of forcibly baptized Jews accused of practicing the Jewish religion secretly.

1919 During a third pogrom in four months, 400 Jews are slaughtered and many Jewish women raped by allies of Simon Petlyura's Ukrainian National Army in Radomysl, district of Kiev.

1942 A ghetto is set up in Kovel, Volhynia, Poland (today Ukrainian S.S.R.), which is divided into two parts: one for the able-bodied men and women, the other for the old and sick who are destined to die.

1,000 Jewish men, women, and children are deported from the Czechoslovakian concentration camp Theresienstadt to Lublin, Poland, and then on to the extermination camp Majdanek, where all of them are killed except one man employed by the Nazis as a watchmaker.

1943 Jewish internees—2,862—from the Westerbork transit camp in the Dutch province of Drenthe are deported to the Sobibor extermination camp in Poland.

A transport with 203 Jews leaves from Vienna for the Theresienstadt concentration camp in Czechoslovakia.

May 26

1171 The whole Jewish community of Blois, France, is burned at the stake following the first blood libel accusation in France.

1905 A pogrom is carried out by Russian soldiers and Cossacks in Minsk, Belorussia, in which Jews are wounded and killed. Many Jewish shops are demolished and plundered.

1942 A deportation transport arrives in Minsk, Belorussian S.S.R., with 1,000 Jewish people from Vienna. They are taken to pits outside the town, where they are immediately shot.

1943 From the Piotrkov Trybunalski ghetto, Poland, 500 Jews are deported to the Starachovice labor camp near Radom, and 40 women and children are murdered.

The SS surrounds the Jewish quarter of Amsterdam, Netherlands, because the majority of Jews have not registered on Nazi demand. The Nazis arrest 3,300 Jews and deport them to the Westerbork transit camp in the Dutch province of Drenthe.

An Aktion lasting three days is carried out against the 6,000 Jews of Sokal, Poland (today Ukrainian

S.S.R.). Many of them are killed and the rest are deported to the Belzec extermination camp.

the inmates, about 2,500, are killed; Sokal is "free of Jews." By hiding, 60 Jews manage to survive.

May 27

1096 Troops of the First Crusade under the command of the count of Leiningen approach Mainz, Germany, and set out to kill the Jews there—in spite of the protection decree issued by the German King Henry IV. The whole Jewish community of 1,300, who have taken refuge in the bishop's castle, is slaughtered. Among the dead are Rabbi Menachem ben David ha-Levi and his whole family.

1942 A convoy with 3,000 Jews leaves from the Theresienstadt concentration camp in Czechoslovakia for the Auschwitz extermination camp in Poland.

A deportation train leaves Vienna with 991 Jews for Minsk, Belorussian S.S.R.

The Jews of Dubno, Volhynia, Poland (today Ukrainian S.S.R.), who had survived the various Aktionen of the Nazis, are confined to a ghetto, where the Nazis carry out a rigid "selection," in which 5,000 Jews are marked as unemployable and are slaughtered and buried in a mass grave.

2,000 Jews who have been deported three weeks before from Dortmund, Germany, and from Czechoslovakia, and assembled in Zamosc in the Polish province of Lublin, are sent to the Belzec extermination camp. Also deported to Belzec are 350 Jews from the Polish town of Laszczov.

1943 In Tluste, Galicia, Poland (today Ukrainian S.S.R.), the Nazis forcibly drive 3,000 Jews from the marketplace to the cemetery, where all of them are massacred.

The last Aktion is carried out in the ghetto of Sokal, Lvov, Poland (today Ukrainian S.S.R.). All

May 28

1349 A fire breaks out in Breslau, Silesia, Germany (today Poland), and the mob exploits the situation to attack the Jews. Only 6 people out of 66 Jewish families survive.

1679 The fifth and last auto-da-fé in one year takes place in Palma de Mallorca, Balearic Islands, Spain. 13 descendants of forcibly baptized Jews are accused of being Judaizers, people who still practice the Jewish religion secretly, and are imprisoned. Their property is confiscated by the Spanish Church and Crown.

1919 In the course of several pogroms, 180 Jews are murdered by the Ukrainian National Army in Litin, Podolia province, Ukrainian S.S.R.

During a raid, 80 Jews are murdered and their property destroyed in Smela, Ukraine, by the Grigoryev Gangs, allies of Petlyura's Ukrainian National Army.

In a pogrom, 400 Jews are murdered by units of the Ukrainian National Army in Trostyanets, Ukraine.

1943 In Lvov province, Poland (today Ukrainian S.S.R.), 600 Jews who have remained in the Grodek Jagiellonski ghetto are shot and buried in mass graves near Artyszczov.

May 29

1241 The Christian populace invades the Jewish quarter of Frankfurt on the Main, Germany. The

Jewish houses are demolished and more than 75 percent of Frankfurt's 200 Jews are massacred, including 3 rabbis. The survivors save their lives by pretending to accept the forced baptism.

1905   In a pogrom lasting three days in Brest Litovsk, Belorussia, many Jews are assaulted and killed, and Jewish shops are looted and destroyed by soldiers and Cossacks.

1919   During a pogrom, 70 Jews are murdered by members of the Ukrainian National Army in Zlatopol, Ukraine.

1938   A law is issued by the Hungarian government reducing the number of Jews permitted in

Page from the Memorbuch *kept by the Jews of Frankfurt from 1629 to 1907, recording the names of communities that have suffered persecution and ending with a prayer for the souls of the martyrs.* (J.N.U.L.)

the professions, administration, business, and industry to 20 percent.

1942   During the first large scale Aktion in Radzivillov near Volyn in the Ukrainian S.S.R., 1,500 Jews are driven out of the town and shot. This Aktion leads to the founding of a resistance movement by the Jews under the leadership of Asher Czerkaski.

For the second time, 3,000 Jews of Opole, Poland, are deported to the Sobibor extermination camp.

The eighth German decree obliges Jews over the age of 6 to wear the Yellow Star with the word "Jew" in the occupied zone of France.

May 30

1096   The Jews of Cologne, Germany, find shelter in the castle of Bishop Hermann III and in the houses of Christian neighbors. Consequently, the soldiers of the First Crusade under the leadership of the count of Leiningen kill only 2 Jewish people who didn't flee. The Jewish quarter is looted and burned and all Torah scrolls are destroyed.

1541   The great auto-da-fé occurs in Sicily, marking the climax of the persecution of the Jews, when 19 Conversos, Jews or descendants of Jews who were forcibly baptized in 1492, are probably burned at the stake.

1938   A transport with 500 Jews leaves from Vienna for the Dachau concentration camp in Bavaria, Germany.

1943   The SS and the Ukrainian police under German command murder 1,100 Jews during the last Aktion in Boryslav, Poland (today Ukrainian S.S.R.).

May 31

Star of David that Jews in occupied France were forced to wear. (Collection Roger-Viollet)

1944 A convoy with 1,000 Jewish men and women leaves from the Drancy transit camp in the German occupied zone of France for the Auschwitz extermination camp. Immediately after arrival, 627 of these deportees are gassed, and only 85 men and 51 women survive until the liberation of the camp in 1945.

The last deportation of Jews from Munkacs, Hungary (today Ukrainian S.S.R.), takes place. The town is now "free of Jews."

1919 During a pogrom carried out by units of Simon Petlyura's Ukrainian National Army, 700 Jews are murdered in Cherkassy on the Dnieper River, Ukraine.

1942 1,000 Jews are deported from Tyszovce, Lublin province, Poland, to the Majdanek extermination camp. Jews have been living there since the fifteenth century under the protection of Polish kings. At the outbreak of the war, 4,000 Jews live in Tyszovce.

An Aktion against several hundred Jews of Stryi, Poland (today Ukrainian S.S.R.), is carried out. It follows repeated manhunts in which young Jewish men have been caught and sent to forced labor.

The SS murders 600 Jews in Parafianov, Kielce district, Poland.

All the patients in the Jewish hospital in Przemyslany, Poland (today Ukrainian S.S.R.), are murdered by the Gestapo.

The SS murders 600 Jews in Luszki, Vilna district, Lithuanian S.S.R.

1944 In the course of three days, 3,500 Jews of the Nyiregyhaza ghetto, Hungary, are deported to the Auschwitz extermination camp in Poland.

JUNE

June 1

1096 Soldiers of the First Crusade invade Trier, Germany. Over the protests of Archbishop Egilbert, they massacre all Jews who do not submit to baptism. One year later the newly baptized are allowed to return to their Jewish faith.

1556 Of the 5 Jews accused of host desecration in Sochaczev, Poland, two are burned at the stake in Polock. One commits suicide in prison, one manages to escape, and the fate of the fifth is unknown.

1906 During a pogrom, 78 Jews are slaughtered and 84 severely injured in Bialystok, Poland.

1940 The Jewish population of Tomaszov Lubelski, Poland, is ordered to resettle in a ghetto set up by the Nazis.

1942 From Cracow, Poland, 2,000 Jews are deported to the Belzec extermination camp.

From Vienna, 1,000 Jews are deported to Minsk, Belorussian S.S.R., where they are driven to pits outside the town and shot by the SS.

The Jews in the German occupied zone of France are obligated to wear the Yellow Star.

1943 Jewish detainees—3,006 of them—are sent from the Westerbork transit camp in the Dutch province of Drenthe to the Sobibor extermination camp in Poland.

June 2

1453 An accusation of host desecration and murder of a Christian boy leads to a trial against the Jewish community of Breslau, Silesia (today Wroclaw, Poland). At the end of the trial, 41 Jews are found guilty and are burned at the stake, the rabbi commits suicide, and the other Jews of the community are expelled from Breslau, after the Christians abducted their children under 7 years in order to baptize them and raise them as Christians.

1938 A transport with 600 Jews leaves Vienna for the Dachau concentration camp in Bavaria, Germany.

Jews represented as desecrating the host (after the Gobelin tapestries in the Cathedral of Sainte-Gudule in Brussels).

1942   The Jews of Ghetto B in Kobryn, in Belorussian S.S.R., are rounded up and deported to Bronna Gora and there killed by the SS. In Ghetto A, a process of selection is carried out. Thus half of the Jewish population of Kobryn is murdered.

In an Aktion that lasts for two days, 3,000 Jews from Hrubieszov, Lublin province, Poland, are captured by the SS and are deported to the Sobibor extermination camp.

The SS and Ukrainian auxiliaries massacre 100 Jews of Belz, in the province of Lvov.

The SS and their Baltic collaborators kill 1,000 Jews in an Aktion in Miory, Latvian S.S.R.

999 Jews are deported from Vienna to Minsk, Belorussian S.S.R.

1944   From Vienna, 1 Jew is deported to the Theresienstadt concentration camp in Czechoslovakia.

June 3

1096   Soldiers of the First Crusade arrive in Xanten, Germany, where Jews from Cologne had been sent by the bishop of Cologne in order to save their lives. During the Kiddush prayer on Shabbat Eve, the crusaders storm the tower in which the refugees are praying. Before the crusaders can begin the slaughter, 60 Jews kill themselves.

Jews from Bonn and Cologne, Germany, fleeing the crusaders, find temporary refuge in Altenahr until the crusaders approach the town and the Jews commit suicide.

1940   The first regulations and measures regarding the Jews in the Netherlands are issued from The Hague: Jews are removed from their posts in government and public service. Before the invasion of the German army about 13,900 Jews lived in The Hague. At the end of World War II only 1,238 will survive. Jews have been living in The Hague since the seventeenth century.

1942   During the final Aktion of the SS, 3,000 Jews in the ghetto of Braslav, Belorussian S.S.R., are murdered. Peasants of the region and the citizens of Braslav are invited to participate. A group of Jewish resistance fighters helps a group of Jews to escape.

The SS murders 200 Jews in Molczadz, Belorussian S.S.R.

1943 The SS and Ukrainian police massacre 900 Jews in Trembovla, Galicia province, Ukrainian S.S.R.

1944 119 people—21 men, 29 women and 69 children—many of them Jews, are burned alive in Pertschup, in the district of Trakaj, in Latvia.

From the Westerbork transit camp in the Dutch province of Drenthe, 496 Jewish detainees are deported to the Auschwitz extermination camp in Poland.

June 4

1919 In Kamenets-Podolsk, in the province of Podolia, 100 Jews are slaughtered in a pogrom lasting six days by soldiers of Petlyura's Ukrainian National Army and local inhabitants.

1940 The German police shoot 29 persons, most of them Jews, in the village of Celiny, Bedzin district, Poland.

1942 The deportations of Jews from the ghetto of Cracow, Poland, begins and lasts two days. Dr. Arthur Rosenzweig, chairman of the Jewish Council, and his family are shot, because the Nazis find him uncooperative during the deportations.

1943 The SS and Ukrainian police massacre 400 Jews in the village of Kozova, Galicia, Poland (today Ukrainian S.S.R.).

1944 From Florence, Italy, 16 Jews are deported to the Auschwitz extermination camp in Poland.

June 5

1670 The Jewish ghetto in Vienna has 4,000 inhabitants, who resettled after the tragedy of March 12, 1421. June 5 is the date set for their expulsion if they don't consent to baptism. But the time limit is prolonged to July 25.

1919 Units of Petlyura's Ukrainian National Army slaughter 27 Jews during a pogrom in Felshtin, in the province of Podolia, Ukraine.

1940 A Jew is among the Poles killed during an Aktion carried out by the Gestapo in Ciezkovice, in the district of Chrzanov, Poland.

1942 A convoy with 1,000 Jewish men, women, and children of foreign nationalities leaves from

Gate leading to the Jewish quarter in Vienna.

the international camp of Compiègne set up by the Nazis in the German occupied zone of France for the Auschwitz extermination camp in Poland. Only 32 people will survive.

Between three and four o'clock in the morning in Czernovitz, Rumania (today Ukrainian S.S.R.), the police deport about 70 sick Jews from the Jewish hospital to Transnistria in cattle cars.

A transport with 1,000 Jews leaves from Vienna for Izbica, Poland.

The synagogue of Ceske Budajovice, Czechoslovakia, is burned down by the Nazis.

1943   In the course of three days, the ghetto of Brody, Lvov province (Ukrainian S.S.R.), is liquidated and nearly 10,000 Jews are deported to the Belzec extermination camp.

The SS and Ukrainian police massacre 700 Jews in Borszczov, East Galicia province, Poland (today Ukrainian S.S.R.).

The last Aktion against the Jews of Drohobycz, Poland (today Ukrainian S.S.R.), begins.

Jewish children, 1,266 under the age of 16, who have been detained in the Westerbork transit camp in the Dutch province of Drenthe, are deported to the Sobibor extermination camp in Poland and immediately gassed.

The SS kills 150 Jewish workers after the liquidation of the camp in the Ruzki factory in Minsk Mazowiecki, Poland.

1944   The Jews of Szekesfehervar, Hungary, and the surrounding area are forcibly assembled in camps and barracks.

June 6

1391   The inhabitants of Seville, Spain, surround the Jewish quarter and set fire to it. They massacre about 5,000 Jewish families and sell many Jewish women and children to the Muslims as slaves. Most of the 23 synagogues of Seville are destroyed or are turned into churches.

1511   During the first auto-da-fé held in Sicily, 8 Spanish Conversos are accused of Judaizing, secretly practicing the Jewish religion, and are executed.

1919   In the second pogrom in six months, 42 Jews are killed in Proskurov, in the region of Podolia, Ukraine, by units of Petlyura's Ukrainian National Army.

1942   In three transports, 5,000 Jews are deported from Cracow, Poland, to the Belzec extermination camp.

In the province of Lublin in Poland, 1,000 Jews from Krasiczyn, and 3,000 Jews from Biala Podlaska, are deported to the Sobibor extermination camp. Jews have lived in Biala Podlaska since the beginning of the seventeenth century.

Almost 4,000 Jews are murdered by SS and local police in Kobryn, Belorussian S.S.R., during an Aktion that lasts for three days. A Jewish resistance movement is organized and starts fighting.

1943   The SS kills the last 300 Jews in the ghetto of Podhaitsy, Ternopol district, Ukrainian S.S.R., and the town is declared "free of Jews."

The Jewish Council and the Jewish militia of the ghetto of Rohatyn, Stanislavov district, Poland (today Ukrainian S.S.R.), prepare a means of escape before the beginning of their "Resettlement" by the SS, building a bunker and storing arms and food in the forest. The SS are informed and they shoot the entire Jewish militia, mutilate their corpses, and hang them up in public as a warning to others. During this Aktion, 1,000 other Jews are also murdered.

The remaining 1,000 Jews of the town of Tluste, Galicia, Poland (today Ukrainian S.S.R.) are killed by the SS and Ukrainian police.

In an Aktion that lasts for four days, 8,000 Jews from Sambor, Lvov province, Poland (today Ukrainian S.S.R.), are either murdered or deported by the SS to the Belzec extermination camp.

The SS and Ukrainian police murder 2,500 Jews in a two-day Aktion in Borszczov, East Galicia, Poland (today Ukrainian S.S.R.).

1944 Arrested by the Nazis in May 1944, 260 Jews from Chania, Greece, and 5 Jewish families from Rethimnon, Greece, are among the passengers aboard a ship that is deliberately sunk near the Greek island of Pholegandros.

From a Jewish home for the elderly in Florence, Italy, 16 people are deported to one of the extermination camps in Poland.

June 7

1884 In Nizhni-Novgorod, Russia, 6 Jewish adults and one Jewish boy are massacred during a pogrom of looting and killing.

1891 Following the accusation of ritual murder against the Jews of Konitz, Germany (today Poland), anti-Jewish agitation breaks out. When a Christian butcher is finally arrested for the homicide, the enraged populace destroys the synagogue. The German emperor sends two infantry regiments to restore order.

1919 In a pogrom that lasts two days, 4 Jews are slain and many Jewish women are raped by units of Petlyura's Ukrainian National Army in Lantskuron, Podolia, Ukraine.

1942 600 Jews of Szczakova, Chrzanov district, Poland, are deported to the Auschwitz extermination camp.

The remaining Jews of Ilya, a village north of Minsk, Belorussian S.S.R., are killed by the SS.

Two days after the liquidation of the ghetto of Braslav, Belorussian S.S.R., a camp is set up by the Nazis for the Jews of the surrounding area. The town mayor announces that all Jews who register voluntarily will gain their freedom. Those Jews who believe the appeal and respond are shot by the SS.

1944 Following an Aktion that lasts for two days, 5,000 Jews from Győr, Hungary, are confined to a camp. The bishop of Győr protests.

Hannah Szenes, 23 years old, born in Budapest, Hungary, is arrested at the Hungarian border. With a group of parachutists she has been sent by the Haganah* from Palestine through Yugoslavia to help the Hungarian Jews organize resistance. She will later be executed by the Hungarian Fascists after unsuccessful interrogation and torture.

The Jews interned in the brickyard of Kosice, Czechoslovakia, are deported by the SS. Included

*Haganah: self-defense organization of the Jews of Palestine founded at the beginning of the British mandate to resist Arab attacks. During the Second World War, the Haganah becomes the network of the Jewish brigade of the British army. At the end of the war the Haganah is dedicated to the fight for independence before giving birth to the Israeli army (Tsahal).

in these deportations are also non-Jews who had tried to help the Jews.

The last Jews from Carpathian Ruthenia, Ukrainian S.S.R., northeastern Hungary, and northern Transylvania, Rumania, are deported to Auschwitz.

June 8

1288 In Bonn, Germany, 104 Jews are slain after an accusation of the ritual murder of a Christian boy from Oberwesel. The accusation spreads into the surrounding area, and the persecution of the Jews spreads as well.

1919 During a pogrom that lasts for six days, units of Petlyura's Ukrainian National Army loot Jewish houses and shops in Dunayevtsky, Podolia province, Ukraine, killing 7 Jews and severely wounding 2.

1942 From Graboviec, Lublin province, Poland, 1,200 Jews are deported to the Sobibor extermination camp.

1943 The SS shoots 100 Jews in Rava Ruska, in the province of Galicia, Poland (today Ukrainian S.S.R.).

From Salonika, Greece, 880 Jews are deported to the Auschwitz extermination camp in Poland.

Two transports with 2,397 and 3,017 Jewish internees, from the Westerbork transit camp in the Dutch province of Drenthe, are deported to the Sobibor extermination camp in Poland.

The SS murders 5,000 Jews during the liquidation of the ghetto of Zbaraz, Poland (today Ukrainian S.S.R.). Only 60 Jews survive the Holocaust.

June 9

1905 Jews are assaulted and killed, and Jewish shops are looted and demolished, during a pogrom in Siedlec and Lodz, Poland, carried out by Russian soldiers and cossacks.

1919 During a pogrom, 12 Jews are massacred, several are gravely wounded, and many Jewish women are raped in Staraya Sinyava, Podolia province, Ukraine, carried out by units linked to Petlyura's Ukrainian National Army under the command of Chepel and Lavorski.

1920 During a four-day siege, 19 Jews are slaughtered, a great many are wounded, and many Jewish women are raped in Berdichev, Volhynia province, Ukraine, by troops of the Ukrainian National Army and their Polish allies.

1942 The SS murders 1,200 Jews of Ivienic, in the district of Novogrodek, Belorussian S.S.R.

Walter Rauff, the official of the RSHA (headquarters of the security of the Reich) responsible for the gas vans, orders the first gassings of German and Austrian Jews using the specially constructed vans, in Riga, Latvia.

From Vienna, 1,006 Jews are deported to Minsk, Belorussian S.S.R.

1943 The SS murders 800 Jews in Skala Podlaska in the province of Galicia, Poland (today Ukrainian S.S.R.).

June 10

1320 The Jewish population of Castelsarrasin, France, numbering about 150, is killed during a two-day massacre carried out by the Pastoreaux,

French soldiers of the Second Crusade against the Muslims of Spain.

1337 German peasants of Franconia and Alsace, called Armleder gangs after the leather bands they wear on their arms, attack the town of Tauberbischofsheim, Germany, for the fourth time and are successful in annihilating the Jewish community.

1648 A band of Chmielnicki Cossacks under the command of Ganja besieges the fortified town of Nemirov, Poland, and slaughters about 6,000 Jews who have taken refuge in the fortress.

BOHDAN CHMIELNICKI EXERCITUS
ZAPOROVIEN PRÆFECTUS BELLI SERVILIS AUTOR
REBELLIUMQ COSACCORUM ET PLEBIS UKRAYNEN
DUX

Bohdan Chmielnicki.

1919 During a pogrom, 73 Jews are slaughtered and 16 wounded by units of Petlyura's Ukrainian National Army, joined by local peasants, in Kitai-Gorod, Podolia, Ukraine.

1942 From Uchanie, Poland (today Ukrainian S.S.R.), 1,600 Jews are deported to the Sobibor extermination camp in Poland, where they are murdered by the SS immediately upon their arrival.

The SS massacres 1,200 Jews in an Aktion in Lachovice, Belorussian S.S.R., but a small number of Jews manages to escape into the forest.

In an Aktion that lasts two days, 1,200 Jews are massacred in Lida, Poland (today Belorussian S.S.R.).

In reprisal for the assassination of Reinhard Heydrich, the Reichsprotector of Bohemia and Moravia, 1,000 Jewish men, women, and children are deported from Prague, Czechoslovakia, to the Majdanek and Sobibor extermination camps.

1943 The ghetto of Ostroviec, in the province of Kielce, Poland, is liquidated. Its 2,000 Jews are collected together and interned in the Ostroviec labor camp.

1944 From Szekesfehervar, Hungary, and its surrounding areas, 50,800 Jews are rounded up and detained in eleven camps on the borders of the town, awaiting further deportations.

June 11

1919 Units of Simon Petlyura's Ukrainian National Army, under the command of Alexander Udovichenko, carry out a pogrom over several days against the Jews in Shargorod, Bessarabia (today Moldavian S.S.R.). It ends with 100 Jews dead and many adults and children mutilated or seriously injured.

1938 Riots and excesses against the Jews occur in the Polish town of Ternopol (today Ukrainian S.S.R.). Many Jews are injured and their property is destroyed.

1940 A ghetto is erected by the Nazis in Bolimov, Poland, in which the Jewish population is forced to resettle.

1942 In a three-day Aktion, 12,000 Jews from Tarnow, Poland, are deported by the SS to the Belzec extermination camp.

1944 The deportation, which lasts several days, of 50,800 Jews from Szekesfehervar, Hungary, to the Auschwitz extermination camp in Poland begins. On the same day, 5,200 Jews from Györ, Hungary, are deported there as well. Jews have been living in Györ since the second half of the sixteenth century.

June 12

1940 All the Zionists of the town of Causani, Bessarabia, Rumania, are arrested and deported by the Soviet authorities to Siberia after the return of Bessarabia to the Soviet Union.

After Bessarabia and Bukovina have been returned to the Soviet Union, Rumanian troops carry out a pogrom against the Jews of Dorohoi, northeast Rumania, and murder 200 of them. Family members are forced to sign declarations saying that the dead were killed by strangers.

Several thousand Jews from Kutno and the surrounding areas, in the province of Lodz, Poland, are crammed into a very small area without sanitary facilities or physicians. Many Jews die of typhoid fever.

1942 From Sosnovice, Katovice province, Poland, 2,000 Jews are deported to the Auschwitz extermination camp.

In two deportation transports which travel two days from the Theresienstadt concentration camp in Czechoslovakia to Trawniki, Poland, 2,000 Jewish men, women, and children die.

1943 The SS and Ukrainian police murder 200 Jews in Kozova, Galicia, Poland (today Ukrainian S.S.R.).

The SS kills 100 Jews in the village of Brzezany, Galicia, Poland (today Ukrainian S.S.R.).

June 13

1919 Units of Petlyura's Ukrainian National Army, under the leadership of hetman Ogorodnikov, massacre 4 Jews during a pogrom in Brussilov, Kiev district, Ukraine.

1938 Jews are injured and Jewish property is destroyed in Przemysl, Poland, during anti-Jewish riots.

1941 Several hundred Jews from Belgorod-Dnestrovski, Bessarabia, Rumania (today Ukrainian S.S.R.), are deported to Siberia by the Soviets. Jews have lived in Belgorod-Dnestrovski since the sixteenth century.

1942 The deportation of the Jews from Czernovitz, Bukovina (today Ukrainian S.S.R.), begins. From the Jewish mental hospital, 70 Jews are assembled and deported to the ghetto of Mogilev, Transnistria, Ukrainian S.S.R. Most of them die on the journey.

Taken from the ghetto of Przemysl, Rzeszov district, Poland are 1,000 Jews; 45 of them are shot by the SS, the others are deported to the Janovska labor camp in Lvov, Poland.

A transport with 1,000 Jews leaves the Theresienstadt concentration camp in Czechoslovakia for the ghetto in Trawniki, Poland.

June 14

1919 Regular troops of the Ukrainian National Army under Commander Alexander Udovichenko carry out a pogrom in Zamekhov, Podolia, Ukraine.

1940 The first deportation transport from Cracow, Poland, arrives with 700 Jews at the Auschwitz extermination camp in Poland.

1942 The ghetto of Tarnow, in the Polish province of Cracow, is divided in two: Ghetto A for forced laborers and Ghetto B for their families. The Jews in Ghetto B die of hunger.

In an Aktion against the ghetto of Dzisna, Poland (today Belorussian S.S.R.), most of the Jews are driven to the sandpits of Piaskowe Gorki, where they are shot by the SS. About 2,000 Jews manage to escape. The majority of them are later captured and shot but the survivors manage to join the 4th Brigade of the White Russian partisans.

A transport with 450 Jews leaves from Dorohoi, Rumania, for Transnistria and later the German concentration camps on the other side of the Bug River.

From Vienna, 996 Jews are deported to Izbica, Poland.

1944 From the Greek island of Corfu, 1,800 Jews are deported to the Auschwitz extermination camp in Poland.

June 15

1281 A pogrom takes place in the town of Mainz, Germany, probably due to a blood libel (the accusation that Jews killed a Christian child in order to use its blood for ritual purposes). Torah scrolls are destroyed, the synagogue is burned down, and the town rabbi, Meir ben Abraham ha-Cohen, is slain.

1919 During a two-day pogrom, carried out by troops under Zaporojski Koche, an ally of Petlyura's Ukrainian National Army, 148 Jews are slaughtered, many are wounded, and several Jewish women are raped in Jaltichkov, Podolia province, Ukraine. On the same day 26 Jews are massacred and many Jewish women and girls are raped in the course of a five-day pogrom in Pereyaslav, Poltava, Ukraine, under command of Zeleny, another of Petlyura's allies.

1942 In Riga, Latvia, the SS orders a second gas van from SS headquarters in Berlin to be able to kill more Jewish ghetto inmates.

In Priluki, Ukrainian S.S.R., the Aktion against the Jews carried out by the SS and the local Ukrainian auxiliaries ends.

About 400 Jews are killed by the SS immediately after being rounded up from various Ukrainian villages and deported to the Lysaja Gora labor camp, Ukrainian S.S.R.

The deportation of 145 Jews from Duisburg, Germany, to the Auschwitz extermination camp begins.

From Vienna, 1,000 Jews arrive in Minsk, Belorussian S.S.R., where they are taken to sandpits and shot by the SS.

1944 The Hungarian Fascist regime orders that all Jews living in Budapest must move to specially marked houses.

June 16

1221 The Jews of Erfurt, Germany, are accused of ritual murder and a crowd of merchants (possibly Frisian) storms the synagogue, threatening baptism or death. The synagogue and the whole Jewish quarter are burned down, and many Jews are tortured and killed. Among the dead are the Levite Schem Tov ha-Levi and the rabbi Samuel Kalonymos and his wife.

1492 King Ferdinand of Aragon, the Spanish king, whose domain includes Sicily, issues the edict that all Jews must leave the country within three months, those remaining being liable to death.

Erfurt synagogue in 1357. (From Jaraczewsky, Geschichte der Juden in Erfurt)

The time limit is pushed back after the Jews pay the king an exorbitant sum.

1938 A transport with 100 Jews departs from Vienna for the Dachau concentration camp in Germany.

1941 Hungarian Fascists deport 3,500 Jews from the ghetto in Subotica, Voivodina, Yugoslavia, to the Bacalmas camp.

1942 The SS murders 300 Jews in an Aktion in Ozmiana, Poland (today Belorussian S.S.R.).

From Bohorodczany, Poland, 1,200 Jews are brought to Stanislav and murdered by Ukrainian police in the Rudolfsmühle (Rudolf's mill).

1943 An unknown number of Jews is deported from Vienna to the Theresienstadt concentration camp in Czechoslovakia.

1944 From Hodmezovasarhely, Hungary, 1,500 Jews are deported to the ghetto of Szeged.

The deportation of the Jews of northern Hungary to the Auschwitz extermination camp is completed.

June 17

1718 During an auto-da-fé held in Coimbra, Portugal, 60 Judaizers, descendants of Jews forcibly baptized some centuries ago who still secretly practice the Jewish religion, are condemned to imprisonment or to the galley. Manuel Rodriguez de Carvalho and Isabella Mendes, 2 Judaizers, are accused of host desecration and are garroted and burned at the stake.

1919 Of the 900 Jews of Dubovo, Ukraine, 800 are beheaded during the most sadistic pogrom in a series of many carried out by units directly under Simon Petlyura and his Ukrainian National Army.

1941 The Jews from the ghetto of Lowicz, in the province of Lodz, Poland, are deported to Warsaw or killed. Lowicz is declared "free of Jews."

1942 The SS encircles the ghetto of Druja, a small town in Belorussian S.S.R., where 1,200 Jews live. During this Aktion all of them are killed except for 50 who manage to flee and join partisans active in the region of Balnia.

The 4,000 Jews of Czernovitz, Bukovina (today Ukrainian S.S.R.), who up till now have been protected by the mayor of the town, Traian Popovici, are deported across the Bug River, where the Nazis kill more than 2,500 of them.

1943 After being deported from Würzburg, Germany, 57 Jews are killed at the Auschwitz extermination camp in Poland.

June 18

1942 In the course of two days, 2,500 Jews from Kolbuszova, Lvov district, Poland, are murdered by the SS and Ukrainian police.

The SS murders 1,200 Jews in Rudnik, Lvov district, Poland (today Ukrainian S.S.R.).

1943 In Germany, 16 Jews from Bamberg and 70 Jews from Nuremberg are deported to the Auschwitz extermination camp in Poland.

1944 The 250 people of the Jewish community of Kalocsa, Hungary, are deported to Auschwitz.

June 19

1941 Three days before the outbreak of war with the Soviet Union, the Rumanians order that, within a half hour, all Jews must evacuate the village of Darabani. The Jews are robbed of their possessions and driven to Dorohoi, 22 miles away.

The Soviets deport all Zionists from Falesti, Bessarabia (today Ukrainian S.S.R.), to Siberia. At the outbreak of World War II, 4,000 Jews lived in Falesti.

1942 The SS deports 800 Jews of Krasiczyn, Lublin district, Poland, to the Sobibor extermination camp.

Classified as "unemployable" by the Nazis, 2,500 Jews are taken from the ghetto of Glebokie, Poland (today Belorussian S.S.R.), and killed in the Borek forest. A number of Jewish resistance fighters originally from the town do battle with the Nazis.

From Nemirov, Poland, 500 Jews are deported to the Belzec extermination camp.

June 20

1230 Jews are massacred in Wiener Neustadt, Austria.

1391 During the Jewish fast commemorating the fall of Jerusalem, the Christian population of Toledo, Spain, attacks the Jewish community. Many Jews are massacred and many others commit suicide. The persecutions spread throughout Spain.

1544 In Tomar, Portugal, where an Inquisition tribunal was installed in 1540, the second and last auto-da-fé against Judaizers, descendants of forcibly baptized Jews who still practice Judaism in secret, takes place. The Inquisition is then abolished.

1734 During a three-day massacre, 20,000 Jews and Poles are killed by the Haidamacks (Cossacks and peasants from the Ukraine) in Uman, near Kiev, Ukraine. The 3,000 Jews in the local synagogue die when it is hit by cannon fire.

1768 Haidamacks, under their leader Gontas, slaughter thousands of Jews in Homel, Ukraine.

1883 During a two-day pogrom, 500 Jewish families are reduced to poverty when their homes and businesses are destroyed in Dnepropetrovsk, Ukrainian S.S.R.

1919 Units under Sokolski massacre 14 Jews and severely wound 10 during a pogrom in Chernigov, Volhynia, Ukraine. In another pogrom, 5 Jews are killed and many wounded in Volodarka, Kiev district, Ukraine, carried out by units under the command of Jelezniak. The units are linked to the Ukrainian National Army.

1942 The SS murders 600 Jews of Snow, district of Novogrodek, Soviet Union.

A ghetto is established for the remaining 2,500 Jews of Nadvorna, Stanislavov district, Poland (today Ukrainian S.S.R.). It is guarded by the German Schutzpolizei (special police) who from time to time break in to kill inmates.

The deportation of 996 Jews from Vienna to the Theresienstadt concentration camp in Czechoslovakia takes place.

1943 The SS shoots 4,000 Jewish inmates when the Germans liquidate the ghetto of Ternopol, Po-

land (today Ukrainian S.S.R.). Only a few manage to escape.

In a large scale Aktion, 5,500 Jews are arrested in Amsterdam, Netherlands, and deported to the Westerbork transit camp in the Dutch province of Drenthe.

1944 Yaakov Edelstein, a member of the Jewish Council of the Theresienstadt concentration camp, and his family in Auschwitz II-Birkenau are shot by the SS.

June 21

1649 The Cossacks of Bogdan Chmielnicki capture Basilei, Ukraine, and massacre several hundred Jewish families.

1919 Troops under the command of Ogorodnikov and Mordalevich, linked to Petlyura's Ukrainian National Army, carry out a pogrom in Brussilov, Kiev province, Ukraine, and 30 Jews are massacred.

1943 The ghetto in Lvov, Galicia, Poland (today Ukrainian S.S.R.), is erected; but within a week it is again liquidated and the SS murders 13,000 Jews in the sandpits of Piaski in the Janovska camp or in the Jewish cemetery.

The SS murders 300 Jewish craftsmen employed by the German administration in Lvov.

The Nazis burn 300 Jews alive in the ghetto of Grodek, Galicia, Poland (today Ukrainian S.S.R.).

In the Auschwitz extermination camp in Poland, 73 Jewish men and 30 Jewish women are selected by Dr. Berger and sent to the Natzweiler camp in Alsace, where they are killed. Their skeletons are sent to the anatomy department of the University of Strasbourg.

1944 From Vienna, 4 Jews are deported to the Theresienstadt concentration camp in Czechoslovakia.

The German authorities load 200 Jews onto old fishing boats in the harbor of Herakles on the isle of Crete, Greece. The boats are conducted to open water and sent to the bottom.

June 22

1239 During the feast of St. Alban, an anti-Jewish riot breaks out in London, England. A Jew is accused of murder and several others are later arrested. The proceedings against them are directed by the prime minister of King Henry III. Several of the Jews are executed.

1639 An auto-da-fé is held in Valladolid, Spain. The Spanish Inquisition condemns 28 persons to be burned at the stake; among them are 10 accused of being Judaizers, descendants of Jews forcibly baptized some centuries ago who still secretly practice the Jewish religion.

1911 Mendel Beilis, a Jew, is accused of the ritual murder of a 12-year-old boy in Kiev, Ukraine. Anti-Jewish excesses begin. After two years in prison, Beilis will be acquitted in a trial on October 28, 1913, defended by the most famous lawyers of Moscow, St. Petersburg, and Kiev.

1941 The German army shoots 300 Jews when it occupies the village Beresteczko, Volhynia, Ukrainian S.S.R., where about 2,000 Jews live. Jews have been living in Beresteczko since 1523.

Lithuanian Fascists carry out a pogrom and kill many Jews in Kaunas.

1942 In Grodek, Belorussian S.S.R., 1,600 Jews are killed in an Aktion by the SS and Baltic collaborators.

The SS murders 2,000 Jews from Smolensk, Ukrainian S.S.R., when they are deported from the ghetto of Sadki in gas vans in the direction of Mogalenschtschina.

In a transport, 1,000 Jewish men, women, and children are deported from the Drancy transit camp in the German occupied zone of France to the Auschwitz extermination camp in Poland. Only 20 of them survive and are liberated in 1945 by the Soviet army.

1943 The Gestapo shoots 80 Jews in a two-day Aktion in Bedzin, Poland.

1944 The 700 Jews from Boryslav, Poland (today Ukrainian S.S.R.), deported to Auschwitz, are killed immediately by the SS.

June 23

1270 In Weissenburg, Germany, 7 Jews are arrested without charges held against them, tortured, and executed.

1298 The Rindfleisch Persecutions, named after the German knight from the Franconian town of Roettingen, annihilated 146 Jewish communities in southern and central Germany. In Windsheim in Franconia 55 Jews are burned at the stake; 900 Jews of the large Jewish community of Würzburg are slain, among them 100 who had sought refuge there from other places. In the little town of Neustadt on the Aisch River, 71 Jews are burned to death.

1475 In the case of Simon of Trent (Italy), a Christian child is found dead and Samuel, a wealthy

A ritual murder as imagined in a fifteenth-century German woodcut: Jews extracting blood from Simon of Trent's body. Each wears the distinguishing circular badge.

Jew, and others of his brethren are falsely accused and subjected to torture. The boy is proclaimed a martyr and the Jews are kept imprisoned and tortured from March to April. On June 23, Samuel is burned at the stake and the others are burned or broken on the wheel. Simon of Trent is venerated as a martyr until the intervention of the Vatican in 1965.

1919   During a pogrom, 45 Jews are slaughtered, many severely wounded, and 35 Jewish women are raped by insurgents under the command of hetmen Tiutiunnik and Mazurenko, allies of Petlyura's Ukrainian National Army, in Skvira, Kiev province, Ukraine. The 9th regiment Strelkovky, under the command of Colonel Shandruck, kills 5 Jews during a pogrom in Verkhova-Bibikovo, Podolia, Ukraine.

1941 After the Germans invade Sokal, Poland (today Ukrainian S.S.R.), where 6,000 Jews live, 8 Jews are shot.

German troops occupy Bereza, near Brest, Belorussian S.S.R. The Jewish population numbers 7,000. Several Jews are killed and many Jewish houses are looted.

1942 The SS murders 850 Jews in Wielopole, in the district of Cracow, Poland.

The first selection for the gas chambers in the Auschwitz extermination camp in Poland takes place on the platform of the train arriving from Paris, France.

In Warsaw, Poland, 10 members of the Jewish ghetto police are shot after being accused of mediating between smugglers of food and arms and German gendarmes. They are among 110 prisoners whom the Germans carry off.

1943 A deportation train leaves Paris for Auschwitz, carrying 1,000 Jews, among them 100 children under the age of 16 and 13 babies, who are all killed upon arrival.

All inmates of the Jewish home for the aged of Moravska Ostrava, Czechoslovakia, are deported to Auschwitz.

The SS deports 1,800 Jews from Strzemieszyce, Kielce district, Poland, to Auschwitz.

A deportation train with 1,018 Jewish people leaves from the Drancy transit camp in the German occupied zone of France for Auschwitz. On their arrival, 518 are gassed; 72 men and 37 women will survive.

June 24

1096 Bishop Hermann III of Cologne, Germany, sends the Jews to take refuge in other towns of his diocese. On June 24 the crusaders approach the town of Neuss near Cologne and slaughter 200 Jews who are hiding there, among them a certain Mar Gedalja and his family.

1298 In Iphofen, Germany, 25 Jews of ten Jewish families are slaughtered during the Rindfleisch Persecutions, so called after their instigator, the German knight Rindfleisch.

1648 When the Cossack hordes of Chmielnicki occupy Homel, Ukraine, they slaughter 2,000 Jewish men, women, and children. The same Cossacks kill 2,000 Jews and 600 Polish Catholics in the Nesterow fortress in Tulczyn, Polish Ukraine (today Ukrainian S.S.R.).

1919 During a pogrom, 15 Jews are slaughtered and a great many wounded by units under the leadership of Zeleny, linked to Petlyura's Ukrainian National Army, in Lukachevka, Kiev, Ukraine. In Kopai-Gorod, Podolia district, Ukraine, 11 Jews are killed and many Jews are wounded by the 7th and 9th regiments of the Blue Division of Petlyura's Ukrainian National Army.

1922 Walther Rathenau, the German minister of foreign affairs, who is of Jewish origin, is assassinated by precursors of the National Socialists in Berlin, Germany. Some of his murderers are caught and sentenced to five years' imprisonment.

1940 From Checiny, Kielce province, Poland, 250 young Jewish men die after being deported to the Eieszanow labor camp. After the Germans invaded Checiny 3,000 Jews had been forced into a ghetto.

1941 After the German troops invade Kobryn, Brest province, Ukrainian S.S.R., 170 Jews are taken to the village of Patryki and killed. After the Soviets took Kobryn on September 20, 1939, many Jews fled there from the German-occupied regions of Poland. At the time of the German invasion, 8,000 Jews are living there.

The Germans occupy Kaunas (today Lithuanian S.S.R.), numbering 30,000 Jews. Lithuanian partisans kill 1,000 Jews and 10,000 Jews are arrested and interned in the Seventh Fort.

1942 Adam Czerniakov, the chairman of the Jewish Council of Warsaw, Poland, is imprisoned for his refusal to cooperate with the Germans in the deportation of the Jews from the ghetto.

1943 A deportation convoy with 151 Jews leaves Vienna for the Theresienstadt concentration camp in Czechoslovakia.

June 25

1096 Soldiers of the First Crusade, under the command of the count of Leiningen, slaughter the Jews of Werlinghofen, Germany, who have fled there from Cologne. Many of them commit suicide before the arrival of the crusaders.

1298 In Rothenburg ob der Tauber, Germany, during the Rindfleisch Persecutions, named for the

German knight who incited the massacres of the Jews in south and central Germany, 57 Jews are killed.

1940 The Nazis set up a ghetto in Bilgoraj, in the district of Lublin, Poland, and begin the deportations of Jews.

1941 After the outbreak of the German-Soviet conflict, German troops occupy Slonim, Grodno province, Poland (today Belorussian S.S.R.), where 15,000 Jews live. The Nazis enact restrictive laws and later begin deportations. Jews first settled in Slonim in the sixteenth century and developed an active cultural life.

Pogroms break out in Iasi, Rumania.

The Germans invade Plunge, Lithuania, where 2,000 Jews live. Arnoldo Pabrescha, the Lithuanian mass murderer, accompanies these German troops and personally takes part in the massacre that annihilates the whole Jewish community.

The German army occupies Radoszkowice, Poland (today Belorussian S.S.R.), and executes many Jews on the charge of being Communists.

The Germans invade Dubno, Volhynia province, Poland (today Ukrainian S.S.R.), where 12,000 Jews live. The Ukrainian population is given permission to deal with the Jews and their property in whatever way they like, which results in murder, rape, and looting.

The German army occupies Vladimir-Volynski, Ukrainian S.S.R. The Jews called the town Ludmir. The Soviets previously occupied the town on September 17, 1939, and deported to Siberia several Jewish personalities known to be Zionists.

The first settlement of Ludmir goes back to the twelfth century, to presumed descendants of the Khazars, a Turkish tribe converted to Judaism in the eighth century.

Lithuanian Fascists slaughter 800 Jews in Kaunas, Lithuania, under the protection of the Germans, who had invaded the day before.

The Nazis occupy the town of Oszmiana, Lithuania (today Belorussian S.S.R.), and a number of Jews are killed.

1942 After 5,000 Jews are massacred, the large-scale Aktion carried out by the SS and Lithuanian volunteers in Lida, Belorussian S.S.R., ends.

The SS murders 6,000 Jews in two days in Lechovicz, in the district of Novogrodek, Belorussian S.S.R.

A Jewish convoy is deported from the Pithiviers transit camp in the German occupied zone of France to the Auschwitz extermination camp in Poland. Only 51 men will survive.

1943 After a Jewish armed resistance in Czestochova, Poland, in which many Jews are killed, the Nazis deport 1,000 Jews to Auschwitz.

The 300 Jews who remain in Stanislavov, Poland (today Ukrainian S.S.R.), working for the Nazis, are shot.

1944 After the intervention of Jewish leaders of Switzerland, Pope Pius XII appeals to Miklós Horthy, the head of state of Hungary, to help the Jews. Other appeals come to Horthy from the king of Sweden and the International Red Cross.

June 26

1096 Troops of the First Crusade reach the German town of Eller and carry out a two-day massacre of the local Jewish community of 300. Only 3 Jews survive.

1221 A band of pilgrims from Friesland bound for the Holy Land storm the Jewish quarter of Erfurt, Germany, and kill 26 Jews.

1919 In the third pogrom within five months, 8 Jews are killed in Kornin, Kiev district, Ukraine, by units under Mordalevitch, linked to the Ukrainian National Army, and local peasants.

1941 Several thousand Jews are shot by Lithuanian Fascists on June 26 and 27 in Kaunas, Lithuanian S.S.R.

When the Germans occupy the Latvian town of Dünaburg where 22,500 Jews live, 5 Jews are shot, the Jewish men are imprisoned and the Jews are forced to leave their homes and town.

In Bereza, near Brest Litovsk (today Belorussian S.S.R.), the synagogue and the surrounding houses are set on fire and many Jews are killed by the SS.

German troops occupy Lutsk, Volhynia province, Poland (today Ukrainian S.S.R.), where 20,000 Jews still live after having survived the Chmielnicki massacres of 1648–49, the pogroms of Petlyura's Ukrainian National Army, the Polish army, and the Soviet army.

1943 The ghetto of Buczacz, Ternopol district, Ukrainian S.S.R., is liquidated by the SS.

The liquidation of the small ghetto of Czestochova, west of Warsaw, Poland, begins, although the Jewish resistance tries to fight. Several hundred Jews are murdered on the spot by the SS, about 1,000 Jews are deported to a camp, and 4,000 Jews are deported to the Hassag labor camp, where they work in a factory.

1943 The ghetto of Dabrova Gornicza, in the province of Katovice, Poland, is liquidated, and about 2,000 Jews are deported to the ghetto of Srodula, a suburb of the Silesian town of Sosnoviec, and then on to the Auschwitz extermination camp. Dabrova Gornicza is declared "free of Jews."

1944 The deportations of the 12,000 Jews from Debrecen, Hungary, to Auschwitz begins. Very few of the deportees will survive.

The SS deports 485 Jews from the towns of Fossoli and Verona in Italy to Auschwitz.

June 27

1096 The Jews from Cologne who have found refuge in Geldern, Germany, are massacred by the crusaders or commit suicide.

1941 German troops occupy Pruzana, in the district of Brest Litovsk, Poland (today Belorussian S.S.R.), where 4,000 Jews live. The Nazis demand a payment of 500,000 rubles, 2 kg of gold and 10 kg of silver from the Jewish community and take hostages whom they threaten to kill if their demands are not satisfied.

For the second time German troops occupy Luboml, Volhynia province, Poland (today Ukrainian S.S.R.), where 3,500 Jews live. The first occupation occurred on September 17, 1939, but after three days they had to give it up to the Soviets. On this day, the Germans drive the Jews out of town and burn down their houses.
   The first Jewish settlement dates back to the year 1516, when the Jews were under the protection of the Polish kings.

German troops take over Kovel, Volhynia province, Poland (today Ukrainian S.S.R.), where 17,000 Jews live. The troops shoot 8 Jews and 200 are driven out of town to an unknown destination.

German and Italian troops attack Falesti, a town in Bessarabia, Rumania (today Ukrainian S.S.R.), burning down houses and killing many Jews.

The Nazis occupy Mir, in the district of Grodno, Poland (today Belorussian S.S.R.), where 3,000 Jews live. The Nazis kill Jews accused of collaborating with the Soviets. Jews have been living in Mir since the sixteenth century, their cultural life flourishing. Famous rabbis and leaders of the Hasidic movement were born here. Some of its yeshivas (schools of Jewish religious learning) were world famous.

1944 From Vienna, 17 Jews are deported to the Auschwitz extermination camp in Poland.

June 28

1244 Several Jews from Pforzheim, Germany, are forced by the judicial council to commit suicide, presumably on the charge of blood libel, using the blood of a Christian child in the Jewish festival of Passover. Their corpses are broken on the wheel as an example to the public.

1286 In the neighboring towns of Boppard and Oberwesel, Germany, 40 Jews are killed following an alleged ritual murder. The Christian child is later canonized and becomes known as *guter* Werner—good Werner. As a result, anti-Jewish riots spread all over the area and many Jews are killed.

1919 During a pogrom, 11 Jews are massacred and many Jewish women are raped when insurgents under the hetman Anghel, allied with Petlyura's Ukrainian National Army, carry out a pogrom in the town of Itchnia, in the district of Chernigov, Ukraine.

1941 The 65 Jews of Unter-Stanestie, Rumania, are divided into groups by the Ukrainian population and led to different places where they are tortured and put to death. Among the massacred are the rabbi of Friedländer and his two sons.

One day after the second occupation of Bialystok, Poland (the first was in September, 1939, after the German invasion of Poland), the German soldiers burn down the local synagogue, killing at least 1,000 Jews who have been locked inside. This day is remembered as "Red Friday."

A concentration camp for 1,500 Jews is set up in Kaunas, Lithuania, in the Seventh Fort, which is guarded by Lithuanian Fascists who carry out executions. The concentration camp is divided into two sections which separate the women and children from the men. In the central prison of Kaunas, 1,869 Jews are imprisoned.

The German troops occupy Zolkiev, Galicia, Poland (today Ukrainian S.S.R.), where 5,000 Jews live. The synagogue is burned down and many Jews are murdered. A Jewish Council is founded. The Jewish community is ordered to pay 250,000 rubles, 5 kg of gold, and 100 kg of silver within three days.

1942 From Vienna, 983 Jews are deported to the Theresienstadt concentration camp in Czechoslovakia.

1,038 Jews from the Beaune-la-Rolande transit camp, in the German occupied zone of France, are deported to the Auschwitz concentration camp in Poland.

The SS shoots 30 Jews when the Germans occupy Krynki, in the province of Bialystok, Poland. Three days later the synagogue is burned down.

In three transports, 5,000 Jews are deported from Czernovitz, Bukovina (today Ukrainian S.S.R.), to the ghetto of Mogilev in Transnistria. The majority of them die on the journey.

1944 The SS shoots 540 Jews near the former paper mill Profintern in the concentration camp in Borisov, Belorussian S.S.R.

During a three-day Aktion, 7,500 Jews from Debrecen, Hungary, are deported to Auschwitz. On this day the deportation of the Jews from southeastern Hungary to Auschwitz is completed.

From Vienna, 38 Jews are deported to Auschwitz.

June 29

1298 In Ochsenfurt, Lower Franconia, Germany, 35 Jewish men, women, and children are massacred; and the only Jewish family of Widdern, numbering 6 people, is slaughtered during the Rindfleisch Persecutions, named after the man who instigated the annihilation of 146 Jewish communities in southern and central Germany.

1494 When a fire breaks out in Cracow, Poland, the crowd uses the opportunity to loot Jewish houses and massacre Jews. Later a decree is issued or-

Polish bishop throwing Hebrew books into the fire. (J. Emden, Séfer Shimush, 1762)

dering all Jews to leave Cracow and to establish a Jewish quarter in the suburb of Kazimierz.

1654 An auto-da-fé is held in Cuenca, Spain, and 57 persons are accused of being Judaizers, descendants of Jews forcibly baptized some centuries before who still secretly practice the Jewish religion. After being garroted, 10 of them are burned at the stake; the others are condemned to imprisonment or to the galley.

1891 Adolf Wolff Buschoff, a Jewish butcher in Xanten, Germany, is accused of blood libel, killing a Christian child in order to use its blood for ritual purposes. He is arrested twice following anti-Semitic agitation by the press and some anti-Semitic representatives of the Parliament, but finally found innocent.

1941 A day after German troops occupy Brazlav, Podolia (today Ukrainian S.S.R.), they drive the 2,500 Jewish inhabitants into the swamps near the town. The Gentile population is allowed to loot the Jews' homes in their absence, until nothing of their property is left. The Jews who are physically unable to make their way out of the swamps are shot by the Nazis.

German troops shoot 300 Jews after they occupy Rovno, in the region of Volhynia, Poland (today Ukrainian S.S.R.), where 30,000 Jews live.

The SS shoots 5,000 Jewish men, supposedly taken for forced labor, after the Germans occupy Brest Litovsk, Belorussian S.S.R., during the German-Soviet conflict.

Thousands of Jews are shot in Iasi, Rumania (former capital of Moldavia), after being taken to the local police station the night before by German and Rumanian patrols assisted by local residents.

German troops occupy Radzivillow, Ukrainian S.S.R., where 3,000 Jews are living. Ukrainians

are given permission to deal with the Jews as they like for three days. Many Jews are killed and Jewish property is looted.

1942 The 2,000 remaining Jews of the ghetto of Olkusz, Cracow province, Poland, are deported to the Auschwitz extermination camp. Kept behind to clean up are 20 Jews who are shot when the job is done.

The ghetto of Slonim in the province of Grodno, Poland (today Belorussian S.S.R.), where 15,000 Jews from the vicinity were forced to resettle, is set on fire by the SS and their collaborators. Many Jews die in the fire and many are caught and murdered outside the town. With help from Jewish resistance fighters, several hundred Jews manage to flee into the forest, where many of them join partisan groups.

1943 Jewish detainees numbering 2,397 are sent from the Westerbork transit camp in the Dutch province of Drenthe to the Sobibor extermination camp in Poland.

1944 1,800 Jews from the Greek island of Corfu arrive at the Auschwitz extermination camp in Poland, where 200 Jewish men are used as forced laborers and the remaining 1,600 are gassed to death.

In a barn near the camp, the SS shoots 6,000 Jews from the Maly Trostyanets concentration camp near Minsk, Belorussian S.S.R.

From Vienna, 28 Jews arrive at Auschwitz; 6 men are detained in the camp and the others are gassed.

Twenty thousand young Jewish women from Hungary are deported from Auschwitz to the Stutthof concentration camp near Danzig.

June 30

1096 The local Jewish population is massacred in Prague, Bohemia (today Czechoslovakia), by troops of the First Crusade, led by Volkmar, who are en route to the Holy Land via the Balkans. In the village of Mörs, Germany, crusaders under the command of the count of Leiningen massacre the Jews who have found refuge there from Cologne. Some survive by submitting to baptism.

1298 In Mergentheim, Germany, 16 Jews are slaughtered in the course of the Rindfleisch Persecutions, named after the German knight who instigated Jewish massacres in 146 places in south and central Germany.

1680 The greatest auto-da-fé in the history of the Spanish Inquisition takes place in Madrid, Spain, when 72 people are accused of being Judaizers, descendants of Jews forcibly baptized some centuries ago who still secretly practice the Jewish religion. The Inquisition condemns 18 of them to be burned at the stake and Charles II, the king of Spain, personally lights the fire. The remaining 54 Judaizers are sentenced to the galley or to life imprisonment.

1706 An auto-da-fé is held in Lisbon, Portugal, during which 60 people are accused of being Judaizers. 6 are burned at the stake as nonrepentants; the rest are sentenced to either doing public penance, to confiscation of their property, or to imprisonment.

1905 During a pogrom in Bialystok, Russia (today Poland), 50 Jews are killed and a great many are injured by defeated soldiers returning from the Manchurian front.

1940 The Rumanian 16th infantry regiment under the command of Major Valeriu Carp, a notorious anti-Semite, arrives in Czudyn, Bukovina, Rumania, where they torture and kill many of the Jewish residents.

1941 The Ukrainian police shoot 200 Jews from Sokal, in Lvov district, Poland (today Ukrainian S.S.R.), near a brickyard outside the town.

2,000 Jews from Lutsk, in the province of Volhynia, Poland (today Ukrainian S.S.R.), are deported and shot.

German troops invade Dobromil, a little town in the province of Lvov. As a welcoming gesture local Ukrainian Fascists round up 132 Jews who are shot by the Nazis in the pit of a salt mine. Their moans are heard throughout the night.

Eight days after the German invasion of Virbalis, Lithuania, where 1,500 Jews live, all the Jewish men are killed. A few days later the Jewish women and children are killed as well.

1944 The last deportation transport of political and Jewish prisoners by the Reichssicherheits-

Sabbath candlestick (after a drawing by Viefers).

hauptamt (State Security Department) from the Fossoli transit camp in Modena, Italy, arrives at the Auschwitz extermination camp in Poland.

From the Drancy camp in the German occupied zone of France, 1,100 Jewish internees are deported to Auschwitz. Immediately after their arrival, 479 of them are gassed; 167 men and 100 women will survive until the liberation of the camp by the Soviet Army in 1945.

JULY

July 1

1096 The Jews of Mehr, Germany, who have taken refuge in the castle, are handed over to troops of the First Crusade. They are all massacred except for some children who are forcibly baptized.

1919 During a five-day pogrom, 20 Jews are slain, a great many wounded, and many Jewish women are raped by units under the command of Zeleny, allied with the Ukrainian National Army, in Rchichtchev, in the Kiev district, Ukrainian S.S.R. More than 170 Jews are slaughtered during a pogrom in Tulczyn, Ukraine.

1940 From Zychlin, Poland, and the surrounding area, 3,500 Jews are resettled in a ghetto in the swamps outside of town. A Jewish Council appointed by the Nazis has to provide workers every day, who very often are arrested and never come back.

Rumanian troops of the 16th infantry regiment, under Major Valeriu Carp, march into Bukovina (today Ukrainian S.S.R.). In the town of Sakarestie, 36 Jews are tortured and shot. The dead and the wounded are buried together in a ditch with the cadaver of a horse on top of them.

1941 Invading German troops imprison 8,000 Jews in Vilna, Poland (today Lithuanian S.S.R.).

Before the Soviets withdraw from Lvov, Poland (today Ukrainian S.S.R.), they kill 2,000 prisoners—Poles, Jews, and Ukrainians. After their withdrawal, the Nazis invade Lvov, and give the Ukrainians three days to deal with the Jewish population. Ukrainians and Poles go into the prisons, find the murdered prisoners, and make the Jews responsible for the crime. In the course of a massacre lasting three days, 2,000 Jews are slain. The Nazis take photographs of the carnage.

After the Soviet withdrawal from Czernovitz, Bukovina (today Ukrainian S.S.R.), where 50,000 Jews live, gangs forcibly enter Jewish homes and drive the families out. Czernovitz is an important Jewish cultural center where many leading Jewish figures were born. Jews have been living there since the fifteenth century.

German troops occupy Riga, capital of Latvia, where 40,000 Jews live. A special squad, assisted by Latvian Fascists, murders 400 Jews and arrests many others. The Jewish community dates back to the sixteenth century. Riga is famous in Jewish history for its cultural developments.

German troops occupy Turka, in the province of Lvov, Poland (today Ukrainian S.S.R.), where 6,000 Jews live.

Occupying German troops and Ukrainian Fascists kill several hundred Jews in Sambor, Poland (today Ukrainian S.S.R.), where 8,000 Jews live. Since the outbreak of World War II the town had been held by the Soviets, who deported many Jews to the Soviet interior. Jews have settled in Sambor since the fifteenth century.

1942 From the ghetto of Opoczno, Kielce province, Poland, housing 3,000 Jews, 400 Jews are deported to the Skarzysko-Kamienna labor camp. Jews have lived in Opoczno since the sixteenth century.

1943 The last deportation of Jews from Brno, Moravia, Czechoslovakia, takes place. Altogether 11,000 Jews from Brno are deported to concentration and extermination camps.

A Jew is shot by the Gestapo in Mochy, in the district of Volsztyn, Poland.

1944 In Aktionen lasting until July 10, those Jews considered to be able-bodied by the SS physicians Dr. Mengele and Dr. Lukas are transported from the Auschwitz II-Birkenau extermination camp in Poland to concentration camps and to ammunition factories in German territory. An additional 4,000 Jewish adults and 80 youngsters between the ages of 14 and 16 are employed to clean up areas that have been bombed. Very few of them will survive.

The Jews from Bonyhad, Hungary, are deported to Pecs, an intermediate station on the way to their next or final deportation.

In a three-day Aktion, 6,000 Jews from Kaposvar, Hungary, and its surrounding area are deported to Auschwitz. Only a few will survive.

A transport with 10 Jews leaves the Theresienstadt concentration camp in Czechoslovakia for the Bergen-Belsen concentration camp in Germany.

July 2

1488 During an auto-da-fé held in Toledo, Spain, 20 men and 7 women are burned at the stake, accused of being Judaizers—descendants of Jews forcibly baptized a century ago who still secretly practice the Jewish religion.

1919 During a second pogrom within two weeks, 15 Jews are slaughtered and 15 severely wounded by units of the Ukrainian National Army, under the command of Jelezniak and Sokolov, in Volodarka, Ukraine.

1940 The Nazis occupying The Hague, Netherlands, issue the order that all Jews of foreign nationalities must register.

1941 German troops occupy Stryj, in the province of Lvov, Poland (today Ukrainian S.S.R.), killing hundreds of its 12,000 Jews with the help of the Ukrainians. Jews first settled there in the sixteenth century.

Slovakian troops and Ukrainian units in German uniforms occupy Bolechov, Poland (today Ukrainian S.S.R.). Jews have been living here since the end of the seventeenth century and many times in history formed the majority of the population. At the beginning of the war the Jewish community had 3,500 members.

The town of Rohatyn, in the province of Stanislavov, Poland (today Ukrainian S.S.R.), where 4,000 Jews live, is occupied by the German army after the outbreak of the German-Soviet conflict. The Jewish community in Rohatyn dates from the eighteenth century.

German troops occupy Korzec (today Ukrainian S.S.R.), where 5,000 Jews live; 500 Jews manage to flee. The first Jews settled in Korzec in the thirteenth century. In the year 1648 almost all its Jewish inhabitants were slaughtered in the massacre by the Chmielnicki Cossacks.

One day after the German invasion, 200 Jews are massacred during a pogrom carried out on the 13,000 Jews of Boryslav, Poland (today Ukrainian S.S.R.) by Ukrainians and the German troops.

The Nazis murder 3,000 Jews in Lvov, Poland (today Ukrainian S.S.R.), during a three-day pogrom styled as "Revenge for Petlyura."

In nearby Lutsk, 1,160 Jews are shot by the Nazis and the local police.

A Jew is shot by the Nazis in Salonika, Greece, for "insulting a representative of the German army."

Several hundred Jews are massacred during a pogrom carried out by the Nazis and Ukrainians in Kamionka-Strumilova, in the district of Lvov, Poland (today Ukrainian S.S.R.), where 4,000 Jews live. Jews have been living here since the fifteenth century.

During a two-day Aktion in Dünaburg, today Latvian S.S.R., the synagogue is burned down with 50 Jews locked inside.

The Nazis kill 7,000 Jews with the help of the Ukrainian Militia during an Aktion in Lvov, Poland (today Ukrainian S.S.R.).

1942   In an Aktion carried out by the Nazis, 850 Jews are victimized in Ropczyce, in the district of Cracow, Poland. Some Jews are murdered and others are deported to the Belzec extermination camp.

1944   The remaining 3,000 Jews of the ghetto of Vilna, Poland (today Lithuanian S.S.R.), who are working as forced laborers, are transported to the nearby forest of Ponary and shot by the SS.

The deportations of 6,500 Jews from barracks in the town of Kaposvar, Hungary, to the Auschwitz extermination camp in Poland begin.

July 3

1919   During a pogrom 6 Jews are massacred and many wounded by troops of Petlyura's Ukrainian National Army in the town of Imerinka, in the district of Podolia, Ukraine. On the same day 9 Jews are slaughtered and many are wounded when insurgents under the hetman Strouk, allied with Petlyura, carry out a pogrom in Bobrik, in the province of Tschernigov, Russia.

1941   German troops occupy Dzisna, Poland (today Belorussian S.S.R.), burning down the synagogue and killing many of the 6,000 Jews. Dzisna's Jewish community was founded in the second half of the eighteenth century.

German troops occupy Novogrodek, in the district of Grodno, Poland (today Belorussian S.S.R.), and the restrictions against the Jewish population begin. At the outbreak of World War II, 6,000 Jews live in Novogrodek, many of them refugees from the German-occupied region of Poland. Jews first settled here in the middle of the sixteenth century.

During a two-day Aktion, 573 Jews are shot at a farm near Ozmiana, Lithuania (today Belorussian S.S.R.).

Two days after German troops have occupied Zloczow, Galicia, Poland (today Ukrainian S.S.R.), 3,500 Jews are massacred in a pogrom organized by Ukrainians with the consent of the Germans. By the outbreak of World War II, 14,000 Jews are living in Zloczow, many of them refugees from western Poland. Jews have lived in Zloczow since the end of the sixteenth century.

With the help of the Ukrainians, the Nazis massacre 400 Jews in Drohobycz, Poland, where 17,000 Jews live. Jews first settled here in the fifteenth century.

Rumanian troops set fire to the Jewish houses in Zgurita, North Moldavia (today Moldavian S.S.R.), and the Jews flee to the open fields, where they are encircled by the Rumanian soldiers who then torture the Jewish women.

In Bialystok, Poland, 300 Jewish intellectuals are murdered by the Nazis in a field outside of town, in one of several massacres that take place during the second occupation which lasts from June 1941 to July 1944 (the first had been in September 1939). The relatives of the murdered are later called the Bereaved of Thursday.

1944   The SS shoots several hundred sick Jewish inmates of the concentration camp situated in the forest near the front between the railway stations of Krynki and Wydreja, in the district of Vitebsk, Belorussian S.S.R.

In the course of a five-day Aktion, 13,000 Jews are deported from Debrecen, Hungary, to the Auschwitz extermination camp in Poland.

From Pecs, Hungary, and the surrounding area, 5,963 Jews interned in the Pecs ghetto are deported to Auschwitz. The number of survivors is not known.

1976   An Air France flight from Tel Aviv to Paris carrying 270 people, including over 100 Jews, is hijacked on June 27 and flown to Entebbe, Uganda. Over the next few days, most of the women, children, and old people are freed. On July 3, Israeli forces attack the terminal and liberate 103 hostages—21 troops and 3 hostages are killed. A Jewish woman who had earlier been released because of illness is taken from her hospital bed and apparently murdered in retaliation.

July 4

1096   The troops of the First Crusade under the command of the count of Leiningen reach Kerpen, Germany, where they slaughter the Jews from Cologne who have found refuge there.

1480   Three Jews from Venice, Italy, are burned at the stake following a blood libel, the allegation that Jews kill a Christian, usually a child, in order to use his blood for religious rituals.

1632   During an auto-da-fé held in Madrid, Spain, in the presence of King Philip IV, his wife, Isabella de Bourbon, and many foreign ambassadors, 7 Judaizers, descendants of Jews forcibly baptized some centuries ago who still practice the Jewish religion in secret, are burned alive, after being arrested for holding a Jewish service; 4 others are burned in effigy.

1919   During a pogrom in Ilinets, Kiev district, Ukraine, 13 Jews are killed, about 60 are wounded, and 8 Jewish women are raped and beaten by units under the command of Volynets. 26 Jews are massacred, many are wounded, and several Jewish women are raped during a two-day pogrom in Brailov, Podolia, Ukraine; and 28 Jews are massacred, 50 are wounded, and many young girls are raped during a three-day pogrom carried out by units under the command of Kasakov and Sokolov in Borchtchagowka, Kiev, Ukraine. All are allies of Petlyura's Ukrainian National Army.

1939   Henceforth, German Jews are subject to the so-called Reichsvereinigung, a national Jewish council headquartered in Berlin, Germany.

1941   Storozynetz, Bukovina, Rumania (today Ukrainian S.S.R.), is the first town the Rumanian army occupies after the outbreak of war with the

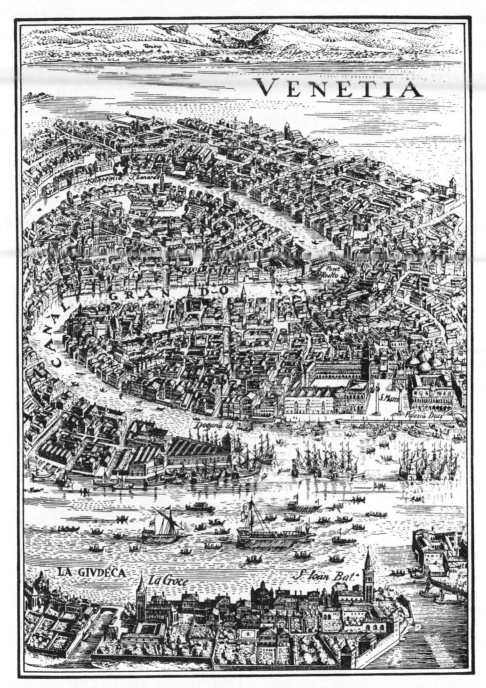

Map of Venice in 1640. Star indicates the ghetto. (From Martin Zeiler, Itineraria Italiæ)

Soviets. The troops take 200 Jews out of their houses and hiding places and shoot them.

In two weeks, 5,000 Jews are murdered by the Nazis and Lithuanian collaborators in Vilna, Poland (today Lithuanian S.S.R.).

All the Jews of Czudyn, Rumanian Bukovina, are massacred during a two-day pogrom by Rumanian troops in cooperation with the rural population.

The Nazis demand 4 kg gold from the Jews and execute 30 intellectuals ten days after their occupation of Bielsk Podlaski, Poland, where 5,000 Jews live, among them many refugees from the German-occupied areas of Poland.

Bielsk Podlaski has an old Jewish community dating back to the fifteenth century. In the year 1564, a pogrom took place in the village after a Jew was falsely accused of having killed a Christian child in connection with Passover.

The German troops organize a pogrom against the 5,000 Jewish people in Zbaraz, Poland (today Ukrainian S.S.R.). All of the Jewish intellectuals are summoned to report to the Gestapo; 70 of them are singled out and shot by the SS in the Lubieniecki forest.

Three days after the German invasion of Przemyslany, in the province of Lvov, Poland (today Ukrainian S.S.R.), where 6,000 Jews live, several hundred Jews are crowded into the big synagogue, which is set on fire by the Nazis.

On the day of the German invasion of Ternopol, Poland (today Ukrainian S.S.R.), a pogrom against the Jewish population of 18,000 is organized and 5,000 Jews are killed with the help of the Ukrainians. The Nazis arrest 1,000 members of the Jewish intelligentsia. Jews have been living there since the sixteenth century. During the Chmielnicki pogroms many were murdered. A number of renowned Jews come from Ternopol.

Pogroms are organized against the Jews by the invading Germans in Grodno, Poland (today Belorussian S.S.R.).

The Nazis of Tilsit kill 111 people of Palanga, 214 from Krottingen, and 201 from Garsden, most of them Jews, in a purge. All the villages are situated in the Lithuanian S.S.R.

During a pogrom carried out by Ukrainian Nationalists and the occupying German troops, 70 Jews are massacred in Tuczyn, in the district of Volnynia, Ukrainian S.S.R., where 3,000 Jews live.

After the Nazis occupy Riga, capital of Latvia, 100 Jews are killed in pogroms.

The SS arrests and kills 3,000 Jews in the fortress of Lubart in Lutsk, Poland (today Ukrainian S.S.R.).

1944 In Hungary, 117 Jews from Köszeg, 800 from Keszthely, and 250 from Sumeg, are deported by the SS to the Auschwitz extermination camp in Poland.

The first deportation transport from the ghetto of Papa, Hungary, where 3,557 Jews have been collected for further deportation, leaves for Auschwitz with 2,565 Jews. Of this group, 300 will survive.

A transport with 15 Jews leaves the Theresienstadt concentration camp in Czechoslovakia for the Bergen-Belsen concentration camp in Germany.

The 6,609 Jews interned in the concentration camp at Szombathely, Hungary, are entrained for further deportation to Auschwitz. More than 3,000 of them are from Szombathely, the rest from neighboring towns. No survivors are recorded.

1945 Anti-Jewish riots break out in Tripoli, Libya, then under British rule. The mob injures and kills many Jews. Jewish property is looted and five synagogues are set on fire.

1946 After the war about 200 Jews return to Kielce, Poland, in order to rebuild the Jewish community there. Anti-Semitic Poles, mostly belonging to Polish nationalist groups, incite a pogrom. The Jews cannot defend themselves because their weapons were confiscated the previous day; 42 Jews are killed, among them 2 children, and about 50 others are wounded.

July 5

1919 In Dunkov, in the district Podolia, Russia, 24 Jews are massacred and 150 more are wounded during a pogrom carried out by units linked to Simon Petlyura's Ukrainian National Army under the leadership of Sokolov.

1941 The Lithuanian police shoot 3,000 Jews during a systematic five-day Aktion in Kaunas, Lithuanian S.S.R.

Fascist death squads murder 1,000 Jews in a two-day Aktion in Edinita, Bessarabia, Ukrainian S.S.R.

In Stryj, Poland (today Ukrainian S.S.R.), 11 Jews are shot by the local population after the withdrawal of the Red Army.

The Ukrainians murder 15 Jews and set the synagogues on fire in Rudki, Poland.

The Ukrainian Auxiliary Police round up and murder 70 Jews in Ternopol, Poland (today Ukrainian S.S.R.). Another 20 Jews are killed in the streets by soldiers and Ukrainians.

The Nazis occupy the village of Liga, in the district of Grodno, Poland, where 15,000 Jews live. They drag the intellectuals and the rabbis, about 200 people, out of the village and take them to Stoniewicze where they are murdered.

In an imitation Aktion, 3 Jews are shot by the Serbian police in Belgrade, Yugoslavia.

When German troops occupy Skalat, Poland (today Ukrainian S.S.R.), 20 of the 4,800 Jews who live there are killed. 200 Jews manage to flee with the withdrawing Soviet army. Jews have been living here since the eighteenth century.

The Ukrainians stage a pogrom against the Jews when the German troops occupy Buczacz, Ternopol, Ukrainian S.S.R., where 10,000 Jews live. Jews have been living there since the sixteenth century. A great number of Jewish intellectuals and notables were born there, including the Israeli Nobel Prize winner S. J. Agnon.

German and Rumanian troops occupy Czernovitz, Bukovina (today Ukrainian S.S.R.). The Task Force 10 starts to murder the Jewish intellectuals.

David-Gorodok, Brest Litovsk, Belorussian S.S.R., where 5,000 Jews live, is occupied by German troops. On demand of the local population, the Nazis order all male Jews over 14 to gather by the church. They are taken outside of town, where they have to dig trenches in which they are then murdered by the SS. A ghetto is set up for the women. Jews have been living here since the sixteenth century.

The Nazis and the newly founded Ukrainian police execute 150 Jews in the prison courtyard during mass arrests in Wlodzimierz, Poland (today Ukrainian S.S.R.).

German troops march into Sarny, in the district of Volhynia, Poland (today Ukrainian S.S.R.), and the SS begins to murder the Jews. Jews have been living here since the beginning of the century. Since the outbreak of the war the Soviets had held Sarny and had dismantled all Jewish institutions. In 1940 they deported 2,000 Jewish refugees from the German occupied regions of Poland to Siberia.

1942 Rumanian troops, allies of the Germans, enter Wiznitz, Bukovina (today Rumania), immediately seizing the Jewish residents and killing 21.

1943 Yizhak Wittenberg, the commander of the Jewish resistance in the Vilna ghetto, Lithuanian S.S.R., is arrested. Members of the Jewish underground movement manage to free him in an attack on the Nazis. The Nazis threaten to destroy the ghetto if Wittenberg is not handed over to them. Wittenberg surrenders himself in order to save the ghetto and the Gestapo murders him.

1944 3,557 Jews, who have been interned in the ghetto of Papa, Hungary, are deported in two transports to the Auschwitz extermination camp in Poland. Only 300 will survive. On the same day 1,286 Jews of Sopron, 650 Jews from Csorna, 50 Jews from Szill, and 500 Jews from the ghetto of Mohacs, all in Hungary, are deported by the SS to Auschwitz.

July 6

1348 During the Black Death epidemic, for which the Jews were thought to be responsible, they were cruelly persecuted everywhere. When the plague reaches Spain, the Jewish community of Tarrega, Catalinia, numbering 300, are slaughtered and their corpses are thrown into a ditch and burned.

1941 German and Rumanian troops occupy Secureni, a small town in Bessarabia (today Moldavian S.S.R.), where 5,000 Jews live. The troops murder 90 Jews who are seized in the streets. Many others commit suicide.

In the district of Polesie, Soviet Union, 400 Jews are taken from Ivaniki. The men are shot by the SS and the women are deported to Pinsk.

The SS murders 250 Jews in Klaszkovce, in the district of Ternopol, Poland (today Ukrainian S.S.R.).

The Nazis shoot 2,000 Jews in the prison of Dünaburg, Latvian S.S.R.

The newly established Ukrainian police begins to murder the Jews in Rohatyn, in the district of Stanislavov, Poland (today Ukrainian S.S.R.).

Two days after the Nazis entered Riga, the capital of Latvia, 400 Jews are liquidated and all the synagogues are destroyed. An auxiliary police troop of Latvians is organized for the purpose of carrying out pogroms.

German troops occupy Druja, a small town in Belorussian S.S.R., where 1,500 Jews live. The SS begins to murder the Jews for allegedly collaborating with the Soviets. Jews have been living in Druja since the sixteenth century.

Ukrainian Nationalists murder 500 Jews in Skalat, Ternopol province, Poland (today Ukrainian S.S.R.), when the Nazis give them a day to get even with the Jews.

After Rumanian troops invade Czernovitz, Bukovina (today Ukrainian S.S.R.), the Germans and Rumanians execute 3,000 Jews from Bila and Klokuczka. They even massacre the inmates of the Jewish psychiatric hospital of Czernovitz.

1943 A transport with 2,417 Jewish prisoners from the Westerbork transit camp in the Dutch province of Drenthe leaves for the Sobibor extermination camp in Poland.

1944 From Sopron, Hungary, and its vicinity, 3,305 Jews have been held in the ghetto of Sopron. They are deported by the SS to the Auschwitz extermination camp in Poland. Only 42 of them will survive.

From Bonyhad in southern Hungary, 1,200 Jews taken to Pecs on July 1, are deported to Auschwitz. Only 70 people will survive. On the same day 120 Jews from Tolna, Hungary, are also sent to Auschwitz.

The deportation of the Jews of western and southwestern Hungary to Auschwitz is completed.

July 7

1320 Les Pastoureaux, crusaders against the Muslims in the south of Spain, massacre 400 Jews, when they reach Jaca in French Basque.

1919 The Jewish community of Zamekhov, Ukraine, is struck by a pogrom carried out by units of Simon Petlyura's Ukrainian National Army under the command of Alexander Udovichenko. On the same day 150 Jews are slain and many Jewish women are gang-raped in Nowogrod-Volynsk, Volhynia, Ukraine, during a four-day pogrom carried out by units under the command of Sokolov, Kolesnitch-enko, and Pogorelov, also linked to the Ukrainian National Army. During a three-day pogrom, 6 Jews are killed, 3 are gravely wounded, and many Jewish women are raped in Michalpol, Podolia, Ukraine, by the 3d regiment of the Haidamacks of the Ukrainian National Army.

1941 Ukrainians kill 1,200 Jews in a forest near the town of Otynia, in the province of Stanislavov, Poland (today Ukrainian S.S.R.).

The SS murders 2,000 Jews in Rodzislav, in the province of Bialystok, Poland, in the course of three days.

Several hundred Jews are arrested and shot by Ukrainian militia during an Aktion in Zloczow, Galicia province, Poland (today Ukrainian S.S.R.).

In Zborov, Galicia, Ukrainian S.S.R., 600 Jews are killed by the Waffen SS, the military SS special-service troops.

In Belzy, Rumania, where 32,000 Jews live, hundreds of Jews are killed in riots caused by the invading Rumanian soldiers, allies of the Germans.

The SS finds 50 Jews through a registry of the Jewish population in Novogrodek, in the district of Grodno, Poland (today Belorussian S.S.R.), and shoots them outside of town.

Jewish houses are burned down and the Jews are murdered when hordes of farmers attack the Jewish community in Balti, Bessarabia, Rumania (today Ukrainian S.S.R.).

German and Rumanian troops occupy Khotin, Bessarabia, where 15,000 Jews live. The SS goes from door to door and murders 2,000 Jews.

1942 During a five-day Aktion in Rzeszow, in the district of Rzeszow, Poland, where 14,000 Jews live, 8,000 Jews of the ghetto are deported to the Belzec extermination camp. The 238 Jews who offer resistance are shot on the spot and another 1,000 Jews are taken into the forest of Rudna and executed by the SS.

The police shoot 3 Jews in Pyzdry, in the district of Wrzesnia, Poland.

July 8

1941 The invading German troops murder 1,000 Jews of the village of Marculesti in Bessarabia, Ukrainian S.S.R.

During mass executions of Jews that span two days, 500 Jews are shot by SS commandos and Rumanian troops in Czernovitz, Bukovina, Rumania (today Ukrainian S.S.R.).

About 140 people, among them many Jews, are shot by the Nazis in the fishing port Liepaja, Latvian S.S.R.

About 1,000 Jews are shot by the SS in the Bikerneku Forest near Riga, Latvian S.S.R.

A group of Rumanian soldiers murders 50 Jews who want to return to their homes in Balti, Bessarabia, Rumania (Ukrainian S.S.R.).

Many Jews are murdered when Rumanian and German troops occupy Brichany, Bessarabia (today Moldavian S.S.R.), where 10,000 Jews live.

German and Rumanian troops occupy Lipcani, Bessarabia (today Moldavian S.S.R.), where 4,000 Jews live. About 800 Jews are murdered by Fascist extermination commandos. The rest of the Jewish population is driven into the forest near Vertyuzhany, from where they are sent on a death march to the camps of Sekiryany and Yedintsy. Those who cannot keep up are shot.

In Vilna, Poland (today Lithuanian S.S.R.), 500 Jews are shot and others are arrested and taken to concentration camps by the Lithuanian Security Service. According to German reports, 500 Jews are shot every day for several days thereafter. Jewish property is confiscated.

The SS kills 3 Jewish women in Zloczow, Galicia (today Ukrainian S.S.R.).

Compulsory marking for Jews in the Baltic States begins.

1944 A transport of several hundred Jews leaves Budapest, Hungary, for the Auschwitz extermination camp in Poland, and the deportation of the Jews from the communities surrounding Budapest is completed.

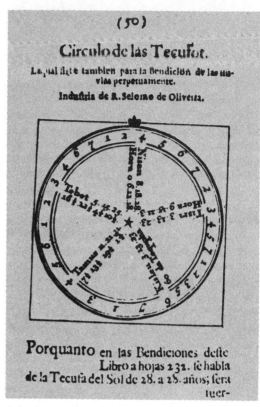

Calendar page from the Orden De Bendiciones, *a prayer book for Marranos who returned to Judaism. Amsterdam, 1687.*

July 9

507 A chariot race takes place in Daphne, near Antiochia (today Turkey), between two rivaling parties, the Greens and the Whites. Suddenly without any apparent reason, the supporters of the Greens, the Byzantine charioteers, destroy the local synagogue and its sanctuaries and massacre the praying Jews.

1391 When a group of marauders and adventurers enter the Jewish quarter of Valencia, Spain,

where 5,000 Jews live, 250 Jews are killed trying to defend the community. The Christian mob violates Jewish women and girls and loots the Jewish houses. A few Jews escape to the mountains and the remaining Jews are forcibly baptized.

1713 An auto-da-fé is held in Lisbon, Portugal. Several persons, accused of being Judaizers—descendants of Jews forcibly baptized some centuries before who still secretly practice the Jewish religion—are condemned to doing public penance. One of the Judaizers is a nun.

1919 Units under the command of Sokolov, a hetman of insurgents linked to Petlyura's Ukrainian National Army, massacre 64 Jews, wound 20, and rape almost every Jewish woman in Novo-Fastov, in the district of Kiev, Ukraine. The same troops massacre 50 Jews and wound 100 during a three-day massacre in Volodarka. During a three-day pogrom, 2 Jews are killed by soldiers under the command of Mordalevitch, in Khamovka, in the district of Kiev, also linked to the Ukrainian National Army.

1941 German soldiers take 150 Jews from Czernovitz, Bukovina (today Ukrainian S.S.R.), to the Pruth River and shoot them. Among them are the Grand Rabbi Dr. Abraham Mark, Cantor Gurman, and several other notables of the town. The day after the execution, several Jews are forced to bury the dead.

The Nazis order the erection of a ghetto for the Jews of Kaunas, in the town Viliampob, Lithuanian S.S.R. The move must be completed within four weeks. The Jews are required to wear the Yellow Star. Jews are imprisoned and shot on the slightest pretext.

The invading Germans kill 80 Jews in Rezehne, Latvian S.S.R.

During a three-day pogrom in Secureni, Bessarabia (today Moldavian S.S.R.), the inhabitants drag the Jews to the Jewish cemetery where they are tortured by the SS and Rumanian troops.

The Jews who return to Balti, Bessarabia, Rumania (today Ukrainian S.S.R.), are deported by the Nazis to concentration camps, 10 Jews who have been taken as hostages are shot. At the time of the German invasion, 15,000 Jews are living in Balti. The Gestapo demands a list of 20 Jewish Communists. When they do not get it, they arrest 44 Jews, among them leading members of the Jewish community, and shoot them.

1944 From Vienna, 5 Jews are deported to the Theresienstadt concentration camp in Czechoslovakia.

1404 The Jews of Salzburg and of Hallein, Austria, arrested on July 4 for alleged host desecration and ritual murder, are sent to the stake. They are burned alive and the corpses of two Jews who committed suicide are burned with them.

1510 The Jews of Berlin are accused of host desecration and the theft of sacred vessels from a church in Knoblauch, a nearby village. 111 Jews are arrested, 51 of them are sentenced to death, and 38 are burned at the stake in the new marketplace. At the diet of Frankfort in 1539, however, all of them will be acknowledged to be innocent.

1919 During pogroms, 43 Jews are massacred and 15 Jewish women and girls are raped in Wachnowa, in the district of Kiev, Ukraine; and 12 Jews are massacred in the town of Woronovitsy, in Podolia, Ukraine, by units under the command of the hetman Tiutiunnik, part of Simon Petlyura's Ukrainian National Army.

Many Jews are massacred and many others are flogged or beaten with sabers when troops under the command of Vitsek and Chepel, allied with Petlyura's Ukrainian National Army, carry out a pogrom in Novo-Konstantinov, Russia.

1941 The SS murders 250 Jews of Dovgaliszek, in the district of Vilna, Belorussian S.S.R.

The Rumanian military authorities round up 400 Jews and shoot 15 male Jews in Belzy, Rumania.

In the course of five days, 1,600 Jews are murdered by the SS in the environs of Riga, today Latvian S.S.R.

Several Jews are killed by the local population in Minsk, Belorussian S.S.R., following an anti-Jewish propaganda campaign.

The Nazis assemble and shoot 150 inmates from the prison in Liepaja, Latvian S.S.R., among them many Jews.

200 Jews are murdered four days after the German invasion, in Chortkov, Poland (today Ukrainian S.S.R.), where 8,000 Jews live. Jews have been living there since the sixteenth century and already in 1648 they suffered severely during the pogroms by the Chmielnicki Cossacks.

1942 A transport of 993 Jews leaves Vienna for the Theresienstadt concentration camp in Czechoslovakia.

After the German invasion of Holland, the Jews of Groningen province have to resettle in the town of Groningen in the north of Holland. Together with the Jews of Groningen they are deported to the Westerbork transit camp in the Dutch province of Drenthe.

1943 During a three-day Aktion, 5,000 Jews are shot by the SS and Ukrainian police in the Kamionka-Strumilova labor camp in the province of Lvov, Poland (today Ukrainian S.S.R.).

During the last Aktion against the 4,000 Jews in the ghetto of Zolkiev, Galicia, Poland (today Ukrainian S.S.R.), many Jews are shot by the SS, and many others are deported to the Belzec extermination camp.

July 11

1919 During a four-day pogrom, 8 Jews are killed, 50 are gravely wounded or mutilated, and Jewish property is pillaged in Janov, Podolia province, Russia, by units under the leadership of Chepel. Units under the command of Sokolski kill 8 Jews in the community of Gorchtchik, Volhynia, Ukraine, during a pogrom. During a pogrom, 148 Jews are massacred and 126 are wounded by units

under the hetmen Kozakov and Sokolov in the town of Novo-Priluki, Kiev district, Ukraine. All are linked to Petlyura's Ukrainian National Army.

1941 The Jews of Balti, Bessarabia, Rumania (today Ukrainian S.S.R.), are interned in the courtyard of the Moldava Bank, from where Rumanian troops drive them into the forests of Rautel where many of them die of hunger and illness.

Several Jews are shot by the SS when they reach Bialystok, Poland.

Several dozen Jews are shot immediately as the SS invade Grodno, Poland (today Belorussian S.S.R.).

The Nazis order that all the surviving Jews of Kaunas, Lithuanian S.S.R., must move to Slobodka, where a ghetto is being erected. At this time a Jewish underground movement develops that consists of 800 members, who manage to flee into the forests of Augustova.

In a civilian detention camp in Minsk, Belorussian S.S.R., 1,050 Jews are liquidated. The male inhabitants of Minsk are taken there, but all are freed soon after, except the Jews. Executions of Jews occur daily. A Jewish Council is established.

1942 The German army raids Athens, Greece, and arrests all Jewish males of 15 years and older for forced labor. They are submitted to such hard conditions that many of them die.

The occupying Germans send 9,000 Jews from Salonika, Greece, to the Leptokarya labor camp.

1944 Hungary, with the exception of the capital, is "free of Jews." SS-Standartenführer (chief of an SS unit) Veesenmayer states: 437,402 Hungarian Jews have been deported to Auschwitz extermination camp in Poland.

The SS sends to the gas chambers 6,000 Jews—children, the old, and the sick—who have been left in the Auschwitz II–Birkenau camp after a general selection. Among them are the deportees, children and adults, from the Theresienstadt concentration camp in Czechoslovakia, who have arrived in several transports in December 1943 and May 1944.

July 12

1462 A case of blood libel occurs in the Austrian town of Rinn, where the Jews are accused of having killed a Christian boy in order to drink his blood for Passover. The stone on which they allegedly murder the child is known as the Judenstein, or the Jews Stone. The accused are later executed.

1555 Pope Paul IV issues the infamous bull, "Cum nimis absurdum" which reinforces remorselessly all the restrictive ecclesiastical legislation against the Jews hitherto only intermittently enforced. This consists of the segregation of the Jews in a special quarter, henceforth called the ghetto; the wearing of the Jewish badge; prohibitions on owning real estate; on being called by any title of respect such as "signor," on the employment by Christians of Jewish physicians, and on dealing in corn and other necessities of life; and the virtual restriction to selling only old clothes and secondhand goods.

1919 During a pogrom, 127 Jews are massacred, many are wounded, and many Jewish women and girls are raped in Petchora, Podolia district, Ukraine, which is carried out by insurgents under hetmen Sokolski and Liakhovich, allies of Petlyura's Ukrainian National Army.

1940 The Zionist Jews of Leova, southwestern Moldavian S.S.R., are arrested by the Soviets and sent to Siberia.

1941 In Minsk, Belorussian S.S.R., a ghetto is set up by the Nazis and the Jews are ordered to wear distinguishing marks.

Several dozen Jews are shot by the invading Germans as they reach Lida, Poland (today Belorussian S.S.R.).

About 300 Jews are shot in the village of Maljuny, Poland, near Wilejka (today Belorussian S.S.R.).

Several hundred Jewish women and girls are abducted from their houses, raped, and shot by the SS during the night in Khotin, Bessarabia, Ukrainian S.S.R.

The SS, who marched into town two weeks before, murders 12 members of the Jewish intelligentsia of Rozana, in the district of Brest, Poland (today Belorussian S.S.R.). Jews first settled here in the beginning of the seventeenth century. In the course of its history Rozana has belonged to Lithuania, Poland, and the Soviet Union. By the time of the German invasion the Jewish community numbers 3,500 people.

On the Sabbath, 3,000 Jewish men from Bialystok, Poland, are arrested by the SS, who drive them out of town and execute them. Their widows are henceforth called the "Sabbath Widows." A ghetto is then established in Bialystok for all the Jews from the neighboring provinces as well as the city—a total of 50,000 Jews.

1942 5,000 Jews are taken from the ghetto in Rovno, in the Volhynia region, Ukrainian S.S.R., to Janova Dolina, where they are murdered by the SS. Some manage to flee into the forest, but only a small number will survive.

July 13

1287 The Christian population slays 19 Jews in Kobern on the Mosel, Germany, following an accusation of ritual murder against the Jews of Oberwesel, whose victim is later known as good Werner.

1561 A Christian girl, the servant of a wealthy and much envied Jewish tax collector, is found dead in Brest Litovsk, Poland (today Belorussian S.S.R.). The tax collector's Jewish servant Abramovich is accused of ritual murder. He is tortured and executed on July 13 in Bielsk, Lithuania.

1919 The Jewish men are flogged and the women are brutally raped when the Brazlav regiment carries out a pogrom in Borivka, district of Podolia, Ukraine; 3 Jews are slain in a two-day pogrom in Rchichtchev, in the district of Kiev, Ukraine, carried out by units under Zeleny; and 80 Jews are slaughtered and 100 are wounded in a pogrom in Brazlav, Podolia, Ukraine, carried out by the hetmen Liachowitsch, Sokolov, and Gromow. All are linked to Petlyura's Ukrainian National Army.

1941 Ukrainian nationalists, together with Nazis, attack Jews in Monasterzyska, in the district of Ternopol, Ukrainian S.S.R., and murder them. Jews have been living here since the middle of the eighteenth century and at the time of the German invasion they number 3,000.

1942 The SS shoots 1,500 Jews in Josefov, a village in Poland.

From Kubin, in the district of Lodz, Poland, 3,000 Jews are deported to the Majdanek extermination camp.

A dozen Jews in the labor camp at Otoczna, in the district of Wrzesnia, Poland, are shot by the Gestapo.

1943 The SS murders 300 Jews in Bolechov, Poland (today Ukrainian S.S.R.).

A transport with 1,988 Jewish prisoners is sent from the Westerbork transit camp in the Dutch province of Drenthe to the Sobibor extermination camp in Poland.

July 14

1683 When the Christian population of the town of Ungarisch-Brod, Bohemia (today Hungary), attacks Brod's small Jewish community, 113 Jews are killed. Austrian troops, who are stationed there to fight the Turks, witness the killings and do not intervene.

1919 In the village of Davidka, Volhynia, Russia, 3 Jews are slain by local peasants and units of Sokolovtsy, an ally of Petlyura's Ukrainian National Army.

1941 In Riga, Latvian S.S.R., 2,300 Jews are killed by the Nazis and the Latvian auxiliary police.

1942 Several thousand Jews, adults and children, from Smolensk, Ukrainian S.S.R., are murdered by the SS in gas vans in the forests between Pasowo and Mogalenschtschina.

A transport with 988 Jews leaves from Vienna for the Theresienstadt concentration camp in Czechoslovakia.

A transport of 1,000 Jewish men, women, and children leaves the ghetto in Theresienstadt, Czechoslovakia, for Minsk. Ten km before the station, the Jews are ordered off the train and are taken in trucks into a nearby forest, where they are shot by the SS. Their corpses are buried in common graves. Of the 35 strong men selected for forced labor, only 2 of them will survive and join the partisans.

In a two-day Aktion in Rovno, Ukrainian S.S.R., 5,000 Jews are massacred by the SS with the help of the local Ukrainian auxiliaries.

1944   In Tallinn, Estonia, 60 Jews, who have helped with the rebuilding of an airport, are driven to a nearby forest and shot.

July 15

1267   A Christian girl is found dead in Pforzheim, Germany, and the local Jews are accused of ritual murder. Three Jewish notables commit suicide, probably forcibly, in order to save the rest of the community. Their corpses are broken on the wheel.

1738   An ex-officer of the Russian navy, Alexander Vosnizi, is converted to Judaism, illegally, by the Jew Baruch Leibov, a tradesman and courtier. Vosnizi is tried and submitted to torture. On July 15, Alexander Vosnizi and Baruch Leibov are condemned to death and burned at the stake in Moscow.

1919   During a four-day pogrom in Murafa, Podolia, Russia, 64 Jews are massacred, many severely wounded, and many Jewish women and girls are brutally raped by the unit under the command of Lubny, and the 9th regiment of sharpshooters, linked to Petlyura's Ukrainian National Army.

1938   A transport of hundreds of Jews leaves Vienna for the Dachau concentration camp in Germany.

1941   In Radzivillov, Volhynia, Ukrainian S.S.R., 28 Jews are arrested and killed by the Nazis for allegedly being Communists.

The Nazis kill 45 Jews, including the Jewish Council of elders, in Belzy, Rumania.

Male Jews numbering 1,150 are arrested in Dünaburg (today Latvian S.S.R.), where they are shot and thrown into previously prepared graves.

1942   From the ghetto in Sassov, Poland (today Ukrainian S.S.R.), 1,000 Jews are deported to the Belzec extermination camp.

From Grybov, West Galicia, Poland, 1,200 Jews are deported to the Novy Sacz transit camp.

During a two-day Aktion, 3,500 Jews from Smolensk, Ukrainian S.S.R., are first taken by the SS to the Sadki ghetto, and are later shot in the forest of Wjasowensk, near Mogalenschtachina.

All inmates of Ghetto B (who are labeled "useless" by the Nazis), of Bereza Kartuska, Poland, are brought to the village of Brona Gora and murdered.

The Central Office for Economic Matters of the SS orders the erection of a camp for women in Majdanek, Poland.

The SS murders 1,000 Jews during an uprising in the ghetto of Molczadz, Belorussian S.S.R.

1943   A transport with 17 Jews leaves Vienna for the Theresienstadt concentration camp in Czechoslovakia.

From the camp in Jasenovac, Yugoslavia, 800 Jews are deported to the Auschwitz extermination camp in Poland, where they are immediately murdered.

1944   The ghetto of Siauliai, Lithuanian S.S.R., is liquidated and part of the population is deported to Stutthof near Danzig.

July 16

1099 After the troops of the First Crusade have conquered Jerusalem, they carry out a massacre of the Muslim and Jewish population. The Jews flee into their synagogue, set it on fire, and die in the flames.

1919 During a pogrom, 63 Jews are slaughtered, 50 are wounded, and an unknown number of Jewish women and girls are raped in Brazlav, Podolia, Ukraine, carried out by units under Liachowitsch, Sokolov, and Gromov, linked to Petlyura's Ukrainian National Army.

Crusaders in Jerusalem. (From a Hebrew illumination of 1170)

1941 The Nazis arrest and shoot 20 Jewish intellectuals in Tuczyn, in the region of Volhynia, Ukrainian S.S.R.

Rabbi Twersky and 57 Jewish doctors, teachers, and lawyers are killed by the SS in Khotin, Ukrainian S.S.R.

In Radzivillov, Ukrainian S.S.R., the synagogue is burned down. Earlier the Torah scrolls have been burned on a special stake.

1942 A transport of 895 Jewish prisoners is sent from the Westerbork transit camp in the Dutch province of Drenthe to the Auschwitz extermination camp in Poland.

The first large-scale raid occurs in the region of Paris, which is occupied by the German army. It assembles all Jews from the ages of 16 to 60 for men, 16 to 55 for women; children between 2 and 16 are to be taken with their parents. According to the calculations of the Nazis, 28,000 Jews will be rounded up in two days. The Jews of French nationality are exempted. The operation is carried out by the French police and in the end 13,000 people are interned in the big sports arena on Boulevard de Grenelle, the Velodrome d'Hiver (known as the Vel d'Hiv). Other Jews are hidden by non-Jewish friends or manage to flee to the "nonoccupied zone."

July 17

1287 Ninety Jewish men, women, and children are slain after the ritual murder accusation against the Jews of Oberwesel, Germany, spreads further and the persecutions reach the Jewish community of Münstermaifeld in the Rhineland.

1349 The Jews of Mainingen, Thuringia, Germany, who have survived the first massacre (on April 10), are caught and burned at the stake.

1648 A slaughter of 600 Jews occurs when the Cossack hordes of Bogdan Chmielnicki capture Pavdocz in the Ukraine.

1919 Many Jews are massacred when units under the command of Volynets, linked to Petlyura's Ukrainian National Army, carry out a pogrom in Teplik, Podolia, Russia.

1941 The Commissar Order calls for "special treatment" of political commissars of the Soviet Army, Jews, and opponents of the Nazi regime, among them Russian prisoners of war.

In Lvov, Galicia province, Poland (today Ukrainian S.S.R.), the Nazis initiate the obligatory wearing of the distinguishing badge for the Jews. Those who do not wear it are shot. The Jews must also pay a 20 million ruble "contribution" to the Nazis.

The SS takes 1,200 Jews from Slonim, Grodno, Poland (today Belorussian S.S.R.), and murders them. The Jews are ordered to pay a fine of 2 million rubles and a "Judenrat," a Jewish Council, is established.

1941 Jews are murdered by the invading Germans and Rumanians in Belgorod-Dnestrovski, Bessarabia (today Ukrainian S.S.R.). About 4,000 Jews manage to flee to Odessa.

Task Force D murders 10,000 Jews in Kishinev, Bessarabia, Rumania (today Moldavian S.S.R.), where 70,000 Jews live, when it is occupied by the Germans and Rumanian troops. Jews have been living in Kishinev since the eighteenth century.

1942 A transport with 995 Jews departs from Vienna for Minsk, Belorussian S.S.R., where they are shot by the SS.

The SS kills 2,500 Jews during an Aktion in Druja, Belorussian S.S.R.

It is the second day of the first-large scale raid in the region of Paris, ordered by the German occupation army and carried out by the French authorities. All those who have not been seized on the first day of the raid are registered and transported to different assembly places, from where they are sent to various concentration camps in the east.

In overcrowded train cars, 928 Jewish internees at Pithiviers, a transit camp in the German occupied zone of France, are deported to the Auschwitz extermination camp in Poland. At the liberation of Auschwitz in 1945, 18 of them are still alive.

From Radomysl, Ukrainian S.S.R., 1,500 Jews are deported to the Dembica labor camp.

July 18

1290 A decree is issued by King Edward I ordering the expulsion of all Jews from English territories by November 1 of the same year. Every Jew left behind is liable to death.

1919 During a pogrom, 20 Jews are massacred by troops under the command of their hetman Chepel, linked to Simon Petlyura's Ukrainian National Army, in Litin, in the province of Podolia, Ukraine.

1941 The SS drowns 40 Jews from Vitebsk, Belorussian S.S.R., in the Dvina River.

From the ghetto in Opatov, Kielce province, Kielce, Poland, 2,000 young men are deported to various labor camps. A small number of them succeed in fleeing to the forests.

1942 The Nazis murder 600 Jews during an uprising led by the Jewish resistance in the ghetto of

Szarkowszczyzna, Poland (today Belorussian S.S.R.). About 1,000 Jews escape into the woods.

1943   A total of 1,000 Jewish men and women are deported from the transit camp of Drancy in the German occupied zone of France to the Auschwitz extermination camp in Poland. Immediately after their arrival, 440 of the deportees are sent to the gas chambers. Only 43 men and 16 women will survive until the liberation of the camp by the Soviet army in 1945.

The last 200 Jews of Miedzyrzec Podlaski, Lublin, Poland, who have been doing forced labor for the Nazis, are shot.

July 19

1648   When the Cossacks of Bogdan Chmielnicki capture Tschernigov, Ukraine, they massacre 2,000 Jews.

1919   Of the 15 Jewish families living in Zhidovska-Grebla, Ukraine, 8 are completely wiped out in a pogrom carried out by units of Simon Petlyura's Ukrainian National Army.

1940   A ghetto is established in Zychlin, Poland, and the Jewish population is forced to move into it.

1942   999 Jewish internees are deported from the Drancy transit camp in the German occupied zone of France to the Auschwitz extermination camp in Poland. Only 16 are still alive at the liberation.

1944   On the isle of Rhodes, Greece, 1,200 Jews are rounded up at German headquarters and deported—with an intermediate station in the Haidar prison in Athens—to Auschwitz.

In his second attempt in one week, Adolf Eichmann manages to deport 1,450 Jewish inmates from the Kistarcsa internment camp in Hungary to Auschwitz despite the opposition of Miklós Horthy, the Hungarian prime minister.

July 20

1648   During a three-day massacre, 12,000 Jews are slaughtered by the Cossacks of Bogdan Chmielnicki in Starodub, Russia.

1941   During a four-day Aktion, 381 people, most of them Jews, are liquidated in Baranowicze, Belorussian S.S.R.

The death march of 1,200 Jews from Lipcani, Bessarabia (today Moldavian S.S.R.), begins. By August 6, all of them are dead.

Ukrainian collaborators indiscriminately murder 800 men, women, and children in the town of Krzemieniec, in the region of Volhynia, Ukrainian S.S.R.

During an Aktion carried out by the security police, 2,000 Jews are arrested and 1,075 are liquidated in Slonim, Poland (today Belorussian S.S.R.).

1942   A transport with 827 Jewish men and women leaves from the Angers transit camp in the German occupied zone of France to the Auschwitz extermination camp in Poland, where 23 of them are immediately gassed. Only 14 will survive.

1,150 Jews of Trzebinia, in Cracow province, Poland, are brought to the collection point Kozienice.

From the ghetto of Kovale Panskie, Poland, 3,000 Jews are deported to the Chelmno extermination camp.

All Jewish patients of the hospitals in Belgrade, Yugoslavia, are murdered by the SS.

1943 From the Hasag camp, 500 Jews are killed in the Jewish cemetery in Czestochova, Poland.

A convoy with 2,209 Jewish prisoners leaves from the Westerbork transit camp in the Dutch province of Drenthe for the Sobibor extermination camp in Poland.

1944 A raid on Jewish children in Paris occurs after the Nazis learn that Jewish children are being hidden by French families.

July 21

1298 In the Jewish community of Rothenburg ob der Tauber, Germany, the remaining 380 Jews are slaughtered in the last of a series of massacres during the Rindfleisch Persecutions, named after the German knight leading the Jew-slaying hordes.

1350 The Jewish community of Minden, Westphalia, Germany, is annihilated during the Black Death Persecutions.

1919 A pogrom takes place in Chemerevtzky, Ukraine, by the "Battalions of Death" commanded by Colonel Palicnko, established by Simon Petlyura, the high commander of the Ukrainian National Army.

1941 Two hundred Torah scrolls are collected from all synagogues and burned during a special ceremony in Kovel, Volhynia, Poland (today Ukrainian S.S.R.).

Heinrich Himmler arranges for the erection of the Majdanek extermination camp near Lublin, Poland.

Several dozen Jews are shot by the invading Nazis in Zhitomir, Ukrainian S.S.R.

1942 The Nazis murder 1,000 Jews during an uprising in the ghetto of Kleck, a town in Belorussian S.S.R.

From Dembica, Cracow province, Poland, 2,500 Jews are deported to the Belzec extermination camp. On the same day the SS begins the deportation to Belzec of 12,000 Jews from the ghetto of Tarnobrzeg, Poland, during a several-day Aktion.

Most of the 2,000 Jews from Rozvadov, Poland, were deported to the Soviet occupied parts of the country. Those who return are rounded up in the marketplace of Rozvadov. Some of them are shot by the SS. The others are taken in cattle cars to Dembica, where the Jews of the area are forcibly concentrated. They are either shot by the SS in the nearby forests or transferred to different camps.

A transport of 931 Jewish inmates leaves from Westerbork transit camp in the Dutch province of Drenthe, for the Auschwitz extermination camp in Poland.

The local Jewish resistance group leads an uprising in the ghetto of Niesviez, Belorussian S.S.R. Many of the resistance fighters and most of the inmates are slaughtered; the death toll is 600. Those who manage to escape join a partisan group.

From the Warsaw ghetto 60 Jews are taken as hostages to the Pawiak prison when the SS learns that a resistance movement exists in the ghetto.

The Gestapo hangs 4 Jews in Leszno, Poland.

1943 All Jewish skilled workers working for the municipality of Drohobycz, Poland (today Ukrainian S.S.R.), are taken outside of town and shot by the SS. The remaining Jews flee to Hungary and to the Carpathian Mountains. About 300 Jews survive.

1944 A transport of 563 Jews leaves Mechelen, Belgium, for Auschwitz.

July 22

1209 Pope Innocent III sends a crusade against the town of Béziers, France, because the mayor is known to be a friend of the Jews and the Albigenses, who are Christian heretics. In the massacre following the conquest of the town, all Christian inhabitants, Catholic and Albigensian alike—as the crusaders can't distinguish between Catholics and others—as well as 200 Jews are exterminated.

1298 The two Jewish families living in Sindelfingen, Germany, numbering 11 people, are slain by the knight Rindfleisch and his hordes during the Rindfleisch Persecutions.

1306 King Philip the Fair orders the expulsion of all Jews from France, except for those who would accept baptism. Because the Jews are only allowed to take the minimum of food and valuables, many die on the roads. Many others are killed by peasants who suspect them of carrying gold and jewelry.

1648 The Cossacks under Chmielnicki slaughter 10,000 Jews of Polonnoye, Ukraine, and refugees from the surrounding countryside, who have found refuge in the fortified castle. Among the victims is the famous Cabalist Samson Ostropole. Several hundred succumb to forced baptism.

1919 A Jew is murdered and Jewish property is looted when the third regiment of Haidamacks, a unit of the Ukrainian National Army, carries out a pogrom in Solobkovtsy, Podolia, Ukraine.

1939 In Prague, Czechoslovakia, where 56,000 Jews live, the Germans establish a central office for Jewish emigration under the leadership of Adolf Eichmann. According to official documents, Jews have been living in Prague since 1091 and have witnessed all the eddies of its changeable history. Famous rabbis, scholars, writers, musicians, and philosophers were born there.

1941 The SS arrests and shoots 80 Jews in the Jewish cemetery in Dubno, Volhynia, Poland (today Ukrainian S.S.R.).

1942 The liquidation of the ghetto in Kovel, Volhynia province, Poland (today Ukrainian S.S.R.), begins, in which 8,000 Jews are killed. The Jews are herded together in the already destroyed major synagogue, and taken outside of town in groups to be massacred. A couple of Jews manage to flee but are murdered by Ukrainian gangs in the nearby forests. Some succeed in fleeing to the Soviet Union, where they join groups of partisans and fight with them against the Nazis and their collaborators.

After the war 40 Jews of Kovel survive. In 1959 the Jewish cemetery is razed by the Soviet authorities in order to use it as an industrial area.

The SS deports 1,200 Jews of Baranov, Poland, to the ghetto of Dembica.

A transport with 260 Jews leaves from Düsseldorf, Germany, for the Theresienstadt concentration camp in Czechoslovakia.

A transport of 1,005 Jews leaves Vienna for Theresienstadt.

From the Drancy transit camp in the German occupied zone of France, 996 Jewish men and women are deported to the Auschwitz extermination camp in Poland. Only 5 from this convoy will survive.

The deportation of the Jews of the Warsaw ghetto to the Treblinka extermination camp begins. In

July, a total of 66,000 Jews are deported to Treblinka and killed by the SS.

The SS murders 6,000 Jews in Kleck, Belorussian S.S.R.

1944 Soviet troops liberate the Majdanek concentration and extermination camp in Poland, where only a small number of Jews are still alive.

Before the arrival of the Red Army, the Nazis withdraw from Lvov, Poland (today Ukrainian S.S.R.). Some Jews have attempted to flee and are shot; the remaining prisoners are dragged along and some are killed on the way. The 33 survivors are transferred to the Plaszow camp.

As the Soviets are approaching Lublin, Poland, the SS starts to evacuate 1,200 Jews from the labor camp by marching them to Kielce, where 180 Jews are killed. The remaining Jews are sent to Auschwitz.

1985 The oldest synagogue in Copenhagen, Denmark, is bombed and dozens of people are wounded.

July 23

1919 During a pogrom, 2 Jews are massacred by units of Simon Petlyura's Ukrainian National Army in Verkhova-Bibikovo, Podolia, Ukraine. In another pogrom, 32 Jews are massacred, 50 are severely wounded or mutilated by saber cuts, and 30 Jewish women are raped in Novo-Konstantinov, Russia, by units under Volynets, allies of the Ukrainian National Army.

1942 The mass gassings in the Treblinka extermination camp in Poland begin when the first transport of Jews arrives and they are killed some hours later.

1944 A transport with 1,700 Jews leaves from Rhodes, Greece, for the Auschwitz extermination camp in Poland.

A Jew is deported from Vienna to the Theresienstadt concentration camp in Czechoslovakia.

July 24

1298 The Jewish community of Würzburg, Germany, is annihilated during the Rindfleisch Persecutions, named after the German knight who instigated them. On the same day over 130 Jews from Tauberbischofsheim, Germany, are burned in Gamburg, also victims of the Rindfleisch Persecutions.

1349 During the Black Death Persecutions, when the Christian mob starts to attack the Jewish quarter of Frankfurt on the Main, Germany, the Jews commit suicide by setting fire to their houses.

1919 Insurgents of Petlyura's Ukrainian National Army slaughter 83 Jews, severely wound or mutilate 30, and rape masses of women while carrying out a pogrom in the town of Ladygine, Podolia, Russia.

1941 In the streets of the town the SS shoots 27 Jews of Vitebsk, Belorussian S.S.R., who do not show up for work, to serve as an example to the others. Extensive executions of Jews follow.

In Liepaja, Latvian S.S.R., 3,000 Jews, most of whom were men, are brought to the lighthouse of Schkede and murdered. On the day of the German invasion 9,000 Jews are living in Liepaja.

1942 Adam Czerniakov, the chief of the Jewish Council of Warsaw, Poland, commits suicide after refusing to cooperate with the Nazis in the deportation of the Jews to the extermination camps.

During a one-week Aktion, 11,000 Jews of Zdunska Vola, Lodz province, Poland, are either murdered or deported by the SS to the Lodz ghetto or to the Chelmno extermination camp.

From the Westerbork transit camp in the Dutch province of Drenthe, 1,000 Jewish inmates are deported to the Auschwitz extermination camp in Poland.

The SS murders 3,000 Jews in the ghetto of the village of Dereczyn, Belorussian S.S.R.

After 1,000 Jews of Vienna arrive in Minsk, Belorussian S.S.R., the SS shoots them in pits near the town.

A train convoy departs with 1,000 Jewish internees of various nationalities from the Drancy transit camp in the German occupied zone of France to Auschwitz. Only 4 men will survive.

The SS murders 3,500 Jews in Dzieciol, district of Novogrodek, Belorussian S.S.R., between July 24 and August 8, 1942.

1943 The labor camp at Nova Vilejka, Poland, is liquidated and the remaining Jews are deported to Vilna, where Jewish resistance fighters start a battle. A number of the resistance fighters flee into the forest.

1944 The Majdanek concentration camp near Lublin, Poland, is liberated by the Soviets. The "Judenlager," the camp of the Jews in the Warsaw concentration camp, is evacuated.

The Nazis deport 1,500 inmates of the Sarvar internment camp, Hungary, to Auschwitz, against the will of Miklós Horthy, the Hungarian head of state.

The 1,700 members of the Jewish community of the island of Rhodes, Greece, are deported to Auschwitz, where only 161 will survive. The first mention of Jews on the island of Rhodes comes in the second century B.C.E. Their history lasts for two thousand years, until the arrival of the Nazis.

July 25

1100 Haifa, Palestine, inhabited predominantly by Jews, is conquered by the troops of the First Crusade. The majority of the Jews is massacred in spite of their courageous resistance. A few manage to escape to Acre or Caesarea.

1644 During an auto-da-fé held in Valladolid, Spain, Don Lope de Vera, a Spanish nobleman who has converted to the Jewish faith, is burned alive.

1648 More than 2,000 Jewish families of Bar, Ukraine, are wiped out after the town is captured by the Cossack hordes of Bogdan Chmielnicki.

1670 The 4,000 Jews of Vienna are expelled on the order of the Austrian emperor Leopold I. Only a small number of them agree to be baptized. The Great Synagogue is destroyed and a church dedicated to St. Margaret is erected on its ruins.

1941 For three days following the anniversary of the death of Simon Petlyura, the Ukrainian leader responsible for the deaths of thousands of Jews who was assassinated in Paris by a Jew called Schwarzbart, 2,500 Jews are murdered in Lvov, Galicia, Poland (today Ukrainian S.S.R.), in retaliation for Schwarzbart's release.

During a three-day Aktion, 600 Jews are shot by the Nazis near the water tower in the military port of Liepaja, Latvian S.S.R.

The Nazis order 700 Jewish men of Oszmiany, Poland (today Belorussian S.S.R.), to gather in the main square, from where they are taken to Bartel and murdered

1942   The SS murders 1,200 Jews in Kossov, Ukrainian S.S.R.

A transport with 200 Jews leaves from Kempten, Germany, to the Theresienstadt concentration camp in Czechoslovakia.

1,135 Jewish prisoners are deported from the Westerbork transit camp in the Dutch province of Drenthe to the Auschwitz extermination camp in Poland.

The Nazis murder 2,000 Jews of the ghetto in Kobryn, Belorussian S.S.R.

The SS murders 840 Jews in Byten, Ukrainian S.S.R.

1944   A small number of Jews are evacuated from the ghetto of Kaunas, today Lithuania, to the west.

July 26

1298   In Krautheim, Baden, Germany, 19 Jews, among them rabbi Eljakim ben Eleasar, are massacred by the German knight Rindfleisch and his followers.

1648   The Cossack hordes of Bogdan Chmielnicki massacre 600 Jews of Ostrog, Ukraine.

1939   Adolf Eichmann, the head of the Jewish division of the Gestapo, opens the Bureau for Jewish Emigration in Prague, Czechoslovakia.

Synagogue in Ostrog, Russia.

1941   After the invasion of the Hungarians, German troops take charge of Stanislavov, Poland (today Ukrainian S.S.R.), where 30,000 Jews live. Jews have been living here since the middle of the seventeenth century. There is an active Jewish community and in particular a flourishing Zionist influence.

The SS slays 250 Jews of Horodec, Poland, in Brianska Gora, Belorussian S.S.R.

A transport with 988 Jews leaves Vienna for the Theresienstadt concentration camp in Czechoslovakia. On the same day 5 Jews are deported from Bacharach, Germany, to the same destination.

The Nazis murder 1,700 Jews in Drohiczyn, Volhynia, Ukrainian S.S.R.

1943   From Dabrova Gornicza, province of Katovice, Poland, 6,000 Jews are deported to the Auschwitz extermination camp.

1944   The last 300 Jewish prisoners of the Redom labor camp, Kielce province, Poland, are deported to Auschwitz, where only a few will survive.

July 27

1298   In Berching, Bavaria, Germany, 35 Jews, among them the Jewish sages Elieser bar Yechiel and Samuel bar Isaac, are massacred in the course of the Rindfleisch Persecutions, named after their instigator, the German knight Rindfleisch. On the same day, after being tortured, more than 130 Jewish men, women, and children are slaughtered or burned in Bamberg, Germany, by Rindfleisch and his hordes. Among the victims are also Jews from France.

1941   The First Regiment of the SS Cavalry reports the execution of 6,504 Jews who had been hiding in the Pripet Marshes, in Poland (today Ukrainian S.S.R.). The search and the executions of the Jews lasted for four days.

A pogrom against the 2,300 Jews of Glinyany, province of Lvov, Poland (today Ukrainian S.S.R.), is organized by the Nazis and Ukrainians. Jews have been living here since the twelfth century, and were victims of massacres in 1624, 1638, 1657, and by the Chmielnicki Cossacks in 1648–49. After the pogrom, the Jews are offered a respite on the condition that they pay a fine of 1 million zlotys. Hundreds of Jews, who are unable to pay, are deported to the Kurwice camp.

1942   The SS murders 1,800 Jews of Dereczyn, Novogrodek district, Belorussian S.S.R.

During a two-day Aktion, 900 Jews of Ignatovka, Volhynia, Soviet Union, are murdered by the SS and the Ukrainian police.

From the ghetto of Rava Ruska, Poland (today Ukrainian S.S.R.), 2,000 Jews are deported to the Belzec extermination camp in Poland and killed.

During a two-day Aktion, 5,680 Jews of the ghetto of Olyka, Ukrainian S.S.R., are murdered by the SS.

A train convoy with 724 Jewish women and 248 Jewish men leaves the Drancy transit camp in the German occupied zone of France for the Auschwitz extermination camp in Poland. Only 12 of them will survive until the liberation of the camp by the Soviet army in 1945.

From Boppard, Germany, 10 Jews are deported to the Theresienstadt concentration camp in Czechoslovakia.

1,010 Jewish prisoners are sent from the Westerbork transit camp in the Dutch province of Drenthe to Auschwitz.

1943   The last Aktion takes place in the ghetto of Czestochova, Poland.

1944   The Nazis murder 450 Jews, originally from Riga, in the Strazdu Mujzha camp near Jugla, Latvia.

July 28

1298   In Mosbach, near Heidelberg, Germany, 55 Jews are massacred during the Rindfleisch Persecutions, named after the German knight Rindfleisch who instigated them.

1648   The Cossack hordes of Bogdan Chmielnicki slaughter 3,000 Jews, among them Rabbi Asher, one of the greatest talmudists and chairman of the Rabbinical Court of Polonnoye, in Konstantinovka, Ukraine.

1670   After the expulsion of the 4,000 Jews of Vienna, one of their synagogues is transformed into the church of St. Leopold, which still exists today. Not one Jew is left in the town and the pope is invited to celebrate the occasion. By imperial decree of Emperor Leopold I, the Jews of Lower

Austria are also expelled, beginning July 28. Jewish settlements have existed in this part of Austria since the year 1391.

1937   The concentration camp at Buchenwald, Germany, is opened.

1941   Jewish men numbering 150 from Smolewicze, Belorussian S.S.R., are shot in the village of Kurovischtscha, 2 km to the east.

All Jews of Brichany, Bessarabia, Rumania (today Moldavian S.S.R.), are conveyed across the Dniester River to the Mogilev camp, where the old Jews are selected to die and the young have to prepare a mass grave for them.

In Vilkaviskis, Lithuanian S.S.R., where 3,500 Jews live, 900 are murdered. A ghetto is erected for the remaining Jewish population. Jews have been living in Vilkaviskis since the fourteenth century.

1942   The SS murders 10,000 Jews of the ghetto of Minsk, Belorussian S.S.R. Of the total, 3,500 of them are German, Austrian, and Czech Jews.

From the Theresienstadt ghetto in Czechoslovakia 1,000 Jews are dispatched to the east. There are no survivors and it is believed that all the prisoners were murdered by the SS in the area of Minsk.

In the course of a last Aktion, 2,000 Jews of Dynov, in the district of Lvov, Poland, are liquidated by the SS.

1943   3,000 Jews who have been hiding in and around Skalat, in the province of Ternopol, Poland (today Ukrainian S.S.R.), are seized and shot by the SS, who comb the forests looking for them.

A convoy with 1,800 Jews leaves from Salonika, Greece, for the Auschwitz extermination camp in Poland.

July 29

1919   During a pogrom, 200 Jews are massacred and many mutilated in Uman, in the district of Kiev, Ukraine, by troops under the command of Sokol, Nikolsk, and Stesiura, linked to Petlyura's Ukrainian National Army.

1941   The SS shoots 400 Jews in Zhitomir, Ukrainian S.S.R.

The Nazis shoot 122 Jews of Belgrade, Yugoslavia. The "Final Solution" to the Jews of Yugoslavia has thus begun.

1942   From Dobromil, Lvov province, Poland (today Ukrainian S.S.R.), 2,600 Jews are deported to the Belzec extermination camp.

A transport with 1,001 Jewish men and women leaves from the Drancy transit camp in the German occupied zone of France for the Auschwitz extermination camp in Poland, where 216 are gassed upon their arrival. Only 5 men are still alive when the camp is liberated by the Soviet army in 1945.

The SS takes 3,000 German Jews from the ghetto of Minsk, Belorussian S.S.R., to ditches outside of town and shoots them.

July 30

1467   When a conference held in the cathedral of Toledo, Spain, between "New Christians" (who are descendants of the Jews forcibly baptized in 1391) and "Old Christians," fails, fighting breaks out between the two groups. The leaders of the New Christians, Fernando de la Torre and his brother, are seized and hanged and the mercantile center of the New Christians is burned down.

1905   Several Jews are killed and many are wounded when a bomb is thrown into the poor

Jewish quarter of Bialystok, Russia (today Poland). Later military patrols systematically fire on the Jewish houses and then search them, killing every Jew they find; 46 Jews are killed and many more are severely wounded.

1941   1,200 Jews of Czernovitz, Bukovina, Rumania (today Ukrainian S.S.R.), are arrested and 682 people are shot with the help of the Rumanian police.

The one-month death march of the Jews of Secureni to Skazinets, a small village in Bessarabia (today Ukrainian S.S.R.) begins.

In the ghetto of Wilejka, Belorussian S.S.R., 350 Jews are killed.

The SS shoots 1,000 Jews from the ghetto of Dünaburg, Latvian S.S.R., near the Dünaburg railway station.

1942   Jewish men in the police internment camp at Nis, Serbia, Yugoslavia, are shot on the nearby hill of Bubanj.

The SS deports 2,000 Jews from the ghetto of Rava Ruska, Poland (today Ukrainian S.S.R.), to the Belzec extermination camp in Poland.

From the ghetto of Javorov, Poland, 100 Jewish girls are deported to the Janovska labor camp.

During a large-scale three-day Aktion, 25,000 Jews of Minsk, Belorussian S.S.R., are massacred by the SS and units of their Belorussian collaborators.

1943   The last 500 Jews of Sassov, Poland (today Ukrainian S.S.R.), who have been interned in a forced labor camp, are shot by the SS in a nearby forest. Several dozen prisoners offer resistance.

1944   From Toulouse, France, 166 Jews are deported to the Auschwitz extermination camp in Poland.

1905   During a two-day pogrom in Kertsh, Crimea, Russia, Jewish shops and houses are looted and 1 member of the Jewish Self Defense is shot.

1919   During a two-day pogrom, in Tulczyn, Ukraine, Russia, 500 Jews are slaughtered, 36 are severely wounded and mutilated, and many Jewish girls and women are raped by units under Liachovitsch, linked to Petlyura's Ukrainian National Army.

1941   Hermann Goering charges Reinhard Heydrich with implementing the "final solution" for the Jews of Europe.

1942   Jewish inmates—numbering 1,007—from the Westerbork transit camp in the Dutch province of Drenthe and 1,049 Jewish men and women from the Pithiviers transit camp in the German occupied zone of France are deported to the Auschwitz extermination camp in Poland.

The 1,000 Jews arriving in Minsk, Belorussian S.S.R., from the Theresienstadt concentration camp in Czechoslovakia are diverted to Baranowicze, where they are crammed into vans and killed by gas.

1943   From the Drancy transit camp in the German occupied zone of France, 1,000 Jewish men and women are deported to Auschwitz, where 727 are gassed immediately. Only 28 men and 18 women will survive.

The twenty-first convoy of 1,563 Jews, among them 208 children, leaves the Mechelen transit camp in Belgium for Auschwitz. Only 40 of them will survive until the liberation of the camp in 1945.

1944   A transport with 178 Jewish inmates leaves the Westerbork transit camp for Auschwitz.

From Drancy, France, 300 Jewish orphans are deported to Auschwitz, where they are gassed.

Of a group on a death march from Warsaw to Zychlin, 20 Jews die of exhaustion in Lowicz, Poland.

1,300 Jews are deported from Drancy to Auschwitz, where 726 of them are gassed immediately. 209 men and 141 women will survive until the liberation of the camp by the Soviet army in 1945.

213 Jewish detainees from the Westerbork transit camp are sent to the Theresienstadt concentration camp in Czechoslovakia.

The twenty-sixth convoy of 563 Jews, among them 47 children, leaves the Mechelen transit camp for Auschwitz. Only 186 will survive until the liberation of the camp a few months later.

Menorah discovered at the entrance to a tomb at Wadi al-Nahal.

AUGUST

August 1

1298 The Jewish community of Meiningen, Thuringia, Germany, is annihilated during the Rindfleisch Persecutions, named after their instigator, the German knight Rindfleisch. Among the victims are the scribe Isaac ben Samuel, his wife Goldlin, and their five children. In the Jewish community of Nuremberg, Germany, the Jews are slaughtered after taking refuge in the town's castle during the same Rindfleisch Persecutions. Among the victims there are Mordochai ben Hillel, author of a highly esteemed rabbinical commentary, and his wife and five children.

1941 The district of East Galicia is incorporated into the General Government of Poland, thus adopting its anti-Jewish laws. The Jewish population is represented by a "Judenrat," Jewish Council.

The Nazis arrest 411 persons in Kishinev, Bessarabia, Rumania (today Moldavian S.S.R.), and shoot them outside of town; 39 of them are only wounded and are brought back to the ghetto.

After the June 23 occupation by the Germans, 6,000 Jews are crowded together in the ghetto of Siemiatycze, Poland. Among them there are 2,000 Jews who have fled from the western parts of Poland and Jews of other smaller towns such as Drohiczyn and Mielnik. Many famous Jewish scholars originated in Siemiatycze. A pogrom against the Jews of Siemiatycze took place in 1905 after Russia lost the war against Japan. A second pogrom was carried out at the end of World War I.

The surviving Jews of Khotin, Bessarabia (today Ukrainian S.S.R.), are shot in Barnova, a village east of the town, after Rumanian soldiers force them to dig their own mass grave.

The SS and their Rumanian allies murder 682 Jews and loot Jewish houses during the systematic annihilation of the Jewish population of Czernovitz Bukovina (today Ukrainian S.S.R.).

1942 1,800 Jews are deported from Vasilishak, Vilna district, Poland (today Belorussian S.S.R.), to Szczuczyn.

All Jewish men between the ages of 14 and 35 are deported by the SS from Rymanov, in the province of Rzeszow, Poland, to the Plaszow labor camp, where many of them are killed.

About 1,000 Jews from Cracow and Lancut, in the province of Rzeszow, Poland, are deported to

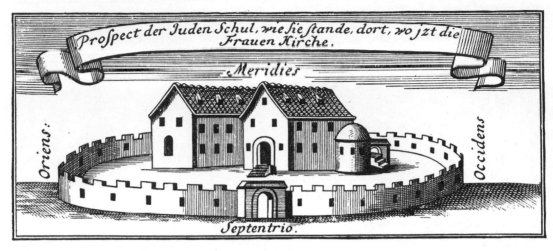

The Nuremberg synagogue, from a German engraving of 1775.

the Falkinia transit camp. The elderly and the children are shot by the SS along the way in the Nechczioli forest while the remaining Jews are sent on.

In a second deportation, 5,000 Jews of Bedzin, Silesia, Poland, are deported to the Auschwitz extermination camp.

1943   On the anniversary of the second deportation of the Jews of Bedzin, Silesia, Poland, begins the liquidation of the Jews from the ghetto in Kamionka, a suburb of Bedzin. This Aktion takes two weeks due to Jewish resistance. The resistance movement of Bedzin started in 1940 and has contacts with the Warsaw ghetto.

The Gestapo shoots 600 Jews during a deportation from the Srodula ghetto in Sosnoviec, Poland.

1944   The Nazis murder 6 Jews and Pardo-Roques, the Catholic philanthropist who has hidden them, in Pisa, Italy.

Several hundred Jews, who earlier marched on foot from the Lublin labor camp to Kielce, Poland, are deported from Kielce to Auschwitz. Upon arrival 200 of them are gassed by the SS.

August 2

1391   In Palma de Mallorca, Balearic Islands, Spain, 300 Jews are massacred, among them their rabbi, En-Vidal Ephraim Gerundi, when a crowd storms the Jewish quarter and the Christian houses where many Jews are hiding. However, 800 Jews find refuge in the castle of Palma and escape on ships to North Africa.

1818   An anti-Jewish riot breaks out in Würzburg, Germany, killing and wounding many Jews. Anti-Semitic students participate, shouting "Hep! Hep!" (acronym for "Hierosolyma perdita est"*), and Christian merchants plunder Jewish shops and attack their owners. The army intervenes in behalf of the Jews but later the 400 Jewish inhabitants are expelled.

Latin for "Jerusalem is lost."

1919 During a two-day pogrom, 11 Jews are slaughtered and 2 Jewish women are repeatedly raped by units under their leader Zeleny, ally of Simon Petlyura and the Ukrainian National Army, in Justingrad-Sokolovka, Kiev district, Ukraine. During a pogrom in nearby Jashkov, 4 Jews are massacred by soldiers under Zelenovtsy, another ally of the Ukrainian National Army.

1940 The Gross-Rosen concentration camp, near Breslau, Silesia, Poland, is established.

1941 Hungary expells the stateless Jews in Carpathian Ruthenia (today Transcarpathian province, Ukrainian S.S.R.).

A fine of 100,000 rubles is imposed on the Jews of Brazlav, Podolia, Ukrainian S.S.R., who have already been deprived of all their property by the Nazis. The Nazis take a great number of Jewish hostages in order to press their demand.

The SS murders 600 Jews in Targovica, Volhynia, Ukrainian S.S.R.

1942 The last Aktion against the 2,500 Jews of Lavoczne, district Stanislavov, Poland (today Ukrainian S.S.R.), is carried out by the SS and the Ukrainian police.

The Nazis arrest 245 Catholic-baptized Jews and send them to the Westerbork transit camp in the Dutch province of Drenthe in response to a message from the Episcopate, indignant of the deportation of Dutch Jews, which has been read in Catholic and Protestant churches.

1943 There is a revolt of Jewish inmates in the Treblinka extermination camp in Poland and about a dozen SS men are killed. Several hundred prisoners manage to flee, but only a very few will survive.

In Salonika, Greece, 367 Jews of Spanish nationality, including Salmon Ezratti, the Spanish vice-consul, are deported. Some are sent to the Auschwitz extermination camp in Poland, some to the Bergen-Belsen concentration camp, from where they will return to Spain six months later after the Spanish government intervenes.

1944 A transport of 222 Jews leaves Verona, Italy, for Auschwitz.

August 3

1492 According to the edict signed on March 31 by the Spanish sovereigns Ferdinand and Isabella, all Jews are to have left Spain by this date. Every non-baptized Jew found in Spain thereafter is subject to death.

1603 During an auto-da-fé in Lisbon, Portugal, Thamar Barrocas, Antonio de Aguilar, Isabella de Valle, and her brother Pedro Serrao are burned at the stake, the last being garroted. Diogo da Assumcao, a Franciscan monk who has converted to Judaism, is also killed.

1648 The Cossack hordes of Bogdan Chmielnicki slaughter 200 Jews of Alik, Ukraine.

1941 The Ukrainians shoot 45 Jews in the village of Otynia, Stanislavov province, Poland (today Ukrainian S.S.R.).

1942 During a four-day Aktion, 12,500 Jews are deported from the ghetto of Przemysl, in the Rzeszow province in Poland, to the Belzec extermination camp, where they are murdered by the SS.

A train convoy with 1,034 Jewish men and women is deported from the Pithiviers transit camp in the

Las pragmaticas del reyno.

TANTO MOTA

✠Recopilació de algũas bu-

las de nueſtro muy ſancto padre: concedidas en fauor dela jurifdicion real: cõ todas las Pragmaticas: τ al gunas leyes: fechas para la buena gouernació del rey no: con algunas otras añadidas que faſta aqui no fue ron impreſſas con las dichas Pragmaticas antiguas: ǧ ſon muy prouechoſas: las quales quié preſto querra hallar: vaya ala tabla alphabetica: nueuaméte aſſimiſ mo añadida: võdc las fallara con eſta ſañal ✠ al prin cipiõpueſta.

Frontispiece of the decree expelling the Jews from Spain.

German occupied zone of France to the Auschwitz extermination camp in Poland, where 482 of them are immediately sent to the gas chambers. Only 7 will survive until the liberation of the camp by the Soviet army in 1945.

From the Westerbork transit camp in the Dutch province of Drenthe, 1,013 Jewish inmates are deported to Auschwitz.

The Jews of Dolina, Galicia, Poland, are deported during a three-day Aktion to Belzec, where they are murdered by the SS.

1943   Members of the Jewish resistance movement in Bedzin, Silesia, Poland, oppose the deportation to Auschwitz by taking up arms and fighting. Many of them are killed and others manage to flee to the forests. Only 150 of the 25,000 Jews of Bedzin will survive.

During a three-day Aktion, 4,000 Jews from Dabrova Gornicza, Katovice province, Poland, are deported to Auschwitz.

1944   Originally from the Riga ghetto, 1,000 Jewish inmates of the Strazdu Mujzha camp near Jugla, Latvia, are shot in the nearby woods by the SS.

The Ostroviec labor camp in Kielce, Poland, is liquidated and 2,000 inmates are deported to Auschwitz. Only a small number of young people manage to save themselves by joining the partisans. They have been in touch with the Jewish resistance movement in the Warsaw ghetto for a year.

From the ghetto of Riga, Latvian S.S.R., 5,000 Jews are deported by ship to the Stutthof concentration camp in Germany.

August 4

1904   In Ostroviec, Kielce, Poland, 22 Jews are wounded, 1 adult and a 2-year-old child are killed, and Jewish shops are broken into during anti-Semitic riots by the workers of the local factory.

1919   During a pogrom, 200 Jews are slaughtered in Golovanevsk, Russia, by units linked to the Ukrainian National Army under the command of Sokolovski.

1941   From Ostrog, Poland (today Ukrainian S.S.R.), 3,000 Jews are arrested and shot in the nearby forests.

One month after the German invasion of Pinsk, Poland (today Belorussian S.S.R.), where 20,000 Jews live, 8,000 Jews are led to prepared graves and murdered. Some people survive and manage to free themselves from the piles of corpses and flee. Jews have been living in Pinsk since the fifteenth century.

1942 From the ghetto of Theresienstadt, Czechoslovakia, 1,000 Jewish men, women, and children are dispatched toward the east. Shortly after the Minsk station the train stops, the carriages are opened by armed SS men and 40 prisoners are chosen to unload the luggage. The 960 people who have to board waiting trucks are killed by the exhaust. Of the 40 selected prisoners, 25 are shot after having unloaded the luggage. The remaining 15 Jews are sent to the Maly Trostinec labor camp; 2 of them will survive.

750 Jews of Pruchnik, Lvov district, Poland (today Ukrainian S.S.R.), are murdered by the SS and the Ukrainian police in the nearby forest.

The first convoy of 998 Jews—among them 140 youngsters under 16—leaves the Mechelen transit camp in Belgium for the Auschwitz extermination camp in Poland. Only 7 deportees in this transport will survive until the liberation of the camp in 1945.

The SS murders 2,750 Jews of Lancut, Poland, in the Falkinia forest.

In the course of the first Aktion, 4,000 Jews are singled out in the ghetto of Sambor, Poland (today Ukrainian S.S.R.), and sent to the Belzec extermination camp.

1943 The deportation of Jews from Sosnovitz-Bendzin, Poland, to Auschwitz takes place.

1944 After they have worked cleaning up rubble in Warsaw, Poland, 3,000 Jewish prisoners from Auschwitz are sent on a death march from Zychlin to the Dachau concentration camp in Germany. About 1,000 of them perish on the way.

Anne Frank, a Jewish girl of 15, is arrested with her parents and her sister. They were hidden in the loft of a house in Amsterdam, Netherlands. On September 2 they are deported to Auschwitz. In December, Anne is sent to Bergen-Belsen concentration camp, where she will die in March 1945.

Anne Frank's diary is a symbol of the tragedy of all those millions of children who lost their lives during the Nazi terror.

August 5

1243 In the Bavarian town of Kitzingen, Germany, several Jewish men and women are tried and tortured, presumably on the charge of using human blood for their feast of Passover. They are executed and their corpses broken on the wheel, where they are left for fourteen days before being allowed to be buried.

1391 Many Jews are massacred, among them a number of prominent members of the community, and almost all the synagogues are set on fire and destroyed during an outbreak of anti-Jewish riots in Toledo, Spain. In Barcelona, Spain, 250 Jews are slaughtered on the first day of similar anti-Jewish riots. The greater part of the Jewish community finds shelter in the governor's castle, but when the mob attacks, some of them commit suicide and others die in battle.

1904 The police wound 20 Jews in Parczev, Poland, when they try to hide a Jewish woman who had been kidnapped and baptized by force.

1934 During a pogrom, 24 Jews are killed, 60 are wounded, 4 buildings are destroyed, and 300 Jewish shops are looted in the Algerian town of

Constantine. The police finally intervene on behalf of the Jews.

1942 During a two-day Aktion, 1,500 Jews from Stavy Sambor, Galicia, Poland, are deported to the Belzec extermination camp, where they are murdered by the SS.

Crammed into train cars, 1,014 Jewish men and women are deported from the transit camp of Beaune-la-Rolande, in occupied France, to the Auschwitz extermination camp in Poland, where 704 of them are immediately gassed. Only 5 men and 1 woman will survive until the liberation of the camp by the Russian army in 1945.

The smaller ghetto of Radom in the province of Kielce, Poland, is liquidated, and in two weeks 30,000 Jews are deported to the Treblinka extermination camp.

1944 "Political" prisoners and 3,521 other Jews are interned in the camp in Sarvar, Hungary, until on August 5 they are deported in freight cars to Auschwitz, under the supervision of an SS captain and 40 SS men.

August 6

1264 In Arnstadt, Thuringia, Germany, 5 Jews are massacred and are mentioned by name in the list of martyrs of the town: Joseph and Kasher, sons of Yechiel ben Chakin; David ha-Cohen from Mainz; Eliezer, the young son of Simon the French; and the learned Shabbetai, son of Samuel.

1919 Units under the command of Mordalevitch massacre 15 Jews during a pogrom in Kornin, Kiev, Ukraine.

1941 Thousands of Jews are shot by the SS in Pinsk, Poland (today Belorussian S.S.R.).

Extermination commandos murder 200 Jews in Orheiu, Bessarabia, Ukrainian S.S.R.

1942 The whole Jewish population of Zdzieciol, a village near Grodno, Soviet Union, numbering 4,500 people, are murdered by the SS.

During a two-day Aktion by the SS, 2,000 Jews of Drohobycz, Poland (today Ukrainian S.S.R.), are deported to the Belzec extermination camp and murdered.

1943 Several dozen armed Jews of Ternopol, Poland (today Ukrainian S.S.R.), are intercepted by the SS. Many die fighting and the rest flee into the forests where they join the partisans.

From the ghetto of Vilna, Lithuanian S.S.R., 1,000 Jews are deported to the Klooga concentration camp in Estonia. During the deportation, fighting breaks out with the Jewish resistance.

1944 The large-scale deportation of the Jews of Lodz, Poland, to the Auschwitz extermination camp begins. The deportations last until the end of the month when 70,000 Jews have been sent to Auschwitz.

The Kaiserwald concentration camp near Riga, Latvian S.S.R., is evacuated; 27,000 Jews from camps east of the Vistula are being sent to Germany.

August 7

1391 The remaining 200 Jews of Barcelona, Spain, who have taken refuge in the "New Castle" in the Jewish quarter, are massacred after the castle is besieged by dockworkers and fishermen.

1941 The Nazis arrest, then murder 2,500 Jews in Utena, Lithuanian S.S.R., outside of town.

Jews have been living in Utena since the sixteenth century.

In the ghetto of Slobodka, near Kaunas, Lithuanian S.S.R., 1,200 Jewish men are arrested and 1,000 of them are then shot.

The SS shoots 5,000 to 6,000 Jews from the ghetto of Dünaburg, Latvian S.S.R., in the nearby village of Poguljanka.

On the pretext of their being Communists, 551 Jews from the ghetto in Kishinev, Rumania (today Moldavian S.S.R.), are shot by Task Force 2 A in a mass execution. The German army with their Rumanian allies occupied Kishinev in July 1941.

1942 The SS murders 1,500 Jews in Lubcz, Novogrodek district, Poland (today Belorussian S.S.R.).

The SS murders 6,000 Jews during the second Aktion in Novogrodek, Grodno district, Poland (today Belorussian S.S.R.). The few survivors are sent to Peresieka to do construction work.

From the Pithiviers transit camp in the German occupied zone of France 1,069 Jews are deported to the Auschwitz extermination camp in Poland. Immediately after their arrival, 794 are gassed. Only 8 will survive until the liberation of the camp by the Soviet army in 1945.

987 Jewish inmates are sent from the Westerbork transit camp in the Dutch province of Drenthe to Auschwitz.

1943 The last transport of Jews leaves Polizei-haftlager (police detention camp) in Hirsch, a quarter in Salonika, Macedonia, Greece, for Auschwitz. The quarter is named for Baron Hirsch, a French philanthropist of the nineteenth century.

August 8

1655 Cossacks and Muscovite troops occupy the town of Vilna, Poland (today Lithuanian S.S.R.), and massacre the Jews who have not fled, as well as many Christian inhabitants. The Jewish quarter is then set on fire, which spreads and destroys the whole town.

1941 330 Jews are killed in the courtyard of the prison in Czortkov, Poland (today Ukrainian S.S.R.).

The Rumanian rural police take 500 Jewish men and 25 Jewish women out of the ghetto of Kishinev, Bessarabia, Rumania (today Moldavian S.S.R.), to perform forced labor.

The Nazis demand 6 kg gold and 12 kg silver from the Jews of Kobryn, Belorussian S.S.R., and make arrangements for the establishment of a ghetto.

About 2,000 Jews are shot by the SS in the prison of Dünaburg, Latvian S.S.R.

112 young Jews of Korzec, Rovno province, Poland (today Ukrainian S.S.R.), are arrested and murdered by the SS outside of town.

1942 After the registration of all members of the Jewish intelligentsia in Krzemieniec, Volhynia, Poland (today Ukrainian S.S.R.), all are shot by the Gestapo and the Ukrainian police.

Hundreds of Jews of Szczebrzeszyn, Lublin province, Poland, are taken to the Belzec extermination camp and killed by the SS.

From the ghetto in Rzeszow, Poland, 1,000 Jewish women and children are brought to Falkinia camp, where they are murdered by the SS.

August 9

1919   During a pogrom, 15 Jews are slain, many severely wounded, and many Jewish women are raped by bands of insurgents under the leadership of the hetman Tiutiunnik, an ally of the Ukrainian National Army, in Talno, Ukraine.

1940   Rumania expels the Jews from the areas it has ceded.

1942   The Nazis deport 1,000 Jews from the ghetto of Tarnogrod, Poland, and 500 Jews of Bilgoraj, Poland, to the Belzec extermination camp, where they are murdered by the SS.

The Nazis deport 1,300 Jews from Karelic, in the district of Novogrodek (today Belorussian S.S.R.), to the Novogrodek camp.

The SS kills 500 Jews in Radun, Novogrodek district, Belorussian S.S.R.

200 young Jews escape the ghetto of Mir, Poland (today Belorussian S.S.R.), and set out for the forests, in order to fight the Nazis as partisans.

1943   The SS murders 8,000 Jews in Krzemieniec, Ukrainian S.S.R., in the course of two days. A number of them manage to flee into the forests.

1944   Leon Kubowitzki, general secretary of the World Jewish Congress, and the Polish government in exile in London ask John J. McCloy, the assistant secretary of war (and after the war high commissioner of Germany) to bomb the railways to Auschwitz.

August 10

1348   During the Black Death Persecutions, the Jews in Savoy, France (probably in Chambéry, where there is still a "Lac des Juifs," a Lake of the Jews), are accused of poisoning wells in order to annihilate the Christians. They are burned at the stake.

1391   The Jews of Gerona, Spain, are massacred by Castilian marauders with the aid of the local population.

1919   During a pogrom, 25 Jews are massacred in Zmerinka, Podolia, Ukraine, carried out by Petlyura's Ukrainian National Army and allied insurgents. 8 Jews are killed and 50 are hanged on special order of Colonel Kovemko, when units of the Ukrainian National Army under his command carry out a pogrom in Vinnitsa, Podolia, Ukraine.

1942   A train convoy with 1,006 Jewish men and women, interned in the Drancy camp in occupied France, is sent to the Auschwitz extermination camp in Poland, where 766 of them are immediately gassed. Only one man survives until the liberation of the camp by the Soviet army in 1945. Another convoy of 559 prisoners, among them 92 Catholic-baptized Jews, including the German philosopher Edith Stein, who was living in a Dutch convent, is sent to Auschwitz from the Westerbork transit camp in the province of Drenthe.

Several hundred Jews are murdered by the SS each day of a two-week Aktion in the ghetto in Krzemieniec, Volhynia, Poland (today Ukrainian S.S.R.). They are driven to a spot near the train station, where they are shot in freshly dug trenches that are to become their graves. The ghetto is then set on fire in order to force out and kill the last hidden Jews.

From the Jewish quarter of Lvov, Poland (today Ukrainian S.S.R.), 40,000 Jews are deported to the Belzec extermination camp and killed by the SS during an intensive two-week Aktion that lasts until August 23. In particular, Jews who are not strong enough to work are deported. Jewish workers are taken away from their jobs only when the number of victims is not enough to fill the trains.

The SS kills 2,400 Jews during a massacre in Kamien Koszyrski, in the province of Volhynia, Ukrainian S.S.R. The Jews actively defend themselves and the Jewish resistance manages to help a few hundred to escape into the forests.

The Nazis deport 1,000 Jews from the ghetto of Zolkievka, Poland, to the Sobibor extermination camp, where they perish.

The deportation of the 40,000 Jews of Lodz, Poland, to Auschwitz begins. It will take two weeks.

1943   From Wadovice, Cracow district, Poland, 2,000 Jews are deported to Auschwitz.

1944   A Jew is shot by the police in Jedlina, a village in the district of Pszcyna, Poland.

August 11

1941   From Czortkov, Poland (today Ukrainian S.S.R.), 100 Jews are brought to the Czarny Las woods and killed.

1942   The SS murders 3,500 Jews in Zelov, province of Lodz, Poland, between now and September 30.

In Lututov, district of Wielun, Poland, 14 Jews are shot by the Gestapo and the police.

The deportations of the Jews from the ghetto of Jaslo, Poland, to the Belzec extermination camp begin. The Jewish community numbers approximately 4,000 at the time of the occupation. Jews first settled in Jaslo in the fifteenth century.

The second convoy of 999 Jews leaves the Mechelen transit camp in Belgium; among the deportees are 147 youngsters under 16. Only 3 people from this transport will survive until the liberation of the camp in 1945.

1944   A deportation convoy ordered by Klaus Barbie, head of the Gestapo in Lyons, France, leaves the city for Auschwitz extermination camp in Poland with 650 people. Among them there are 308 Jews, of whom 128 are gassed upon arrival. The other deportees are members of the resistance. Only 32 men and 16 women will survive until the liberation of the camp by the Soviet army in 1945.

1945   Several Jews are killed during a postwar pogrom in Cracow, Poland, against the few Jewish survivors of the Nazi genocide. It is instigated and carried out by Poles belonging to reactionary Polish organizations.

August 12

1391   In Burgos, Spain, 78 Jews are massacred when anti-Jewish excesses break out.

1940   The Nazis arrest 300 Jews of Szczebrzeszyn, Poland, and intern them in a labor camp. Jews have been living in Szczebrzeszyn since the sixteenth century. At the outbreak of the war there are 3,000 Jews living there.

1941   The Nazis establish a ghetto in Lomza, a town in northeast Poland. At the start of World War II, 11,000 Jews are living in Lomza.

1942   The SS murders 27 Jews in Praszka, district of Wielun, Poland.

The SS murders 800 Jews in Korczyn, district of Lvov, Poland.

A deportation convoy of 1,007 Jewish men and women departs from the transit camp of Drancy, in the German occupied zone of France, for the Auschwitz extermination camp in Poland. Immediately, 705 are sent to the gas chambers. Only 10 survive until the liberation of the camp by the Soviet army in 1945.

The SS murders 250 Jews in Polanka, Novogrodek, Belorussian S.S.R.

Immediately after arrival in Auschwitz, 550 Jews are gassed. They had been sent from Dabrova Gornicza, Katovice province, Poland, to Auschwitz.

The SS murders 450 Jews in Jodlova, province of Cracow, Poland.

In the course of three days, 2,500 Jews from Oliki, Soviet Union, are murdered by the SS and Ukrainian police.

During a 6-day Aktion, 8,000 Jews are deported to Auschwitz from Sosnoviec, suburb of Srodula, Katovice province, Poland.

120 Jews of Sarajevo, the capital of Bosnia and Herzegovina in central Yugoslavia, originally considered useful, are sent to Auschwitz. Only 4 of Sarajevo's 9,000 Jews deported to concentration camps will survive.

1,250 Jews are murdered within a few hours after being deported by the SS from Bobrka (today Ukrainian S.S.R.) to the Belzec extermination camp. 200 Jews are shot immediately.

August 13

1942 The SS murders 2,000 Jews in Lanovitz, Volhynia, Soviet Union.

For the first time, the Swiss police hand over Jewish refugees who had entered Switzerland.

The few remaining members of the Jewish community of Rymanov, in the district of Rzeszow, Poland, are sent to the Belzec extermination camp and killed by the SS; thus Rymanov is "free of Jews." Jews had been living in Rymanov since the beginning of the fifteenth century.

A convoy of 997 Jews leaves Vienna, Austria, for the Theresienstadt concentration camp in Czechoslovakia.

About 2,000 Jews are deported from the ghetto of Grodek Jagiellonski, in the province of Lvov, Poland (today Ukrainian S.S.R.), to Belzec.

After a night raid in the ghetto of Gorlice in southeastern Poland, 700 Jews are murdered by SS and Ukrainian police after being brought to the village of Garbic. Some manage to escape into the forests.

August 14

1919 140 Jews are slaughtered during a pogrom in Belaya-Tserkov, Ukraine, by units of Simon Petlyura's Ukrainian National Army under the leadership of Sokol and Sokolovski.

1941 Following a night raid on the ghetto of Minsk, Belorussian S.S.R., several thousand Jews are killed after being told they were going to a labor camp.

The entire 3,000-member Jewish population of Lisko, Poland, is deported by the Nazis to Zaslaw and killed along with the Jews of that town.

The last Jews of Banat, Yugoslavia, are arrested. These 2,500 men, women, and children are then brought to Belgrade, where all the men over the age of 14 are incarcerated in the Topovske Supe prison.

1942 The SS murders 7 Jews with hydrocyanic acid at the Chanska train station, in the district of Majkop, Ukrainian S.S.R.

The SS kills 405 Jews after being deported from the village of Sakod, Poland, to the Chelmno extermination camp. Another 1,400 Jews are killed by the SS at Chelmno after being deported from the ghetto of Sieradz, Poland.

The SS murders 1,000 Jews in Lenino, a village in the Ukrainian S.S.R.

A transport of 991 Jewish men and women leaves the Drancy internment camp in German-occupied France, for the Auschwitz extermination camp, Poland, where 875 are gassed immediately. Only 1 man from the entire convoy will survive.

The Jewish ghetto of Gorlice, Poland, is established after the outbreak of the German-Soviet war in June 1941. On August 14, the ghetto is surrounded by German and Ukrainian units and 700 old and infirm people are selected and shot.

From the Westerbork transit camp in the Dutch province of Drenthe, 505 Jewish prisoners are deported to Auschwitz.

In the second large-scale deportation, 70,000 Jews are deported from the Warsaw ghetto to the Treblinka extermination camp, where they are murdered by the SS.

1943 The SS shoots 360 Jews in Borszczov, East Galicia, Poland (today Ukrainian S.S.R.).

August 15

1940 Adolf Eichmann presents the "Madagascar Plan" to his superior Reinhard Heydrich in Berlin. The plan is to obtain the island of Madagascar in the peace treaty with France and deport all Jews there.

1942 The SS murders 1,500 Jews in Torysk, Volhynia, Ukrainian S.S.R.

The SS murders 2,350 Jews of Mir, district of Novogrodek, Poland (today Belorussian S.S.R.). Some of them offer resistance and 150 of them manage to flee.

The SS kills 3,500 Jews after being deported from the ghetto of Gostynin, Poland, to the Chelmno extermination camp.

A transport with 1,000 Jews, among them 700 children, leaves from the Tenje camp, near Esseg, Hungary, for the Auschwitz extermination camp in Poland.

The Nazis liquidate the ghetto of Lask, in the province of Lodz, Poland. They take 3,500 Jews to a church outside of town where they have to spend several days under terrible conditions; 800 skilled workers are then taken to the ghetto of Lodz and the remaining 2,700 Jews are deported to Chelmno.

The third convoy of 1,000 Jews—among them 172 children under the age of 16—leaves the Mechelen transit camp in Belgium for Auschwitz. Only 3 members of this convoy will survive until the liberation of the camp in 1945.

August 16

1919 During a major pogrom, 105 Jews are brutally slain, 20 are severely wounded, and 10 Jewish women are raped in Lipovets, Podolia, Russia, by the 8th Ukrainian division.

During a three-day pogrom, 166 Jews are massacred and 10 Jewish women are raped in Pestchanka, Podolia, by soldiers of the 1st regiment of the Blue Division, a unit of Petlyura's Ukrainian National Army.

1942 The Nazis and Ukrainian volunteers murder 2,000 Jews in Pohost, Volhynia, Ukrainian S.S.R.

1943 All Jewish inhabitants of the ghetto of Sosnoviec, Poland, with the exception of 1,000 people, are deported to the Auschwitz extermination camp.

A revolt by Jewish prisoners of the Krychov labor camp in Poland is brutally suppressed by the SS.

A large-scale Aktion is carried out in Bialystok, Poland, under the personal supervision of the leader of the SS and the Lublin police, Odilo Globocnik. A Jewish resistance movement takes shape immediately after the planned Aktion becomes known among the Jewish population. They manage to smuggle many Jews out of the town, and the resistance fighters, hiding in the forest, launch several attacks on the Germans. The Jewish resistance takes up position in bunkers and do battle with the Nazis, until all the Jewish fighters are killed. After the battle the Nazis deport 40,000 Jewish men and women to the Treblinka and Majdanek extermination camps. Bialystok is thus "free of Jews."

The Jewish resistance fighters remaining in the forests continue their warfare against the Nazis and most of them are killed. Only about 950 Jews from Bialystok survive the Nazi regime, as partisans or fugitives in the forests, under false names hidden by Polish friends, or as survivors of one of the numerous concentration camps.

1944 A convoy with 16 Jews leaves Vienna for the Theresienstadt concentration camp in Czechoslovakia.

August 17

1298 During the Rindfleisch Persecutions, named after the German knight from Roettingen, Germany, who leads this series of massacres, his followers reach the village of Kleingarlach near Heilbronn. The Jewish community, numbering at least 140 members, among them one French family, is annihilated.

1915 Leo Max Frank, a Jewish engineer from Atlanta, Georgia, is accused of killing a thirteen-year-old girl and is arrested despite the lack of evidence. As the trial proceeds, the anti-Semitism of the local population and of the jury becomes obvious. The newpapers launch an anti-Semitic campaign and in this atmosphere Frank is convicted and sentenced to death. Governor Slanton commutes the sentence to life imprisonment. On August 17, an armed mob abducts Frank from prison and, chanting anti-Semitic slogans, lynches him. Other Jews are also attacked and many flee the state. In March 1986, Frank will be posthumously exonerated.

1917 When the Russians invade Kalusz, in East Galicia, incredible atrocities against the Jews, Poles, and Ruthenians take place. Little girls are stripped, raped, and quartered. Machine guns are set up in the street and everything that moves is shot.

1919 During a pogrom 9 Jews are massacred by units of the Ukrainian National Army under its high commander Simon Petlyura in Janov, Podolia, Russia. During a pogrom in Brazlav, Podolia, carried out by units under Tiutiunnik, an ally of the Ukrainian National Army, 7 Jews are slaughtered, 100 are injured, and almost every Jewish woman and girl is raped.

1941 The Nazis shoot 80 Jews in the village of Kurovischtscha, near Smolewicze, Belorussian S.S.R.

1942 A transport with 997 Jews, mainly from Poland, leaves from Paris for the Auschwitz extermination camp in Poland and are gassed. Among them are 27 children under the age of 4.

The Schutzpolizei (special police) arrest 700 Jews of Stary Sacz, Poland, and deport them to the Belzec extermination camp. Also deported to Belzec are 600 Jews of Biecz, Poland.

A convoy of 1,000 Jewish men and women are deported from the Drancy transit camp in the German occupied zone of France to Auschwitz, where 878 of them are gassed immediately. Only 3 men live to see the liberation of the camp by the Soviet army in 1945.

During a two-day Aktion, 2,400 Jews are killed by the SS after being sent from Drohobycz, Poland (today Ukrainian S.S.R.) to Belzec.

From the Westerbork transit camp in the Dutch province of Drenthe, 506 Jewish inmates are deported to Auschwitz.

During the eleven day liquidation of the larger ghetto of Radom, in the province of Kielce, Poland, 16,000 Jews are sent to the Treblinka extermination camp. The remaining 4,000 Jews are retained in a part of the ghetto which is transformed into a labor camp.

A convoy with 1,003 Jews leaves Vienna for Minsk, Belorussian S.S.R.

The SS shoots 1,700 Jews in Lomazy, Poland, during a two-day Aktion.

1944   The last transport of 51 Jews leaves Drancy for the Buchenwald concentration camp in Germany. Only 35 men and 4 women survive until 1945 when the camp is liberated by the U.S. Army.

The last convoy of Jews, half-Jews, and Jewish partners of mixed marriages leaves Drancy for Auschwitz.

August 18

1917   The Jewish quarter of Salonika, Greece, is burned down. Thousands of Jewish families are left homeless and have to camp in tents.

1919   During a pogrom, 40 Jews are massacred and many women are raped in Trysolie, Ukrainian S.S.R., by insurgents under their hetmen Zeleny and Sokolov, allies of Petlyura's Ukrainian National Army.

1941   In the course of an Aktion lasting two days, 5,000 Jews from the ghetto of Dünaburg, Latvian S.S.R., are shot in nearby Zolotaja Gorka.

The Ukrainian police take 2,000 Jews out of the ghetto of Kolomyja on the Prut River in the Ukraine, and, intending to shoot them, drive them to a forest nearby. But the Hungarian commander in chief prevents the execution.
Kolomyja has been occupied by Hungarian troops, allies of the Germans, since July 4, 1941. In September 1941, the Hungarians are forced to withdraw from the town and hand it over to the Germans, leaving the 15,000 Jews living there unprotected. The vital Jewish community of Kolomyja dates back to the seventeenth century. It suffered greatly during the massacres by Chmielnicki's Cossacks; on September 17, 1939, all cultural and religious life is halted when, after the partition of Poland, the town becomes part of the Soviet Union.

In a selection, 3,000 Jews from the ghetto of Kaunas, Lithuanian S.S.R., are taken to the so-called 9th Fortress, where they are massacred.

1942   The SS murders 1,200 Jews in Kurzanhradek and 3,000 Jews in Luniniec, both in Polesia, Soviet Union.

The Nazis send 1,500 Jews of Przystak, Poland, and 1,100 Jews of the village of Garbatka, Poland, to the Belzec extermination camp. The SS murders 200 on the spot.

The Nazis establish a ghetto in the suburb of Sosnoviec in Srodula, Katovice province, Poland.

From the Tenje camp, near the town of Esseg, Hungary, 1,300 Jews are deported to the Jasenovac extermination camp and killed. Only 10 Jews survive the Jasenovac camp.

The fourth convoy of 999 Jews—among them 287 children—leaves the Mechelen transit camp in Belgium for the Auschwitz extermination camp in Poland. They will all be murdered there.

1943   The police shoot a Jewish woman in Poreba, district of Zawiercie, Poland.

The last convoy of Jews from the Hirsch transit camp in the Hirsch district of Salonika, Greece, arrives at Auschwitz.

1944   Adolf Eichmann has three representatives of the Jewish Council of Budapest, Hungary, arrested.

August 19

1287   Two young Jews, Eleasar and Mose ha-Levi, are massacred in Braubach on the Rhine, Germany, following the alleged ritual murder of a Christian child in the nearby town of Oberwesel.

1338   The Jewish community of Wolfsberg, Carinthia, Austria, is accused of host desecration and in the aftermath more than 70 Jewish men, women, and children are massacred.

1919   One Jew is killed and 5 are injured during a three-day pogrom in Jivatov, district of Kiev, Ukrainian S.S.R., by units under the command of Zelenovtsy, an ally of Petlyura's Ukrainian National Army.

1941   In the area of Szumowa, the Nazis murder 1,500 Jews from Zambrov, a town in the province of Bialystok, Poland.

1942   During the large-scale extermination campaign against the Jews of Otvock in Warsaw province, Poland, 7,000 Jews are deported to the Treblinka extermination camp. The Jews in Otvock put up fierce resistance and 2,000 Jews are shot by the SS on the spot, but 700 Jews manage to escape into the forest.

A train convoy with 1,000 Jewish men and women are deported from the Drancy transit camp, in the German occupied zone of France, to the Auschwitz extermination camp in Poland, where 817 men and women are gassed immediately. Only 5 will survive until the liberation of the camp by the Soviet army in 1945.

The Nazis deport 2,400 Jews from the ghetto of Grodek, province of Galicia, Poland (today Ukrainian S.S.R.), to the Belzec extermination camp in Poland. About 50 Jews are shot and the wounded are buried alive by the SS.

Over three days, 17,000 Jews from Lutsk and the surrounding area in Poland (today Ukrainian S.S.R.), who are living in the Lutsk ghetto, are taken out to the hills of Polanka and shot by the SS.

1943   In four days, the ghetto of Bialystok, Poland, is liquidated.

1944   The last convoy leaves the Haidar transit camp, a police detention camp in the Haidar quarter in Athens, Greece, taking mainly Greek but some foreign Jews to Auschwitz.

August 20

1941   The Gestapo murders 350 Jews of Korzec, in the province of Rovno, Ukrainian S.S.R.

After the Nazis invade Minsk, Belorussian S.S.R., where 60,000 Jews live, a ghetto consisting of small wooden houses is erected. The Jewish community of Minsk dates back to the fourteenth century.

After the 3,000 Jews of the Banat, Yugoslavia, area have been deported to Tasmajdan near Belgrade, the Nazis declare the area of the Banat, situated between the Theiss River in the west and the Rumanian border in the east, "free of Jews."

1942 A convoy with 997 Jews leaves Vienna for the Theresienstadt concentration camp in Czechoslovakia.

The deportation of the Jews of Radzyn, Poland, to the Treblinka extermination camp begins. At the outbreak of the war about 3,500 Jews are living in Radzyn. About half of them will be deported. Jews have been living in Radzyn since the fifteenth century.

In the course of three days, 8,000 Jews of Falenica, Poland, are deported to Treblinka. From Rembertov, Poland, 2,000 Jews are deported to the same extermination camp. All are killed by the SS.

During a four-day Aktion, 21,000 Jews are deported from the ghetto of Kielce, Poland, to Treblinka. The ghetto is thus essentially liquidated and the remaining 2,000 Jews are moved to a labor camp.

Another convoy with 1,000 Jewish men and women leaves the ghetto of Theresienstadt, Czechoslovakia, for the east. The destination of the transport still remains unknown because no survivor has ever been found. It is supposed that those deported were murdered in the area of Minsk, Belorussian S.S.R., by the SS.

1943 The SS murders 100 Jews in Koziany, Belorussian S.S.R.

The ghetto of Glebokie, Belorussian S.S.R., is to be liquidated, but Jewish resistance groups have already been formed to fight the Nazis. In order to crush the resistance and to make flight from the ghetto impossible, the Nazis set the ghetto on fire. In the course of two days, 3,500 Jews are murdered by the SS and the Lithuanian police. Nevertheless, some young men manage to flee and find refuge with the Kaganovitch partisans. About 60 out of the 6,000 inhabitants survive the Nazi era.

August 21

1321 Accused of poisoning the wells to cause an epidemic, the entire Jewish community—160 people—of Chinon, a town in central France, is burned at the stake on an island outside the town. For centuries afterward the island is known as Ile des Juifs.

1941 The 2,500 Jews of Czyzev, Poland, are driven out of the ghetto and murdered.

1942 During a two-day Aktion, 320 Jews are murdered by the Nazis in Krasnodar, Ukrainian S.S.R.

1,008 Jewish inmates of the Westerbork transit camp in the Dutch province of Drenthe are deported to the Auschwitz extermination camp in Poland.

The SS deports 4,000 Jews from the ghetto of Turka, Poland (today Ukrainian S.S.R.), and 800 Jews from Goraj, Poland, to the Belzec extermination camp.

A train convoy crammed with 1,000 Jewish men and women leaves the Drancy transit camp in the German occupied zone of France for Auschwitz, where 892 of them are gassed immediately. Only 7 men survive the atrocities of the camp until the liberation by the Soviet army in 1945.

During the liquidation of the ghetto of Wieruszov, Poland, 80 Jews are shot by the police.

In the course of a large-scale Aktion carried out by the Nazis in Minsk Mazoviecki, Poland, where 6,000 Jews live, 1,000 Jews are shot by the SS and about 4,000 Jews are deported to the Treblinka extermination camp and killed. Jews had been living in this town since the fifteenth century.

August 22

1614 The Jewish quarter of Frankfurt, Germany, is attacked by a crowd led by the baker Vincent Fettmilch. The fighting lasts three days and many Jews are killed or wounded, their synagogues desecrated. In the aftermath the Jews are expelled from Frankfurt.

1648 The 40,000 Jews of Narol, Poland, are seized by the Cossack hordes of Bogdan Chmielnicki, who carry out a terrible massacre. Among the victims are refugees from the surrounding villages who had sought shelter from the marauding cossacks.

1941 The Nazis shoot 760 people, among them 60 children, receiving care in the hospital of Dünaburg, Latvian S.S.R., in Aglona, nearby. Among them are many Jews.

The Nazis arrest 900 Jews in Dubno, Volhynia, Poland (today Ukrainian S.S.R.), then take them to the Jewish cemetery and shoot them. The Nazis then set up a Jewish Council to execute all the orders from the Gestapo.

Attack on the Jewish quarter of Frankfurt instigated by Vincent Fettmilch, 1614.

Coming from Rovno, the Nazis march into Stolin, Pinsk district, Poland (today Belorussian S.S.R.), and abolish the Ukrainian administration. They impose the payment of a tribute of 1,000,000 rubles on the Jews and take hostages In order to enforce their demand. Henceforth, Jews are shot in the street every day, either by Ukrainian policemen or by the SS.

1942   The SS deports 1,500 Jews from Sarnaki, Poland, via Siedlce, to the Treblinka extermination camp. On the same day 10,000 Jews are deported from the ghetto of Siedlce, in eastern Poland, to the same extermination camp and are killed by the SS. A number of Jews manage to hide.

Almost 12,000 Jews from Zdunska Vola in central Poland are arrested by the SS and deported to Treblinka during a three-day Aktion.

All 6,900 Jews of Losice, Poland, are deported to Treblinka and killed by the SS. Jews have been living in Losice since the seventeenth century.

Every Jew living in the rural area surrounding Wielun, province of Lodz, Poland, is herded by the Nazis into St. Augustine Church in Wielun, where they are left without food and water for days. The sick, the weak, and the old are murdered by the SS inside the church and the remaining 10,000 are deported to the Chelmno extermination camp.

1944   Two Jews are deported from Vienna to the Auschwitz extermination camp in Poland.

August 23

1349   The Black Death Persecutions reach Cologne, Germany, and the mob attacks the Jewish population. Although the Jews defend themselves, most of the Jewish community perishes when a fire breaks out. Among the dead is Rabbi Israel Thann.

1648   The Jewish population of Koric, Ukraine, is massacred by the Cossack hordes of Chmielnicki.

1919   During a pogrom, 5 Jews are massacred and 2 Jewish girls are raped by units of the Ukrainian National Army under the high command of Simon Petlyura, in the village of Chibene, Ukraine. On the same day, a major pogrom is carried out in nearby Pogrebitche, by units under Zeleny. The Jewish death toll is between 300 and 400; 100 Jews are wounded and many rapes occur. In addition, 200 Jews are slaughtered and several young Jewish women are mutilated and raped when insurgents under the hetmen Zeleny and Sokolov, also allies of the Ukrainian National Army, carry out a pogrom in Tetiev, Ukraine.

1940   The Nazis single out 1,000 young Jewish men between 18 and 25 in Czestochova, Poland, and are sent to a forced labor camp in Ciechanov, Poland. None of them will survive.

1942   The Gestapo shoots 16 Jews, among them 2 women and a child, in Warta, Poland, during their deportation.

Several hundred Jews from the ghetto of Mir, Baranowicze district, Poland (today Belorussian S.S.R.), are shot by the SS.

The Nazis murder 2,000 Jews from the ghetto in Mordy, Poland, during a so-called Aktion.

The largest deportation of the 40,000 people in the Jewish quarter of Lvov, Poland (today Ukrainian S.S.R.), to the Belzec extermination camp— where they all are murdered by the SS—ends.

The liquidation of the ghetto of Zdunska Vola, Poland, begins. The SS murders 550 Jews immediately. About 7,000 Jews are deported to the Chelmno extermination camp and 1,000 men are sent to the ghetto of Lodz.

A Cossack of Chmielnicki's hordes.

1943 From Bialystok, Poland, 1,260 Jewish children arrive at the Theresienstadt concentration camp in Czechoslovakia, and are then deported to the Auschwitz extermination camp in Poland.

1944 The Drancy concentration camp near Paris, France, is liberated and 1,500 prisoners are set free. From this concentration camp, more than 61,000 people were sent to the extermination camps in the east.

August 24

1349 During the Black Death Persecutions, the entire Jewish community of Mainz (with 6,000 members, the largest in Germany) is annihilated, when the Jews set fire to their houses.

1919 During a pogrom, 14 are massacred, 35 are injured, and many Jewish women are brutally raped in Jivatov, Ukraine, by units under Sokolov and other detachments of the Ukrainian National Army.

1920 Hungarian soldiers murder 10 Jews in Czelldomolk, Hungary.

1929 Arabs murder 67 Jewish inhabitants of Hebron, Palestine, incited by the mufti of Jerusalem, Amin el-Husseini.

1941 Jews from Smolewicze, Belorussian S.S.R., numbering 1,500, are shot on the Gorodischtsche mountain.

1942 The SS murders 300 Jews in Czartorysk, Volhynia, Ukrainian S.S.R.

The Nazis deport 1,000 Jews from the ghetto of Warta, Poland, to the Chelmno extermination camp, where they are murdered.

The SS deports 1,500 Jews from the ghetto of Chorostkow, East Galicia, Poland (today Ukrainian S.S.R.), to the Belzec extermination camp, and then murders them.

The remaining Jews of Lvov, Poland (today Ukrainian S.S.R.), are crowded into a ghetto bounded on one side by a railway embankment and on the other by a wooden fence and barbed wire. Many Jews are shot by the SS and many die of starvation and disease.

The remaining 10,000 Jews of Novy Sacz, Poland, are sent to Belzec and killed by the SS during a four-day Aktion.

All inhabitants of the ghetto of Krzemieniec, Poland (today Ukrainian S.S.R.), are shot, except for 1,500 young, able-bodied Jews who are deported to a labor camp in Bialokrynica. Only 14 Jews of Krzemieniec survive the war.

The SS murders 2,000 Jews of the ghetto of Janov, Soviet Union.

1,000 Jewish men and women are deported from the Drancy transit camp in the German occupied zone of France to the Auschwitz extermination camp in Poland, where 908 of them are gassed immediately upon arrival. Only 3 men survive until the liberation of the camp by the Soviet army in 1945.

Another convoy with 519 Jewish internees leaves the Westerbork transit camp in the Dutch province of Drenthe for Auschwitz.

The SS and the Schupo (security police) shoot 150 Jews in the course of the liquidation of the ghetto in Zdunska Vola, Poland.

1943 A transport with 1,001 Jewish inmates of the Westerbork transit camp are deported to Auschwitz.

1944 The labor camp at Mielec, Galicia, Poland, is liquidated and 1,000 Jews are shot by the SS. The remaining 2,000 Jews are sent to Wieliczka.

August 25

1255 A Jew in Lincoln, England, is victim of a blood libel and he is tortured and hanged. In the aftermath, many of his neighbors are arrested on the same charge and taken to London, where 18 of them are hanged and the others are acquitted. The allegedly murdered child has become known as St. Hugh of Lincoln.

1941 During a night raid, several thousand Jews are taken from the ghetto of Minsk, Belorussian S.S.R., and murdered.

Within two and a half months 5,000 Jews are murdered when the Nazis begin the internment of the Jews of Belgrade, Yugoslavia.

The SS takes 350 Jews from Buczacz, Ternopol district, Ukrainian S.S.R., to the hills one mile outside of town and murders them. After this massacre a ghetto is established in Buczacz.

1,400 Jews of Tykocin, Poland, are taken to prepared ditches and murdered there by the SS and the Polish police. Only about 200 Jews manage to flee to the ghetto of Bialystok, where later they and the inhabitants of Bialystok's ghetto will be mur-

Tomb of St. Hugh in Lincoln Cathedral, from Tovey, Anglia Judaica, 1738.

dered. The Jewish community came into existence at the beginning of the sixteenth century.

1942 The SS deports 1,000 Jews from the Theresienstadt concentration camp in Czechoslovakia to Minsk-Trostyanets, where they are immediately shot by the SS.

The SS takes 1,000 Jews of Jedlinsk, in the province of Kielce, Poland, to Pionka and murders them.

In the course of three days, 3,000 Jews are murdered by the SS and the Ukrainian police in Maczev, Volhynia, Ukrainian S.S.R.

In two days, 1,200 Jews are murdered in Ludvipol, Poland, by the SS and the Ukrainian police.

The SS murders 1,000 Jews of Ossovo, Ukrainian S.S.R.

Another convoy, with 1,000 Jewish men and women, leaves the ghetto of Theresienstadt in Czechoslovakia for Minsk, Belorussian S.S.R., where they are loaded into vans and killed by exhaust gasses. Their corpses are hurriedly buried in common graves in the nearby woods. The SS singles out 22 able-bodied men and sends them to the Maly Trostyanets labor camp, where 20 of them are slain. The other 2 men manage to flee to the partisans and 1 is later killed in action. The story of this convoy is related by the only survivor.

A large-scale deportation of the Jews of Miedzyrzec Podlaski, Poland, begins. At the outbreak of the war 12,000 Jews are living there. In December 1939 the Nazis brought into the town another 2,000 Jews from neighboring towns and 1,000 Jews from Slovakia, thus increasing the population to 15,000. In the first deportation convoy to the Treblinka extermination camp are 5,000 Jews. They have been living in Miedzyrzec Podlaski since the seventeenth century.

From the ghetto in Bochnia, West Galicia, Poland, 2,000 Jews are deported to the Belzec extermination camp, where they are murdered by the SS.

The fifth convoy of 995 Jews—among them 232 children—leaves the Mechelen transit camp in Belgium for the Auschwitz extermination camp in Poland. Only 26 of these people will survive until the liberation of the camp in 1945.

1943 The last 3,200 Jews of Bolechov, Poland (today Ukrainian S.S.R.), are deported to the camp at Stanislavov.

In Ratne, Ukrainian S.S.R., 2,300 Jews are murdered by the SS and the Ukrainian police.

In the course of two days, 3,200 Jews of Berezna, Ukrainian S.S.R., are murdered by the SS.

1944   The remaining Jews in the camp at Kielce, Poland, are sent to Auschwitz and the Buchenwald extermination camp in Germany. Kielce is officially declared "free of Jews."

August 26

1725   An auto-da-fé is held in Llerena, Spain, involving among others Samuel Rodriguez from Bayonne and many of his family members. They are accused of being Judaizers, descendants of Jews forcibly baptized who still adhere to the Jewish faith. Most of them are executed and some are condemned to prison.

1941   The Nazis take 8,000 Jews of and surrounding Zarasai, Lithuanian S.S.R., into a forest near Dusetai and murder them.

1942   The Nazis first intern 4,000 Jews living in the vicinity of Wloszczowa, Poland, in the ghetto of Wloszczowa and then deport them to the Treblinka extermination camp.

In the course of two days, 7,000 stateless Jews are arrested in Vichy France.

A transport with 1,002 Jewish men and women leaves from the Drancy transit camp in the German occupied zone of France for the Auschwitz extermination camp in Poland, where 937 are gassed immediately. Only 32 men from this convoy will survive until the liberation of the camp by the Soviet army in 1945.

The SS murders 800 Jews in Rokitno, Polesie, Soviet Union.

In the course of 3 days, 6,000 Jews are murdered by the SS and the Ukrainian police in Kostopol, Poland.

In two raids carried out by the Nazis, on August 26 and 28, 11,000 Jewish men, women, and children from the German occupied zone of France are sent to the Drancy transit camp to await their further deportation to the extermination camps in Poland.

1943   From Krimilev, province of Kielce, Poland, 400 Jews are deported to the Auschwitz extermination camp.

The ghetto of Zaviercie in southern Poland is liquidated and the Jews are sent to Auschwitz. For passive resistance, 100 Jews are shot, and 500 Jews remain in a labor camp.

1944   An uprising against the Nazis takes place in Banska Bystrica and Novaky in Czechoslovakia. A significant number of Jews participate in the fighting.

1952   Stalin orders mass arrests of Jewish artists and the closing of all Yiddish institutions. Of those arrested, 26 are members of the Jewish Anti-Fascist Committee, and they play an important role in Jewish cultural life; they are secretly executed on August 26, accused of "Jewish nationalism" and of cooperation with Western espionage.

August 27

1349   The Jewish community of Rothenburg ob der Tauber, Germany, is annihilated during the Black Death Persecutions.

1919   During a pogrom, 1 Jew is slain and 3 Jewish girls are raped by units under the command of Volynetz, an ally of Petlyura's Ukrainian National Army, in Tsibulev, near Kiev, Russia (today Ukrainian S.S.R.); 3 Jews are slain and many wounded by flogging in a pogrom carried out by units of the Ukrainian National Army who stay for twelve days in Zamekhov, Podolia, Ukrainian S.S.R.

1941 Having fled to Hungary, 18,000 foreign Jews are arrested and sent to the Polish border, into the hands of the SS, who drive them to Kamenets-Podolski, Ukrainian S.S.R. From there they, and the approximately 5,600 Jews remaining in the Kamenets-Podolski area are forced to march to a row of bomb craters about 10 miles away and are shot by the SS and Ukrainians.

1942 Deported to the Belzec extermination camp are 8,000 Jews of Wieliczka, in the province of Cracow, Poland, and its surrounding area. 500 Jews are sent to the Stalova-Wola labor camp and another 200 to the Plaszow concentration camp. Thus, Wieliczka is "free of Jews." Jews have been living there since the fourteenth century.

A convoy with 965 Jews leaves Vienna for the Theresienstadt concentration camp in Czechoslovakia.

The SS murders 1,800 Jews in Bereznica, Polesie, Belorussian S.S.R.

The ghetto of Sarny, Volhynia, Poland (today Ukrainian S.S.R.), is overcrowded, with 14,000 Jews from Sarny and the surrounding area. The Nazis start to liquidate the ghetto and thousands of Jews are taken out and shot.

August 28

1919 During a three-day pogrom, 25 Jewish women are raped and many Jews are wounded by sabers and whips used by Ukrainian troops in Jabocritch, Podolia, Ukraine.

During a pogrom, 24 Jews are killed in Vassilivtchin, Kiev district, Ukraine, by units of Pet-

lyura's Ukrainian National Army led by the two hetmen Zeleny and Sokol. In the town of Guermanovka, also in the district of Kiev, 114 Jews are massacred and many Jewish women are raped during a pogrom carried out by units under the command of Diakov and Zeleny.

1942 During a two-day Aktion, 2,500 Jews from the ghetto of Novy Targ, West Galicia, Poland, and 1,200 Jews arrested in Mikuliuce, Ternopol province, Poland, are all deported by the SS to the Belzec extermination camp and are murdered there.

The SS murders 1,600 Jews in Rafalovka, Volhynia, Ukrainian S.S.R.

The Nazis deport 600 Jews of Sobkov, in the province of Kielce, Poland, to the collecting point at Jedrzejov.

A transport with 608 Jewish inmates of the Westerbork transit camp in the Dutch province of Drenthe leaves for the Auschwitz extermination camp in Poland.

The SS and Ukrainian police murder 1,800 Jews in Wlodzimierz, Poland (today Ukrainian S.S.R.).

The Nazis slay 2,800 Jews in Dabrovica, Volhynia, Ukrainian S.S.R., in the course of mass executions. The Jews resist and over 1,000 escape into the forests.

From the ghetto of Czortkov, Poland (today Ukrainian S.S.R.), 2,000 Jews are deported to the Belzec extermination camp. In Czortkov, 500 people—children, the sick, and the old—are shot.

When the ghetto is finally liquidated, Sarny, Volhynia, Poland (today Ukrainian S.S.R.), is "free of Jews." The Jewish cemetery is destroyed and the gravestones are used as paving stones. A small group of Jews manages to flee into the forests where they fight the Bandera Gangs, Ukrainian nationalists who are collaborating with the Germans against the Soviet Union. After the war, 20 of these Jewish partisans return to Sarny.

The SS deports 2,000 Jews from the ghetto of Skavina, West Galicia, Poland, and 2,700 Jews from the ghetto of Zloczow, East Galicia, Poland (today Ukrainian S.S.R.), are deported to Belzec, where the Germans murder them immediately.

A convoy with 1,000 Jewish men and women leaves from the Drancy transit camp in the German occupied zone of France for Auschwitz, where 929 are gassed immediately. Only 8 men will survive until the liberation of the camp by the Soviet army in 1945.

1944 Thousands of Jewish prisoners from the camps at Narva, Tallinn, and Klooga in Estonia are deported by ship to the Stutthof concentration camp near Danzig. Hundreds of them die on the way.

August 29

1919 During a pogrom, 60 Jews are massacred in Vassilkovo, in the district of Kiev, Ukraine, carried out by units allied with Petlyura's Ukrainian National Army under the leadership of the hetmen Zeleny and Sokolski.

1941 German troops murder 3,016 Jews of Czernovitz and its vicinity in Bukovina (today Ukrainian S.S.R.).

1942 The SS murders 1,800 Jews in Zoludek, district of Novogrodek, Belorussian S.S.R.

The Yugoslavian Nazis report to Berlin that they have achieved the Final Solution to the Jewish Question in Serbia. Out of the 23,000 Jews of Serbia, 20,000 have been murdered.

The SS murders 400 Jews in Byten, Ukrainian S.S.R.

A group of 100 Jews from Sassov, Poland, and 472 Jews from Olesko, situated in East Galicia (today Ukrainian S.S.R.), are deported to the Belzec extermination camp, where they are all murdered by the SS.

The large-scale three-day Aktion against the Jews of Ternopol, Poland (today Ukrainian S.S.R.), begins; 4,000 Jews are seized and deported to Belzec.

The sixth transport of 1,000 Jews—among them 179 children—leaves the Mechelen transit camp in Belgium for the Auschwitz extermination camp in Poland. Only 34 persons of this convoy will survive until the camp is liberated in 1945.

1981 During a Bar Mitzvah service, two men armed with automatic weapons and hand grenades attack a synagogue in Vienna, Austria, killing two people and wounding about 20 others.

August 30

1941 The SS shoots 40 to 50 children of the nursery school in Zhitomir, Ukrainian S.S.R.

600 Jews from the ghetto of Vitebsk, Belorussian S.S.R., are shot in the Ilovskji pit, a ravine near Vitebsk. The children are buried alive.

The remaining 8,941 Jews in the district of Balti in Bessarabia, Rumania (today Soviet Union), are interned in three camps and afterward deported to Transnistria.

After several Jews have been murdered by the SS in Smolensk, Ukrainian S.S.R., a ghetto is set up. Jews have been living there since the end of the fifteenth century.

1942   From Kielsztyglov, in the district of Lodz, Poland, 400 Jews are deported to the Chelmno extermination camp.

The seven-day Aktion against the Jews of Szumsk, Volhynia, Poland (today Ukrainian S.S.R.), ends. The SS has murdered 4,500 Jews.

About 2,500 people, the entire Jewish population of Kock, Lublin province, Poland, are deported to Parczev, where they are murdered by the SS along with the local Jewish population. Jews have been living in Kock since the seventeenth century and many famous scholars were born there.

With the help of the Ukrainian police, the Nazis murder 1,000 Jews in Wisnievicze, Volhynia, Soviet Union.

The SS murders 700 Jews in Wisznievo, district of Novogrodek, Belorussian S.S.R.

1944   The deportation of the inmates from the ghetto of Lodz, Poland, to the Auschwitz extermination camp begins.

August 31

38 A.D.   Anti-Jewish riots break out when the Jews refuse to obey the order from the Roman prefect Flaccus to set up a statue of Emperor Caligula in the synagogue of Alexandria, Egypt.
   400 Jewish houses are looted and entirely demolished and the Jews are forcibly concentrated in one quarter, where they suffer from overcrowding and hunger. Jews who leave the quarter in search of food are tortured to death; 38 Jewish elders are publicly whipped and several of them die.

1919   When the Ukrainian National Army recaptures Kiev, Ukraine, from the Bolsheviks, 35 members of the newly formed Jewish Self Defense are summoned by Levka, the head of the unit. They are disarmed, marched out of town, and murdered.

1941   The Germans take 3,000 Jews from the ghetto of Minsk, Belorussian S.S.R., and murder them.

1942   Jewish inmates numbering 560 are sent from the Westerbork transit camp in the Dutch province of Drenthe to Auschwitz. Several hundred Jews from Zbaraz, Poland (today Ukrainian S.S.R.) are deported to the Belzec extermination camp.

In the course of an Aktion in Skalat, Ternopol province, Poland (today Ukrainian S.S.R.), 500 Jews are crammed into cattle cars and sent to the town of Ternopol. From there they are sent in a deportation transport to Belzec.

A transport with 967 Jews leaves Vienna for Minsk, Belorussian S.S.R.

A deportation train with 1,000 Jewish men and women leaves the Drancy transit camp in occupied France for Auschwitz, where 961 are gassed immediately. Only 18 survive until the liberation of the camp by the Soviet army in 1945.

1943   A convoy with 1,004 Jewish inmates leaves the Westerbork transit camp for Auschwitz.

SEPTEMBER

September 1

1592 Severe persecutions against the Jews begin when Archbishop Salikowski orders the erection of a church in Lvov, Poland.

1739 An auto-da-fé is held in Lisbon, Portugal, and 47 persons are accused of being Judaizers, descendants of Jews forcibly baptized some centuries ago who still adhere to the Jewish faith. Of the group 4 men and 8 women are burned alive as nonrepentants and the other 35 are sentenced to life imprisonment.

1903 50 Jews are massacred, many are injured, and many Jewish homes are destroyed during a pogrom in Homel, Ukraine, carried out by workers and supported by soldiers stationed there.

1939 Germany invades Poland. The Sicherheitsdienst, secret service, starts its activities in Poland. The Nazis occupy Wolbrom in the province of Cracow, where 5,000 Jews are living. The entire Jewish population is sent on a three-day march to Zawierce, during which they are beaten and tortured. Jews have been living in Wolbrom since the seventeenth century.

At the outbreak of World War II, prominent Jews of Prague, Czechoslovakia, are taken as hostages and deported to the Buchenwald concentration camp in Germany.

1941 All Jews living in the German Reich are ordered to wear the Judenstern, the Yellow Star.

1942 The Nazis send 5,000 Jews from the ghetto of Wloszczova, Poland, to the Treblinka extermination camp, where they are murdered immediately.

A convoy of 1,000 Jewish men, women, and children leaves the Theresienstadt ghetto in Czechoslovakia for Raasika, Estonia. Upon its arrival, 120 men and 75 women are singled out and sent to the Jagala concentration camp, where the men will perish. The 75 women will be sent on to an ammunition factory near Hamburg; 45 of them will survive. The remaining 805 Jews are deported to Kalevi-Liva, where they are shot by SS men and buried in mass graves.

Jakob Kaplan, a member of the Jewish Council of Wlodzimierz, Poland (today Ukrainian S.S.R.), commits suicide with his wife and son when the

197

Nazis demand from him a list of 7,000 Jews to be deported. An Aktion begins in the ghetto of Vladimir-Volynski: 18,000 Jews are murdered during two weeks, only 4,000 are left.

Dr. Henryk Landsberg, the chairman of the Jewish Council in Lvov, Poland (today Ukrainian S.S.R.), and all the other council members, are hanged in retaliation for the killing of an SS man. Another 175 Jews are shot. The first chairman of the Jewish Council, Dr. Parnes, has also been murdered.

In the course of two days, 3,500 Jews of Uscilug, Volhynia, Ukrainian S.S.R., are murdered by the SS and the Ukrainian police.

In Poland, 800 Jews from Mikolasov, Stanislavov district (today Ukrainian S.S.R.), hundreds of Jews from Zbaraz, East Galicia, and 3,000 Jews from Stryj, Lvov province (today Soviet Union), are deported to the Belzec extermination camp. The Jews from Zbaraz are murdered upon arrival.

The SS murders 1,700 Jews from Poryck, Volhynia, Ukrainian S.S.R.

The seventh convoy of 1,000 Jews, including 344 children, leaves the Mechelen transit camp in Belgium for the Auschwitz extermination camp in Poland. Only 15 persons of this convoy will survive until the liberation of the camp in 1945.

1943 During a four-day Aktion, 8,000 Jews of the Vilna ghetto, Lithuanian S.S.R., are deported to a labor camp. About 200 resistance fighters succeed in escaping into the forests, where they join the partisans.

1944 120 Italian Jews, who have been interned in the only concentration camp in Italy, Risiera di San Sabba near Trieste, are deported to Auschwitz.

September 2

1629 During an auto-da-fé held in Lisbon, Portugal, several people are accused of being Judaizers, descendants of Jews forcibly baptized some centuries ago who still practice the Jewish faith in secret.

1939 The Nazis occupy Zaviercie, Katovice district, Poland, where 7,000 Jews live. All Jewish men between the ages of 17 and 50 are ordered to gather in the marketplace, where they are detained and tortured for nine days.

The Nazis erect the Stutthof concentration camp in the vicinity of Danzig. Several hundred prominent Jews are taken there soon after, most of whom die soon.

1941 The SS murders 1,500 Jews of Zaremby Kasztelanskie, province of Bialystok, Poland, outside of the town.

1942 Crammed with 1,000 Jewish men and women, the twenty-seventh convoy leaves France for the Auschwitz extermination camp in Poland. The deportees were interned in the Drancy camp in the German occupied zone of France, where they awaited deportation to one of the extermination camps in the east of Europe. Immediately, 877 of them are gassed, and only 30 men from the entire convoy will survive till 1945.

The Nazis kill 700 Jews during an uprising in the ghetto of Lachva, Belorussian S.S.R. Jewish resistance is active and with its help 120 Jews escape into the forests.

In Strzegowo, district of Mlawa, Poland, 20 Jews are hanged by the Gestapo and the local police.

After the liquidation of the Jewish ghetto of Lublin, Poland (erected by the Nazis in March 1941), 2,000 of the 4,000 surviving Jews are killed by the

Nazis. The ghetto population of 34,000 has been reduced by several deportation transports to the concentration and extermination camps.

1943   The fifty-eighth deportation convoy, with 1,000 Jewish men and women who have been interned in Drancy, leaves for Auschwitz. Immediately, 662 of the deportees are gassed; only 13 men and 3 women will survive until the liberation of the camp in 1945.

The Nazis send 3,500 Jews of the ghetto of Przemysl, province of Rzeszow, Poland, and 2,000 Jews of the ghetto of Tarnov, province of Cracow, Poland, to Auschwitz. Another 3,000 Jews from Tarnov are sent to the Plaszow-Cracow concentration camp.

From Vienna, 20 Jews are deported to the Theresienstadt concentration camp in Czechoslovakia.

September 3

1189   During the coronation of King Richard I (the Lionhearted) in London, the Jewish notables who have come to show their allegiance and respect are mistreated and prevented from entering the palace. The incited mob storms the Jewish quarter, sets fire to the houses, and massacres about 30 Jews.

1919   During a pogrom, 4 Jews are massacred and many are wounded in Tsibulev, near Kiev, Ukraine, by units under the hetman Sokolov, an ally of Simon Petlyura's Ukrainian National Army.

1939   The Nazis murder 3 Jews in Rekszovice, Poland.

The Wehrmacht (regular German forces) shoots 80 Jews during a two-day Aktion in Zloczev, district of Sieradz, Poland.

The Nazis murder 4 Jews in Lelow, district of Wloszczowa, Poland.

The Wehrmacht murders 150 Jews in Czestochova, near Warsaw, Poland.

1941   The imprisonment of the Jews of Sarajevo, Yugoslavia, begins. About 3,000 Jews are sent to the camps at Jasenovac, Loborgrad, and Djakovo, where they are murdered together with the Jews of the neighboring villages.

The first gassing takes place in the Auschwitz extermination camp in Poland.

1942   The first large-scale Aktion against the Jews in Dzialoszyce, Cracow province, Poland, takes place, and 1,000 Jews are murdered on the spot. Two convoys with 8,000 Jews are deported to the Belzec extermination camp and another 1,000 Jews are sent to the Plaszow concentration camp in Cracow. In Dzialoszyce, a Jewish resistance movement begins to take shape. The Jews have been living there since the eighteenth century. By the time of the German invasion the Jewish community numbers 7,000 and makes up 80 percent of the population.

The SS and Ukrainian policemen round up 500 Jews from Brzozdovce, Ukrainian S.S.R., 4,000 Jews of Dzialoszyn, Poland, and 2,000 Jews from Bolechov, Poland (today Ukrainian S.S.R.), and deport them to Belzec.

The SS murders 1,400 Jews in Lachva, Polesie, Belorussian S.S.R.

1943   A convoy of 3,000 Jews leaves the ghetto of Bochnia, Poland, for Auschwitz, where they are murdered upon arrival.

1944   From the Westerbork transit camp in the Dutch province of Drenthe, 1,019 Jewish inmates are deported to Auschwitz.

September 4

1553 On the Jewish high holy day of Rosh Hashanah (the New Year), the Talmud and all Jewish books are confiscated and burned by the Inquisition in Italy.

1883 During the outbreak of a pogrom in Novomoskovsk, Russia, almost all Jewish homes are destroyed and completely looted.

1939 The Germans occupy Sosnowiec, a town in the province of Katovice in southern Poland. At the outbreak of World War II, 28,000 Jews are living there. On the day of the German invasion, 13 Jews are murdered by the Nazis.

In the history of Jewish martyrdom this day is known as Bloody Monday. It is the first day of the German occupation of Czestochova, a town 205 km southwest of Warsaw in Poland. The Germans organize a pogrom in the course of which some hundred Jews are slain. Jews have been living in Czestochova since the eighteenth century. By the time of the German invasion the Jewish community has 30,000 members.

1941 During an Aktion, 1,000 Jews of Zambrov, Poland, are murdered by the Nazis in the area of Rutki-Kosaki.

1942 The day after the Belorussian militia shuts off the ghetto of Lachva, Belorussian S.S.R., and begins to make preparations for the massacre of the 2,000 Jewish inmates. The Jews offer fierce resistance and set fire to their houses; 600 manage to escape, but 500 of them will be killed. The 100 survivors meet in the forest to fight as partisans. The rest of the people in the ghetto perish.

A convoy with 1,013 Jewish men and women leaves the Drancy transit camp in the German occupied zone of France for the Auschwitz extermination camp in Poland. Upon arrival, 959 of them are sent to the gas chambers. Only 28 from this convoy will survive until the liberation of the camp in 1945.

The SS executes 100 elderly Jews and sends 2,000 Jews to the Belzec extermination camp from the Sambor ghetto in the province of Lvov, Poland (today Ukrainian S.S.R.).

The Nazis send 2,000 Jews from Skole, Poland, 2,000 Jews from Chodorov, Ukrainian S.S.R., 3,000 Jews from Lesko, Ukrainian S.S.R., 1,000 Jews from Rozdol, Poland, and 500 Jews from Mikolayov, Ukrainian S.S.R., to Belzec. The Jews of Chodorov, Rozdol, and Mikolayov are murdered upon arrival.

1944 On a transport, 2,087 Jewish inmates of the Westerbork transit camp in the Dutch province of Drenthe are sent to the Theresienstadt concentration camp in Czechoslovakia.

September 5

1939 In Chmielnik, district of Stopnica, Poland, 14 Jews are burned alive at the stake.

German troops occupy Plonsk, Poland, where 8,200 Jews live. The Jewish community of the town came into existence when the princess of Masovia invited them to settle there and Jews attained high positions in trade and business. Many Jewish scholars originate from Plonsk, among them Rabbi Abraham Yekuthiel Lichtenstein and Rabbi Zevi Ezekiel Michaelsohn, as well as famous Zionist activists such as David Ben-Gurion, a prime minister of Israel. Only a few Jews from Plonsk survive the Holocaust.

The Wehrmacht (regular German forces) shoots 87 Jews of the villages Chrzanov and Jaworzno at the train station of Trzebinia, Poland.

1942 The children, the old, and the sick of the ghetto in Lodz, Poland, are deported and murdered during a seven-day Aktion.

Deported to the Treblinka extermination camp are 3,200 Jews from Sokolka, Poland.

The Nazis deport 500 Jews from Zydaczov and 500 Jews from Zurawno, Poland, to the Belzec extermination camp, where they are murdered within hours of their arrival.

1943 During a two-day Aktion, 2,500 Jews are murdered in Pilica, Poland. The remaining Jewish population is deported to the Auschwitz extermination camp.

1972 During the summer Olympics in Munich, West Germany, 8 terrorists break into the Olympic Village and murder two members of the Israeli Olympic team. Before being killed, 9 other members of the team are held hostage for 18 hours. The Olympic Games are suspended for one day.

September 6

1705 An auto-da-fé is held in Lisbon, Portugal, in which 60 people are accused of being Judaizers, descendants of Jews forcibly baptized some centuries ago who still secretly practice the Jewish religion. One of the accused is burned alive and the others are condemned to lifelong penance and imprisonment.

1939 The Nazis occupy Gorlice, a town in southeastern Poland where 5,000 Jews live, and take Jewish hostages. Jews have been settled there since the beginning of the eighteenth century.

1941 All Jews are forbidden to leave the two ghettos of Vilna, Lithuanian S.S.R. A second Jewish Council is established.

1942 The Nazis start to liquidate the ghetto of Wolbrom, in the province of Cracow, Poland, and all Jews are driven to the train station. The Germans then select 2,000 old and sick Jews and send them to the nearby forest, where they are shot and buried in mass graves. The remaining 2,000 Jews are deported to the Belzec extermination camp.

The Nazis deport 1,000 Jews from the ghetto of Biala Podlaska, Poland, to the Treblinka extermination camp, where they are murdered several hours after their arrival.

1943 On this day and September 8, a total of 5,007 Jews of the Theresienstadt ghetto, Czechoslovakia, are deported to the Auschwitz extermination camp in Poland. They are all accommodated in the yet unfinished part of the Birkenau camp, the "family camp." On March 8 and 9, 1944, the surviving 3,792 prisoners of this transport are gassed.

1986 During Sabbath services at a synagogue in Istanbul, Turkey, gunmen burst in and massacre 21 worshipers, then pour gasoline over the corpses and set them on fire. The name of the synagogue is Neve Shalom: "place of peace."

September 7

1939 The Wehrmacht (regular German forces) murders 7 Jews and one of them is burned alive in Zgierz, a village southwest of Warsaw, Poland.

The Germans occupy Aleksandrov (Lodzki) in central Poland, where 3,500 Jews are living. The Gestapo and the police shoot 60 Jews. The synagogue, containing the Torah scrolls, is burned down. All religious books from private houses are confiscated and brought to the synagogue. Many Jews who do not want to lose their books, and try to save them, are killed.

German troops occupy Pultusk, Poland, where 9,000 Jews live, and kill 14 Jews. The Jewish community in Pultusk has existed since the second half of the fifteenth century. The Jews were protected by a special tolerance edict dating from the sixteenth century issued by Polish King Sigismund II Augustus. The names of great scholars are associated with Pultusk, such as Rabbi Joshua of Kittno and Rabbi Jakob Grodzinski.

1942   Hundreds of Jews from Kuty, 20 Jews from Zablotov, 200 Jews from Zabie, 4,500 Jews from Sniatyn, and Jews from the Kolomyja ghetto, all in the Ukrainian S.S.R., and the Jews from Sinolin, 100 Jews from Roznow, 500 Jews from Pistyn, and 800 Jews from Jablonov, all towns in Poland, are deported to the Belzec extermination camp in Poland. The Jews of Kolomyja, Zabie, Roznow, Pistyn, and Jablonov are murdered some hours after their arrival.

The SS and members of the Ukrainian police take 1,300 Jews of Poczasov, Ukrainian S.S.R., from the town and murder them.

A train convoy with 1,000 Jewish men and women from the Drancy transit camp in the German occupied zone of France leaves for the Auschwitz extermination camp in Poland, where 889 of them are gassed immediately after their arrival. Only 34 men will survive until the liberation of the camp in 1945.

The Jews of the ghetto of Kossov, Ukrainian S.S.R., are driven to the main square, while German and Ukrainian police units search the houses for hidden Jews. They discover 150 people and shoot them on the spot; 600 Jews are deported to Belzec.

1943   A convoy with 987 Jewish inmates of the Westerbork transit camp in the Dutch province Drenthe leaves for Auschwitz.

1944   From Vienna, 29 Jews are deported to Auschwitz. After the selection, 4 Jewish women remain in the camp; all of the others are gassed.

September 8

1939   German troops occupy Lodz, a city in central Poland, where 233,000 Jews live. Many of them manage to flee to the Russian occupied part of Poland. At times the Jewish population constituted a third of the total population of the city. All Jewish organizations are represented and Jewish newspapers are published in Lodz.

The Nazis murder 60 persons, most of them Jews, in Konskie, Poland.

In Trzebinia, Poland, 150 Jews are murdered by the Wehrmacht (regular German forces).

The Wehrmacht shoots 41 Jews in the village of Krasnosielc Lesny, Poland.

The German army occupies the town of Skiernievice, Poland, where 4,500 Jews live. Jews have been living in Skiernievice since the second half of the sixteenth century. Among them were famous Jewish scholars such as Rabbi Meir Yehiel Levi Holzstock.

The Germans occupy Ostrov Mazoviecka, Poland, where 7,000 Jews live, and organize a pogrom in the course of which 50 Jews are murdered.

Some Jews are shot when German troops march into Zyrardov, Poland, where the Jewish community numbers 3,000 people.

German troops murder 150 Jews and burn down the synagogue when they occupy Rypin, Poland, where 2,500 Jews are living. Rypin is incorporated into the German Reich and made part of the province of Danzig.

1942   During a three-day Aktion, 2,000 Jews in Horodenka, Ukrainian S.S.R., are murdered by the Schutzpolzei (special police) with the help of the Ukrainian police.

A convoy with 1,000 Jews leaves the Theresienstadt concentration camp in Czechoslovakia for Minsk-Trostinetz, Belorussian S.S.R., where they are shot on arrival.

Another convoy with 1,000 Jewish men and women leaves the Theresienstadt ghetto for Brest Litovsk. From there they have to change to open wagons which take them 10 km past the Minsk railway station. Armed SS men surround the train, the Jews are ordered to get off, and they are robbed of all their property. The SS singles out 44 able-bodied Jews to unload the baggage. All other Jews are loaded into trucks and murdered by the exhaust fumes. Their corpses are buried in the forests of Maly Trostyanets in common graves. The 44 remaining men are brought to the Maly Trostyanets camp, where hundreds of Jews are already interned. They are either shot, hanged, or murdered in some other way by the SS. When the Soviet army is approaching the camp, it is set on fire; 25 prisoners manage to flee but only 4 will survive.

The eighth transport of 1,000 Jews—among them 238 children—leaves the Mechelen transit camp in Belgium for the Auschwitz extermination camp in Poland. Only 34 persons of this convoy will survive until the liberation of the camp in 1945.

1943 A convoy with 3,442 Jews leaves Moravska Ostrava in Moravia, Czechoslovakia, for Auschwitz, where they are murdered upon arrival.

September 9

1899 Alfred Dreyfus, a French officer of Jewish origin accused of high treason, is tried a second time before the court-martial in Rennes, France. On September 9 the court confirms the sentence of the first trial, but his prison term is reduced from life to ten years. In 1906, the plot of anti-Semitic officers against Dreyfus is discovered and the Court of Appeals pronounces that the evidence against Dreyfus is completely unsubstantiated.

Dreyfus will be reinstated in the French army. The Dreyfus Affair raises strong anti-Semitic emotions which result in riots in several parts of France—on the other hand the trial and the subsequent anti-Semitism inspire in Theodor Herzl, French correspondent of a Viennese newspaper, the idea of the need for a Jewish state.

1939 The 300 male Jews of Gelsenkirchen, Germany, are deported to the Sachsenhausen concentration camp.

The Germans occupy Plock, Poland, where 10,000 Jews are living. Jews have been living there since the first half of the thirteenth century and the community is one of the oldest in Poland. The Polish kings have supported Jewish artisans, although in the sixteenth and eighteenth centuries several accusations of ritual murder were raised against the Jews. Great Jewish scholars such as Rabbi Zevi

Captain Dreyfus listening to the charges against him.

Hirsch Munk, Zelig Isaac Margolioth, and many others originated from this town. At one time Jewish political organizations are headquartered here and many writers, such as Shalom Asch and Max Eljowicz, and Zionist leaders such as Nahum Sokolow and Yizhak Gruenbaum live here. Only about 100 Jews will survive the Holocaust by joining partisan groups or forging identity papers.

The synagogue on Dekert Street in Sosnoviec, Poland, is burned down.

The Wehrmacht (regular German forces) arrests and murders 44 Jews in Bedzin, Poland, where 25,000 Jews are living in the Jewish quarter. The old marketplace is set on fire, including 56 houses and the synagogue. Several hundred Jews are burned to death when the German soldiers and the SS hinder anyone from putting out the fire or escaping it. Jews settled in Bedzin in the seventeenth century. It became an industrial town where many Jews worked in the metal industry.

The Germans occupy Lowicz, central Poland, where 4,500 Jews are living. The male Jews are rounded up in the marketplace and locked into the synagogue, where they are tortured for two days. Jews have been living in Lowicz since the beginning of the sixteenth century.

The Gestapo shoots 175 people, most of them Jews, in the yard of the courthouse in Bydgoszcz, Poland.

1942   The SS murders 300 Jews of Swiniuchy, Ukrainian S.S.R., outside of town.

The Nazis murder 2,000 Jews of the village of Kurzeniec, near Minsk, Belorussian S.S.R.

In Lukaczin, Ukrainian S.S.R., 1,800 Jews are murdered by the SS and the Ukrainian police. Also 150 Jews in Bludov, Ukrainian S.S.R., are shot by the SS.

A train convoy with 1,000 Jewish men and women leaves the Drancy transit camp in France for the Auschwitz extermination camp in Poland, where 909 of them are gassed upon arrival. Of the 81 who are not selected to be sent to the gas chambers immediately, 42 will survive till the liberation of the camp in 1945.

German extermination commandos murder 1,800 Jews from Kislowodsk in the Caucasus, in Mineralnyye Vody, Soviet Union.

German extermination commandos murder 2,000 Jews of Jesentuki, a town in the Soviet Caucasus.

The Nazis deport 300 Jews from Bamberg, Germany, to the Theresienstadt concentration camp in Czechoslovakia. They will all perish.

1943   A convoy with 10 Jews leaves Vienna for Theresienstadt.

September 10

1349   The few Jews who have survived the March massacre in the Jewish community of Constance, Germany, are burned at the stake. The Jewish community of Constance has thus ceased to exist.

1939   In Grygrov, district of Wegrov, Poland, 11 Jews are murdered by the Wehrmacht (regular German forces).

The Wehrmacht murders 13 Jews in Mszczonov, Poland.

In Ostroviec, district of Kielce, Poland, 10 Jews are murdered by the Wehrmacht.

The Wehrmacht shoots 43 persons, most of them Jews, in Piatek, district of Leczyca, Poland.

1942   The SS murders 200 Jews in Blihusz, near Vilna, Poland.

On the eve of Rosh Hashanah, the Nazis deport 533 Jews from Nuremberg, Germany, and 990 Jews from Vienna to the Theresienstadt concentration camp in Czechoslovakia. Only 27 Jews of Nuremberg will survive the war.

From Malgoszcz, Poland, 800 Jews are sent to the transit camp at Jendrzejov, Poland.

The Germans intern 8,000 Jews of Sanok and the surrounding area in the district of Rzeszov, southeastern Poland, in the ghetto of Sanok. The old and sick Jews are taken to a nearby forest and shot. From the ghetto, 5,000 Jews are sent to the Belzec extermination camp, together with a convoy of 8,000 Jews from the ghetto of Tarnow, province of Cracow. There has been a Jewish community in Sanok since the end of the sixteenth century. Under the rule of King Augustus II and King Augustus III, the Jewish community obtained privileges and flourished. The critic and educator Benzion Katz was born there. At the outbreak of the war more than 5,000 Jews are living in Sanok.

The SS murders 750 Jews of Horodna and 550 Jews of Plotnice, both villages in Polesie, Poland.

The Nazis execute members of the Jewish Council of Stolin, in the Pinsk district of Poland (today Belorussian S.S.R.). The old and sick are shot in their beds. The rest are lined up in the marketplace and taken in groups of 500 to the nearby forests of Dolin and are shot there in spite of their fierce resistance. Only a few manage to flee into the forests, where they try to contact the partisans. Ukrainian farmers deliver the Jews to the Germans. The captured Jews are hanged in public.

1943 The Nazis meet with resistance by the Jews in Miedzyrzec Podlaski, Poland. The SS murders 5 Jews.

September 11

1902 Riots and anti-Jewish excesses break out in Czestochova, Poland. Jewish houses are demolished, shops entirely looted, and Jews are beaten up in the streets. The military has to intervene and about 200 of the rioters, among them two priests, are arrested.

1939 German troops occupy the town of Kaluszyn, Poland, where 6,500 Jews live. Many of them are locked in the big church and tortured for three days. Jews have been living in Kaluszyn since the seventeenth century.

The Nazis burn 40 Jews alive in Solec on the Vistula River, Poland.

The security police shoot 5 Poles and 1 Jew in Zdunska Vola, a town southwest of Warsaw, Poland.

The Wehrmacht (regular German forces) murders 12 Jews in the village of Tuchov, near Tarnow, Poland.

During a pogrom, 65 Jews are murdered when the Germans occupy the village of Wyszkov, Poland. Wyszkov has a theological seminary (yeshiva). The future commander of the Warsaw ghetto uprising, Mordecai Anielewicz, was originally from Wyszkov.

1942 On this Rosh Hashanah, 1,600 Jews of Grodek, Belorussian S.S.R., are murdered by the Nazis. About 400 survivors are sent to the ghetto of Krasnoye.

In Druszkopol, Volhynia, Ukrainian S.S.R., 1,200 Jews are murdered by the SS and Ukrainian police.

The thirty-first deportation train of 1,000 Jewish men and women leaves the Drancy transit camp in the German occupied zone of France for the Auschwitz extermination camp in Poland. Immediately, 920 are gassed; only 13 men will survive till the liberation of the camp in 1945.

The SS murders 3,600 Jews within two days in Stolin, Poland (today Belorussian S.S.R.).

The liquidation of the 10,000 Jews in the ghetto of Lida, district of Novogrodek, Poland (today Belorussian S.S.R.), begins. It will take nine days. Many Jews are murdered and the others are deported to the Treblinka extermination camp.

Jews numbering 235 leave the ghetto of Horochov, district of Luzk, Poland, to join the partisans in the forest who are fighting against the Germans.

From the Westerbork transit camp in the Dutch province of Drenthe 874 Jewish inmates are deported to Auschwitz.

1943   Jews are deported from the Theresienstadt concentration camp in Czechoslovakia to Auschwitz.

The liquidation of the ghettos of Minsk, Belorussian S.S.R., and Lida, Belorussian S.S.R., begins and will last for three days.

September 12

1939   The Wehrmacht (regular German forces) murders 32 Jews in Kozmice, Poland.

The Wehrmacht murders 6 Jews in the village of Stara Wies, district of Limanowa, Poland.

In Mordarka, Limanowa, Poland, 5 Jews are murdered by the Nazis.

The Germans invade Grojec, central Poland, and all male Jews between the ages of 15 and 55 are herded together in the marketplace and marched 60 km to Rava Mazoviecka. Those who cannot walk are shot on the way. On the day of the Ger-

man invasion the town numbers about 5,200 Jews. Jews have been living in Grojec since the eighteenth century.

1942   The SS murders 1,200 Jews of Vysoko, Polesie, Poland (today Belorussian S.S.R.), outside of town.

On the first day of the Jewish New Year, 5,000 Jews from the ghetto of Stanislavov, Poland (today Ukrainian S.S.R.) are rounded up and deported to the Belzec extermination camp. A great number of Jews are shot on the spot.

The ninth convoy with 1,000 Jews—among them 228 children—leaves the Mechelen transit camp in Poland. There will be only 20 survivors of this convoy when the camp is liberated in 1945.

September 13

1939   The first Aktion against the 4,000 Jews of Mielec, Poland, begins on the eve of Rosh Hashanah, the Jewish New Year. The Germans set a synagogue on fire and push 20 Jews into the burning building; those who try to escape are shot. The slaughterhouse is set aflame and Jews pushed in. The Jews who are in the mikveh (the ritual bath) are shot when German soldiers force their way in. The Jewish community of Mielec was founded in the seventeenth century.

German troops occupy Tomaszov Lubelski, a town in eastern Poland where 6,000 Jews live. The synagogue is burned down and 500 Jewish houses are destroyed. The Nazis stay for only two weeks before handing it over to the Soviets. Jews have been living here since the beginning of the seventeenth century, and in 1648 they were victims of the Chmielnicki Cossacks.

1940   The Gestapo threatens the 4,000 Jews of Luxembourg with deportation unless they leave the country the next day—which is Yom Kippur. Jews have been living in Luxembourg since the second half of the thirteenth century.

1941 The Nazis shoot 398 Jews in the town of Kaganovitsch, Soviet Union, during a three-day Aktion.

In the ghetto of Smolewicze, Belorussian S.S.R., 250 Jews are shot.

The first Aktion against the 2,000 Jews living in Arnhem, Gelderland province, Netherlands, takes place. In retaliation for sabotage, several hundred Jews are arrested and sent to the Mauthausen concentration camp in Austria, never to return. Jews have been living in Arnhem since the middle of the thirteenth century.

In the course of a three-day Aktion, 3,000 Jews are murdered by extermination commandos in Hancewicze, Belorussian S.S.R.

1942 The last large-scale deportation of Jews from the Warsaw ghetto is sent to the Treblinka extermination camp. Each day the convoys transport between 5,000 and 7,000 Jews to Treblinka, where they are killed—a total of 300,000 Warsaw Jews.

During the liquidation of the ghetto in Checiny, Poland, many Jews are shot and more than 1,000 are deported to Treblinka, where they are murdered.

From Brzesko, Poland, 3,000 Jews are sent to the Belzec extermination camp and murdered.

The SS murders 500 Jews in Miody, Vilna district, Lithuanian S.S.R.

1944 The last convoy of 279 Jewish prisoners is deported from the Westerbork transit camp in the Dutch province of Drenthe to the Bergen-Belsen concentration camp. Among the deportees are Anne Frank and her family.

September 14

1928 Anti-Jewish agitation arises in Petrovo Selo, the Banat, Yugoslavia, due to rumors of ritual murder. Troops are instructed to watch over the Jewish houses night and day. A number of rioters are arrested. They admit that they intended to murder all the Jewish inhabitants of Petrovo Selo.

1939 The Nazis burn down the synagogue and burn Jewish religious books and Torah scrolls in the marketplace of Lezajsk, Poland, deliberately choosing this day, Rosh Hashanah.

The Gestapo shoots 7 Jews in Nove Miasto, Warsaw province, Poland.

The police shoot 3 Jews in the Jewish cemetery of Dzigorzev, district of Sieradz, Poland.

In Aleksandrov, Poland, 45 Jews are arrested, tortured, and murdered by the Wehrmacht (regular German forces).

The Gestapo murders 14 Jews in Pultusk, a town north of Warsaw, Poland.

A number of Jews are murdered during a pogrom when the Nazis occupy Bilgoraj, Lublin province, Poland, where 5,000 Jews live. Jews have been living there since the seventeenth century, including such famous Jewish writers as the Nobel Prize winner Isaac Bashevis Singer.

1942 A convoy with 992 Jews leaves Vienna for Minsk, Belorussian S.S.R.

902 Jewish inmates are sent from the Westerbork transit camp in the Dutch province of Drenthe and 1,000 Jewish men and women from the Drancy

Jewish betrothal in Nuremberg, from Kirchner, Judisches Zeremoniell, *1726.*

transit camp in occupied France are all deported to the Auschwitz extermination camp in Poland. Immediately after their arrival, 893 of the Jews from Drancy are gassed. Only 45 of this convoy will survive until the liberation of the camp in 1945.

700 Jews are sent from the ghetto of Gorlice in southeastern Poland to the Belzec extermination camp.

The Warsaw ghetto is made smaller and the Nazis restrict it to 35,000 Jews. With the help of the Jewish underground organization, Zydowska Organizacja Bojowa (ZOB), another 20,000 people remain in the ghetto illegally. The underground begins to prepare for the last fight.

1943   From the Westerbork transit camp, 1,005 Jewish inmates are deported to Auschwitz.

From Westerbork, 305 Jewish inmates are deported to the Theresienstadt concentration camp in Czechoslovakia.

September 15

1935   The Nuremberg Laws against the Jews, signed by Rudolph Hess, are published. The German Jews lose all their civil rights.

1939   The Wehrmacht (regular German forces) shoots 2 Jews in Visla Vielka, Poland.

On the second day of the Jewish New Year, another synagogue is burned down in Mielec, Poland, and some Jews are killed in the flames.

A number of Jews are murdered, the synagogue is burned down, and Jewish property is plundered when the German troops occupy the town of Kutno, Poland, where 6,700 Jews live. The Jewish community dates back to the fifteenth century.

1941   During an Aktion that lasts several days, 1,500 Jews from the ghetto of Vilna are shot in Ponary, Poland (today Lithuanian S.S.R.).

The Nazis murder 8,000 people, most of them Jews from the area of Golina, Slupca, and Konin, in the Biskupi Vygoda forest near Kazimierz, Poznan province, Poland. Many are shot and many others are burned alive.

1942   In the course of three days, some of the 4,000 Jews of Kalusz, province of Stanislavov, Poland (today Ukrainian S.S.R.), are either murdered on the spot or deported to the Belzec extermination camp, along with the 1,500 Jews of the ghetto of Kamionka-Strumilova, province of Lvov (today Ukrainian S.S.R.).

The Nazis deport 500 Jews from the village of Dobra, Poland, to the Treblinka extermination camp, where they are murdered on arrival.

From the area of Rozvadov, Poland, 450 Jews are sent to the Rozvadov labor camp, where they perform extremely hard work at the steel mill of Stalova Vola. Those people not strong enough for the work are shot. About 1,000 Jews perish in this camp.

The tenth transport of 1,048 Jews, among them 264 children, leaves the Mechelen transit camp in Belgium for the Auschwitz extermination camp in Poland. Only 17 will survive until the liberation of the camp in 1945.

1943   A Jew is deported from Vienna to the Theresienstadt concentration camp in Czechoslovakia.

The Nazis surround the ghetto of Vilna, Lithuanian S.S.R., and battle the Jewish underground.

1944   The liquidation of the ghetto of Lodz, Poland, is complete. Most of the 70,000 Jews are gassed in Auschwitz.

September 16

1939   The Nazis murder 6 Jews in Jarczev, district of Lukov, Poland.

On the day of the German invasion, 16 Jews are arrested in Wloclawek, southeast of Bydgoszcz, Poland. They are taken to prison, murdered, and buried in a mass grave in the Jewish cemetery.

Two days after the German invasion of Przemysl, Rzeszow province, Poland, 500 Jews are shot. Two days later the Germans hand the town over to the Soviets. At the outbreak of the war 20,000 Jews are living in Przemysl; the Jewish community dates back to the middle of the sixteenth century.

1942   From the ghetto of Jedrzejov, Kielce province, Poland, 6,000 Jews are sent to the Treblinka extermination camp. Only 200 Jews remain in the ghetto.

A forced labor camp for Jews is set up in Pustkov, Kielce province, Poland.

SS men and Ukrainian auxiliaries deport 1,400 Jews from the ghetto of Radziechov, Ukraine, to the Belzec extermination camp, Poland.

A deportation train with 1,003 Jewish men and women from the Drancy transit camp in the German occupied zone of France is sent to the Auschwitz extermination camp in Poland, where 856 of them are immediately sent to the gas chambers. Only 33 men and 1 woman will survive until 1945.

The eleventh transport of 1,742 Jews, including 523 children, leaves the Mechelen transit camp in Belgium for Auschwitz. Only 30 will survive until the liberation of the camp in 1945.

1943   In the course of two days, 24 Jews are sent from Merano, Italy, to Auschwitz.

Southern Transylvania, belonging to Rumania, is briefly occupied by some Hungarian units, led by ultrarightist officers. In the town of Sarmas, a group of local anti-Semites, under the leadership of a certain Varga and his wife, plans the elimination of the Jewish community of the town. The 126 Jewish residents of Sarmas are taken to a nearby hill, where they are all massacred by the police, under the command of a Hungarian captain.

September 17

1394   An edict is issued on Yom Kippur—the highest Jewish holiday, the Day of Atonement—by Charles VI, king of France, ordering the explusion of all Jews from French Territories.

1920   Units of the Ukrainian National Army, under the command of Khmara, carry out a pogrom in the town of Vinograd in the district of Kiev, Ukraine. The number of Jewish victims is unknown.

1939   The Germans occupy Zychlin, Lodz province, Poland, where the 3,500 Jews make up half the town's population.

The Germans occupy Tarnobrzeg, Rzeszov province, Poland, and at once incite pogroms against the 3,800 members of the Jewish community. Jews settled there in the early seventeenth century and

according to old documents, the entire Jewish population was murdered in 1655.

1941   German troops enter the town of Lomza, Poland, after the outbreak of the Soviet-German war and two months later erect the Jewish ghetto. At this time 11,000 Jews live in Lomza. A large-scale Aktion is undertaken by the German Troops and 3,000 Jews are killed.

The general deportation of German Jews begins.

1942   The ghetto of Kalusz, Poland (today Ukrainian S.S.R.), is liquidated, and all Jews are either murdered or deported. A very few manage to flee to Stanislav but are later caught and killed. Kalusz is "free of Jews."

The Jews of Sokal, Lvov province, Poland (today Ukrainian S.S.R.), have been deported to do forced labor and suffer under economic restrictions and assaults on their lives. On September 17, a large-scale Aktion takes place in the course of which 2,000 Jews are deported to the Belzec extermination camp.

The first transport of four with 200 Jews from Moravska Ostrava, Moravia province, Czechoslovakia, is carried out. A total of 8,000 Jews are deported from Moravska Ostrava and its vicinity.

1943   Lejzor Stolicki, the chief of the Jewish ghetto police who has continuously supported the Jewish partisans in the forest, is killed during the last Aktion carried out in the ghetto of Lida, Poland (today Belorussian S.S.R.). The Jews who remain in the ghetto are murdered, but 300 Jewish partisans who join the Soviets in fighting the Germans will survive the Nazi era.

1944   The 3,600 Jewish forced laborers employed in the copper mines of Bor, 124 miles southeast of Belgrade, Yugoslavia, are marched to

Mohacs under the escort of 100 Hungarian guards. Only a few are saved by Yugoslavian partisans. Most of them are deported to the German concentration camps of Flossenbürg, Sachsenhausen, and Oranienburg. Only a few will survive.

September 18

1349 Duke Albrecht of Austria gives protection to 330 Jews from Diessenhofen, Winterthur, and other small towns in his territory (today Switzerland), and allows them to stay in his fortress at Kyburg. When he gives in to the pressure of these towns a few weeks later, the Jews are burned at the stake on September 18.

The Jewish community of Wetzlar, Germany, is annihilated following the accusation of well poisoning.

1939 Per the agreement with the Nazis on the division of Poland, Soviet troops occupy Dubno, Volhynia, Poland (today Ukrainian S.S.R.). Jews settled here in 1532. In 1648 the Chmielnicki Cossacks massacred the Jewish population. During the following centuries the community flourished again, but after the Soviets seize power on September 18, 1939, all Jewish institutions are dissolved and all leaders of the Jewish community are deported to Siberia. The Jews are expropriated of all their possessions.

1941 From the ghetto of Krupki, Belorussian S.S.R., 1,900 Jews are brought to the peat pits outside the town and shot.

1942 The ghetto of Piaski, a suburb of Kovel, Volhynia province, Poland (today Ukrainian S.S.R.), is liquidated and Kovel is declared "free of Jews."

The Nazis send 1,004 Jewish inmates of the Westerbork transit camp in the Dutch province of Drenthe and a deportation train with 1,000 Jews from the Drancy camp in the German occupied zone of France to the Auschwitz extermination camp in Poland. Immediately after their arrival, 859 of the Jews from Drancy are gassed. Only 21 men of this convoy will survive until the liberation of the camp in 1945.

1942 During a two-day Aktion, 1,200 Jews are murdered by the SS in Biten, district of Novogrodek, Poland.

1943 2,000 Jews, among them Soviet Jewish prisoners of war, are deported from the ghetto of Minsk, Belorussian S.S.R., to the Sobibor extermination camp in Poland, and murdered.

September 19

1939 The Wehrmacht (regular German forces) murders 100 Jews in the village of Lukov, east of Warsaw, Poland.

1941 From Lipniszki, district of Novogrodek, Belorussian S.S.R., 500 Jews are deported to Ivje to do forced labor.

The Nazis murder all the Jews of Shitomir, Ukrainian S.S.R., who could not flee in time. The exact number is not known but probably amounts to 15,000 victims.

1942 The first deportation of the 5,000 Jews of Parczew, province of Lublin, Poland, to the Treblinka extermination camp begins. Several hundred Jews manage to flee into the forests, where they form a partisan group under the command of a Jewish officer of the Polish army, Alexander Skotnicki. About 150 Jewish partisans survive the war. Jews have been living in Parczew under the protection of Polish kings since the sixteenth century.

A convoy of 1,000 Jews from the Theresienstadt concentration camp in Czechoslovakia is deported to Minsk-Trostyanets, Belorussian S.S.R., where they are shot on arrival.

About 3,000 Jews of the ghetto of Brody, Poland (today Ukrainian S.S.R.), are arrested and deported to the nearby Belzec extermination camp, where they are all murdered. Jewish resistance groups remain active.

1944   In the Klooga labor camp in Estonia, a four-day Aktion takes place due to the approaching Soviet troops and about 3,000 Jews are murdered. Among the dead are 1,500 Jews from Vilna, Poland.

A second group of 2,500 Hungarian Jewish laborers leaves the copper mines of Bor, 124 miles southeast of Belgrade, Yugoslavia. On the way several hundred of the starving men are shot. After a mass execution on October 7, the rest of the group will be deported to the German concentration camps at Buchenwald and Flossenbürg, where most of them will perish.

September 20

1540   The first auto-da-fé of Conversos (forcibly baptized Jews) is held in Lisbon, Portugal, after the establishment of an Inquisition tribunal there. The Lisbon Inquisition will become the country's most active.

1939   A decree is issued by Reinhard Heydrich to all Gestapo divisions, which employs the code word "Special Treatment," meaning the actual physical destruction of people. The decree affects mainly Jews.

The advancing Wehrmacht (German regular forces) arrests and murders 33 Jews in Sieradz, Poland.

A Jew is murdered by the Nazis in the village of Grodzisk, Poland.

1942   From Szczekociny, province of Kielce, Poland, 3,000 Jews are deported to the Radomsk labor camp.

All 3,000 Jews of Zaleszczyki, Poland (today Ukrainian S.S.R.), are ordered to be ready within 24 hours for their deportation to the Tluste ghetto. Part of them are sent to Tluste, part to the Belzec extermination camp, where 350 Jews from Bialy-kamien are deported on the same day. Some Jews from Zaleszczyki manage to flee into the forests.

1943   The twenty-first convoy of 1,433 Jews, among them 89 children, leaves the Mechelen transit camp in Belgium for the Auschwitz extermination camp in Poland. Only 51 will survive until the liberation of the camp in 1945.

September 21

1287   In Kirn, near Bad Kreuznach, Germany, 6 Jews are slain. The slaying probably follows the accusation of ritual murder (killing a Christian child in order to use its blood for the festival of Passover) against the Jews of the town of Oberwesel, after which Jews are slain in several places in the vicinity.

1348   The Jews of Zurich, Switzerland, are accused of well poisoning and ritual murder. Except for a few who are driven out of town, the people of the Jewish community are burned at the stake. A law is issued on the same day that no Jew is ever to be allowed to return to Zurich.

1939   Reinhard Heydrich, the chief of Reichs-Sicherheitshauptamt (Reich Security Headquar-

Ceremony on the eve of Yom Kippur, from a woodcut of Augsburg, 1530.

ters) in Berlin, presents the plan to create the ghettos in Poland.

The Nazis order that all communities in Poland with less than 500 Jews are to be dissolved and that the Jews have to resettle in ghettos in the towns and in the area between Lublin and Nisko.

1941 The SS and Lithuanian volunteers murder 3,500 Jews in Aishishak, Vilna province, Lithuanian S.S.R.

1942 On this Yom Kippur, 1,200 Jews from Suchedniov, 1,200 Jews from Sendziszov, and 6,000 Jews from Wegrov, Poland, are deported during a three-day Aktion in Wegrov to the Treblinka extermination camp.

On the Jewish holiday of Yom Kippur, 1,000 Jews from the ghetto of Rohatyn, and 1,000 Jews from the ghetto of Podhaitsy, Ukrainian S.S.R.—where 3,000 Jews are living—are sent to the Belzec extermination camp. Jews have been living in Podhaitsy since the seventeenth century.

On Yom Kippur, 600 Jews from Kamionka-Strumilova, a town in the province of Lvov, Poland (today Ukrainian S.S.R.), are taken from town and murdered near the Bug River in Zabuze.

On Yom Kippur, a deportation train of 2,000 Jewish men and women—among them about 1,000 non-French Jews—leaves the Pithiviers transit camp in the German occupied zone of France. Another convoy of 713 Jewish inmates of the Westerbork transit camp in the Dutch province of Drenthe leaves on the same day. All are deported to the Auschwitz extermination camp in Poland.

On Yom Kippur, in Rakov, Belorussian S.S.R., the SS assemble about 100 Jews and shoot them.

On Yom Kippur, 700 Jews are murdered by the SS in Chodel, province of Lublin, Poland.

In the course of an Aktion that lasts from September 21—Yom Kippur—to September 29, 1942, five convoys with a total of 10,000 Jews are sent from the Theresienstadt ghetto in Czechoslovakia, supposedly to the area of Minsk and Trostinec in Belorussian S.S.R. Nobody knows of any survivors.

1943 The last 400 Jews of Kobylnik, district of Vilna, Lithuanian S.S.R., are murdered by the SS.

From the Westerbork transit camp 979 Jewish inmates are deported to Auschwitz.

1944 From Vienna, 2 Jews are deported to the Theresienstadt concentration camp in Czechoslovakia.

September 22

1287 In the village of Lahstein, Germany, 6 Jews are massacred in connection with the ritual murder accusation against the Jews of Oberwesel, Germany.

1928 In Massena, New York, one day before Yom Kippur Eve, a four-year-old child disappears. The Ku Klux Klan alleges that the Jews have kidnapped the child to use his blood for the Yom Kippur services. Several Jewish citizens, including the town rabbi, are then questioned at the police station and the Jewish community is harassed by people peering in the windows in search of the child. On Yom Kippur Eve, the doors of the synagogue are blocked and there are riots, but the child is found alive and well the next day.

1939 By agreement, the Germans hand over Brest Litovsk, Poland (today Belorussian S.S.R.), to the Soviet Union. The Jewish community dates back to the fourteenth century, and 30,000 Jews are living there now. The Soviets immediately start to arrest and deport the leaders of the Jewish community to Siberia, and to liquidate the Jewish institutions.

The 3,000 Jews of Lancut, Poland, are driven out of town toward the San River, which marks the Soviet border, and are forced to swim across the river. Many of them drown, and many others are shot by the Nazis. The Jewish community of Lancut dates back to the middle of the sixteenth century.

1941 The SS murders 1,200 Jews in Wiloczan, district of Vilna, Lithuania.

On Rosh Hashanah, the day of the Jewish New Year, the ghetto of Pruzana, Poland (today Belorussian S.S.R.), has to be enlarged to accommodate 2,000 Jews from the surrounding area and 2,000 Jews from Bialystok.

On Rosh Hashanah, Monsignor Dr. Josef Tiso, president of the Slovakian Republic—a satellite state created by the Germans after their occupation of Czechoslovakia in 1938—orders the Jews to wear the Yellow Star.

On the Jewish New Year, the Nazis murder 28,000 Jews from Vinnitsa, Ukrainian S.S.R., and its vicinity who are living in the Vinnitsa ghetto. Among them are 2,500 Jews of Litin, district of Podolia. The Jewish communities of Vinnitsa and of Litin date back to the sixteenth century.

1942 Another convoy with 1,000 Jews—most of them elderly Jews from Czechoslovakia—is sent from the Theresienstadt ghetto to the east. There are no survivors and it is assumed that they have been sent to Minsk and murdered there.

In Aleksandia, Volhynia, 2,000 Jews are murdered by the SS and Ukrainian police.

The SS burns 225 Jews in their houses in Syrokomia, province of Lublin, Poland.

Of the 7,000 Jews living in the ghetto of Opatov, Kielce province, Poland, 1,800 are arrested and deported to the camps in the district of Lublin. Jews have been living in Opatov since the middle of the seventeenth century.

In Poland, 2,500 Jews from Jadovo, 2,000 Jews from Sokolov Podlaski, and 7,500 Jews from Wegrov, are deported to the Treblinka extermination camp. Only 100 Jews are left in Wegrov. In Sokolov Podlaski, 500 Jews hide but are found by the Nazis and shot. Of the 700 Jews who manage to flee into the forests, most are also murdered by the Nazis. Only a small number of Jews of Sokolov Podlaski succeed in joining the partisans.

September 23

1648 The Cossacks led by Chmielnicki capture the town of Pilaviez, Ukraine, and massacre the Jewish population.

1938 The synagogue of Cheb, Sudentenland, Czechoslovakia, is burned down in the course of an Aktion. The Nazis, who will occupy this area in October, burn down the synagogue in Marienbad as well.

1939 On Yom Kippur in Sokolov Podlaski, Poland, where 4,000 Jews live, 20 Jews are murdered and the synagogue is burned down by the Nazis. The Jewish community dates back to the sixteenth century.

On Yom Kippur the Nazis arrest Rabbi Mendel Morgenstern of Wegrov, Poland, where 6,000 Jews are living, and torture him to death. Jews first settled in Wegrov in the sixteenth century under the protection of Polish kings.

1942 The SS burns 1,800 Jews in their homes in Motel, Polesie, Belorussian S.S.R.

A deportation train of 1,000 Jews from the Drancy transit camp in the German occupied zone of France is sent to the Auschwitz extermination camp in Poland. Immediately, 475 are gassed; only 30 will survive until the liberation of the camp in 1945.

A large-scale Aktion—lasting for the following twelve days—begins in the ghetto of Czestochova, 205 km southeast of Warsaw, Poland. The Nazis send 40,000 Jews to the Treblinka extermination camp. On September 23, 5,000 Jews from the ghetto of Kosov Lacki, and 10 Jews from Szydloviec, are deported to Treblinka as well.

A convoy with 1,980 Jews leaves the Theresienstadt concentration camp in Czechoslovakia for Minsk-Trostyanets, Belorussian S.S.R., where they will be shot.

In the course of a seven-day Aktion, 16,000 Jews from Lodz, Poland, are deported to the Chelmno extermination camp and murdered.

All Jews over the age of 50 and under the age of 14—a total of 64 people—are shot during the first liquidation in the concentration camp at Brazlav, Poland (today Ukrainian S.S.R.), by the German and Rumanian guards of the camp.

Deported to the transit camps at Biala Podlaska, are 2,100 Jews from Janov Podlaski, Poland, and 1,200 Jews from Konstantinovka, Ukrainian S.S.R.

From Tuczyn, Volhynia, Ukrainian S.S.R., 3,500 Jews are taken outside of town and murdered.

The SS murders 210 Jews in Ostronek, province of Lublin, Poland.

1943 The ghetto of Vilna, Lithuanian S.S.R., with 40,000 inhabitants, is liquidated. The Jewish men are sent to Estonia, the young Jewish women to Latvia. Old people and children are deported to the Majdanek concentration camp in Poland. The remaining 3,000 Jews are put to work on motor vehicle repairs for the Wehrmacht (German regular forces).

The Gestapo orders all Jews of the ghetto of Tuczyn, a town near Rovno, Ukrainian S.S.R., to gather at the gate of the ghetto. The Jews, who know what awaits them, set their houses on fire and offer fierce resistance. Many of them are killed, but 2,000 Jews manage to flee into the forests. Most of them are seized by Ukrainian farmers and handed over to the Germans. Only 15 Jews from Tuczyn will survive the war.

1944 Further deportations of the Jews of Slovakia take place after the uprising in Banska Bystrica, Czechoslovakia, which was organized by the Czech resistance with the help of American parachutists.

September 24

1752 In an auto-da-fé in Lisbon, Portugal, 12 Conversos, descendants of Jews forcibly baptized some centuries ago, are accused of Judaizing, secretly practicing the Jewish religion. Three of them are burned at the stake as nonrepentants, and the others are sentenced to terms of imprisonment.

1941 One day after the Jewish New Year, the Jews of the ghetto of Vilkaviskis, Lithuanian S.S.R., are taken out of the ghetto and murdered by the SS.

1942 In two days, 1,200 Jews are deported from Sterdyn, province of Lublin, Poland, to the Treblinka extermination camp.

A convoy of 1,287 Jews from Vienna leaves for the Theresienstadt concentration camp in Czechoslovakia.

1943 SS officer Herbert Kappler demands 50 kg of gold from the Jews of Rome, to be delivered within thirty-six hours. He takes 200 Jewish hostages whom he threatens to kill if his demand is not satisfied. On September 24, the Jews pay the exorbitant sum.

September 25

1941 After the arrival of the first SS Cavalry Brigade in the region of Polesie in the Soviet Union, their commander Fegelein orders: "Every partisan must be shot. All Jews are to be regarded as partisans and must be shot. Jewish women and children are to be driven into the swamps."

The SS murders 1,000 Jews in the village of Olkieniki, Polesie, Belorussian S.S.R.

1942 4,000 Jews from Kaluszyn, Poland, and 700 Jews from Stanslavov, Poland (today Ukrainian S.S.R.), are deported to the Treblinka extermination camp.

A deportation convoy with 928 Jewish inmates of the Westerbork transit camp in the Dutch province of Drenthe and another with 1,004 Jewish men and women of various nationalities from the Drancy transit camp in the German occupied zone of France leave for the Auschwitz extermination camp in Poland. Only 15 people of the Drancy convoy will survive until the liberation of the camp in 1945.

Two days after Yom Kippur all the Jews of Ivanovo, Poland (today Belorussian S.S.R.), are murdered.

Jews have been living in Ivanovo since the seventeenth century.

1944   The Jewish inmates of the concentration camps in the area of Riga, Latvia—such as Kaiserwald and Salaspils—are deported by ship to the Stutthof concentration camp near Danzig, Poland. Those who are sick are shot in the camps or in the nearby forests.

September 26

1941   From Orsha, Belorussian S.S.R., 3,000 Jews are shot in the local Jewish cemetery.

A selection of 3,000 Jews of the ghetto of Kaunas, Lithuanian S.S.R., is made, and they are murdered in Fortress 9.

The Jews of Svieciany, Lithuanian S.S.R., are driven by SS extermination commandos into the nearby forest of Polygon, where about 8,000 Jews are murdered. However, armed resistance is offered by the Jews, and several hundred manage to escape into the forest.

1942   Two convoys totaling 4,004 Jews leave the Theresienstadt concentration camp in Czechoslovakia for Minsk and Maly Trostyanets, Belorussian S.S.R., where they are shot.

The Gestapo shoots about a dozen Jews of the Otoczna labor camp in Poland.

The second deportation of Jews from the town Biala Podlaska, Poland, begins when 4,000 Jews are transferred to the ghetto of Miedzyrzec and from there to the Treblinka extermination camp. On the same day, 2,000 Jews from the ghetto of Siedlce, Poland, are deported to Treblinka.

The Nazis deport 1,500 Jews from the village Skala Podlaska, and 2,100 Jews from Jezierzany, both in Poland (today Ukrainian S.S.R.), to the Belzec extermination camp.

The SS murders 250 so-called working Jews in Belzec.

September 27

1939   After the incorporation of the Polish town of Aleksandrov Lodzki into the Third Reich, all Jews are deported to Glovno in the "General Government." The Jewish cemetery is leveled to the ground.

1942   Thirty Jewish men and women are driven into a minefield in Galibicy, near Demidov, Soviet Union. Immediately, 8 people are torn to pieces and the others are mutilated and wounded. Some hours later, the survivors are driven into the minefield once more and they all perish.

Via Wolkowysk, 600 Jews from Parcevo, province of Bialystok, Poland, are deported to the Auschwitz extermination camp.

From Kock, province of Lublin, Poland, 3,000 Jews are sent to the Lukov transit camp.

In 3 days, 5,000 Jews are deported from Zvolen, province of Kielce, Poland, to the Treblinka extermination camp.

The Nazis deport 13,000 Jews from the ghetto of Kozienice and the surrounding area, Kielce province; 2,500 Jews from Parysov, Lublin province; and 1,000 Jews from the village of Kolbiel (all in Poland), to Treblinka.

1943   After the fall of Mussolini, the Greek island of Corfu is occupied by the Germans. At the outbreak of the war, 2,000 Jews are living on Corfu;

their settlement dates back to Byzantine times. Now anti-Jewish laws are introduced.

1944 A transport with 20 Jews leaves the Theresienstadt concentration camp in Czechoslovakia for Bergen-Belsen in Germany.

September 28

1939 The Nazis order 10,000 Jews to assemble on a sports field in Jaraslav, Rzeszow province, Poland, from where they are driven across the San River into Soviet-occupied territory. The Jews have to leave all of their possessions behind. In May 1940, most of them will be deported by the Soviets to Siberia; several hundred of them will survive. Jews have been living in Jaroslav since the sixteenth century.

1942 From the Westerbork transit camp in the Dutch province of Drenthe, 610 Jewish inmates, and a convoy of 904 Jewish men and women from the Drancy transit camp in the German occupied zone of France are deported to the Auschwitz extermination camp in Poland. Only 18 men of the Drancy convoy will survive until the liberation of the camp in 1945.

In the ghetto of Kossov, Ukrainian S.S.R., the Nazis circulate the message that all Jews in hiding will not be harmed if they give themselves up, but will be allowed to remain in the ghetto. All Jews who heed the announcement are murdered.

1944 A transport with 2,499 Jews leaves the Theresienstadt concentration camp for Auschwitz.

September 29

1349 Accusing them of well poisoning, the townspeople of Krems and of Stein, Austria, threaten

the Jews of Krems, one of the most important Jewish communities in Austria. The Jews of Krems set fire to their own houses and die in the flames. Only a few manage to flee to the castle of Krems.

1891 Several Jews are massacred during a pogrom in Starodub, Russia, on the eve of Yom Kippur.

1939 The Germans occupy Warsaw, Poland, whose 393,950 Jews comprise a third of the total population. Jews have been living there since the end of the fourteenth century. Their history has been as changeable as that of the city, which has belonged to Poland, Prussia, Russia, and again to Poland.

Several days after the German invasion of Wyszkov, Poland, the entire Jewish population of 5,000 is rounded up and forced to cross the Soviet border. They are driven toward the east, where they are left to their own fate.

1941 After the German army occupies the town on September 27, all the Jews of Kiev, Ukrainian S.S.R., and the surrounding area are summoned to register with the German authorities. Those who assemble near the Jewish cemetery on the order of the Nazis are driven to the ravine of Babi Yar. Here, according to the official SS report, 33,771 Jews are machine-gunned on this and the following day.

1942 A transport with 2,000 Jews leaves the Theresienstadt concentration camp in Czechoslovakia for the Maly-Trostyanets concentration camp in Belorussian S.S.R.

The Nazis murder 1,000 Jews in the town of Wolozyn, Soviet Union.

In the course of an uprising in Serniki, Volhynia, Poland (today Ukrainian S.S.R.), 850 Jews are murdered by the Nazis; 150 Jews flee into the forests. Only 10 of them will survive.

The Nazis murder 150 Jews in the village of Kobylniki near Minsk in Belorussian S.S.R.

In the course of a raid, the last 2,000 Jews of Amsterdam, including all the members of the Jewish Council, are arrested by the Nazis and sent to the Westerbork transit camp in the Dutch province of Drenthe.

1943 In Kiev, Ukrainian S.S.R., 325 Jews and Soviet prisoners of war are forced to dig up and burn the corpses of the victims of the Babi Yar massacre of September 1941, in order to eliminate all traces of the mass murder. Though they are in chains, they revolt, and 311 are murdered by the Nazis the next day.

The SS takes 680 prominent Jews, who are under the personal protection of the Reichskommissar (deputy of the Reich), from the castle of Barneveld in the Dutch province of Gelderland and drives them to the Westerbork transit camp in the province of Drenthe.

1944 A transport with 1,500 Jews leaves the Theresienstadt concentration camp in Czechoslovakia for the Auschwitz extermination camp in Poland.

September 30

1337 On the false accusation of host desecration, a small army set up by the aldermen of Deggendorf, Bavaria, Germany, and commanded by the knight Hartmann massacres the defenseless Jews and burns their corpses. The Jews' houses are looted and the looted property is divided among their murderers.

1939 Several Jews are murdered when the German troops occupy Novy Dvor (Mazoviecki) near Warsaw, Poland, where 4,000 Jews live. The Jewish community dates back to the beginning of the eighteenth century.

1941 The SS murders 300 Jews in Troki, district of Vilna, Lithuania.

When the Germans invade Tallinn, Estonia, 1,000 Jews are massacred.

The preparations for the creation of the ghetto in Riga, Latvia, are complete. With the Jews from the rural areas who have survived the massacres organized by the Einsatzgruppen (special killing squads), the inmates of the ghetto number 30,000.

1942 The Jews offer fierce resistance against the Nazis in Korzec, Volhynia, Poland (today Ukrainian S.S.R.). About 2,000 Jews are murdered by the SS and Ukrainian police.

The Nazis murder 400 Jews of the village of Koziany near Minsk, Belorussian S.S.R.

From Magierov, Lvov province, Poland, 900 Jews are deported to Rava Ruska.

Deported to the town of Stryj are 2,100 Jews from Rozdol, and 1,000 Jews from Zydaczov, Poland.

From Ternopol, East Galicia, Poland (today Ukrainian S.S.R.), 1,000 Jews are deported by the Nazis to the Belzec extermination camp.

A convoy of 210 Jews leaves the Drancy transit camp in the German occupied zone of France for the Auschwitz extermination camp in Poland. All of them will be murdered there.

On the day of the Sukkot feast (Feast of Tabernacles), the ghetto of Zelechov, Poland, is liquidated and the Jews are sent to the Treblinka extermination camp. Several hundred Jews man-

Procession with palms during Sukkoth, the Feast of Tabernacles. (German engraving, 1748)

age to flee, and together with Poles and Russians, they fight in partisan units. Many of them are killed in action and only a very few survive. At the outbreak of the war the town numbers 5,500 Jews. The Jewish community dates back to the seventeenth century. On the same day, 4,000 Jews from the ghetto of Parysov and its vicinity, 2,150 Jews from Laskaczev, and 2,500 Jews from Mordy, are deported to Treblinka.

1943 An Aktion against the Jews in Czortkov, Poland (today Ukrainian S.S.R.), ends after six weeks. The SS has murdered 46,000 Jews.

OCTOBER

October 1

1939 In Wloclawek, in central Poland, all the synagogues of the Jewish community, which numbers 13,500, are burned down. With the active help of the ethnic Germans, several hundred Jews are arrested and deported.

1941 In Ponary, Poland (today Lithuanian S.S.R.), at least 2,000 Jews, originally from the Vilna ghetto, are shot.

In Siedlce, eastern Poland, a ghetto is set up toward which the Jews are forced to pay a very high "contribution."

On Yom Kippur the 5,000 Jews of Sarny, Volhynia, Poland (today Ukrainian S.S.R.), are registered. They all have to wear the Yellow Star.

As a first anti-Jewish measure against the 3,250 Jews living in Utrecht, Netherlands, 3 Jewish professors at the University of Utrecht are removed from their posts. The Jewish community dates back to the fourteenth century.

In Jasenovac, southeast of Zagreb, Yugoslavia, another concentration camp is set up, where 20,000 Jews will eventually perish.

1942 In the course of three days, the 10,000 Jews of Luboml, Poland (today Ukrainian S.S.R.), and the vicinity are rounded up. In the subsequent massacre, thousands are slaughtered by the SS in the town and the surrounding forests.

A convoy with 1,290 Jews leaves Vienna for the Theresienstadt concentration camp in Czechoslovakia.

Blowing the shofar on New Year's Day. (Dutch engraving, 1695)

In Legionovo, Warsaw province, Poland, 700 Jews are murdered by the SS.

From the ghetto of Chmielnik, Kielce province, Poland, 1,000 young Jews are deported to the Skarzysko-Kamienna labor camp. Another 500 Jews are sent to the Hasag labor camp in Czestochova where they will all perish.

In Drohobycz, Poland (today Ukrainian S.S.R.), a ghetto is set up where the Jews of Drohobycz and the neighboring villages are interned.

The 2,000 Jews of Busko Zdroj, Poland, and the surrounding area, concentrated in the Busko Zdroj ghetto, are deported to the Treblinka extermination camp. On the same day, 1,000 Jews from Radzyn, Poland, and 2,200 Jews from Bialobrzeg, Poland, are deported to Treblinka.

Deported to the Parczev camp are 1,500 Jews of Czemierniki, in the province of Lublin, Poland.

1943   The deportation of the 6,500 Danish Jews is scheduled for Rosh Hashanah. The Nazis only succeed in arresting 500 Jews; the Danish Resistance sends the remaining 6,000 Jews on fishing boats across the Belt Strait to safety in Sweden.

1944   A transport with 1,500 Jews leaves the Theresienstadt concentration camp for the Auschwitz extermination camp in Poland.

October 2

1919   For two days Petlyurian units of the Ukrainian National Army carry out a pogrom in the town of Dymar, Podolia, Russia. 4 Jews are massacred and many are wounded; several Jewish women and girls are raped.

1939   The Jews of Pultusk, Warsaw province, Poland, are driven to the other side of the Narev River, where Soviet-occupied territory begins. On the way to the border, many Jews are murdered. A number of the survivors find shelter in Bialystok. (In May and June 1940, some of the Jews will be deported by the Soviets to Siberia.)

The Germans order the Jewish population of Rozvadov, Poland, to leave town within twenty-four hours. The Jews are sent across the San River to the Soviet-occupied part of Poland from where they are scattered all over the country, some even as far as Siberia.

1940   After the majority of the Jewish population has been deported to Warsaw, 3,000 Jews remain in the ghetto of Wloclawek, Central Poland. They die from lack of food and sanitation. The buildings of the Jewish community are destroyed and the children have to be taught in the cemetery.

The ghetto of Warsaw, capital of Poland, is set up. All the Jews of Warsaw are herded in, 13 people to a room, and thousands remain unsheltered in the streets. Hunger spreads, as the daily rations contain only 184 calories. The ghetto is guarded on the outside by German and Polish police; inside the Jewish police are responsible for keeping order. Leaving the ghetto is punishable with death.

1941   Several synagogues in Paris are blown up by the Gestapo.

1942   Luboml, Poland (today Ukrainian S.S.R.), is declared "free of Jews," its last 10,000 Jews having been murdered.

The last 11 Jewish patients of the insane asylum of Kovin, Yugoslavia, are shot by the Nazis.

The 4,000 inmates of the ghetto of Sobienie Jeziory, Poland, both from the town itself and the surrounding area, are deported to the Treblinka extermination camp, where they are murdered upon arrival.

In the course of an Aktion that lasts two days, 4,000 Jews from the ghetto of Radzymin, Poland, are deported to Treblinka, where they are murdered. Radzymin is declared "free of Jews." Jews have been living there since the seventeenth century.

The SS murders 11,000 Jews from the ghetto of Bielsk Podlaski, Poland.

3,000 Jews of Belzyce, Lublin province, Poland, are sent to the Majdanek extermination camp. The ghetto of Belzyce is turned into a concentration camp.

A convoy with 1,014 Jews leaves from the Westerbork transit camp in the Dutch province of Drenthe for the Auschwitz extermination camp in Poland.

First sent to Opoczno, 250 Jews from Bialoczev, in the province of Kielce, Poland, will then be deported to an extermination camp.

October 3

1648 The Cossacks of Bogdan Chmielnicki begin the siege of Lvov, Galicia, Poland, which lasts until October 26. In the course of it, 6,000 Jews will die of hunger and epidemics.

After the conquest of Brody, Ukraine, the Chmielnicki Cossacks begin a massacre of the Jewish population of the town. In the course of two weeks, 6,000 Jews are cruelly slaughtered.

1940 The Nazis issue the order that the cafés of The Hague, Holland, display signs reading: JEWS NOT WANTED!

1941 In Kremenchug, Ukrainian S.S.R., all elderly Jewish men are killed by the SS.

The Jews of Secureni, Bessarabia, Rumania (today Moldavian S.S.R.), who have survived the pogroms of July and the death march, have been crowded together in a concentration camp which is now liquidated. They are deported to Transnistria.

1942 The Nazis have rounded up 13,000 Jewish men, women, and children in the course of large-scale raids. They are taken to the Westerbork transit camp in the Dutch province of Drenthe. The camp is so overcrowded that thousands have to sleep on the floor, without mattresses or blankets. Food and sanitary facilities are badly lacking.

The resettlement of the 310,000 Jews of Warsaw into the ghetto is completed.

The Polish representative at the Vatican, Ambassador Papée, gives precise details of the gassings to the cardinal secretary of state.

From the ghetto of Wislica, Kielce province, Poland, 3,000 Jews are deported by the Nazis to the Treblinka extermination camp. This marks the end of the Jewish community of Wislica, which dates back to the beginning of the sixteenth century. During the Swedish War (1656), 50 Jewish families were murdered by the soldiers of Stefan Czarniecki.

On the same day, 600 Jews from Rembertov, Warsaw province, Poland, are also deported to Treblinka.

The SS deports 4,500 Jews of the ghetto of Kolomyia, Ukrainian S.S.R., to the Belzec extermination camp in Poland.

1944 In the town of Zwolle, Netherlands, 3 Jews who have been in hiding are discovered by the Nazis and murdered.

1980 A bomb explodes outside a synagogue in Paris, killing 4 people and wounding 9.

The Jewish cemetery in Brody, Austria. (From Pennell, *The Jew at Home*)

October 4

1940 An order of the Vichy government, the Statute on Jews of foreign nationalities and on the Jewish race, divests all Jewish refugees in nonoccupied France of their rights. A week before, the Gestapo introduced the same measures in the occupied zone of France.

1941 In the ghetto of Kaunas, Lithuanian S.S.R., 3,000 Jews are singled out and taken to Fortress no. 9, where they are murdered.

The deportations of the Jews from the ghetto of Kishinev, Bessarabia (today Moldavian S.S.R.), to the camps of Transnistria begin. On October 4 about 6,000 persons are deported. In the following days the number of deportees is between 700 and 1,000 per day.

About 2,000 Jews, all inmates of the ghetto of Zagare, Lithuanian S.S.R., are murdered. The Aktion lasts for two days. Young people offer fierce armed resistance.

1942 From Lubycza Krolevska, Poland (today Ukrainian S.S.R.), 2,300 Jews are deported to the Belzec extermination camp in Poland.

For the Jews of Wolomin, Poland, this day signifies the beginning of the end. In the course of a purge that lasts until October 6, 600 Jews are shot by the SS. The remaining 2,400 Jews are deported to the Treblinka extermination camp, where they are murdered upon arrival. Wolomin, whose Jewish population has comprised about 30 percent of the total population, is "free of Jews." On the same day 1,000 Jews from the village of Ludvisin are also deported to Treblinka, and murdered upon arrival.

1944 A transport with 1,500 Jews leaves the Theresienstadt concentration camp in Czechoslovakia for the Auschwitz extermination camp in Poland

The Jews of the ghettos of Berdichev, Volhynia, Ukrainian S.S.R., are murdered. The Jewish community dates back to the sixteenth century. By the time of the Nazi invasion 30,000 Jews are living there.

October 5

1737 An auto-da-fé is held in Lisbon, Portugal, in which figures Antonio José da Silva, one of the best-known comedy writers of his time, and his wife and mother. They are accused of being Judaizers, descendants of Jews forcibly baptized some centuries ago who still practice the Jewish religion in secret. Although King José I himself intervenes on his behalf, da Silva is condemned to death by the Inquisition. He is garroted and his corpse is burned at the stake. His mother and his wife publicly abjure the Jewish faith.

1938 From this day on, the passports of all Jews in the German Reich, including Austria and the Sudetenland, are marked with a J. This is the idea of Dr. Rothmund, the chief of police of Switzerland, and it makes emigration even more difficult.

On Yom Kippur eve, the Jews of the 4th district of Vienna are ordered to turn in the keys to their houses. They are taken to the Ostbahnhof (eastern railway station) and sent without passports toward Czechoslovakia to the Danube River, where they are embarked on ships.

1941 500 Jews from Przemyslany, Poland (today Ukrainian S.S.R.), are taken into the forest and murdered.

In Swierzan Novy, in the district of Novogrodek, Poland, 500 Jews are murdered by the SS.

The SS shoots 1,300 Jews from Otynia, Poland (today Ukrainian S.S.R.), in the village of Povolutsch, Soviet Union.

1942 From the Westerbork transit camp in the Dutch province of Drenthe, 2,012 Jewish inmates are deported to the Auschwitz extermination camp in Poland.

In the ghetto of Czestochova, Poland, the Aktion that began on September 23, 1942, is completed. The SS has shot 2,000 Jews and deported 25,000 Jews to the Treblinka extermination camp. A small number of Jews remain in the "Smaller Ghetto."

On the same day a convoy with more than 1,000 Jews leaves the Theresienstadt concentration camp in Czechoslovakia for Treblinka. All of the deportees are gassed upon arrival.

During an Aktion, 500 Jews from the ghetto of Chortkov, Poland (today Ukrainian S.S.R.), and 1,000 Jews from Tluste, Poland (today Ukrainian S.S.R.), are deported to the Belzec extermination camp. In Tluste itself, 150 Jews have been murdered.

The Nazis begin an Aktion in Radzivillov, Ukrainian S.S.R. Several hundred Jews are murdered by the SS and some commit suicide. About 500 Jews flee into the forest where they are caught by Ukrainian farmers who turn them over to the Nazis.

A convoy with 544 Jews leaves Vienna for Minsk, Belorussian S.S.R.

All 5,000 Jews in the district of Dubno, Poland (today Ukrainian S.S.R.), are shot by the SS on this day and the next.

1943 A transport with 53 Jews leaves the Theresienstadt concentration camp for Auschwitz.

October 6

1938 In Slovakia anti-Semitism becomes open. Anti-Jewish decrees are put into force and measures are taken against the Jewish population.

1941 The deportation of Jews from Prague, Czechoslovakia, to the Theresienstadt concentration camp begins and lasts for several months.

1942 From the ghetto of Biala Podlaska, Poland, where the Jews of the surrounding area have also been forcibly resettled, 1,200 Jews are deported to the Treblinka extermination camp, where they are killed some hours after their arrival. On the same day, 3,000 Jews from Wolomin, 4,000 Jews from Miedzyrzec Podlaski, 800 Jews from Zarki, and 8,000 Jews from Chmielnik, are deported to Treblinka by a special task force of German police and Ukrainian auxiliaries.

The SS murders 500 Jews in the course of an Aktion in Warkovicze, Volhynia, Poland. About 800 flee into the forests. Young men offer organized resistance.

The SS continues the shooting of the Jews from the district of Dubno, Poland (today Ukrainian S.S.R.), which began on October 5. In these two days, 5,000 Jews are shot.

1944 In the course of an Aktion, 529 Jews who have been doing forced labor in the copper mines of Bor, Yugoslavia, are shot by the SS.

A transport with 1,550 Jews leaves the Theresienstadt concentration camp in Czechoslovakia for the Auschwitz extermination camp in Poland.

October 7

1939 The Nazis shoot 48 Jews from Swiecie, northern Poland, in an Aktion that lasts for two days.

1941 In an Aktion lasting two days, 7,000 Jews from the ghetto of Borisov, Belorussian S.S.R., are shot in a ravine near the airport.

1942 The SS murders 700 Jews in Lisoviki, province of Lublin, Poland.

From the ghetto of Koniecpol, Poland, 1,600 Jews are deported to the Treblinka extermination camp. On the same day 2,000 Jews from Lagov, Poland, and the surrounding area are also deported to Treblinka, where they are murdered upon arrival.

1943 A deportation convoy with 1,000 Jewish men and women leave the Drancy transit camp in the German occupied zone of France for the Auschwitz extermination camp in Poland. Only 33 will survive until the liberation of the camp in 1945.
On the same day, a convoy of 21 Jews leaves Vienna for Auschwitz.

From the Theresienstadt concentration camp in Czechoslovakia, 1,260 Jewish children arrive at Auschwitz. They are gassed on the same day. The children originated in Bialystok, Poland, from where they were deported to Theresienstadt on August 23, 1943.

General Jürgen Stroop—responsible for the destruction of the Warsaw ghetto—arrives in Athens, Greece. All Jews are ordered to register and to come to the synagogue. This registration is the first step toward the deportation of the Jews in March 1944. Many Jews hide with the help of the Greek Orthodox Church as instructed by Archbishop Damaskinos.
The Jewish community dates back to the sixth

century B.C. By the time of the German invasion, Athens has 3,000 Jewish inhabitants and their number is increased by 3,000 refugees from Salonika.

1944 About 2,000 Hungarian survivors of forced labor in Bor, Yugoslavia, who have been on a march since September 19, are told to stop in Cservenka, Hungary. There the SS prepares for a mass execution in order to free the roads for the withdrawing Axis forces. On October 7 and 8, about 1,000 of them are shot. The survivors continue their march on the same day. They are sent to the German concentration camps Buchenwald and Flossenbürg, where all but a handful perish.

In the course of an uprising, the Jewish special detachment in Auschwitz burns down crematories, kills a number of SS men, cuts through the barbed wire, and flees. Many of them are killed by the SS; very few will survive.

October 8

1941 In Poligon, the SS murders 100 Jews of Koltynian, near Vilna, Poland, today Lithuanian S.S.R.

The SS begins the systematic liquidation of the 16,000 Jews of Vitebsk, Belorussian S.S.R., with the murder of 3,000 Jews. The Jewish community dates back to the sixteenth century. Famous personalities like the artist Marc Chagall are from Vitebsk.

1942 A large-scale Aktion begins against the Jews of the ghetto of Skarzysko-Kamienna, Kielce province, Poland. Most of them—more than 2,000 people—are deported to the Treblinka extermination camp. On the same day more than 1,000 Jews from Theresienstadt concentration camp in Czechoslovakia are deported to Treblinka. They are gassed upon arrival.

The SS murders 88 Jews from Kamionka, province of Lublin, Poland.

The SS and the Lithuanian police murder 1,100 Jews in two days in Hajduczok, district Vilna (today Belorussian S.S.R.).

The SS takes 900 Jews of Demidavka, near Kiev, Ukrainian S.S.R., to the nearby forest and shoots them.

1943 On Yom Kippur eve, the ghetto of Liepaja, Latvian S.S.R., is liquidated; 816 Jews are murdered on the spot; the others are deported to various concentration camps.

1944 At dawn, 200 Jewish men on a death march from Crvenka to Sombor, Yugoslavia, are murdered by the Nazis near Sombor.

October 9

1920 A pogrom breaks out in Vilna, Poland (today Lithuanian S.S.R.), lasting three days. The Polish army which enters the town after the withdrawal of the Soviet Red Army starts to massacre the Jews, of whom 80 are shot, others buried alive or drowned. Most of the victims live in the suburb of Lipovka.

1939 The SS shoots 800 people, most of them Jews, among them women and children, in Dobrcz, district of Bydgoszcz, Poland.

1941 The deportation of the Jews in Bukovina, Rumania (today Ukrainian S.S.R.), begins. Jews from the towns of Radautsi, Suczawa, Gurahumora, Kimpolung, and Dorna Watra are one after the other deported to the concentration camps in Transnistria, a total of 40,000 souls. Many of them die on the march; those who are too weak to keep up are mercilessly shot. Deportations continue on

October 10. On the same day the entire Jewish population of Burduyeni, Rumania, is deported to Transnistria.

1942 In the course of two days, 900 Jews are murdered by the SS and the Ukrainian police in Mylanov, Volhynia, Ukrainian S.S.R.

On this and the preceding days, the Nazis arrest 75 Jews in Rotterdam, Netherlands. They are deported to the Westerbork transit camp in the province of Drenthe, and from there to camps in Germany.

The Nazis deport 1,703 Jews from the Westerbork transit camp to the Auschwitz extermination camp in Poland.

A convoy with 1,306 Jews leaves Vienna for the Theresienstadt concentration camp in Czechoslovakia.

About 14,000 Jews are deported from the ghetto of Radomsko, Lodz province, Poland, to the Treblinka extermination camp, where they are murdered. During the final Aktion, many young Jews flee into the forests where they become partisans.
   On the same day begins the liquidation of the ghetto of Przedborz, Kielce province, Poland, in the course of which 4,500 Jews are deported to Treblinka.

1943 The surrender of Italy in September 1943, and the subsequent division of Italy into a southern part occupied by Allied forces and a northern part occupied by German forces, make the Jews in the north victims of the Final Solution. On October 9 a raid is carried out by the Nazis on the Jews of Trieste. The only concentration camp in Italy, Risiera di San Sabba, is nearby, and after the raid about 600 Jews are interned there. From there they will be deported to the extermination camps in the east, mainly to Auschwitz.

1944 A transport with 1,600 Jews leaves Theresienstadt for Auschwitz.

1982 Rome's main synagogue is attacked. A two-year-old boy is killed, and 34 people are wounded.

October 10

1290 After the expulsion of the Jews from England, a boat carrying poor Jews from London sails down the Thames River to the coast. At the mouth of the Thames, the captain has the anchor cast and tells the Jews to disembark and rest on a sandbank. However, when the tide comes in, the ship sails off, leaving the Jews behind to be drowned. The culprits are subsequently tried and hanged.

1941 In the course of an Aktion that lasts several days, about 400 elderly Jews are shot by the SS in the military harbor of Riga, Latvian S.S.R.

The Nazis order the Jews of Czechoslovakia to leave their homes and to resettle in ghettos in fourteen towns that have been chosen for this purpose.

The SS shoots 2,000 Jews on the way from Bogdanovka to Darnica in southern Transnistria (today Ukrainian S.S.R.).

1942 Two transport convoys leave the Mechelen transit camp in Belgium for the Auschwitz extermination camp in Poland. Arriving at Auschwitz will be 1,679 deportees, among them 487 children, but only 54 of them will survive until the liberation of the camp in 1945.

From Bursztyn, Stanislavov district, Poland, 4,000 Jews are deported to the Belzec extermination camp.

October 11

1941 A deportation train carrying Jews from Suczawa, Bukovina, passes through the train station in Czernovitz, capital of Bukovina. The train is stopped by the Nazis and Rumanian guards to unload the corpses of those who have died during the journey in the cold, overcrowded cars. The train then continues its way to the ghetto of Czernovitz.

The Nazis shoot 400 Jews in Belgrade, Yugoslavia.

The Jews of Czernovitz (today Ukrainian S.S.R.), are confined to a ghetto and their property is confiscated. Ultimately they will be deported to Transnistria.

1942 In the course of an Aktion against the ghetto of Ostroviec, Kielce province, Poland, 11,000 Jews are rounded up and deported to the Treblinka extermination camp, where they all perish. The Jewish community dates back to the eighteenth century.

About 4,200 Jews of Lubartov, Lublin province, Poland, are deported to the extermination camps of Sobibor, Belzec and Majdanek, where they all perish. Among them are 1,000 Jews who one year before had been deported from Slovakia to Lubartov. Lubartov is declared "free of Jews." For more than a year, a Jewish partisan unit fights in the forests, led by Samuel Jegier and Mietek Gruber.

From Bicheva, Lublin province, 3,000 Jews are deported to the Belzec extermination camp.

1944 In the course of an Aktion, SS men shoot 208 young Jews of Ujvidek, Yugoslavia, who have been working on the railway; 12 Jews survive.

From Venice, Italy, 20 mentally ill Jews are interned in the infamous concentration camp Risiera di San Sabba near Trieste. By evening, 5 or 6 of them have already been murdered by SS soldiers guarding the camp.

Risiera di San Sabba is the only Nazi concentration camp on Italian territory.

October 12

1285 In Munich, Germany, the Jews are accused of a ritual murder. On Friday evening when all the Jews have assembled in the synagogue, the mob storms the building. When the Jews refuse to be baptized, the mob sets the synagogue on fire and everyone in it perishes in the flames.

1939 Following a decree by Hitler, the Nazis order that in all areas of Poland occupied by the Germans, so-called Jewish Councils have to be established to serve as liaisons between the German authorities and the Jews.

In Chrzanov, district of Cracow, Poland, a Jew is shot by the Wehrmacht (German regular forces).

1941 In Stanislavov, Poland (today Ukrainian S.S.R.), during the Jewish High Holidays, German troops drive about 10,000 Jews to the Jewish cemetery. After having been forced to dig their own graves, they are shot by the SS.

The wholesale murder of the Jews of Dnepropetrovsk, Ukrainian S.S.R., by the SS lasts for two days.

Shmuel Kruh, president of the Jewish Council of Czortkov, Poland (today Ukrainian S.S.R.), is executed for disobeying Nazi orders.

1942 From Rospsza, province of Lodz, Poland, 600 Jews are taken to the transit camp at Trybunalski.

From the Westerbork transit camp in the Dutch province of Drenthe, 1,711 Jewish inmates are deported to the Auschwitz extermination camp in Poland.

The SS and the Ukrainian police murder 2,000 Jews in Zdolbunov, Volhynia, Ukrainian S.S.R.

In the course of an Aktion against the Jews of the ghetto of Mlava, Warsaw province, Poland, which lasts until the end of the month, 6,500 Jews are deported to the Treblinka extermination camp. On the same day the deportations of the 4,500 Jews from Przedborz, in the province of Kielce, come to an end.

1944 A convoy with a great many Jewish internees leaves the concentration camp at Risiera di San Sabba in northern Italy, established by the Nazi occupation army. The destination is unknown, but it is presumably one of the extermination camps in the east.

A transport with 1,500 Jews leaves the Theresienstadt concentration camp in Czechoslovakia for Auschwitz.

October 13

1726 An auto-da-fé is held in Lisbon, Portugal, in which a cleric is accused of Judaizing, secretly practicing the Jewish religion. He is burned at the stake.

1939 The supreme command of the German army orders that the Jews of Lodz, Poland, must furnish 600 workers every day.

1941 The Jews of Storozynetz, Bukovina, Rumania (today Ukrainian S.S.R.), who have been deported to Transnistria, are sent on to Marculesti on foot. They arrive in complete exhaustion, reduced in number by hunger and the bullets of the German and Rumanian guards.

The SS murders 350 Jews in Verba, Volhynia, Ukrainian S.S.R.

1942 1,900 Jews are sent from Ivaniska, Kielce province, Poland, to the Treblinka extermination camp.

1942 The SS murders 1,800 Jews in Mizocz, Ukrainian S.S.R.

October 14

1542 Sentenced to death by the Inquisition, 20 New Christians, descendants of forcibly baptized Jews, are burned at the stake in Lisbon, capital of Portugal.

1905 A pogrom breaks out in Kamenskoye, Russia, and lasts two days; 3 Jews are slaughtered, and 150 Jewish families are reduced to poverty.

1938 In Vienna, from this day on, synagogues are defiled and Torah scrolls are burned every day.

1942 When another Aktion is carried out in the ghetto of Kobryn, Belorussian S.S.R., the Jews organize self-defense. The invading Germans are attacked and a great battle commences; 100 Jews manage to flee into the forests where they join the partisans. Except for a small group of workers who will be killed later, Kobryn is "free of Jews."

The SS murders 1,000 Jews from the ghetto of Antonopol, Belorussian S.S.R.

In Bereza Kartuska, Poland, the members of the Jewish Council collectively commit suicide. This is their response to the Nazi order that all Jews gather the next day to be deported for forced labor in the Ukraine. Before their suicide, they inform

Pogrom in Kiev, c. 1875. A Jew is being beaten by the crowd while soldiers watch. (Collection Roger-Viollet)

the Jewish community of the true nature of the fate that awaits them.

About 450 Jews from the ghetto of Grodek, Poland (today Ukrainian S.S.R.), are deported to the Belzec extermination camp.

The SS murders 300 Jews in Kamien Koszyrski, Volhynia, Ukrainian S.S.R.

1943 From Grosec, a district of Warsaw, Poland, 3,000 Jews are deported to Bialobrzeg.

An uprising occurs in the Sobibor extermination camp in Poland under the leadership of Alexander Pechersky in which Jews attempt to flee. Eleven SS men and 200 Jews are killed; 400 Jews manage to escape.

October 15

1941 In the course of an Aktion, Nazis shoot the entire Jewish population of Roslawlj, Ukrainian S.S.R.

The third law on residence restrictions prohibits Jews in the General Government, Poland, from leaving their assigned residence.

A convoy with 1,005 Jews leaves Vienna, Austria, for Lodz, Poland.

1942   In the course of the liquidation of the ghetto of Brest Litovsk, Poland (today Belorussian S.S.R.), many Jews are shot and the majority are sent to the Treblinka extermination camp by the SS. Earlier some young people formed a resistance group, led by Hana Ginsberg. A small number of Jews manage to escape into the surrounding forests where they join the partisans. After the war only 200 of the 30,000 Jewish inhabitants of Brest Litovsk remain.

On the same day, 3,000 Jews from Ciechanoviec, 1,000 Jews from Sienna, and a convoy with 1,000 Jews from the Theresienstadt concentration camp in Czechoslovakia are deported to Treblinka. All members of the Theresienstadt convoy are gassed upon arrival.

In The Hague, Netherlands, the Nazis declare the Jews of Holland to be without any rights.

The SS murders 2,500 Jews from the ghetto of Drohiczyn, Volhynia (today Ukrainian S.S.R.).

In Sokal, Poland (today Ukrainian S.S.R.), a ghetto is set up. Among the 5,000 Jewish inmates are Jews from the villages of Steniatyn, Radziechov, Lopatyn, Witkov, Tartakov, and Mosty Vielkie. The inmates suffer terribly from the lack of water, as there are only four wells in the ghetto.

The SS arrests and shoots 3,000 Jews from the ghetto of Ostrog, Volhynia (today Ukrainian S.S.R.), near town, but 800 Jews manage to flee into the forests. Many of them are rounded up by Ukrainian farmers and handed over to the Nazis. Others are caught by the Bandera gangs (Ukrainian Nationalists) and murdered. Only 60 Jews, 30 of whom had fled to the Soviet Union, survive the war.

The Nazis begin the destruction of Ghetto A (for artisans and workmen) in the town of Bereza, Belorussian S.S.R. During their last session, several members of the Jewish Council commit suicide. The Jews set the ghetto on fire. The Nazis succeed in rounding up 1,800 Jews, whom they drive out of town and murder. Bereza is "free of Jews."

In the course of an Aktion, 1,500 Jews of Anapol, Poland (today Ukrainian S.S.R.), are murdered by the SS.

The SS murders 2,300 Jews of Antopol, Poland.

The SS murders 2,600 Jews in Bereza Kartuska, Poland, in the course of the final Aktion.

1943   In Trieste, Italy, the Risiera di San Sabba camp is set up, in which several thousand Jews and Italian resisters will be murdered. The prisoners are interned in an old factory.

1944   Miklós Horthy, the head of state of Hungary, resigns and the rightists take power. Anti-Jewish violence breaks out in Budapest and in the countryside. Members of the Fascist Arrow Cross slaughter 160 Jewish laborers at Pusztavam.

October 16

1746   An auto-da-fé is held in Lisbon, Portugal, in which figure 6 people accused of being Judaizers, descendants of Jews forcibly baptized some centuries ago who still practice the Jewish religion in secret—3 of them are burned at the stake, 3 are burned in effigy.

1941   The German army occupies the town of Odessa, capital of the Ukrainian S.S.R. On the first day of their occupation two special commando units kill 8,000 Jews.

Half of the Jewish population, 2,200 Jews of Kossov, Ukrainian S.S.R., are driven into the hills behind the Moskalovka Bridge and murdered.

The Nazis begin the deportation of 5,000 Jewish men, women, and children from Prague, Czechoslovakia to the Lodz concentration camp in Poland in five convoys.

1942 From the ghetto of Bereza Kartuska, Poland, 3,500 Jews are murdered.

From Zolkievka, Poland, 1,800 Jews are deported to the Auschwitz extermination camp. On the same day Auschwitz receives 675 Jews from Mechelen, Belgium, and 1,710 Jews from the Westerbork transit camp in Drenthe, Holland.

All 12,000 Jews of Zamosc, Poland, are rounded up in the market square. They are forced to march to Izbica, about 25 km away. Many of them are shot on the way by the SS. The remaining Jews are deported to the Belzec extermination camp, where they all perish.

1943 After the surrender of Italy on September 8, and the subsequent division of the country into the southern part under Allied rule and the northern part under Nazi occupation, the Jews living in the German-occupied regions are submitted to the Final Solution.

On October 16, the Jewish quarter of Rome is surrounded by German soldiers and over 1,000 Jews are arrested in a house-to-house search. They are directly dispatched to Auschwitz. Only 16 of them will survive.

1944 A transport with 1,500 Jews leaves the Theresienstadt concentration camp in Czechoslovakia for Auschwitz.

October 17

1660 An auto-da-fé is held in Lisbon, Portugal. Several people are accused of being Judaizers, descendants of Jews forcibly baptized some centuries before who still practice the Jewish religion in secret. All of them are executed.

1939 The first deportation of Czech Jews takes place. Of the 7,000 Jews of Moravska Ostrava, in the province of Moravia, 1,200 are deported to Nisko, Poland, where they are forced to set up the Zarzecze labor camp. The Jewish community dates back to the beginning of the sixteenth century.

1941 In the course of an Aktion, 1,400 Jews from Sarajevo, capital of Yugoslavia, are arrested and deported to concentration camps in Croatia, where they perish.

The SS murders 900 Jews of Ostrozec, Volhynia, Poland.

1942 500 Jews of Kazanov, province of Kielce, Poland, are taken to the collecting point Sienna.

1,800 Jews are deported from Lipsko, province of Kielce, to the Treblinka extermination camp.

In the course of an Aktion in the ghetto of Buczacz, Poland (today Ukrainian S.S.R.), 300 Jews are killed and 1,500 are deported to the Belzec extermination camp. On the same day are deported to Belzec 3,000 Jews from Sambor, and 2,000 Jews from Stryj, Poland (today Ukrainian S.S.R.).

All Jewish inmates of the Buchenwald concentration camp in Germany, except 200 who are doing construction work, are deported to the Auschwitz extermination camp in Poland.

1943 The remaining 500 Jews of Zaviercie, Katovice province, Poland, interned in a forced labor camp, are murdered by the SS.

1944 Adolf Eichmann returns to Budapest, Hungary, where he begins the forced settlement of the Jews in two large ghettos.

October 18

1905 Pogroms against the Jewish population break out in several districts of Russia, organized by the authorities, supported by the army, the local police—especially by the "Black Hundreds"*—and hooligans. They last four or five days. In Kiev, 27 Jews are slaughtered, 300 wounded; in Odessa, 302 Jews are murdered, several thousand wounded; in Minsk, 42 Jews are killed, several hundred wounded; in Rostov-on-Don, 16 Jews are murdered, 40 wounded; in Simferopol, 42 Jews are murdered; in Orel, 6 Jews are wounded; in Kremenchug, a great many Jews are killed, even more are severely wounded; in Cherson, Jewish houses and shops are devastated and looted. In some of these towns, members of the Jewish Self-Defense are killed.

1941 In the course of an Aktion, 3,500 Jews from Belgrade, capital of Serbia, Yugoslavia, are deported to forced labor camps where they all perish.

About 8,000 Jews from Zhdanov, Ukrainian S.S.R., who have been interned in a military camp, are murdered.

1942 The remaining 600 Jews of Zakszuwek, province of Lublin, Poland, are murdered by the SS.

The SS kills 2,250 Jews from Nove Miasto, province of Warsaw, Poland, in the course of an Aktion.

Taken to the collecting point at Staszov, are 1,500 Jews from Pielancz, province of Kielce, Poland.

The Nazis deport 700 Jews from the village of Siennica, and 800 Jews from Seciny, Poland, to the Treblinka extermination camp.

*Black Hundreds: The local branches of the Union of Russian People (Sayuz Russkavo Naroda), an anti-Liberal, anti-Semitic organization founded in 1905.

1943 The Nazis deport 1,015 Jews from Rome to the Auschwitz extermination camp in Poland. This is the first deportation of Jews from Rome to Auschwitz.

October 19

1298 In the course of the Rindfleisch Persecutions, named after the German knight who instigated them, more than 140 Jews are massacred in Heilbronn, Germany. On the same day the hordes of Rindfleisch slaughter the only Jewish family in Neckarsulm, Germany: Vivis, his wife Meilin, and their granddaughter Meilin.

Dedication page of Shornik, *by Maxim Gorki, in memory of the victims of the Kishinev pogrom, illustrated by E. M. Lilien.*

1704 An auto-da-fé is held in Lisbon, Portugal, in which Diego Nunes Ribeiro is accused of being a Judaizer, a descendant of Jews forcibly baptized some centuries ago who still secretly practices the Jewish religion. He does penance and is reconciled with the Church, but finally he flees to England.

1905 Pogroms against the Jewish population break out in several districts of Russia, organized by the authorities, supported by the army, the Cossacks, the local police, and hooligans, lasting two to five days. Jewish property is demolished and looted and synagogues are desecrated. In Jelissavetgrad 11 Jews are massacred, 150 are wounded; in Kishinev 29 Jews are slaughtered, 56 are severely wounded; in Nikolayev several Jews are killed; in Feodociya 11 Jews are slaughtered, 11 are mutilated; in Saratov several Jews are murdered, 80 are severely wounded; in Romny 7 Jews are massacred, 20 are severely wounded; in Solotonoscha 1 member of the Jewish Self Defense is killed, several Jews are wounded; in Nezhin 30 Jews are beaten up; in Novozybkov 2 members of the Jewish Self Defense are slaughtered, 19 Jews are wounded.

1941 A convoy with 1,003 Jews leaves Vienna for Lodz, Poland.

1942 2,000 Jews from Mielnica, district of Ternopol, Ukrainian S.S.R., are deported to the ghetto of Borszczow.

The Nazis deport 1,327 Jews from the Westerbork transit camp in the Dutch province of Drenthe to the Auschwitz extermination camp in Poland.

A convoy with more than 1,000 Jews leaves the ghetto of Theresienstadt, Czechoslovakia, for the Treblinka extermination camp in Poland. They are gassed upon arrival.

In the ghetto of Pinczov, Poland, 3,000 of the 3,500 Jews are arrested and deported to Treblinka, but 100 Jews manage to flee and join the partisans.

The Jewish community dates back to the sixteenth century. On the same day more than 1,000 Jews from the Theresienstadt concentration camp are deported to Treblinka and are gassed upon arrival.

The SS murders Jews of Dubienka, of Lublin, Poland.

1943 A convoy with 1,007 Jews leaves the Westerbork transit camp for Auschwitz.

1944 A transport with 1,500 Jews leaves the Theresienstadt concentration camp for Auschwitz.

October 20

1905 Pogroms against the Jewish population break out in several districts of Russia, organized by the authorities and supported by the army, the local police, and by hooligans. They last three days. Jewish shops and houses are entirely demolished and looted. In Aleksandrovsk 7 Jews are killed, 46 are wounded; in Mariupol 22 Jews are slaughtered; in Jusovka 12 Jews are massacred, about 100 are wounded or mutilated; in Uman 3 Jews are murdered, many are wounded; in the neighboring villages Bogopol, Golta, and Olviopol, 13 Jews are massacred and a number are injured; in Tomsk many women are raped, several Jews are massacred, many are mutilated or wounded.

1939 The first convoy for the swamps of Nisko, Poland, leaves Vienna with 912 Jews.

In Lublin, Poland, a special administration for forced labor is established, which is entitled to round up Jews.

1941 From Turek, province of Lodz, Poland, 3,500 Jews are sent to Kovale Panskie to do forced labor.

In the course of an Aktion lasting five days, 7,000 Jews from the ghetto of Vitebsk, Belorussian S.S.R., are shot by the SS in trenches at Ilowskji, near the Vitba River.

The 8,000 Jews of Borisov, Belorussian S.S.R., are taken out of the ghetto and murdered by the SS.

By order of Helmut Rauca, the commander of the ghetto of Kaunas, Lithuanian S.S.R., the Jews must bring their documents and gather on the Democratic Square. A large-scale Aktion against the inmates of the ghetto follows.

The SS takes 100 Jewish prisoners of war from the Darnica POW camp and they are shot in a forest north of the camp. Darnica is situated near Kiev, Ukrainian S.S.R.

Task Force D, under the command of Otto Ohlendorf, murders 8,000 Jews in Odessa, Ukrainian S.S.R.

1942   A convoy with 995 Jews leaves Mechelen, Belgium, for the Auschwitz extermination camp in Poland.

German police and Ukrainian auxiliaries surround the ghetto of Opatov, province of Kielce, Poland. In the course of three days several hundred Jews are murdered and 6,000 Jews are selected and deported to the Treblinka extermination camp, where they perish. The police take 500 Jews to the Sandomierz labor camp, while several dozen are kept back to inventory their expropriated goods, after which they are led to the Jewish cemetery and executed.

The remaining Jews of Kubyn, province of Lublin, Poland, are murdered by the SS.

From Zbaraz, Poland (today Ukrainian S.S.R.), 1,000 Jews are taken from the ghetto and deported to the Belzec extermination camp. Several hundred Jews are deported to the labor camp at Janowska.

1944   The systematic Aktionen against the remaining Jews of Hungary begin at 5 A.M. All Jewish males between 16 and 60 are ordered to prepare for departure within one hour. They are hastily organized into labor companies. Some die on the way; others are tortured to death by units of the Arrow Cross.

1981   A truck bomb explodes outside a synagogue in Antwerp, Belgium, killing 3 people and wounding 106.

October 21

1905   Pogroms against the Jewish population break out in several districts of Russia, organized by the authorities and supported by local officials and hooligans, lasting between one and three days. Jewish property is demolished and looted and synagogues are desecrated. In Orsha 30 Jews are slaughtered, 20 Jews are wounded or mutilated; in Winniza 4 members of the Jewish Self Defense are killed, 13 Jews are wounded; in Dnepropetrovsk 100 Jews are massacred, several hundred are wounded; in Ovidiopol 13 Jews are murdered, 25 are wounded; in Polatzk 12 Jews are murdered, 50 Jews are gravely wounded; in Schmerinka, 2 Jews are killed; in Klintsy 2 Jews are slain, 5 Jews are wounded; in Surasch 4 members of the Jewish Self Defense are massacred, a great number of Jews are wounded; in Balta 2 members of the Jewish Self Defense are killed, 58 Jews are wounded; in Rasdelnaja 12 Jews are slaughtered and 32 are mutilated; in Mogilev, a Jew is shot dead and several Jews are heavily wounded; in Woronesch several Jews are wounded; anti-Jewish riots break out in Werkievka and Dymar.

1941   From Adamov, province of Lublin, Poland, 850 Jews are deported to the Lukov transit camp.

The entire Jewish community of Kaidanovo, southwest of Minsk, Belorussian S.S.R., a total of about 2,000 people, are murdered. Several dozen organize a partisan group and escape into the forests from where they will fight the Nazis.

The SS murders 1,200 Jews in Kasdanov, Volhynia, Ukrainian S.S.R.

A convoy with several hundred Jewish men, women, and children leaves Prague, Czechoslovakia, for the Lodz concentration camp in Poland.

1942 After the SS liquidates the Bodzentyn ghetto, Kielce province, Poland, the 1,350 Jewish inmates are driven away to the town of Suchedniov.

From Paradysz, Kielce province, 300 Jews are sent to the Opoczno transit camp.

3,000 Jews from the ghetto of Skalat, Ternopol district, Poland (today Ukrainian S.S.R.), are deported to the Belzec extermination camp and 153 Jews are shot on the spot. On the same day the remaining Jews of Szczebrzeszyn, Lublin province, Poland, arc deported to Belzec.

1943 The ghetto of Minsk, Belorussian S.S.R., with its 2,000 Jewish inmates, is liquidated.

October 22

1648 The Chmielnicki Cossacks occupy the village of Tomaszov Lubelski, Poland, and the Jewish population is completely exterminated.

1905 Pogroms against the Jewish population lasting two days break out in several districts of Russia, organized by the authorities and supported by the army, the local police, and local hooligans. Jewish shops and houses are entirely demolished and looted, their owners thus reduced to poverty; synagogues are desecrated. In Strascheny a Jewish

child is massacred and many Jews are wounded; in Akkerman 8 Jews are massacred, 8 others are severely injured.

1940 The Nazis deport about 15,000 German Jews from the towns of the Rhineland to internment camps at the foot of the Pyrenees in France. Later on, some of the Jews are deported to Drancy, France, and from there to extermination camps in Poland; the rest disappear into other camps.

1941 The smaller ghetto of Vilna, Poland (today Lithuanian S.S.R.), is liquidated. The Jews are taken to the nearby Ponary forest where they are murdered by the Nazis.

From Czernovitz and other villages of the district 8,000 Jews are assembled in Czernovitz, Bukovina, Ukrainian S.S.R. They are marched to Marculesti from where they are deported to different camps. Those who don't walk fast enough are shot by the accompanying German soldiers.

1942 From Klevov, Kielce province, Poland, 500 Jews are deported to the Drzewice transit camp.

The last five convoys with a total of 8,000 Jewish men, women, and children, leave the Theresienstadt ghetto in Czechoslovakia for the Treblinka extermination camp in Poland. They are gassed upon arrival.

On the same day are deported to Treblinka 1,500 Jews from Dzevice, 400 Jews from Nove Miasto, 22,000 Jews from the ghetto of Piotrkov Trybunalski, and 1,900 Jews from Ilza, all in Poland.

Outside of Schnodnica, Poland (today Ukrainian S.S.R.), 1,000 Jews are murdered by the SS and the Ukrainian police.

In Kimeliszek, district of Vilna, Poland (today Lithuanian S.S.R.), 250 Jews are murdered by the SS.

1944 The second announcement concerning the remaining Jews of Budapest, Hungary, is issued. All Jewish males between 16 and 60 years of age who were recruited two days earlier are now called up; so are all Jewish women between 18 and 40. By October 25, an estimated 25,000 Jewish males and 10,000 Jewish females have been registered.

October 23

1541 The Portuguese Inquisition holds an auto-da-fé in Lisbon. Five people found guilty of adhering to the Jewish faith are burned at the stake. One of them is Goncalo Eannes Bandarra, who thinks himself to be a prophet.

1905 Pogroms against the Jewish population break out in several districts of Russia, organized by the authorities and supported by the local police and hooligans, which last up to two days. Jewish houses and shops are entirely demolished and looted, their owners reduced to poverty. In Tschernigov a Jew is murdered, 20 Jews are gravely injured; in Starodub 2 Jews are killed, 15 are severely injured; in Kalarasch 60 Jews are put to death, 75 are mutilated, and 200 are injured; in Rjetschiza 7 Jews are massacred, 12 are gravely wounded.

1940 Deported to the Sobibor extermination camp are 1,000 Jews from Maczevice, province of Lublin, Poland.

1941 A convoy with 991 Jews leaves Vienna for the ghetto of Lodz, Poland.

In retaliation for an explosion in Rumanian headquarters, 5,000 inhabitants of Odessa, Ukrainian S.S.R., 90 percent of them Jews, are murdered. Many of them are hanged in public parks. A further 19,000 Jews are arrested on the same day and taken to the harbor, where gas is poured on them and they are burned alive.

1942 A transport with 800 Jews from Slovakia arrives at the Auschwitz extermination camp in Poland.

The SS murders 106 Jews from the ghetto of Ozmiany, Lithuania (today Belorussian S.S.R.).

1,000 Jews from Leczna, Poland, are sent to the Belzec extermination camp. By the outbreak of the war, 2,300 Jews are living in Leczna. The Jewish community dates back to the beginning of the sixteenth century.

From the Westerbork transit camp in the Dutch province of Drenthe, 988 Jewish inmates are deported to Auschwitz.

1943 The 1,007 Jews who were deported from Rome some days before are gassed in Auschwitz.

1944 A transport with 1,715 Jews leaves the Theresienstadt concentration camp for Auschwitz.

October 24

1492 In Mecklenburg, Germany, 24 Jews, among them 2 women, have been falsely accused of host desecration by a priest. They are burned at the stake and the site of the pyre becomes known as the Judenberg (Jews' Hill).

1905 Pogroms against the Jewish population break out in Kursk and Tschigirim, Russia, organized by the authorities and carried out by local peasants under the cover of the police. Jewish shops and houses are entirely demolished and looted.

1941 In the course of an Aktion in Komarno, Poland (today Ukrainian S.S.R.), 600 of the 2,500 Jewish inhabitants are murdered by the Nazis. The

Ein grawsamlich geschicht Geschehen zu passaw Von den Juden als hernach volgt:

Hye stilt Cristoff acht partickel des sa cramet auß der kirche, legt das in sein teische, hat sy darinne drei tag behalte

Hye schuer er die sacrament den juden auff den tisch die vnuermayligt gewe sen sein, darumb sy in ein guldē geben

Hye tragen die judē vn schulklopffer, die sacrament yn ir synagog, vnd vber antwurten dye den Juden.

Hye stecht pfeyl Jud das sacrament auff irem altar als plut daraus gangen das er vn ander juden gesehen haben.

Hye teylten sy auß dye sacramēt schick ten swen partickel gen p̄ag. swē gen salcspurg, swen yn die Newenstat

Hye verpaēten sy die sacramēt versiu chen ob vnser glaub gerecht wer flogē auß dem offen swen engel vñ ij taubē

Hye vecht man all Juden zu passaw die dy sacramēt gekaufft verschickt ge stolen vnd verprant haben.

Hye furt mā sy für gericht, verurtaylt die vier getaufft, fachel mano kolman vnd walich, sein gehopft worden.

Hye zereyst man den pfeyl vnd vettel die das sacramēt behytltē, dz darnach gestochen vnd verprant haben.

Hye verpaent man sy mit sampt dē ju den, die yn irem glauben blyben, vnd vmb das sacrament gewyst haben.

Hye wirt der Cristoff des sacramēts verkauffer, auff einem wagē zeryssen mit gluenden zangen.

Hye hebt man an sw pawen, vnserm herren zu lob eyn gotzhaus, Auß der juden synagog rc.

German broadside, c. 1480, telling the story of the alleged desecration of the host in Passau, Germany, in 1478. 1. Christoff Eisengreisshamer, a Christian, steals eight consecrated wafers from St. Mary's Church. 2. He sells them to Jews, identified by their circular badge, for one gulden. 3. The Jews take the host to the synagogue. 4. In reenactment of the Crucifixion, they stab the wafers, from which blood flows. 5. They send some of the wafers to Prague and Salzburg. 6. When they try to burn the remaining wafers, on which the face of a child has appeared, two angels and two doves fly out of the oven. 7. The Jews are arrested. 8. They are found guilty and two of them are beheaded. 9. Others are tortured with burning pincers and then burned at the stake. 10. All the Jews who knew of the desecration are burned to death. 11. Christoff is torn to pieces with red-hot pincers. 12. The synagogue is turned into a church.

Jewish community dates back to the sixteenth century.

1942 Two transports with 1,172 Jews—among them 321 children—leave the Mechelen transit camp in Belgium for the Auschwitz extermination camp in Poland. Only 41 of them will survive until the liberation of the camp in 1945.

The remaining Jewish population of the Wlodava ghetto, Lublin province, Poland, is deported to the Sobibor extermination camp, where they perish. Several hundred Jews manage to flee into the forests where they join a partisan group under the command of Yehiel Grynszpan. They cooperate with Soviet and Polish partisans to battle the Nazis.

From Ciepielov, province of Kielce, Poland, 500 Jews are deported to the Treblinka extermination camp.

In the course of five days, 2,500 Jews from the ghetto of Sokal, Poland (today Ukrainian S.S.R.), are deported to the Belzec extermination camp.

1944 From Bolzano, Italy, 87 Jews are deported to the Auschwitz extermination camp in Poland.

October 25

1905 Anti-Jewish excesses break out in Rjepki, Russia. Jewish shops and houses are looted and demolished. The entire Jewish community, 286 families, is reduced to poverty.

1939 In Jaroslav, Poland, Jews are driven across the San River into Soviet territory.

1941 In the course of an Aktion lasting two days, 16,000 Jews from Odessa, Ukrainian S.S.R., are tied together in groups of 40 to 50 persons, then thrown into antitank trenches and shot. This massacre is carried out by the Rumanians with the help of Einsatzgruppe XI (killing squad).

The SS massacres 300 Jews in Starodub, in the region of Briansk, Soviet Union. Some young Jews offer armed resistance.

1942 From Esseg, Hungary, 350 Jews are deported to the Treblinka extermination camp.

In Norway, all Jewish men over the age of 16 are arrested. A total of 209 people are sent by ship from Oslo to Stettin, from where they are deported to the Auschwitz extermination camp in Poland.

1943 The SS murders 2,000 Jews in the Janowska camp in Lvov, Poland (today Ukrainian S.S.R.).

October 26

1648 The Cossack army of Bogdan Chmielnicki reaches Pinsk, Poland, and massacres the 40 Jews who remain. The greater part of the Jewish community of Pinsk managed to flee earlier.

1664 In the town of Coimbra, the Portuguese Inquisition holds a huge auto-da-fé involving 237 people mainly accused of Judaizing, secretly practicing the Jewish religion. They are deprived of their civil rights and their wealth and are required to do public penance.

1905 Pogroms against the Jewish population break out in Krivoi Rog and Bajramtscha, Bessarabia, Russia, organized by the authorities and covered up by the local police. Peasants and hooligans loot and burn the Jewish quarters. In Krivoi Rog 4 Jews are massacred, 25 are severely wounded; in

Bajramtscha 2 Jews are tortured to death, 5 are severely injured.

1939 Jews from Brno, Czechoslovakia, are deported toward the East, to the Lublinland in Poland, where most of them perish.

The second convoy leaves Vienna with 672 Jews for the swamps of Nisko in the district of Lublin.

Jews from Prague, Czechoslovakia, are deported to Lublinland, where most of them perish.

According to a decree by Hitler, Nasielsk, a village in Warsaw province, Poland, whose Jewish community numbers 3,000 members, is annexed to East Prussia. The Jewish community dates back to the middle of the seventeenth century.

1941 A convoy with several hundred Jewish men, women, and children leaves Prague for the Lodz concentration camp in Poland.

1942 From Monasterzyska, Poland (today Ukrainian S.S.R.), 2,800 Jews are deported to the ghetto of Buczacz (today also Ukrainian S.S.R.).

The first convoy with 1,866 Jews leaves the ghetto of Theresienstadt, Czechoslovakia, for the Auschwitz extermination camp in Poland. Upon arrival, 1,619 men, women, and children are gassed. Singled out are 215 young men and women who are sent to the concentration camp of the I. G. Farben Buna Company at Monowice-Auschwitz III; 28 of them will survive the war.

In the course of two days, 1,800 Jews are murdered by the SS in Krasnobrod, province of Lublin, Poland.

From the Westerbork transit camp in the Dutch province of Drenthe, 841 Jewish inmates are deported to Auschwitz.

1943 3,000 Lithuanian Jews from Kaunas, Lithuanian S.S.R., are deported to the Klooga concentration camp in Estonia.

October 27

1765 The last public auto-da-fé is held in Lisbon, in which New Christians are accused of Judaizing.

1905 A pogrom occurs in Semenovka, Russia. Looting and burning of Jewish property accompanies the slaughter of the Jews—11 are massacred, 11 are gravely wounded.

1940 In Kalisz, central Poland, 300 old and sick Jews are crammed into especially constructed gas trucks. They are suffocated by the SS and their corpses buried in the forest.

1942 The ghetto of Opoczno, Kielce province, Poland, is liquidated and about 2,500 Jews are deported to the Treblinka extermination camp, where they are all murdered. Only 120 Jews are left in the ghetto to be used for various labor. A small number manage to flee into the forests where they join the partisans.

On the same day are deported to Treblinka 4,000 Jews from Przysucha and some neighboring villages and 4,000 Jews from Miedzyrzec Podlaski, Poland. Several hundred Jews from Miedzyrzec Podlaski manage to escape into the forests and offer resistance to the Nazis.

October 28

1938 Deported from Germany are 15,000 Polish-born Jews. The old and the sick, who cannot bear the hardships of the evacuation, die.

1939 German troops occupy Piotrkov Trybunalski, Poland, whose Jewish community numbers 16,000. Many Jews are killed when the Nazis round up the Jews of the town and its vicinity. The Jewish community dates back to the middle of the sixteenth century. It includes several distinguished Jewish organizations in the fields of culture and sports.

In Wloclawek, Poland, the distinguishing badge for Jews, the Yellow Star, is introduced.

1941 A convoy with 998 Jews leaves Vienna for Lodz, Poland.

Dr. Erhard Wetzel from the office of racial questions of the Ministry of Eastern Territories proposes "gassing camps" for Riga, Latvia, and Minsk, Belorussian S.S.R.

Nazi extermination commandos murder 2,000 Jews in Lachovice, Belorussian S.S.R.

The SS shoots 1,600 Jews in the village of Pestschannoje, district of Kremenchug, Ukrainian S.S.R.

The SS murders 2,000 Jews in Lida, Poland (today Belorussian S.S.R.).

1942 A labor camp is set up for the remaining Jews of Kaluszyn, Warsaw province, Poland. In the course of its construction, several Jews are murdered.

From Hrubieszov, Lublin province, Poland, 2,000 Jews are deported to the Sobibor extermination camp and murdered. Another 200 Jews are sent to the Budzyn labor camp, where nearly all of them perish. In summer 1941, an underground movement took shape in Hrubieszov, which set up bases in the forests where escaped Jews found shelter. From there Jews went to Vilna and Warsaw, where they joined the underground movements. Some of them also joined the Polish resistance.

In an Aktion, 6,000 Jews are deported from the ghetto of Cracow, Poland, to the Belzec extermination camp. The patients in the Jewish hospital, the old age home inmates, and the 300 Jewish children at the Jewish orphanage are murdered by the SS on the spot.

During an Aktion lasting two days, 3,500 Jews from Kamionka-Strumilova, Poland (today Ukrainian S.S.R.), are deported to Belzec and murdered. The remaining 3,000 Jews are murdered nearby by the SS and the Ukrainian police.

1943 1,000 Jews from the Drancy transit camp in the German occupied zone of France are deported to the Auschwitz extermination camp in Poland. Immediately upon arrival, 613 of them are gassed; 45, among them 3 women, survive until the liberation of the camp by the Soviet army in 1945.

1944 An uprising against the Nazis in Banska Bystrica, Slovakia, Czechoslovakia, takes place with the help of the partisans and parachutists. A number of Jews participate. This day marks the fall of Banska Bystrica, the center of the Slovakian resistance movement. Subsequent anti-Jewish measures are taken. The Jews are rounded up and sent to Sered, from where they are gradually deported to Auschwitz.

A transport with 2,038 Jews leaves the Theresienstadt concentration camp in Czechoslovakia for Auschwitz.

October 29

1941 In the course of an Aktion lasting two days, 3,000 Jews are shot by the SS in a sandpit near the village of Srednjaja Poguljanka, in the district of Dünaburg, Latvian S.S.R.

1942 In the course of an Aktion lasting for three days, 7,000 Jews from Hrubieszov, province of Lublin, Poland, are deported to the Sobibor extermination camp.

3,200 Jews from Sandomierz, Kielce province, Poland, are deported to the Belzec extermination camp. At the outbreak of the war 2,500 Jews are living in Sandomierz and another 2,500 Jews from the surrounding area are resettled in the town. The Jewish community dates back to the twelfth century. On the same day 180 Jews from Drohobycz, Poland (today Ukrainian S.S.R.), are shot during the Aktion by the SS and 2,300 are deported to Belzec.

The remaining 800 Jews of Radomysl, Ukrainian S.S.R., are murdered by the SS.

In the course of the final Aktion against the ghetto of Kamionka-Strumilova, Poland (today Ukrainian S.S.R.), 3,500 Jews are murdered by the SS and the Ukrainian police.

2,000 Jews from Biala Ravska, Warsaw province, and 2,500 Jews from Przysucha, province of Kielce, Poland, are deported to the Treblinka extermination camp.

The SS kills 1,800 Jews from Maydan Tatarski, Poland, and deports 200 to the Majdanck concentration camp.

The SS deports 400 Jews from Kamiensk, province of Lodz, Poland, via Radomsk to Treblinka.

The remaining 900 Jews of Ulanov, district of Lvov, Poland, are murdered by the SS and the Ukrainian police.

Over four days, 20,000 Jews are taken outside Pinsk, Belorussian S.S.R., and murdered by the SS.

1943 From Zavichost, province of Kielce, Poland, 2,000 Jews are deported to the Belzec extermination camp.

October 30

1941 The SS shoots 200 Jews from Ioda, district of Scharkovschtschina, Belorussian S.S.R.

A considerable number of Jews are rounded up by the Nazis in Pushkin, Ukrainian S.S.R., and shot.

The SS murders 5,000 Jews in the town of Niesviez, Belorussian S.S.R.

1942 A convoy with 659 Jewish inmates of the Westerbork transit camp in the Dutch province of Drenthe leaves for the Auschwitz extermination camp in Poland.

About 600 Jews from Garvolin, province of Lublin, Poland, are deported to Zelechow, in the Warsaw province.

Last day of the deportation of the Jews of Rava Mazoviecka, province of Warsaw, Poland, to the Treblinka extermination camp.
   On the same day are deported to Treblinka 800 Jews from Czmielov, 500 Jews from Konev, 2,200 Jews from the Skarzysko-Kamienna camp, and 1,200 Jews from Pokrzyvnica, all in the province of Kielce.

A second convoy with 1,500 Jews from Podhaitsy, Ternopol district, Ukrainian S.S.R., leaves for the Belzec extermination camp in Poland.

The remaining Jews of Belchatov, Lodz province, Poland, are deported to the Chelmno extermination camp.

October 31

1939   Anti-Jewish riots break out in Vilna, Poland (today Lithuanian S.S.R.), which abate only with the arrival of Polish troops. 50 Jews are injured; one Lithuanian policeman, probably intervening on behalf of the Jews, is killed; and all Jewish shops are plundered and devastated. Subsequently a Polish nationalist is condemned to death, and another is sentenced to 15 years imprisonment.

1941   In Kleck, Belorussian S.S.R., 4,000 Jews are murdered by extermination commandos.

A massacre of the Jews deported from Kishinev, Rumania (today Moldavian S.S.R.), begins on the banks of the Dniester River. The executioners are members of the Rumanian rural police and German soldiers. They murder 53,000 people.

Several hundred Jewish men, women, and children are deported from Prague, Czechoslovakia, to the Lodz concentration camp in Poland.

1942   The Nazis carry out an Aktion against the Jews of the ghetto of Konskie, Kielce province, Poland. The ghetto was set up in December 1941 and houses Jews from the smaller towns of the surrounding area as well. The Nazis deport 9,000 Jews to the Treblinka extermination camp where they are murdered. The Jewish community dates back to the sixteenth century under the protection of Polish King Sigismund III.

On the same day are deported to Treblinka 1,200 Jews from Koprzyvnica, province of Kielce; all the Jews of Przytyk, Radom province; and 7,000 Jews from the ghetto of Tomaszov Rawski, province of Lodz, all in Poland.

In the ghetto of Riga, Latvian S.S.R., 195 Jews are shot, 45 of them on the charge of assisting an escape and 150 for being unfit. On the same day, the SS shoots 42 Jewish policemen and 108 Jews in the central prison.

1942   Two transports with a total of 1,937 Jews—among them 137 children—leave the Mechelen transit camp in Belgium for the Auschwitz extermination camp in Poland. Only 85 of them will survive until the liberation of the camp in 1945.

NOVEMBER

November 1

1349 By the order of the duke of Brabant, all Jews, including the baptized ones, are executed in Brussels, capital of Brabant (today Belgium). The duke believes that the Jews poison the wells in order to annihilate the Christians. The Jewish community of Brussels existed since 1260.

1504 In order to compel King Wladislaw of Bohemia to expel the Jews from Pilsen, the people of the small town of Hostau accuse the local Jews of stealing from a church and force them to name the Jews of Pilsen as their accomplices. The Jews of Pilsen are expelled by King Wladislaw on November 1.

1939 In Plock in the Polish province of Warsaw, a ghetto is set up and a Jewish Council is appointed. The Jews are not allowed to leave the ghetto. The Jewish Council has to provide a list of old and sick Jews, who are then taken from old-age homes and hospitals and sent away. They will never return.

1941 The Hadjerat-M'Guil concentration camp in the Sahara, in French Algeria, contains 170 prisoners, who are building the Trans-Sahara Railroad under horrendous conditions. After being brutally tortured, 9 inmates, including 2 Jews, are murdered.

The deportations of Jews from Czernovitz, Bukovina, Rumania (today Ukrainian S.S.R.), toward the east begin. In the course of two weeks 30,000 Jews will be deported.

1942 From Sopockinie in the district of Bialystok, 1,200 Jews are deported to the assembly point at Kielbasin, Poland.

From Grodek, Ukrainian S.S.R., 3,800 Jews are taken to Bialystok. Some days later they will be deported to the Treblinka extermination camp in Poland.

The Plonsk ghetto houses 8,000 local Jews and about 4,000 Jews from smaller towns in the vicinity. On November 1 the deportations to the Auschwitz extermination camp begin. The evacuation of the ghetto will last for five weeks.

In the course of two days, 4,000 Jews of Kossov, Ukrainian S.S.R., are murdered by the SS and the Ukrainian police. Some of them are killed on the spot, others are deported to the Belzec extermination camp.

The Germans surround the ghetto of Pruzana, Poland (today Belorussian S.S.R.). The intelligentsia of the village—teachers, physicians, etc.— are gathered together with their families in the office of the Jewish Council. In order not to fall into the hands of the SS, 41 of them take poison and commit collective suicide.

In Huszcz, Volhynia, Ukrainian S.S.R., 950 Jews are murdered by the SS and the Ukrainian police.

November 2

1941 The Nazis send 998 Jews from Vienna, and several hundred Jews from Prague to the ghetto of Lodz, Poland.

1942 The SS murders 3,000 Jews in the course of a final Aktion against the Jewish community of Kamien Koszyrski, Volhynia, Ukrainian S.S.R.

A transport with 7,000 Jews leaves the Wolkowysk camp in Grodno province, Poland (today Belorussian S.S.R.), for the Treblinka and Auschwitz extermination camps in Poland.

The entire population of the ghetto of Rozana, district of Brest, Poland (today Belorussian S.S.R.), is deported to Wolkowysk. Many people die on the long journey. The survivors will remain there only for a short time: at the end of November they will be deported to Treblinka and murdered.

In Krzeszov, Poland, the SS murders 500 Jews.

The deportation of the Jews of Siemiatycze, Bialystok province, Poland, to Treblinka begins. About 7,000 Jews are sent to Treblinka. A Jewish resistance movement takes shape and enables 200 people to escape into the forests where they will join

the partisans. Only 80 Jews from Siemiatycze will survive.

The Jews of Marcinkowce, province of Bialystok, actively resist the Nazis who are arresting Jews to deport them to extermination camps. The Nazis kill 360 Jews on the spot.

From the Lomza ghetto, Poland, 7,000 Jews are sent to the Zambrov camp. The rest of them are brought into the nearby forest of Galczyn, where they are executed. Lomza is declared "free of Jews."

In Ciechanov, Poland, 2 Jews are hanged by the Gestapo.

A convoy with 954 Jews leaves from the Westerbork transit camp in the Dutch province of Drenthe for Auschwitz.

The following are deported to Treblinka: 8,000 Jews from the ghetto of Sokolka, 1,000 Jews from Goniadz, 5,000 Jews from the ghetto of Krynki, 3,500 Jews from the ghetto of Wysokie, 2,500 Jews from the ghetto of Grajewo, 3,000 Jews from the ghetto of Skidel, 2,000 Jews from Zabludov, 5,000 Jews from Bielsk Podlaski and other hiding places, 2,000 Jews from the Zambrov labor camp (all of them in the province of Bialystok, Poland); and 1,500 Jews from Szczuczyn, 4,000 Jews from the Grodno ghetto, and 2,500 Jews from the ghetto of Wolkovysk (all Soviet Union).

Two thousand Jews from Prampol, 600 Jews from Josefov, 3,000 Jews from Tarnogrod, 4,000 Jews from the Bilgoraj ghetto, and 3,200 Jews from Novy Korczyn (all in Poland); and 2,500 Jews from Zloczow and 2,000 Jews from the Brody ghetto (in Ukrainian S.S.R.) are deported to the Belzec extermination camp.

1943 The ghetto of Riga, the capital of the Latvian S.S.R., is liquidated. The old and very young inmates are murdered on the spot. The remaining Jews are deported to the Kaiserwald concentration camp nearby.

1944 Over five days, 76,000 Jews from Budapest are driven by the SS, Hungarian Fascists, and rural police out of town in the direction of Vienna. Nearly 10,000 Jews will die on the way.

November 3

1941 The SS murders 600 Jews in Turez, Novogrodek district (today Belorussian S.S.R.).

In the course of two days, 2,500 Jews from Gomel, Belorussian S.S.R., interned in a camp near Monastyrek, are shot in an antitank trench near Leschtschinec.

1942 In the course of the final Aktion against the Jews of Zaklikov, Lublin province, Poland, 2,000 Jews are murdered.

The deportation of 2,000 Jews from Radoszyn, district of Kielce, Poland, and 7,000 Jews from the ghetto of Tomaszov Rawski, district of Lodz, to the Treblinka extermination camp begins.

1943 After the surrender of Italy, the country is divided, with the south occupied by the Allies and the north occupied by the Germans. The Jews living in the north now fall victim to the Final Solution. During an Aktion by the Germans on November 3, 300 Jews from Genoa and 100 Jews of foreign nationalities are deported.

In the course of three days, 3,000 Jews are arrested in Radoszyce, Poland, and deported to Treblinka.

The SS murders 2,500 Jews in the Lipova Street camp in Lublin, Poland.

About 3,000 Jews are murdered by the SS and Latvian police in Riga, the capital of Latvian S.S.R.

In a massacre in the Majdanek concentration camp in Poland, 14,000 Jews from the Lublin region and another 4,000 inmates of the camp are murdered by the Nazis.

1944 400 Jews from Sered, Slovakia, are deported to the Auschwitz extermination camp in Poland.

November 4

1940 In The Hague, Netherlands, the Nazis order that all Jewish civil servants be suspended.

1941 In Lubavich, a town in Smolensk province, Soviet Union, a ghetto is set up by the Nazis and 483 Jews are shot.

1942 From the Drancy transit camp in the German occupied zone of France, 1,000 Jewish men and women are deported. They are sent to the Auschwitz extermination camp in Poland. Immediately after their arrival, 639 of them will be gassed. Only 4 men will survive until the liberation of the camp.

The last remaining Jews of Kossov, Ukrainian S.S.R., are deported to the Kolomyja ghetto where they are murdered with the Jews of the ghetto. Kossow is declared "free of Jews."

From the ghetto of Brzezany, Poland, today Ukrainian S.S.R., 1,000 Jews are deported to the Belzec extermination camp.

1943 The Nazis shoot 815 Jews originally from the ghetto of Liepaja, Latvian S.S.R., in the Riga ghetto.

The SS sends 2,800 Jews from the Szebnie labor camp in East Galicia, Poland, to Auschwitz.

November 5

1337 In the village of Parchein in the German province of Mecklenburg, 2 Jews are slain.

1648 The Chmielnicki Cossacks besiege the village of Zamosc, Poland, for two weeks. Many of the population, which is primarily Jewish, starve to death.

1941 The SS murders 400 Jews in Swiercna, district of Novogrodek, Belorussian S.S.R.

1942 The 7,000 surviving inmates of the Piaski ghetto near Trawniki, Poland (today Ukrainian S.S.R.), originally from Theresienstadt and Germany, are deported to the Sobibor extermination camp, where they will all perish.

After a selection in the Sokolka ghetto, Bialystok province, Poland, most of the Jews are deported to the Kielbasin camp and from there to Treblinka. Some of them are shot on the spot. The remaining Jews will eventually be deported to the Treblinka extermination camp.

The second deportation of Jews from the Chmielnik ghetto, Kielce province, Poland, begins. The Jews have learned of the Aktion beforehand. Some of them hide in the shelter of the ghetto, some of them escape into the forests. Only a small number are deported to Treblinka or murdered.

The SS and the Ukrainian police arrest 600 Jews in Boryslav, Poland (today Ukrainian S.S.R.). They are stripped naked and in the cold of winter deported to the Belzec extermination camp.

From the Stopnica ghetto in Poland 3,000 Jews are forced to march toward Szczecin. Many of them are shot on the way. The survivors will be sent by train to Treblinka. 400 children and old people are shot in Szczecin cemetery, and 1,500 men are deported to the Skarzysko-Kamienna labor camp.

1943 In the Krychov labor camp in Poland, an uprising takes place in the course of which 1,500 Jews are murdered.

In the course of four days, 14,000 Jews of the Poniatova labor camp in Poland are murdered. Some Jews offer resistance.

In Siauliai, Lithuanian S.S.R., an Aktion against Jewish children begins. Two members of the Jewish Council who attempt to save the children are sent with them to an extermination camp.

November 6

1941 The Nazis begin a large-scale Aktion against the Jews of Nadvorna, in the district of Stanislawow, Poland (today Ukrainian S.S.R.), in the course of which half of the 5,000 Jews are murdered. The Jewish community in Nadvorna dates back to the eighteenth century.

German troops take 18,000 Jews from Rovno, Ukrainian S.S.R., to a pine forest near the town and shoot them. The rest of the Jewish population of Rovno is forced into a newly erected ghetto.

1942 In a final Aktion in Chelm, southeast of Lublin, Poland, the remaining Jews are deported to the Sobibor extermination camp. Chelm is declared "free of Jews."

The SS murders 900 Jews of Koszyce, Cracow province, Poland.

About 1,200 Jews from the Komarno ghetto in Poland (today Ukrainian S.S.R.), are deported to the Belzec extermination camp, where they will be murdered. Komarno is declared "free of Jews."

A convoy with 465 Jewish inmates of the Westerbork transit camp in the Dutch province of Drenthe and 1,000 Jewish men and women from the Drancy transit camp in occupied France leaves for the Auschwitz extermination camp in Poland.

1943 In the Szebnie labor camp in East Galicia, Poland, 500 Jews are shot by the SS.

Deported to Auschwitz are 2,000 Jews of Ciechanov, Warsaw province, Poland.

In a raid in Florence, Italy, 200 Jews are arrested and deported to one of the extermination camps in the east of the Reich. Only 5 of the 200 deportees will return after the war; all the others will be murdered in the camps.

November 7

1939 After the Wartheland is annexed to the German Reich, more than 2,000 Jews are deported from Poznan to the General Government.

1941 The SS takes 3,000 Jews from Kalwarja, in the district of Minsk, Belorussian S.S.R., out of town and shoots them.

In the course of an Aktion lasting several days, the SS murders 20,000 Jews in the town of Bobruisk, Belorussian S.S.R.

From the ghetto of Minsk, the capital of Belorussian S.S.R., 12,000 Jews are deported to Tuchinka, where they are shot by the SS.

In the course of three days, about 8,000 Jews—mainly women and children—from the ghetto of Dünaburg, Latvian S.S.R., are taken to nearby Poguljanka and shot by the SS and Latvian volunteers.

The Jews of Darabani, Dorohoi, Targu-Jiu, and Turnu-Severin, Rumania, are conducted on foot to Transnistria, where most of them will perish.

The SS takes 350 Jews from Hermanovice, Poland, to Szarkowszczyzna to do forced labor.

1942 In the course of two days, 1,300 Jews of the Jaworow ghetto, Lvov province, Poland (today Ukrainian S.S.R.), are sent to the Belzec extermination camp, where 200 Jews are shot on the spot. Another 200 Jews escape into the forests where they form partisan groups. The most celebrated units are commanded by Artur Henner and Henry Gleich. They will all be killed in action.

In Kuty, Stanislawow province, Poland (today Ukrainian S.S.R.), 18 Jews are still alive. On November 7, 16 of them are murdered, while 2 manage to escape.

In Poland, 3,700 of the 4,000 remaining Jews in the Konskie ghetto, 1,500 Jews from the Miedzyrzec Podlaski ghetto, 3,000 Jews from the Lukov ghetto, and 6,000 Jews from the Staszov ghetto, are deported to the Treblinka extermination camp, where all of them will be murdered.

1944 Hannah Szenes, the poet and Haganah fighter from Budapest, Hungary, is executed. She was sent by the Haganah in Palestine with a group of parachutists to organize Jewish resistance in Hungary. Crossing the border on June 7, she was arrested by the Hungarian police. Despite brutal torture, she would not talk.

November 8

1939 The deportation of the Jews from Sierpc, Warsaw province, Poland, begins when this area is annexed to the German Reich. About 1,800 Jews are sent on a march toward Warsaw, while

500 Jews remain in Sierpc, where they are confined to a ghetto.

1941 The Jews of Lvov, East Galicia (today Ukrainian S.S.R.), are concentrated in a ghetto. At the same time, the SS takes old or sick people out of the town and shoots them.

In Krjupow, a village in the district of Krementschug in the Soviet Union, SS men shoot a 14- and 15-year-old girl after raping them.

1942 From Zbaraz, Poland (today Ukrainian S.S.R.), 1,000 Jews are deported to the Belzec extermination camp.

The ghetto of Staszov, Kielce province, Poland, is liquidated. Hundreds of Jews are shot on the spot. The rest—about 5,000 people—are sent to Belzec. A small group manages to escape into the forests.

1944 The death march of 25,000 Jews to Hegyeshalom near Budapest, Hungary, begins. Under unimaginably terrible conditions, these Jews who are being "loaned" to the Reich for forced labor are marched from various internment camps in the Hungarian countryside toward the checkpoint for their further deportation. Many die of hunger and exhaustion.

November 9

1938 On the night of November 9–10, the infamous Kristallnacht ("Night of Broken Glass"), synagogues, chapels, cemeteries, and Jewish shops are destroyed and set on fire in Germany and annexed Austria. This is in revenge for the assassination of the secretary of the German legation in Paris, by Herschel Grynszpan.

1941 The Nazis take 1,500 Jews from Mir, in the district of Grodno, Poland (today Belorussian S.S.R.), and murder them. For the remaining 850 Jews a ghetto is set up.

1942 The second deportation of the last few hundred Jews of Dzialoszyce, Cracow province, Poland, begins. A number of Jews manage to escape into the forests where they join the Polish underground movement.

A deportation convoy with 1,000 Jewish men and women leaves the Drancy transit camp in the German occupied zone of France for the Auschwitz extermination camp in Poland. On arrival, 900 of them will be sent to the gas chambers. Only 15 of them will survive until the liberation of the camp.

Deported to the Belzec extermination camp are 1,100 Jews from the ghetto of Skalat, Ternopol province, Poland (today Ukrainian S.S.R.).

From the ghetto in Piaski, Poland (today Ukrainian S.S.R.), 4,000 Jews are deported to the Majdanek extermination camp, where they are murdered immediately after their arrival.

1943 The SS murders 600 Jews in Postavy, near Vilna, Lithuania.

November 10

1938 The day after Kristallnacht (see November 9, 1938), all over the Reich 35,000 Jews are arrested. Many of them are sent to the Dachau, Buchenwald, and Sachsenhausen concentration camps in Germany. The worst maltreatment will occur in Buchenwald.

1941 In Charkov, Ukrainian S.S.R., two Jewish girls are hanged by the SS in the Jewish cemetery of Lysa Gora.

From Bielica, Novogrodek district, Belorussian S.S.R., 750 Jews are driven to the ghetto of Zdzieciol, which is liquidated the same day.

1942 Promising that their lives will be spared, the Nazis lure Jews out of the forests surrounding Szydloviec, Kielce province, Poland, back into the ghetto. The Jews have no chance of surviving the winter in the forests and return. Immediately afterward, 5,000 of them are sent to the Treblinka extermination camp.

The Nazis shoot 70 Jews from the ghetto of Bochnia, in Galicia, Poland. Then 500 Jews from Bochnia and 1,000 Jews from the Komarov ghetto are deported to the Belzec extermination camp.

From the Mlava ghetto, Poland, 6,300 Jews are deported to Treblinka, where they will be murdered within a few hours of arrival.

From the Westerbork transit camp in the Dutch province of Drenthe, 758 Jewish inmates are deported to the Auschwitz extermination camp in Poland.

November 11

1938 Shortly before the proclamation of the Independent Slovakian State, organized gangs assault the synagogues in its capital, Bratislava. They also beat up Jews and do not allow Jewish students to enter the university. At the outbreak of the war, about 17,000 Jews live in the city.

1939 The Nazis arrest 600 Jews in Ostrov Mazoviecki, Warsaw province, Poland. They are taken to a nearby forest and murdered.

The Nazis deport all the members of the Jewish Council of Lodz, Poland, to the Radogoszcz camp.

1942 The SS murders 100 Jews in Berezov, Polesia, Belorussian S.S.R.

In the ghetto of Slutsk, Belorussian S.S.R., 5,000 Jews are murdered. Jews have been living there since the thirteenth century. On the day of the German invasion there are nearly 9,000 Jewish inhabitants.

From Jastary, Vilna province, Lithuanian S.S.R., 900 Jews are deported to the Kielbasin internment camp.

From the town of Leczna, Lublin province, Poland, 1,000 Jews are sent to the Sobibor extermination camp, where they all will be murdered.

From the Drancy transit camp in the German occupied zone of France, 745 Jews are deported to the Auschwitz extermination camp in Poland. Immediately on arrival, 599 will be gassed, only 2 men will survive until 1945.

1943 During an all-day roll call, 300 Jews die of exhaustion in the Theresienstadt concentration camp in Czechoslovakia.

A group of Jews is arrested by the Nazi occupation forces during a raid on the Carmine Church in Florence, Italy. They are deported to the extermination camps in the east.

A convoy with 91 Jews leaves Vienna for the Theresienstadt concentration camp.

November 12

1939 Wilhelm Koppe, the chief of police of the Wartha district, orders that Poznan, west Poland, has to be made free of Jews. Jews have been living there since the thirteenth century. On the day of the German invasion, there are 1,500 Jewish inhabitants.

1941 In Gorodok, Belorussian S.S.R., on the Vorobjevy Mountain, all Jewish men and women are shot by the SS. Their children are buried alive.

500 Jews of Kamionka-Strumilova, Poland (today Ukrainian S.S.R.), are taken outside of town and shot.

In two convoys, 3,000 Jews of Dorohoi, Rumania, are deported to Transnistria.

The Majdanek concentration camp near Lublin, Poland, is set up.

1942 From Krzeszov, district of Lublin, 500 Jews are deported to the Belzec extermination camp.

The last Aktion against the Jews of Luzk in Volhynia, Ukrainian S.S.R., begins. In one week, some of the Jews are murdered on the spot, some are deported to the Treblinka extermination camp, and altogether 20,000 Jews are murdered. On the same day, 2,500 Jews from Grajewo, Poland, are deported to Treblinka.

In Leczna, district of Lublin, 2,500 Jews are murdered by the SS.

November 13

1940 From the Zaviercie ghetto, in the Polish province of Katowice, 500 young men are sent to several labor camps in Germany. None of them will survive.

1942 A total of 1,500 Jews falls victim to the last Aktion against the Jewish community of Kniszyn, district of Bialystok, Poland. Some of them are murdered on the spot, others are deported to the Treblinka extermination camp.

For two weeks the Nazis pursue Jews who have fled from the Drohobycz ghetto, Poland (today Ukrainian S.S.R.), even searching the houses of Poles. Anybody they seize is shot in the forest of Bronica.

An Aktion against the Jews of the Vladimir Volynski ghetto in Poland (today Ukrainian S.S.R.), begins. In the course of ten days, 2,500 Jews will be massacred.

1943 Several thousand Jews of the Riga ghetto, Latvian S.S.R., are murdered by the Germans before the advance of the Soviet troops. Several thousand Jews are deported to Germany.

The SS takes away 2,000 Jews from Dobiecin, Warsaw province, Poland, and murders them.

November 14

1941 The first large-scale Aktion in Zaleszczyki, district of Ternopol, Poland (today Ukrainian S.S.R.), is organized. It begins with the murder of 800 people, and many young Jews are arrested and sent to the Kamionka labor camp. On the day of the German invasion, the Jewish community numbers 5,000 members.

There is an Aktion against the Jews of Slonim, Poland (today Lithuanian S.S.R.), with the participation of Lithuanians and Belorussians. They take 9,000 Jews out of the ghetto and massacre them near Czepielov. Only a few Jews manage to escape.

1942 In the course of three days, 6,000 Jews from the ghetto of Grodno, Poland (today Lithuanian S.S.R.), are rounded up by the SS and Latvian auxiliaries. They are deported to the Auschwitz extermination camp.

From Makov Mazoviecki, Warsaw province, Poland, 500 Jews are deported to the Treblinka extermination camp. Jews have been living in this town since the sixteenth century. At the time of the German invasion, the Jewish population numbers 3,500.

1943   Italian Fascists murder 3 Jews in the streets of Ferrara, Italy.

November 15

1491   In La Guardia, near Toledo, Spain, 6 Jews and 5 Conversos accused of killing Christians with the help of black magic are condemned to death. The next day they will be burned at the stake.

1938   Jewish children are expelled from German schools.

1939   The Jews of Rypin, in central Poland, are resettled in Warsaw, Ciechanov, and other towns. Two Jewish cemeteries are destroyed. Some Jews manage to cross the border and flee into the Soviet Union, where they will be deported to Siberia.

1940   All the Jews in Legionovo, district of Warsaw, Poland, are sent to Ludwiszyn.

Jews from Warsaw, Poland, and the provinces are concentrated in a very small area. In the following weeks 4,000 Jews from Sochaczev are added to the Warsaw ghetto.

1941   From Czernovitz, the capital of Bukovina, Rumania (today Ukrainian S.S.R.), 30,000 Jews are sent to Transnistria. The mayor of Czernovitz, Traian Popovici, who is a friend of the Jews, prevails upon the German authorities to allow 4,000 Jews to remain.

The SS shoots 500 Jews from Kolomyia, Ukrainian S.S.R.

In the course of a large-scale Aktion in Sarajevo, the capital of Bosnia-Herzegovina, Yugoslavia, 3,000 Jews are arrested and deported to various concentration camps, where they will perish. Only a small part of Sarajevan Jewry will survive, joining partisan groups or managing to escape to Italy.

1942   From Klementov, Kielce province, Poland, 3,500 Jews are deported to the Sandomierz camp.

In a final Aktion, 2,300 Jews in Dembica, province of Cracow, Poland, are murdered by the SS.

The last 350 Jews of Holonie, Belorussian S.S.R. are murdered by the SS.

Deported to the Belzec extermination camp are 4,000 Jews from the Zamosc ghetto in Poland. They will be murdered within a few hours of arrival. Another transport with 3,000 Jews leaves the Tarnov ghetto for Belzec to meet the same fate.

A transport with 3,800 Jews of Tyszviec, province of Lublin, Poland, leaves for the village of Piatidin, where they are murdered.

From the Gniewoszov ghetto in Poland 1,000 Jews are deported to the Treblinka extermination camp.

1943   The last 1,200 Jews of Budzanov, district of Ternopol, Ukrainian S.S.R., are murdered by the SS and the Ukrainian police.

A deportation transport with 1,149 Jewish internees from the Westerbork transit camp in the Dutch province of Drenthe leaves for the Auschwitz extermination camp in Poland.

November 16

1491   In La Guardia, Spain, 5 Jews are arrested and accused of having killed a child, whose body will never be found. The 3 who are forcibly baptized Jews are garroted and burned. The others are torn to pieces. The instigator of the persecution, the Dominican Tomás de Torquemada, wants to strengthen anti-Jewish sentiments in Spain.

1941 From Brno, Moravia, Czechoslovakia, 1,000 Jewish men, women, and children are deported to the Minsk ghetto in Belorussian S.S.R. Only 12 of them will survive.

1942 During an Aktion lasting two weeks, 15,000 Jews are murdered in Wlodzimierz, Poland (today Ukrainian S.S.R.).

761 Jewish internees of the Westerbork transit camp in the Dutch province of Drenthe are sent to the Auschwitz extermination camp in Poland.

1943 From the Westerbork transit camp, 995 Jewish internees are deported to Auschwitz.

fled to the fortress at Kiburg. All 330 are burned at the stake.

1918 Units of Simon Petlyura's Ukrainian National Army and groups of partisans reach the town of Bobrovitsy, in the district of Tschernigov. The pogrom they unleash causes the death of 9 Jews; a great many others are wounded or mutilated.

1942 The last Jews of Krasnik, Lublin province, Poland, are deported to the Belzec extermination camp. Several hundred of them manage to escape into the forests. Two partisan units are organized to fight the Nazis. Eduard Forst is the leader of the one called Berek Joselowicz.

1942 The last labor squad of 30 Jews in the Treblinka extermination camp, Poland, is shot by the SS.

November 17

1278 Jews are being arrested throughout England in a house-to-house search. The charge is "coin clipping," which means cutting off the edges of the coins and melting down the metal. Among the 680 Jews who are imprisoned in the Tower of London, many are Jewish notables. Their properties are confiscated by the Crown and 293 of them are sentenced to death and hanged.

1301 The Jews of Renchen in the province of Baden, Germany, are accused of ritual murder. Subsequently the Jews Noach ben Meir, Kalonymos, son of the rabbi Yehuda ben Eleazar, and Yerachniel ben Meschullan are broken on the wheel.

1349 The destiny of their brethren all over Europe strikes the Jews from Winterthur, Diessenhofen, and other villages in Switzerland who have

November 18

1648 The town of Kamenets-Podolski, Ukraine, is captured by the hordes of Chmielnicki. In the course of three days, 10,000 Jews will be slaughtered.

1940 The Germans set up a ghetto in Lask, province of Lodz, Poland. At the outbreak of World War II, the town numbers about 4,000 Jews. Jews have been living there since the early seventeenth century.

1942 From Makov Mazoviecki in the province of Warsaw, Poland, 4,000 Jews are deported to the Warsaw ghetto.

In the course of three days about 5,000 Jews from the Lvov ghetto, Poland (today Ukrainian S.S.R.), are deported either to the Belzec extermination camp or to the Janovska labor camp, where they will perish. This is the last transport from Lvov. Henceforth, the remaining Jews are shot.

A transport with 4,000 Jews leaves from the Przemysl ghetto in the province of Rzeszow, Poland, for the Belzec extermination camp.

1944 Enzo Hayyim Sereni is murdered in the Dachau concentration camp in Germany. An Italian pioneer in Palestine, the Haganah had him parachute into the German-occupied part of Italy. Captured immediately after landing, he was sent from camp to camp until finally being shot in Dachau.

November 19

1941 The Nazis crowd 54,000 Jews into the Bogdanovka concentration camp, in southern Transnistria, on the Bug River, Ukrainian S.S.R.

Over two days, 5,000 German, Austrian, and Czech Jews are deported from Minsk, capital of Belorussian S.S.R., to Tuchinka, where they will be massacred.

1942 In the course of an Aktion in Drohobycz, Poland (today Ukrainian S.S.R.), several hundred Jews are murdered in the streets by the SS. Among them is the famous writer and painter Bruno Schulz. This day becomes known as "Black Thursday."

The Jewish population of Wyszgorod, Warsaw province, Poland, is rounded up and transported to Czerwinsk and Novy Dvor, from where they will be deported to the Treblinka extermination camp. Wyszgorod is thus "free of Jews." The Jewish community was founded in the fifteenth century.

1943 The Nazis liquidate the Janowska labor camp in Lvov, Poland (today Ukrainian S.S.R.). Almost all of the Jewish prisoners are shot.

November 20

1939 Out of a total of 20,000 Jews in Kalisz, district of Posen, Poland, 19,300 are deported to various places in the province of Lublin. Jews first settled in Kalisz in the twelfth century, when they enjoyed privileges by the Polish kings.

1941 In the course of two days, 500 Jews from the ghetto of Vilna, Poland (today Lithuanian S.S.R.), are shot in Ponary by the SS.

1942 From the Westerbork transit camp in the Dutch province of Drenthe, 726 Jewish internees are deported to the Auschwitz extermination camp in Poland.

The Nazis shoot 120 Jews in Wisznice, Poland.

A transport with 3,200 Jews from Szebrzeszyn, province of Lublin, Poland, leaves for the Belzec extermination camp.

Several hundred Jews are murdered by the SS and Ukrainian police in an Aktion against the Jews of the Glinyany ghetto, in the province of Lvov, Poland (today Ukrainian S.S.R.).

1943 The sixty-second deportation transport leaves France with 1,200 Jewish internees from the Drancy camp in the German occupied zone for Auschwitz. Immediately on arrival, 914 persons are sent into the gas chambers. Only 31— among them 2 women—will survive until 1945.

1944 Havivah Reik is murdered in Kremnica, Slovakia, Czechoslovakia. She was sent from Palestine by the Haganah to help organize a Jewish resistance movement in Slovakia. She is captured by the Germans, imprisoned, tortured, and finally executed.

From Vienna, 4 Jews are deported to the Theresienstadt concentration camp in Czechoslovakia.

All Jews remaining in Bratislava, the capital of Slovakia, have to assemble in the inner court of the town hall to be deported to the Sered labor camp.

November 21

1918   In Lvov, Galicia, Poland (today Ukrainian S.S.R.), Polish soldiers organize a pogrom against the Jewish population. They massacre 72 Jews, wound 443, set the synagogues and the houses in the Jewish quarter on fire, and tear the Torah scrolls.

1942   A convoy with 4,000 Jews from the ghetto of Suchedniov and 1,500 Jews from the ghetto of Szczekociny, Poland, leaves for the Treblinka extermination camp. They are murdered within a few hours of their arrival.

1943   From Borgo San Dalmazzo, Italy, 325 Jews are deported to the Auschwitz extermination camp in Poland.

November 22

1348   After the annihilation of the Jewish communities of the Rhineland, the Black Death Persecutions spread to Bavaria and Swabia, provinces in southern Germany. The first Jewish community to perish in these massacres is Augsburg in Bavaria on November 22.

Seal of the Jewish community of Augsburg, 1298. It shows a double-headed eagle and a medieval Jewish hat.

1942   In the course of an Aktion, 2,500 Jews from the ghetto of Zolkiev, in Galicia, Poland (today Ukrainian S.S.R.) are deported to the Belzec extermination camp, where they will be murdered.

In Serokomea, Poland, the SS shoots 200 Jews.

The SS murders 900 Jews on the spot in Dunilovicze, near Vilna, Lithuania.

1943   The Germans send 100 patients from the Jewish mental hospital in Berlin to the Auschwitz extermination camp in Poland.

1944   A Jew is deported from Vienna to the Theresienstadt concentration camp in Czechoslovakia.

November 23

1939   The wearing of the Yellow Star becomes obligatory for the Jews in Poland.

1941 A deportation transport with 995 Jews leaves Vienna for Riga, the capital of Latvian S.S.R.

1942 From Strzygov, district of Warsaw, Poland, 850 Jews are deported to the Auschwitz extermination camp.

650 Jews from Oszmiany, Belorussian S.S.R., are shot in a forest near the Aglejby estate.

In the course of five days, 10,000 Jews from the Szydloviec ghetto in Poland are deported to the Treblinka extermination camp, where they are murdered within a few hours of arrival.

1943 Jewish resisters numbering 150 manage to escape from Kaunas, Lithuanian S.S.R., into the forests, where they fight against the SS. Many of them will die in combat.

November 24

1605 The Jews of Bochnia, Poland, and its vicinity are expelled by the Polish King Sigismund III Vasa after the flight of a Jew from Bochnia and two of his relatives, who are accused of host desecration. The whole Jewish community is held responsible and expelled.

1941 The SS shoots 300 Jews in Kozlowstchine, district of Baranowicze, Belorussian S.S.R.

A ghetto is set up in Theresienstadt, Czechoslovakia. Until the end of World War II, about 75,000 Jews will pass through this ghetto and concentration camp.

About 18,000 Jews are crammed into the Akmechetka concentration camp, in southern Transnistria, Ukrainian S.S.R.

1942 A transport with 709 Jewish internees from the Westerbork transit camp in the Dutch province of Drenthe leaves for the Auschwitz extermination camp in Poland.

The Mlava ghetto, in the province of Warsaw, Poland, is liquidated. A small group of Jewish workers, useful to the Germans, are spared for the time being.

1944 The last 200 Jews of the Piotrkov Trybunalski ghetto, in the province of Lodz, Poland, are deported to the Buchenwald and Bergen-Belsen concentration camps.

November 25

1696 In an auto-da-fé in Coimbra, Portugal, 14 men and women are burned alive and 4 are burned in effigy. They were accused of being Judaizers, secretly practicing Judaism.

1940 The *Patria*, a British passenger ship with 1,771 passengers without visas—European Jews trying to escape Nazi persecution by emigrating "illegally" to Palestine—is not allowed by the British authorities to dock in Haifa, Palestine. The ship is blown up and 257 people are killed; the survivors are saved by the people onshore.

1941 The Nazis massacre 3,000 Jews in Rechitsa, Belorussian S.S.R. The Jewish community of Rechitsa is one of the oldest in the area.

1942 By ship, 531 Jewish women and children are taken from Bergen, Norway, to Stettin, Poland, from where they will be deported to the extermination camps in Poland.

A transport with 400 Jews from the ghetto of Sassov, Poland (today Ukrainian S.S.R.), takes them to the Zloczow ghetto, where they will perish along with the Jews of Zloczow.

The ghetto of Siedlce, Poland, is liquidated after it has been shrunk by the deportations. Of the remaining Jews, 2,000 are deported to the Treblinka extermination camp, where they will perish. Only a forced labor camp with 500 prisoners will remain in Siedlce.

1943 40 Jews are murdered in the course of the liquidation of the Gomel concentration camp in Belorussian S.S.R.

1944 The German police hang 4 Jews in Ciechanov, Poland.

November 26

1942 The Nazis deport 250 Jews from Brody, Ukrainian S.S.R., to the Belzec extermination camp; 20 Jews are shot on the spot.

In Sarnova, district of Rawicz, Poland, 2 Jews are hanged by the SS because they tried to escape.

The Jews of the transit camp under the special custody of the police in Berg, Norway, are transported by ship to Swinemunde. From there they are sent to the Auschwitz extermination camp in Poland with Hungarian women and children.

1944 Despite intervention by the Portuguese embassy, which tried to protect Sephardic Jews, the Jewish forced laborers in Budapest are deported to Sopron, Hungary, to build the East Wall for the defense of Vienna. Many will die of exhaustion, hunger, and mistreatment.

Heinrich Himmler, the head of the SS, orders the destruction of the crematoria in the Auschwitz extermination camp in Poland.

November 27

1095 At the Council of Clermont-Ferrand, France, Pope Urban II proclaims the First Crusade. This date is of great importance not only to the Christians, but also to the Jews, for the Crusades will degenerate into armed pilgrimages that leave a bloody trail of massacres of Jews across Europe and the Orient on the way to liberate Jerusalem.

1941 In The Hague, the Netherlands, the Nazis order the establishment of Jewish quarters in all large towns, where the Jews from smaller towns in the surrounding areas are to be resettled.

1942 From the Buczacz ghetto, district of Ternopol, Ukrainian S.S.R., 2,500 Jews are deported to the Belzec extermination camp. Shot in the ghetto itself are 250 Jews.

From the ghetto of Tlumacz, Poland, 2,000 Jews are deported to Belzec.

November 28

1939 Suvalki, in the Polish province of Bialystok, is annexed to the German Reich. As the Germans want a town "free of Jews," the 6,000 Jewish inhabitants are deported to the towns of Biala Podlaska, Lukov, Miedzyrzec-Podlaski, and Kock.

1940 In the Netherlands, all Jews are dismissed from civil service despite a protest letter from the Protestant churches.

1941 From Vienna, 999 Jews are deported to Minsk, the capital of Belorussian S.S.R.

1942   At the outbreak of World War II, the Jewish population of Mosciska, in the district of Lvov, Poland (today Ukrainian S.S.R.), numbers 2,500 people. They are deported to Belzec extermination camp where they will be murdered immediately.

1943   The SS deports 420 Jews from the ghetto of Dünaburg, Latvian S.S.R., to Riga.

1944   Members of the Arrow Cross, the Hungarian Fascist organization, break into a block of houses in Budapest, dragging several hundred Jews into the street. Some of them are shot on the spot, the others are sent to the ghetto.

Lamp discovered at Khirbat Sammaka, near Carmel.

labor camps in the province, where most of them will perish from the harsh treatment.

November 29

1941   In the ghetto of Riga, Latvian S.S.R., about 600 Jews are killed by the SS, who march them to their execution.

In Kertsh on the Crimean Peninsula, the SS massacres 4,500 Jews.

The SS and Ukrainian police massacre 1,500 Jews from Boryslav, Poland (today Ukrainian S.S.R.), after they are taken to the neighboring forest.

1942   From Glusk, in the province of Lublin, Poland, 750 Jews are deported to Piaski.

The SS and Ukrainian police murder 1,000 Jews from Szczerzec, in the province of Lvov, Poland.

Over three days, 10,000 Jews from the Zvolen ghetto in Poland are deported to the Treblinka extermination camp, where they will be murdered within a few hours of arrival.

1944   Several thousand Jewish workers from Budapest are taken to the Fertorakos camp and other

November 30

1941   10,600 Jews are taken from the Riga ghetto, Latvian S.S.R., to a nearby forest, where they are shot by the Einsatzgruppe A (killing squad) of the SS. In the ghetto hospital, on Ludzac Street, about 30 Jewish children are murdered by the SS by being thrown out of the windows of the second floor. Also 15 Jews are shot in the Jewish cemetery of Riga.

1942   From the Westerbork transit camp in the Dutch province of Drenthe, 826 Jewish internees are deported to the Auschwitz extermination camp in Poland.

In the Proskurov ghetto in the Ukrainian S.S.R., 7,000 Jews are massacred by the SS with the help of the Ukrainian police.

In Goraj, Poland, the SS shoots 30 Jews.

1943   A transport with 46 Jews leaves Vienna for the Theresienstadt concentration camp in Czechoslovakia.

DECEMBER

December 1

1652 An auto-da-fé takes place in Lisbon, Portugal. On the charge of secretly practicing Judaism, Manuel Fernandez Villareal is sentenced to death and burned alive.

1939 From Chelm, Poland, 1,018 Jews arc deported to Sokal. The SS shoots 440 on the way. Jews have been living in Chelm since the fifteenth century and developed a flourishing cultural life. Some well-known rabbis originated in Chelm.

The space allotted to the Jews in Lodz, Poland, is reduced. They have to leave their houses and ethnic Germans move in.

The deportations to the east of the Jews from Wloclawek, Poland, begin. Most of them will be deported to Warsaw. Hundreds of them will perish on the way.

1940 Having arrived at Chelm, Poland, 600 Jews are shot by the SS.

1941 The Nazis shoot 300 old and sick Jews in the ghetto of Riga, Latvian S.S.R.

1942 In Stryj, Poland (today Ukrainian S.S.R.), a ghetto is set up. The Jews of Stryj begin to realize what is going to happen to them. Some young people venture to flee across the Carpathian mountains to Hungary.

The ghetto of Sambor (today Ukrainian S.S.R.), is evacuated and closed down. The inhabitants are interned in a labor camp in Lvov.

The labor camp in Karczev, Poland, in which 400 Jews from Otvock have been interned, is liquidated. All the Jews that have remained alive are murdered.

The Nazis set up a ghetto in Zloczow, Poland (today Ukrainian S.S.R.); all the Jews from the neighboring towns of Sassov and Bialykamien are interned there. Many of them will die of hunger and exhaustion.

The remaining Jews of Glinyany, Poland (today Ukrainian S.S.R.), are deported to the ghetto of Przemyslany. Later they will be massacred there along with the Jews of Przemyslany. Only 20 will survive the Holocaust.

1943 A deportation transport with 25 Jews leaves Vienna for the Auschwitz extermination camp in Poland.

December 2

1264 A convert who has taken the name Abraham appears in the small town of Sinzig, Germany, preaching Judaism. He is immediately arrested and imprisoned. As he refuses to die as a Christian, he is cruelly tortured and burned alive at the stake.

1941 The first deportation of Jews of Brno, the capital of Moravia, Czechoslovakia, begins. Jews have been living in Brno since the thirteenth century. At the outbreak of World War II the Jewish community numbers 11,000.

In the course of two days, 420 Jewish families are executed by the SS in Slavjansk, near Doneck, Ukrainian S.S.R.

1942 About 800 Jews of Krosno, Poland, have escaped the general deportations by hiding themselves. One by one they have been discovered by the SS and crowded into a ghetto that is evacuated on December 2, 1942. All the inmates are deported to the Belzec extermination camp.

The Nazis deport 2,500 Jews from Krasne, Poland (today Ukrainian S.S.R.), to the Rzeszow ghetto.

December 3

1918 In Holleschau, Czechoslovakia, armed gangs of soldiers force their way into the houses and shops of Jews and start looting and burning. In the riots two Jews are killed.

1939 The town Nasielsk, Warsaw province, Poland, is declared "free of Jews": in September and October most of the Jewish inhabitants have been deported to various places in the east, like Biala Podlaska, Lublin, and Warsaw, where they share the fate of their Jewish brethren.

1941 The Nazis murder 400 Jews in the ghetto of Riga, Latvian S.S.R.

From Vienna, 995 Jews are deported to Riga.

The extermination camp Jumpravas Muiza (Jungfernhof) in Vidzeme, Latvian S.S.R., is opened. Part of the Jews from Vienna who have been deported to Riga are sent on to Jumpravas Muiza.

1942 The SS kills 800 Jews of Lubeczov, Polesie, Belorussian S.S.R.

A transport with 1,000 Jews leaves from Podkamia, Poland (today Ukrainian S.S.R.), for the Brody ghetto.

December 4

1941 The SS murders several hundred Jews in Feodosiya, a port on the Crimean Peninsula. Most of the 3,500 Jews living there manage to escape. Jews have been living there since the thirteenth century.

The Hungarian occupation army hands over the town of Horodenka, Ukrainian S.S.R., to the Nazis. The Jewish population is called to assemble in the synagogue under the pretext of being vaccinated against typhus; the able-bodied among them are then singled out, while the others are taken outside of town, shot, and buried in mass graves.

1942 The SS deports 600 Jews from Krosno, in the province of Galicia, Poland, to the Belzec extermination camp.

A transport with 812 Jewish inmates leaves the Westerbork transit camp in the Dutch province of

Drenthe for the Auschwitz extermination camp in Poland.

800 Jews from the Radom labor camp, Kielce province, Poland, are deported to Szydlowiec, where they will be murdered.

1943 A considerable number of Jews of Pskov, Soviet Union, are transported into a forest and murdered there by the SS.

December 5

1349 Victims of the Black Death Persecutions, 500 Jews are murdered in Nuremberg, Germany. Some of the Jews are slain, the others are burned at the stake. Many are tortured before being killed.

1939 The Nazis begin to burn down the synagogues and to confiscate Jewish property in Cracow, Poland, which they occupied on September 17. At this time 60,000 Jews are living in Cracow. Jews first settled there in 1335 under the protection of Polish kings.

1941 The Jews of Ghetto 2 in Novogrodek, Belorussian S.S.R., are taken out of the town and murdered.

In the course of four days 6,500 Jews are deported from Kolo, province of Lodz, Poland, to the Chelmno extermination camp.

1942 The town of Plonsk, province of Warsaw, Poland, is declared "free of Jews." From November 1 to December 5, 1944, 12,000 Jews have been deported in four transports from the Plonsk ghetto to the Auschwitz extermination camp. Only a few Jews will survive.

December 6

1348 The Jewish community of Lindau, a town on the Bodensee in Germany, is reached by the Black Death Persecutions. All Jews are either slain or burned at the stake.

1705 An auto-da-fé is held in Lisbon by the Portuguese Inquisition. One Portuguese is burned alive for being Jewish, which he affirms proudly even until his last breath.

1920 In the village of Voltchkii in the district of Kiev, Ukrainian S.S.R., a pogrom is carried out by units linked to Petlyura's Ukrainian National Army; 6 Jews are slain and 3 others severely wounded.

1940 The Nazis arrest 300 Jews in Mlava, Warsaw province, Poland, from where they are deported to the transit camps Miedzyrzec Podlaski, Lubartov, and Lublin.

Page from a Converso prayer book with a special prayer in memory of those burned at the stake. (1687)

1941 The SS takes 8,000 Jews—old people, women, and children—from the ghetto of Riga, Latvian S.S.R., to the nearby forest of Rumbuli and shoots all of them.

1942 The SS deports 1,500 Jews from the Novy Dvor ghetto in Poland to the Auschwitz extermination camp.

1943 From Milan and Verona, Italy, 212 Jews are deported to Auschwitz.

December 7

1941 In the course of two days, 450 men are murdered in Riga, Latvian S.S.R., on the grounds of a factory called Quadrat. Among them are many Jews.

The Jews of Novogrodek, in the district of Grodno, Poland (today Belorussian S.S.R.), are forced to assemble in the yard of the courthouse, where the SS carries out a selection of 400 Jews who are shot in the trenches of the nearby village of Skrydlewo. For the remaining Jews a ghetto is set up.

1942 In the ghetto of Rava Ruska, Ukrainian S.S.R., an Aktion by the SS and the Ukrainian police begins. Over five days almost 3,000 Jews are sent to the Belzec extermination camp.

1943 Sent to Auschwitz are 1,000 Jewish men and women from the Drancy transit camp in the German occupied zone of France. Immediately after their arrival, 661 deportees are sent into the gas chambers. Only 42 men and 2 women will survive until the end of the war.

December 8

1348 The entire Jewish community of the small town of Reutlingen in Württemberg, Germany, is annihilated in the course of the Black Death Persecutions. They are accused of planning to destroy Christian people by poisoning their water and thus spreading the plague.

1596 Accused of Judaizing, 4 members of the famous Converso family of Carvajal are burned at the stake in Mexico City, Mexico, by the Spanish Inquisition.

1940 A ghetto is set up in Skiernievice, Poland, where 4,500 Jews are interned and another 2,000 Jews from Lodz are also resettled there.

1941 All Jewish women and children of Belgrade, the capital of Yugoslavia, are ordered to register with the police. About 6,000 people from Belgrade and Banat province are taken to the transit camp set up in the industrial area of Sajmiste.

From the ghetto of Riga, Latvian S.S.R., 1,500 weak and old Jews are murdered by the SS in the forest of Bikerneku near Riga. Some of them are shot, some are asphyxiated in gas vans.

In the Chelmno extermination camp in Poland the extermination of Jews begins. The first victims are from neighboring areas in the Wartheland.

1942 A transport with 927 Jewish internees from the Westerbork transit camp in the Dutch province of Drenthe leave for the Auschwitz extermination camp in Poland.

In an Aktion that lasts for four days, all 4,000 Jews of Makov Mazoviecki, Warsaw province, Poland, are deported to the Treblinka extermination camp.

From the ghetto of Rohatyn, Stanislavov district, Poland (today Ukrainian S.S.R.), 1,250 inmates, including the medical staff of the Jewish hospital, are deported to the Belzec extermination camp.

December 9

1941 The SS takes 800 Jews from the "Smaller Ghetto" of Riga, Latvian S.S.R., to the nearby forest of Rumbuli where they are gassed in vans. By this date 25,000 Jews from the ghetto of Riga have been massacred. Among them is the famous historian Simon Dubnow.

1942 A convoy with 2,500 Jews leaves Luga Wola, in the province of Bialystok, Poland, for the Auschwitz extermination camp.

Walter Rauff, SS commander of Tunisia, is infuriated that only 120 Jewish workers have followed his order and registered rather than the 3,000 he had expected. The same day German soldiers storm the crowded synagogue of Tunis. Men are taken away for forced labor. Many women and children are manhandled by the soldiers.

December 10

1600 In an auto-da-fé, 14 Portuguese "New Christians," the term then employed for the descendants of forcibly baptized Jews, are brought to trial in Lima, Peru, then a Spanish possession. Two of them will be burned at the stake, a third in effigy.

1920 The town of Ivankov, district of Kiev, Ukrainian S.S.R., is again struck by a pogrom carried out by units of Petlyura's Ukrainian National Army; 8 Jews are massacred, another 2 severely wounded.

1941 A transport with 1,000 Jews from the Kovale-Panskie camp in Poland, all originally from

the surrounding area, leaves for the Chelmno extermination camp. In the nearby forest they are asphyxiated in gas vans by the SS.

In the course of an Aktion in Brcko, Bosnia and Herzegovina province, Yugoslavia, 150 native Jews and 200 Jews from Austria are driven by the SS to the Sava River where they are brutally massacred.

1942 The last Jews of Mlava, district of Warsaw, Poland, who were used for extremely hard labor, are deported to the Treblinka extermination camp.

1943 The Jews of the Rumanian village of Mihova were deported to the Tarasika labor camp on the Bug when Bukovina was occupied by German and Rumanian troops. Now the surviving inmates of the camp are murdered by the German troops when the Soviet army breaks through the front lines.

December 11

1939 Over three days, 15,000 Jews are expelled from Kalisz, Poland, and sent to various cities in the General Government, such as Cracow, Warsaw, and Rzeszow.

In the course of a two-day Aktion, the Jews from Poznan, Poland, are deported to Ostrov Lubelski and other towns. Poznan is officially declared "free of Jews," although small groups of Jewish forced laborers are still employed there.

1941 About 1,200 Jews from Ciechanov, in central Poland, are deported to the Nove Miasto ghetto. A number of Jews are shot on the way by the SS.

December 12

1505 In Ceske Budejovice, Bohemia, Czechoslovakia, 10 Jews fall victim to a blood libel. A shepherd accuses them of having murdered a Christian girl. The Jews are imprisoned and submitted to torture from November 20 to December 12, when they are burned at the stake. Some years later the shepherd will confess on his deathbed that he lied and that the Jews were innocent.

1939 The Nazis order that all Jewish men between the ages of 14 and 60 have to do two years of forced labor. Labor camps are set up in the General Government in Poland and the Warthegau, Germany. Most of the internees will die as a result of the cruel treatment and physical exhaustion.

After Lodz is annexed to the German Reich, in three days about 8,000 Jews are deported from Lodz to the General Government.

1941 The SS murders 200 Jewish patients of the psychiatric hospital in Nowinki, district of Minsk, Belorussian S.S.R. Some of them are gassed, some of them shot.

The SS shoots 26 Jews from the prison of Newel, Belorussian S.S.R., in the village of Pjatino.

1941 In Paris, a house-to-house raid is carried out by the German occupation army in order to arrest Jewish intellectuals and notables. Among the 1,000 Jews arrested are René Blum, the brother of the former prime minister of France, Roger Masse, brother of Senator Pierre Masse, and Jean-Jacques Bernard, son of author Tristan Bernard.

The municipal police arrest and execute several hundred Jews who try to bring food to the starving inmates of the ghetto of Chmielnik, in the Polish province of Kielce.

1942 A transport with 757 Jewish internees of the Westerbork transit camp in the Dutch province of Drenthe leaves for the Auschwitz extermination camp in Poland.

The 500 Jewish craftsmen remaining in Lutsk, Volhynia, Poland (today Ukrainian S.S.R.), are murdered by the SS. However, a small number manage to escape into the forest. Only 150 Jews from Lutsk will survive, by hiding, until the end of the war.

The SS deports 2,000 Jews of the ghetto of Novy Dvor and 2,000 Jews of the ghetto of Czerwinsk, both villages in the province of Warsaw, Poland, to Auschwitz.

Jews being burned at the stake in the marketplace, from a pamphlet published in Frankfurt in 1510.

December 13

1918 For seven days soldiers of Petlyura's Ukrainian National Army occupy Bobrinskaia in the province of Kiev. They murder 11 Jews and wound and mutilate a great number.

1939 The last 65 Jews of Gniezno, in the province of Poznan, Poland, are murdered by the SS. Originally the town numbered 150 Jews.

1941 In an Aktion that lasts for three days, 14,300 Jews from Simferopol, Ukrainian S.S.R., are murdered by the SS.

The last 6 Jews of Warnsdorf, Germany, are arrested and deported to Riga, Latvian S.S.R., where they will all perish.

The SS murders 90 Jews in Bachtshisarai, on the Crimean Peninsula, Ukrainian S.S.R.

A ghetto is set up in Wolkowysk, Poland (today U.S.S.R.). After the German occupation, a pogrom is carried out by the local Polish population. Jews have been living in Wolkowysk since the sixteenth century.

1942 From Wyszgorod, Warsaw province, Poland, 2,700 Jews are deported to the Auschwitz extermination camp. The SS shoots 620 Jews beforehand.

1943 All the remaining Jews of Vladimir-Volynski, Poland (today Ukrainian S.S.R.), are murdered by the SS. In the course of the liquidation about 30 armed Jews offer resistance to the Nazis. Half of them are killed, the others manage to escape into the forest.

December 14

1941 The SS murders 76 Jews in Karasubazar, Ukrainian S.S.R.

The SS brings 975 Jews from the Polish village of Dabie to the forest of Chelmno, where they are asphyxiated in specially constructed gas vans.

The deadline for the Jews of Lvov, Poland (today Ukrainian S.S.R.), to move to the Jewish district established by the Nazis on November 8, arrives. In the resettlement Aktion of December 14, all Jews who did not obey the order and stayed in their homes, are shot.

1942 From Novy Dvor, Warsaw province, Poland, 4,000 Jews are deported to the Auschwitz extermination camp.

1943 A Jew is deported from Vienna to the Theresienstadt concentration camp in Czechoslovakia.

In Drohobycz, Poland (today Ukrainian S.S.R.), 200 Jews are shot by the SS and Ukrainian police.

December 15

1647 Isaac de Castro Tartas is killed in Lisbon, reciting the Shema, the Jewish prayer affirming the Oneness of God. Tartas lived in Brazil. On a visit to Bahia, which belonged to the Kingdom of Portugal, he was arrested by the myrmidons of the Inquisition and sent to Lisbon. He maintains his Jewish faith to the end and with 5 others is burned alive. Another 60 people are sentenced to life imprisonment.

1658 An auto-da-fé is held in the Portuguese town of Pôrto, and 90 Judaizers, people accused of secretly practicing the Jewish faith, are tried. 6

men and 1 woman are burned at the stake. The others are only sentenced to prison.

1941 In an Aktion that lasts for two days, 3,500 Jews from Liepaja, Latvian S.S.R., are massacred by the SS and Latvian collaborators.

3,000 Jews are shot in Fortress 9, in Kovno, Lithuanian S.S.R., by the SS and Lithuanian volunteers.

1942 In the forest of Suchodebski in Lanieta, Poland, The police shoot 10 Jews from Gostynin and Wloclawek.

1943 A transport with 2,504 Jews leaves from the Theresienstadt concentration camp in Czechoslovakia for the Auschwitz extermination camp in Poland.

December 16

1941 From Dabie, Poland, 1,600 Jews are deported to the Chelmno extermination camp.

In a two-day Aktion in Yalta, a port on the Black Sea, 1,500 Jews are massacred by the SS.

1943 From December 16 to 20, a number of transports leave the Theresienstadt concentration camp in Czechoslovakia. About 6,000 Jews, family by family, are sent to the Auschwitz extermination camp in Poland. Along with the families deported in September, they are to serve Nazi propaganda, to show the visiting Red Cross teams that "Jews are not mistreated in Auschwitz." When they are no longer useful, they will be gassed, on March 7, 1944.

December 17

1531 A bull issued by Pope Clement IV establishes the Inquisition in Portugal. Most of the victims will be "New Christians," Jews who were forcibly baptized in 1492 in Spain and their descendants, who secretly continue to adhere to their old faith. Many seek refuge in Portugal, whose kings are more tolerant than the Royal House of Spain. Several hundred thousand Spanish and Portuguese Jews will fall victim to the Inquisition.

1595 A great auto-da-fé is held in Lima, Peru, where the Inquisition Tribunal was established in 1571. There, 10 people are accused of Judaizing, secretly practicing Judaism, and 4 of them are burned at the stake. Before being burned, 3 are garroted and one, called Francisco Rodriguez, is burned alive.

1942 The SS shoots 231 Jews of the ghetto of Biala Podlaska, Poland.

The SS kills 557 Jews after an uprising in the Kruszyna labor camp in Poland.

The SS kills 3,000 Jews in the ghetto of Baranovicze, Belorussian S.S.R.

1943 The last deportation transport of the year leaves Drancy in France with 850 Jewish men and women. Their destination is the Auschwitz extermination camp in Poland. Immediately after their arrival, 505 deportees are gassed. Only 26 of them, among them 4 women, will survive until the liberation of the camp in 1945.

December 18

1941 The SS massacres 1,500 Jews in Yalta, on the Crimean Peninsula, Soviet Union.

1943 From the ghetto and concentration camp of Theresienstadt, Czechoslovakia, 2,503 Jews are deported to the Auschwitz extermination camp in Poland.

1942 In a second deportation, 3,500 Jews from Radzyn, Poland, are sent to the Treblinka extermination camp. Several small Jewish resistance groups are organized in the surrounding forests, and fight against the Nazis under the leadership of the Ha-Shomer ha-Za'ir.*

December 19

1942 The Aktion against the ghetto of Slonim, Poland (today Ukrainian S.S.R.), begins. At the time 10,000 Jews are living in the ghetto.

The 3,000 Jews interned in the Dworzec labor camp, Poland (today Belorussian S.S.R.), revolt against the SS. All of them are murdered.

German soldiers shoot the young Jew Victor Nataf in Tunis, Tunisia, accused of having signaled Allied planes flying over Tunis. His execution is meant to be a warning.

December 20

1348 The Jews of the small town of Horb on the Neckar River in Württemberg, Germany, fall victim to the Black Death Persecutions. They are burned at the stake, probably for alleged well poisoning, the most common accusation of the era.

1632 Nicolas Antoine, a French pastor from a Catholic family who has converted to Judaism, is declared insane, but is later summoned to court. He is executed in Geneva, Switzerland, on this date.

1939 A ghetto is set up in Lodz, Poland, in which the Jews from Lodz itself and the surrounding areas are settled. From the lack of space and sanitary facilities, epidemics break out and food soon becomes scarce.

December 21

1625 In 1618 an Edict of Faith was published in Rio de Janeiro, Brazil, by an Inquisitor specially dispatched from Lisbon, Portugal, resulting in many arrests of New Christians accused of Judaizing. Consequently many of them flee to Spanish territory. On this date, some of these refugees are tried in an auto-da-fé in Lima, Peru. Ten of them are "reconciled," which means doing public penance, confiscation of their property and deprivation of their civic rights. 4 are burned at the stake, 2 of them garroted beforehand.

1680 An auto-da-fé is held in Toledo, Spain. Accused of Judaizing are 21 people, all of them Portuguese, who had fled the Inquisition in their own country. Two of them, Balthasar Lopez Cardoso and his cousin Felipa Lopez, who remain steadfast until the end, are burned alive at the stake. The others are garroted first.

1942 From Krukienice, Poland (today Ukrainian S.S.R.), 700 Jews are brought to the Javorov collection point for deportation.

December 22

1941 The mass murders in Vilna, Poland (today Lithuanian S.S.R.), are complete; 32,000 Jews have been massacred.

*Leftist Zionist youth movement.

The SS drives 900 Jews from Zablotov, Poland (today Ukrainian S.S.R.), outside the town, then shoots them and hurriedly buries them in pits. In Zablotov itself, 100 Jews are shot on the same day.

1942   A group of Jewish resistance fighters attacks the Cyganeria Club in Cracow, Poland, which is frequented by German officers. The armed Jewish resistance movement was organized in 1940 and began to sabotage German installations. Its leaders in Cracow are Shimon Draenger and Dolek Liebeskind. They are in contact with the Warsaw ghetto through their mediator Yizhak Cukierman, who has been active in the Cracow ghetto as well.

In the cemetery of Rava Ruska, Ukrainian S.S.R., the SS shoots Jewish children along with 40 adults.

December 23

1736   The last victim of the Peruvian Inquisition, condemned for Judaizing, is Ana de Castro. He is burned at the stake, probably denounced to the Inquisition by personal enemies.

1942   The last Jews remaining in Pinsk, Poland (today Belorussian S.S.R.), are 150 Jewish craftsmen, who are driven to the Jewish cemetery, where they are shot and buried.

1943   A group of Jews who are burning corpses under the surveillance of the Gestapo in Fortress no. 9 in Kaunas, Lithuanian S.S.R., overpower their guards and escape. The Jewish underground movement sends them into the forest of Rudnicka from where they operate against the Germans.

December 24

1496   The king of Portugal, Manuel I, orders the expulsion of all Jews from Portuguese territory.

Because many Spanish Jews fled to Portugal in order to escape the Inquisition, this is especially fatal. They have to leave within ten months, after which every Jew will be killed and his property confiscated by the Crown.

1939   The Nazis burn down the synagogue of Siedlce, Poland, where Jews have been living since the sixteenth century, including famous authors and rabbis. At the outbreak of World War II, the Jewish community numbers 15,000, almost half of the total population.

1942   On Christmas Eve several thousand Jews are rounded up in the ghetto of Stanislavov, Poland (today Ukrainian S.S.R.), and taken to the courtyard of the prison. They have to spend the Christmas holidays outside without shelter and many die from the cold. Several of them are shot.

In Cracow, Poland, 20 Jewish resistance fighters, among them their leader Dolek Liebeskind, are killed in a battle with the SS. Two days earlier they bombed a German club in Cracow.

The SS takes 218 Jewish workers from the Kopernik labor camp near Minsk Mazoviecki, Poland, and shoots them.

1943   64 Jews escape from the ghetto of Kaunas, Lithuanian S.S.R. The SS will capture and murder 45 of them.

1944   Budapest is encircled by Soviet forces. The terror of the Arrow Cross, the Hungarian Fascist organization, reaches its climax. They force their way into an orphanage of the International Red Cross and the Jewish Council and shoot 3 women and 3 children. Later on another 5 children and a teacher will be murdered.

December 25

1881 Persecution of Jews intensifies in Warsaw, the capital of Poland. The army as well as civilian authorities turn against the Jews.

1939 The Germans round up the Jews of Czestochova, Poland, and carry out a pogrom. The synagogue is burned down.

1941 In the ghetto of Riga, Latvian S.S.R., 36 Jewish policemen are shot.

1942 In the course of an uprising in the Sobibor extermination camp in Poland, 4 Jews escape into the nearby forest. However, they will be betrayed and shot by the SS.

The SS massacres 2,500 Jews in the ghetto of Postavy, Lithuanian S.S.R.

The Great Synagogue of Warsaw in the nineteenth century.

December 26

1684 The Spaniard Antonio Cabicho and his clerk Manoel de Sandoval die in the flames of the stake erected by the Portuguese Inquisition in an auto-da-fé in Lisbon. They remain steadfast until the end, loudly proclaiming their adherence to the Law of Moses.

1941 100 Jews who have been waiting at the gate of the ghetto in Lvov, Poland (today Ukrainian S.S.R.), to be picked up for labor, are taken by the Gestapo to the Jewish cemetery and shot.

1942 The SS takes 800 Jews of Krakowiec, Poland (today Ukrainian S.S.R.), to the Javorov collection point.

The SS murders the last Jews of Biala Podlaska, in the province of Lublin, Poland.

December 27

1348 The Black Death Persecutions continue. When the mob threatens the Jews of Esslingen, a village on the Neckar River in Germany, the Jews set fire to their own houses and their synagogue and die in the flames.

1939 From Aleksandrov Lodzki, in the province of Lodz, Poland, 3,500 Jews are deported to Zgierz and from there to the Chelmno extermination camp.

1942 The last living Jew of Kaluszyn, in the province of Warsaw, Poland, is shot in the street after having been denounced by a Pole whose reward is a bottle of vodka.

A transport takes 2,500 Jews of Komarno, Poland (today Ukrainian S.S.R.), to the Rudki collection point for deportation.

The SS and Ukrainian police shoot 1,500 Jews, and an unknown number of inmates of the ghetto are buried alive in the cemetery of Grodek, Poland (today Ukrainian S.S.R.)

1943 In the forest near the village of Sawtschonki, in the Vitebsk region of Belorussian S.S.R., 30 Jews are killed when their hiding place is discovered and blown up.

December 28

1235 Five young children of a miller in Fulda, Germany, are killed on Christmas when their parents are absent; suspicion falls on 2 Jews and the rumor spreads that they killed them in ritual murder. It is said that the Jews drew the blood from the corpses and keep it in waxed bags to preserve it for Passover. With the help of some crusaders, the enraged townspeople attack the Jewish community of Fulda and massacre 34 Jewish men and women.

1941 The SS shoots 60 Jews in the ghetto of Charkov, Ukrainian S.S.R.

The SS shoots 600 Jewish children in the forest of Rumbuli, near Riga, Latvian S.S.R.

From Sniatyn, Poland (today Ukrainian S.S.R.), 200 Jews are driven into the forest of Potoczek where they are forced to dig their own graves in the frozen earth. Afterward they are shot by the SS and Ukrainian police.

In Berezino, near Minsk, Belorussian S.S.R., 1,000 Jews are shot by the SS and local auxiliary police after being tortured. The children are buried alive.

In Kirovograd, Ukrainian S.S.R., all Jewish men and women, old as well as young, are shot by the SS. Babies and small children are buried alive. Jews in the prison who try to escape are shot.

1942 1,500 Jews of Szremsk, in the province of Warsaw, Poland, are sent to Mlava to do forced labor.

2,500 Jews of Kamieniec Litewski, in the district of Polesie, Belorussian S.S.R., are deported to the Pruzany camp.

December 29

1348 During the Black Death Persecutions, the Jews of Colmar on the Rhine, France, fall victim to the general "Jewslaying." On the allegation of having poisoned the wells in order to spread the plague, they are burned at the stake.

1939 About 2,500 Jews, the entire Jewish population of Pulavy, a town in the province of Lublin, Poland, are deported to Opole Lubelskie. From there they will be deported in May 1942 to the Sobibor extermination camp.

1940 In the town of Glovno, Poland, the Jewish population is forced to leave their homes and resettle in the ghetto established by the Nazis.

1944 The Jewish members of the Bajczy-Szilinszky resistance movement are arrested and killed in Budapest, Hungary, by members of the Fascist Arrow Cross. On the same day the Arrow Crossers force their way into several houses under Swedish protection, drag out more than 100 Jewish men and women, and shoot them.

December 30

1941 The SS massacres 400 Jews in Dshankoi on the Crimean Peninsula.

The massacres of the Jews of Simferopol on the Crimean Peninsula are finished. Every Jew is dead.

1944 On the road between Kryry and Branica-Rudziczka in the province of Katowice, Poland, 36 prisoners, among them 18 women, who are too exhausted to continue, are shot by the SS. They are on an evacuation march from the Auschwitz extermination camp. Some of the victims are Jews.

In an Aktion in Budapest, members of the Arrow Cross, the Hungarian Fascist organization, drag 40 Jews out of their houses and shoot them.

SS men and members of the Arrow Cross invade the Bethlen Square Hospital in Budapest, Hungary. They round up 28 young Jewish women whom they later shoot at a school for girls.

December 31

1918 Units commanded by Kozyr-Zyrko stationed in the town of Ovrutch, Volhynia, Ukrainian S.S.R., until January 2, carry out a pogrom against the Jewish inhabitants. Kozyr-Zyrko and his troops belong to Simon Petlyura's Ukrainian

Menorah found on a tomb near Jaffa.

National Army. They massacre 18 Jews and rape many Jewish women.

1919 The town of Gochevo, in the province of Volhynia, suffers from a pogrom carried out by insurgents under Kozyr-Zyrko. They massacre 2 Jews.

1942 From the ghetto of Czortkov (today Ukrainian S.S.R.), 1,000 Jews are taken and sent to various labor camps in the district. Most of them will be murdered in July 1943.

The SS murder 150 Jews in Iwje, Belorussian S.S.R.

1944 On the night of December 31, members of the Arrow Cross, the Hungarian Fascist organization, storm the Ritz Hotel in Budapest, Hungary, which is under international protection. They drag O. Komoly, the president of the Zionist organization, out of the hotel and murder him.

BIBLIOGRAPHY

Adler, H. G. *Der Kampf gegen die Endlösung der Judenfrage* (The Struggle against the Final Solution to the Jewish Question). Bonn, 1958.

Anchel, Robert. *Les Juifs de France* (The Jews of France). 1946.

Apenszlak, Jacob, and Polakiewicz, Moshe. *Armed Resistance of the Jews in Poland.* New York, 1944.

Arad, Yitzhak. *Ghetto in Flames: The Struggle and Destruction of the Jews in Vilna in the Holocaust.* Hoboken, N.J.: Ktav, 1980.

———.*The Partisan.* New York: Holocaust Publications, 1979.

Baer, Yitzhak. *A History of the Jews in Christian Spain.* 2 vols. Philadelphia: Jewish Publications Society, 1961.

Bednarz, Wladyslaw. *Das Vernichtungslager zu Chelmno am Ner* (The Chelmno extermination camp on the Ner River). Warsaw, 1946.

Berman, Adolf. "The Fate of Jewish Children in the Warsaw Ghetto," in *The Catastrophe of European Jewry,* edited by Yisrael Gutmann and Livia Rothkirchen. Hoboken, N.J.: Ktav, 1976.

Bernadac, Christian. *Le Train de la Mort* (The train of death). Paris: Empire, 1970.

Blumenthal, Nachman, ed. *Yitzkor Baranow: A Memorial to the Jewish Community of Baranow.* Jerusalem, 1964.

Bourdrel, Philippe. *Histoire des Juifs en France* (History of the Jews in France). Paris: Albin Michel, 1974.

Braham, Randolph, L. *The Politics of Genocide. The Holocaust in Hungary.* 2 vols. New York: Columbia University Press, 1981.

Brann, Marcus. *Geschichte der Juden in Schlesien* (History of the Jews of Silesia). Breslau, 1896.

Centre de Documentation Juive Contemporaine. *Tableau Chronologique des Convois de Deportation, Paris.*

Chazan, Robert. *Medieval Jewry in Northern France.* Baltimore: Johns Hopkins University Press, 1973.

Cocatrix de, A. *The Number of Victims of the National Socialist Persecution.* Arolsen, West Germany: International Tracing Service, 1977.

Crimes of the Fascist Occupants and their Collaborators Against Jews in Yugoslavia, The. Belgrade, 1957.

Czech, Danuta. *Deportation und Vernichtung der griechischen Juden in Hefte von Auschwitz–II* (The deportation and extermination of Greek Jews according to the Archives of Auschwitz–II). 1970.

Datner, Szymon. *Walka i zaglada bialostockiego ghetta* (The uprising in the Bialystok ghetto). Lodz, 1946.

——— et al. *Genocide 1939–1945.* Warsaw, 1962.

Donati, Guiliana. *Ebrei in Italia: Deportazione, Resistenza* (The Jews in Italy: Deportation and resistance). Florence, 1975.

Dubnow, Simon. *History of the Jews in Russia and Poland from the Earliest Times until the*

Present Day. 3 vols. Philadelphia: Jewish Publication Society, 1946.

Ehrlich, Ernst Ludwig. *Judenfeindschaft. Von der Spätantike bis zum Mittelalter. Ein historischer Rückblick* (Anti-Semitism from antiquity to the Middle Ages. A historical perspective). Vienna, 1980.

Eidelberg, Shlomo. *Jews and the Crusaders.* Madison: University of Wisconsin Press, 1977.

Elbogen, I.; Freimann, A; and Tykocinsky, H. *Germania Judaica.* Vol. 1 (1963), vol. 2 (1968). Tübingen, Germany.

Feig, Konnilyn G. *Hitler's Death Camps—The Sanity of Madness.* New York: Holmes & Meier, 1981.

Ferencz, Benjamin B. *Less than Slaves: Jewish Forced Labor and the Quest for Compensation.* Cambridge: Harvard University Press, 1979.

Files of Nazi criminals and their trials. Vienna: Jewish Documentation Center.

Fraenkel, Josef, ed. *The Jews of Austria, Essays on Their Life, History and Destruction.* London: Vallantine, Mitchell, 1967.

Friedman, Saul S. *Pogromchik: The Assassination of Simon Petlyura.* New York: Hart Publishing Co., 1976.

Friedmann, Tobia. *Schupo und Gestapo Kriegsverbrecher von Stanislau vor dem Wiener Volksgericht* (Police and Gestapo who committed war crimes before the Vienna Tribunal). Haifa, 1957.

Gilbert, Martin. *Atlas of the Holocaust.* New York: Macmillan, 1982.

Gold, Hugo. *Geschichte der Juden in der Bukowina* (History of the Jews of Bukovina). Vols. 1 and 2. Tel Aviv, 1958.

Gold, Hugo. *Geschichte der Juden in Österreich* (History of the Jews of Austria). Tel Aviv, 1971.

Graetz, Heinrich. *History of the Jews.* 12 vols. Philadelphia Jewish Publication Society, 1891–98. Originally published as *Geschichte der Juden.* Leipsig.

Gurland, H. J. *Lekorot ha-Gezairot al-Yisroel* (The persecutions against Israel). 1887–89.

Gutman, Yisrael. *The Genesis of Resistance in the Warsaw Ghetto.* Yad Vashem Studies. Vol. 9. Jerusalem, 1973.

Hannover, N. N. *Abyss of Despair.* New Brunswick, N.J.: Transation Books, 1983. Originally published as *Yeven Mezullah.* Israel, 1945.

Hausner, Gideon. *Justice in Jerusalem.* New York: Schocken Books, 1978.

Hay, Malcolm. *Europe and the Jews.* Boston, 1960.

Heer, Friedrich. *God's First Love.* New York: Weybright and Talley, 1970. Originally published as *Gottes erste Liebe.* Munich/Esslingen, 1967.

Hilberg, Raul. *The Destruction of the European Jews.* New York: Holmes & Meier, 1985.

———, ed. *Documents of Destruction, Germany and Jewry 1933–1945.* London, 1972.

Hilberg, Raul, and Staron, Stanislaw. *The Warsaw Diary of Adam Czerniakow.* New York: Stein & Day, 1982.

Holl, Adolf. *Religionen* (Religions). Stuttgart: Ullstein Bucher, 1981.

Jacobsen, H. A., and Dollinger, H. *Geschiednis van de Tweede Wereldoorlog in foto's en documenten* (History of World War II in documents and photographs). Baarn, Netherlands, 1962.

Jewish Encyclopedia, The. New York, 1903.

Jong de, Louis. *The Netherlands and Auschwitz.* Yad Vashem Studies. vol 7. Jerusalem, 1968.

Joods Historisch Museum Amsterdam. *Documenten van de Joodenverfolging in Nederland 1940–1945* (Documents on the persecution of Jews in the Netherlands). Amsterdam, 1965.

Katz, Robert. *Death in Rome.* New York: Macmillan, 1967.

Kayserling, Meyer. *Geschichte der Juden in Spanien und Portugal.* (History of the Jews in Spain and Portugal). Vols. 1 and 2. Hildesheim, West Germany, 1978.

Kempner, Robert M. W. *Edith Stein und Anne Frank. Zwei von Hunderttausend. Die Enthüllungen uber die NS-Verbrechen in Holland vor dem Schwurgericht in München.* (Two among a hundred thousand: Revelations on the Nazi crimes in Holland before the Munich Tribunal). Freiburg–Basel–Vienna, 1968.

———. *Eichmann und Komplizen.* (Eichmann and his accomplices). Frankfurt on the Main, 1961.

Kirsch, J. P.; Göller, Emil; and David, E. *Römische Quartalshrift für christliche Altertum-*

skunde und für Kirchengeschichte. (Catholic quarterly on Christian antiquity and eccliastic history). Vol. 34. Freiburg im Breisgau, 1926.

Klarsfeld, Serge. *Additif au Mémorial de la Déportation des Juifs de France*. Paris, 1981.

Kogon, Eugen. *Der SS-Staat* (The SS state). Munich, 1979.

Kossoy, Edward. *Handbuch zum Entschädigungsverfahren* (Handbook on reparations procedure). Munich, 1958.

Krausnick, H., and Wilhelm, H. H. *Die Truppe des Weltanschauungs-krieges—Die Einsatzgruppen der Sicherheitspolizei und des SD 1938–1942* (Soldiers in the war of ideology: The killing squads and the security police in the Intelligence Service 1938–1942). Stuttgart, DVA.ST., 1981.

Kreppel, J. *Juden und Judentum von heute* (Jews and Judaism today). Vienna, 1925.

Mark, Bernhard. *Der Aufstand im Warschauer Ghetto* (The Warsaw ghetto uprising). Berlin, 1959.

Meisl, Josef. *Geschichte der Juden in Polen und Russland* (History of the Jews in Poland and Russia). Vols. 1 and 2. Berlin, 1921.

Moser, Jonny. *Die Judenverfolgung in Österreich 1938–1945* (The persecution of the Jews in Austria). Vienna, 1966.

Novitch, Miriam. *Il Passaggio dei Barbari* (The passage of the barbarians). Paris, 1967.

Ostrowski, Wiktor. *Anti-Semitism in Byelo-Russia*. London, 1960.

Paris, Edmond. *Genocide in Satellite Croatia: A Record of Racial and Religious Persecution*. Chicago, 1961.

Piotrowski, Stanislaw. *Hans Frank's Diary*. Warsaw: Pan Stwowe Wydawnietwo Naukowe, 1961.

Poliakov, Léon. *The History of Anti-Semitism*. New York: Vanguard, 1975.

Poliakov, Léon, and Wulf, Joseph. *Das Dritte Reich und die Juden* (The Third Reich and the Jews). Munich: Saur, 1978.

Reitlinger, Gerald. *The Final Solution: The Attempt to Exterminate the Jews of Europe 1939–1945*. New York: Barnes, 1961.

Rosenberg, Dr. Artur. *Beiträge zur Geschichte der Juden in Steiermark* (Contribution to the history of the Jews of Styria). Vienna and Leipzig, 1914.

Rosenkranz, Herbert. *Verfolgung und Selbstbehauptung. Die Juden in Österreich 1938–1945* (Persecution and reaction of the Jews of Austria). Vienna, 1978.

Roth, Cecil. *A History of the Jews in England*. 3rd ed. Oxford. Clarendon Press, 1964.

———. *A History of the Marranos*. Salem: Ayer, 1975.

Roth, Cecil, ed. *Encyclopedia Judaica*. Jerusalem: Keter, 1971–82.

Rothkirchen, Livia. *The Destruction of Slovak Jewry: A Documentary History*. Jerusalem, 1961.

Runciman, Steven. *A History of the Crusades*. 3 vols. Cambridge: Cambridge University Press, 1951.

Runes, Dagobert D. *The War Against the Jew*. New York, 1953.

Sabille, Jacques. *Les Juifs de Tunisie sous Vichy et l'Occupation* (The Jews of Tunisia under Vichy and the Occupation). Paris, 1954.

Scheffler, Wolfgang. *Judenverfolgung im Dritten Reich* (The Persecution of Jews in the Third Reich). Berlin, 1979.

Schepansky, Israel. *Luach ha-shoah shel yahadut Polin* (The Calendar of the Holocaust of the Polish Jews). New York, 1974.

Schneider, Gertrude. *Journey into Terror: The Story of the Riga Ghetto*. New York: Irvington, 1979.

Schoenberner, Gerhard. *Der gelbe Stern* (The Yellow Star). Munich, 1978.

Shatzky, Jacob: *Gezarot 1648* (The Decrees of 1648). Vilna, 1938.

Stein, A. *Die Geschichte der Juden in Böhmen* (The History of the Jews in Bohemia). Brunn, 1904.

Szende, Stefan. *Der letzte Jude aus Polen* (The Last Jews in Poland). Zürich, 1945.

Tcherikower, Elias. *Anti-Semitism and Pogroms in the Ukraine 1917–1918*. New York, 1923.

———. *The Pogroms in the Ukraine in 1919*. New York, 1965.

Totenbuch Theresienstadt (Book of the Dead of Theresienstadt). Vol. 1: "Deportierte aus Osterreich" (The Deportees from Austria).

Trial of the Major War Criminals before the International Military Tribunal. Nuremburg 14

November 1945–1 October 1946. Nuremburg, 1947.

Trunk, Isaiah. *Judenrat*. New York: Stein & Day, 1977.

"Unsere Ehre heisst Treue"—Kriegstagebuch des Kommandostabes Reichsführer SS—Tätigkeitsberichte der 1. and 2. SS–Inf.–Brigade, der 1. SS–Kav.–Brigade und von Sonderkommandos der SS ("Our Honor Means Loyalty"—A War Diary of the First SS Cavalry Brigade and the Special Commandos of the SS). In *Zeitgeschichte in Dokumenten*. Vienna, 1965.

Wellers, Georges. "La Déportation des Juifs en France." *La Monde Juif*, no. 99 (July–September), 1980. Magazine of the Centre de Documentation Juive Contemporaine.

Wiesenthal, Simon. *The Murderers Among Us*. New York: McGraw-Hill, 1967. Originally published as *Doch die Mörder leben*. Munich and Zürich, 1967.

Yad Vashem. *Black Book of Localities Whose Jewish Population was Exterminated by the Nazis*. Jerusalem, 1965.

Zentrale Stelle der Landesjustizverwaltung Ludwigsburg: Sammlung UdSSR, 6 Hefte (Central Office for the Ludwigsburg Department of Justice; documents of USSR collection, 6 pamphlets). Ludwigsburg, 1970.

INDEX OF PLACES

Salaspils, near Riga, Latvia
1943: *May 5, May 10*
Salonika (Saloniki), Greece
1917: *August 18*
1941: *April 15, July 2*
1942: *July 11*
1943: *February 6, March 3, March 13, March 14, March 15, March 17, April 5, June 8, July 28, August 2, August 7, August 18*
Salzburg, Austria
1404: *July 10*
Sambor, Lvov province, Poland, today Ukrainian S.S.R.
1941: *July 1*
1942: *August 4, September 1, October 17, December 1*
1943: *March 14, April 14, June 6*
Samgorodok, Kiev district, Ukraine
1919: *March 13*
Samothrace (isle), Greece
1943: *March 3*
Sandomierz, Kielce province, Poland
1942: *October 29*
1943: *January 10*
1944: *January 16*
Sanniki, Poland
1942: *April 17*
Sanok, Poland
1942: *September 10*
Santarém, Portugal
1531: *January 26*
Sarajevo, Bosnia and Herzegovina, Yugoslavia
1941: *April 16, September 3, October 17, November 15*
1942: *August 12*
Saratov, Russia
1905: *March 17, October 19*
Sarmas, Rumania
1943: *September 16*
Sarnaki, Lublin province, Poland
1942: *August 22*
Sarnova, Rawicz district, Poland
1942: *November 26*
Sarny, Volhynia, Poland, today Ukrainian S.S.R.
1941: *July 5, October 1*

1942: *April 4, August 27, August 28*
Sarvar, Hungary
1944: *July 24, August 5*
Sassov, province of Lvov, Poland, today Ukrainian S.S.R
1942: *July 15, August 29, November 25*
1943: *July 30*
Satoraljaujhely (Ujhely), Hungary
1944: *May 11*
Saulgau, Germany
1349: *February 19*
Savoy, France
1348: *August 10*
Sawtschonki, Belorussian S.S.R.
1943: *December 27*
Saxony, Germany
1942: *May 12*
Schaffhausen, Switzerland
1349: *February 20, February 22*
Schaulen, see Siauliai
Scheibbs, Austria
1945: *April 19*
Schkede, Latvia
1941: *April 24*
Schmerinka, Russia, today Ukrainian S.S.R.
1905: *October 21*
Schneidemühl, Germany, today Pila, Poland
1940: *March 12*
Schodnica, Lodz province, Poland
1942: *October 22*
Seciny, Warsaw province, Poland
1942: *October 18*
Secureni, Bessarabia, today Moldavian S.S.R.
1941: *July 6, July 9, July 30, October 3*
Segovia, Spain
1474: *March 16*
Semenovka, Russia
1905: *October 27*
Semlin, see Sajmiste
Sendziszov, Cracow province, Poland
1942: *September 21*
Serbia, constituent republic of Yugoslavia
1942: *August 29*
Sered, Slovakia, Czechoslovakia
1942: *March 25*
1944: *October 28, November 3*
1945: *January 6*

Tunis, Tunisia, Africa
  1942: February 24, December 9, December 19
Turek, Lodz province, Poland
  1941: October 20
Turez, Novogrodek district, Belorussian S.S.R.
  1941: November 3
Turka, Lvov province, Poland, today Ukrainian S.S.R.
  1941: July 1
  1942: January 1, August 21
Turnu-Severin, Rumania
  1941: November 7
Turobin, Poland
  1942: May 12
Tykocin (Tiktin), Bialystok province, Poland
  1941: August 25
Tyszovce, Lublin province, Poland
  1942: May 22, May 31
Tyszviec, Lublin province, Poland
  1942: November 15

Überlingen, Germany
  1332: March 5
Uchanie, Poland, today Ukrainian S.S.R.
  1942: April 10, June 10
Uchomir, Podolia, Ukraine
  1919: March 11, April 3
Ujazd, Poland
  1943: January 6
Ujhely, see Satoraljaujhely
Ujvidek, Yugoslavia
  1944: October 11
Ulanov, Lvov province, Poland
  1942: October 29
Ulm, Germany
  1349: January 30
Uman, Kiev district, Ukraine
  1734: June 20
  1919: May 12, July 29
Ungarisch-Brod, Bohemia, today Hungary
  1683: July 14
Ungvar (Uzhorod), Ukrainian S.S.R.
  1944: April 21, May 13
Unter-Stanestie, Rumania
  1941: June 28

Urmini, Podolia district, Ukraine
  1919: May 21
Uscilug, Volhynia, Ukrainian S.S.R.
  1942: September 1
Utena, Lithuanian S.S.R.
  1941: August 7
Utrecht, Netherlands
  1941: October 1
  1942: February 9
  1943: April 10
Uzhorod, see Ungvar

Vakhnovkha, see Wachnowa
Valencia, Spain
  1391: July 9
Valladolid, Spain
  1639: June 22
  1644: July 25
Valréas, Dauphiné department, France
  1247: March 27
Varnsdorf, see Warnsdorf
Varosmajor, Hungary
  1945: January 14
Vasilishak, Vilna district, Belorussian S.S.R.
  1942: August 1
Vassilivtchin, Kiev district, Ukraine
  1919: August 28
Vassilkovo, Kiev district, Ukraine
  1919: February 7, August 29
  1920: May 1
Vatican, Italy
  1942: October 3
Venice, Italy
  1480: July 4
  1944: October 11
Verba, Volhynia, Ukrainian S.S.R.
  1941: October 13
Verkhova-Bibikovo, Podolia, Ukraine
  1919: June 23, July 23
Verona, Italy
  1943: December 6
  1944: June 26, August 2
Vichy France
  1942: August 26